Leadership and Power

Leadership and Power

Identity Processes in Groups and Organizations

Edited by
Daan van Knippenberg and Michael A. Hogg

SAGE Publications
London ● Thousand Oaks ● New Delhi

First published 2003
Reprinted 2005

SAGE Publications Ltd
1 Oliver's Yard
55 City Road
London EC1Y 1SP

SAGE Publications Inc.
2455 Teller Road
Thousand Oaks, California 91320

SAGE Publications India Pvt Ltd
B-42, Panchsheel Enclave
Post Box 4109
New Delhi 100 017

British Library Cataloguing in Publication data

A Catalogue record for this book is available from
the British Library

ISBN 0 7619 4702 6
ISBN 0 7619 4703 5 (pbk)

Library of Congress Control Number: 2003102342

Typeset by C&M Digitals (P) Ltd, Chennai, India
Printed in Great Britain by Athenaeum Press, Gateshead

Table of Contents

Chapter 14

Chapter 15

Chapter 16

References

Index

List of Contributors

Robert Baron is Professor of Psychology at the University of Iowa. He has published widely on topics in group influence including papers on group polarization, conformity and indoctrination procedures. He (with Norbert Kerr) is the author of *Group process, group decision, group action* (Open University Press, 2003).

Martin M. Chemers is the Dean of Social Sciences and Professor of Psychology at the University of California at Santa Cruz. Prior to this appointment he was the Henry R. Kravis Professor of Leadership and Organisational Psychology and Director of the Kravis Leadership Institute at Claremont McKenna College. He was previously on the faculties of the Universities of Illinois, Delaware, Washington, and Utah where he was chair of the Department of Psychology. Since receiving his PhD in Social Psychology from the University of Illinois in 1968, he has been an active researcher and has published seven books and many articles on leadership, culture and organizational diversity. Dr Chemers' books have been translated into German, Japanese, Swedish, Spanish, and Portuguese. His most recent book, *An integrative theory of leadership* (Lawrence Erlbaum Associates) was published in autumn 1997. The Japanese edition was published in 1999.

Kevin Crawley was, from 1980 to 1990, Co-Director of Unbound, Inc, a residential counselling center for former members of totalist groups. He wrote 'Reintegration of exiting cult members with their families: A brief intervention model' (Cultic Studies Journal, vol. 7, no. 1), with Diana Paulina and Ron White. He is currently an interactive specialist with the City of Iowa City.

David De Cremer obtained his PhD in 1999 with highest honours at the University of Southampton. He was the recipient of the British Psychology Society Award for 'Outstanding PhD in Social Psychology'. From September 1999 to 2001 he was first assistant professor and subsequently associate professor of organizational behavior at the Department of Economics and Business Administration at Maastricht University, The Netherlands. Currently he is associate professor of psychology at the Department of Experimental Psychology, Maastricht University, and obtained a research fellowship from the Netherlands Organization for Scientific Research (NWO) for the period 2001-2006. His main research interests include social dilemmas, leadership, the psychology of distribution rules, and the relationship between self and procedural justice.

Carsten K.W. De Dreu (PhD, University of Groningen, 1993) is Professor of Organizational Psychology at the University of Amsterdam. His research is concerned with social conflict, negotiation, and group decision making. His work has been published in the major outlets in both social and organizational psychology. Carsten de Dreu is currently Associate Editor of *Group Processes and Intergroup Relations*, and of *Journal of Organizational Behavior*.

Alice H. Eagly is a Professor of Psychology at Northwestern University. Earlier she served on the faculties of Purdue University, University of Massachusetts in Amherst, and Michigan State University and Faculty Fellow in the Institute for Policy Research and held visiting professor appointments at University of Tuebingen, Harvard University, and University of Illinois. Eagly earned her doctoral degree in social psychology from the University of Michigan and her bachelor's degree from Harvard University. She has published widely on the psychology of attitudes, especially attitude change and attitude structure. She is equally devoted to the study of gender. In both of these areas, she has carried out primary research and meta-analyses of research literature. She is the author of *Sex differences in social behavior: A social role interpretation* (Lawrence Erlbaum Associates, 1987) and, with co-author Shelly Chaiken *The psychology of attitudes* (Harcourt Brace Jovanovich, 1993) and the co-editor of two volumes. Eagly is also the author of numerous journal articles, chapters, notes, and reviews in her research specialities. She has served as president of the Midwestern Psychological Association, president of the Society of Personality and Social Psychology, and chair of the Board of Scientific Affairs of the American Psychological Association. She has received several awards, including the Distinguished Scientist Award of the Society for Experimental Social Psychology, the Donald Campbell Award for Distinguished Contribution to Social Psychology, the Gordon Allport Award of the Society for the Psychological Study of Social Issues, and the Citation as Distinguished Leader for Women in Psychology from the American Psychological Association.

Margaret Foddy is Professor of Psychology and Sociology at Carleton University in Ottawa, Canada. Her research is concerned with social dilemmas, status relations in groups, and the social psychology of the self. Her most recent books are edited volumes, *Resolving social dilemmas* (with Smithson, Schneider & Hogg) (Psychology Press, 1999), and *Self and identity: Personal, social and symbolic* (with Kashima & Platow) (Lawrence Erlbaum, 2002).

Diana M. Grace is a PhD student at the Australian National University. Her primary area of research is self-categorization and social influence in children. She has published journal articles and chapters on the topics of categorization, social influence, and stereotyping.

Stephanie A. Goodwin is an assistant professor of psychology and women's studies at Purdue University. She received her PhD in social and personality psychology from the University of Massachusetts at Amherst where she first became interested in the study of social power. In addition to her research on social power and judgment, she is investigating the role of non-conscious processes in inter-group biases.

Rosalie J. Hall received her PhD in Industrial/Organizational Psychology from the University of Maryland in 1988. She has been at the University of Akron (USA) since that time and is currently an Associate Professor in the Department of Psychology, and a member of the Institute for LifeSpan Development. Her work focuses on issues of interpersonal perceptions in organizational settings, and research methodology and statistics.

Alex Haslam is Professor of Social and Organisational Psychology at the University of Exeter. Formerly an associate editor of the *British Journal of Social Psychology*, he is currently editor of the *European Journal of Social Psychology* and serves on the board of a number of international journals. His most recent book is *Psychology in organizations: The social identity approach* (Sage, 2001).

Michael Hogg is Professor of Social Psychology at the University of Queensland, an Australian Research Council Professorial Fellow, and a Fellow of the Academy of the Social Sciences in Australia. He is editor of the journal *Group Processes and Intergroup Relations*, and series editor of Essential Texts in Social Psychology. He has a PhD from Bristol University, and has held research and teaching positions at Bristol University, Macquarie University, the University of Melbourne, Princeton University, the University of California, Los Angeles, and the University of California, Santa Cruz, and the University of California, Santa Barbara. Michael Hogg's research is in the areas of group processes, intergroup relations and self-conception, and he has been closely associated with the development of the social identity perspective. He has published 200 scholarly books, chapters and articles on these topics. Leadership, the topic of his contribution to this book, has been a core research topic of his for over a decade.

Nick Hopkins is a social psychologist at Dundee University and has research interests in social influence, stereotyping and the organization of collective action. These interests are pursued in *Self and nation* (co-authored with Steve Reicher and published by Sage, 2001) which explores the strategic construction of national identity in political mobilization. Current research addresses the reception of such identity constructions and their consequences for action.

Roderick M. Kramer is the William R. Kimball Professor of Organizational Behaviour at the Graduate School of Business, Stanford University. His current research interests are trust and distrust in organizations, organizational paranoia, cooperation, and organizational creativity. He is the author or co-author of over 75 scholarly articles. His research has appeared in numerous academic journals and books, including *Administrative Science Quarterly, Annual Review of*

Psychology, *Journal of Personality and Social Psychology*, *Journal of Experimental Social Psychology*, *Journal of Conflict Resolution*, *Research in Organizational Behavior*, and *Organizational Behavior and Human Decision Processes*. He is also co-editor of a number of books, including most recently *Negotiation as a social process*, with David M. Messick (Sage Publications, 1995), *Trust in organizations: Frontiers of theory and research*, with Tom Tyler (Sage Publications, 1996), *The psychology of the social self*, with Tom Tyler and Oliver John (Lawrence Erlbaum Publishers, 1999), and *Power and influence in organizations*, with Margaret Neale (Sage Publications, 1998). He has been an Associate Editor for *Administrative Science Quarterly*, and has served on the editorial boards of *Organization Science* and *Organizational Behavior and Human Decision Processes*. He has been a visiting professor at the Kennedy School of Government at Harvard University, Oxford University, London Business School, and the Kellogg Graduate School of Management at Northwestern University. He earned his PhD in social psychology from the University of California Los Angeles in 1985.

Robin Martin is an Associate Professor of Psychology and Director of the Centre for Organizational Psychology at the University of Queensland. He has research interests in both social and organizational psychology. He received his doctorate from the Open University with a thesis examining the effects of social categorization on minority influence. Following this he spent five years as a research fellow at the MRC/ESRC Social and Applied Psychology Unit at Sheffield University. During that time he was involved in projects examining the psychological and organizational implications of computer-controlled technology in manufacturing organizations. After leaving Sheffield, he held lecturing positions at the University of Wales, Swansea, and at Cardiff University. Following a sabbatical visit to the University of Queensland, he moved to his present position in 2000. In addition to his academic work, he has acted as a management consultant to a large number of public and private organizations. Robin's research interests are in attitude change, persuasion, majority and minority influence, workplace motivation and leadership, teamwork, and job relocation.

Sik Hung Ng is Professor of Social Psychology and Head of the Department of Applied Social Studies at the City University of Hong Kong. He is author of *The social psychology of power* (Academic Press, 1980), and, with James Bradac, *Power in language: Verbal communication and social influence* (Sage, 1993).

Robert G. Lord received his PhD in organizational psychology from Carnegie-Mellon University in 1975. He has been at the University of Akron since that time and is currently a professor in the Department of Psychology. He is a fellow of the Society for Industrial and Organizational Psychology and a founding fellow of the American Psychological Society. He has published extensively on topics related to motivation, self-regulation, social cognition, leadership processes, leadership perceptions, information processing. He co-authored *Leadership and information processing: Linking perceptions and performance*,

(Routledge, 1991) with Karen J. Maher and co-edited *Emotions in the workplace: Understanding the structure and role of emotions in organizational behavior* with Richard Klimoski and Ruth Kanfer (Jossey-Bass, 2002). He also served as associate editor of the *Journal of Applied Psychology*.

Diana Paulina was from 1980 to 1990, co-director of Unbound, Inc, a residential counselling center for former members of totalist groups. She has taught at High School Level. She wrote *Reintegration of exiting cult members with their families: A brief intervention model* with Kevin Crawley and Ron White. She currently is Vice President at Avalon Network inc.

Michael Platow is a senior lecturer in the School of Psychology at the Australian National University. His research uses social identity and self-categorization principles to study the social psychology of distributive and procedural justice, leadership, trust, social influence, and the self. Some lessons from this work are applied in his recent book *Giving professional presentations in the behavioral sciences* (Psychology Press, 2002).

Stephen Reicher is a social psychologist at the University of St Andrews. He has a general interest in group processes, especially mass social behavior, alongside more specific interests in political rhetoric and leadership. His most recent text on these issues (jointly with Nick Hopkins) is *Self and nation* (Sage, 2001) which analyses the use which politicians and activists make of national categories in order to mobilize their constituencies.

Scott Reid is an Assistant Professor in the Department of Communication at the University of California, Santa Barbara. Scott's research is framed by interests in intergroup relations, social identity, language, and power.

Cecilia L. Ridgeway is Professor of Sociology at Stanford University. She received her PhD in sociology from Cornell University. She is particularly interested in the role that social hierarchies in everyday interaction play in the larger processes of stratification and inequality in a society. Current projects include empirical tests of status construction theory, which is a theory about the power of interactional contexts to create and spread status beliefs about social differences. Other work addresses the role of interactional processes in preserving gender inequality despite major changes in the socioeconomic organization of society. In addition to research and teaching, she is currently the editor of *Social Psychology Quarterly*.

Tom Tyler is a University Professor of Psychology at New York University. His research explores authority dynamics in political, legal, and work organizations. In particular, he studies the role of procedural justice in shaping people's attitudes, feelings, and behaviors in groups, organizations, and societies.

Gerben A. van Kleef (MA, University of Amsterdam, 2000) is a PhD student in Organizational Psychology at the University of Amsterdam. His main stream of research concerns the interpersonal effects of emotions in negotiation.

Barbara van Knippenberg is Assistant Professor at the Psychology Department of the Vrije University in The Netherlands. Barbara's research interests include power and leadership, influence tactics, justice and identity processes in organizations.

Daan van Knippenberg is Professor of Organizational Behavior at the Rotterdam School of Management, Erasmus University Rotterdam, The Netherlands. Daan van Knippenberg's research is in the area of group processes (leadership, influence, diversity, decision making, performance; organizational identifications). In addition to the present volume, he co-edited *Social identity at work: Developing theory for organizational practice* (Psychology Press, 2003) with Alexander Haslam, Michael Platow, and Naomi Ellemers, and edited a special issue on social identity processes in organizations of *Group Processes and Intergroup Relations* together with Michael Hogg.

Karen Weeden is a PhD candidate in organizational psychology at the University of Queensland. She graduated from the Open University and obtained an MSc from the University of Hull. She is currently working on her dissertation research, which focuses on emotion, cognition and appraisal in the workplace. She is also interested in inter-group relations between leaders and followers, narratives, and implicit theories in organizations.

1 Identity, Leadership, and Power: Preface and Introduction

DAAN VAN KNIPPENBERG
AND MICHAEL A. HOGG

The study of leadership and power has always been a core concern for the social and behavioral sciences. Leadership is inextricably tied to group membership. Studying leadership therefore inevitably leads to questions concerning the social psychology of leadership. Somewhat surprisingly, however, for several decades leadership research has held a very modest position within social psychology. Recently, all this has changed, and leadership and power have re-emerged as important research themes in social psychology. These recent developments have been paralleled by, and fed into, developments in leadership research in the organizational sciences. This reinvigorated interest does not just pick up where earlier social psychological research left off, but approaches leadership and power from a new perspective. Although analyses vary in specific focus and emphasis, they have in common the fact that they are informed by social categorization theories which highlight individuals' social identity as group members and the role of social categorization processes in perceptions of and expectations about people and groups. This emphasis on social categorization and identity is paralleled by a similar development in the organizational sciences, where identity and the self-concept have gradually assumed center stage in behavioral research on leadership (e.g., Lord, Brown, and Freiberg, 1999; Shamir, House, and Arthur, 1993). This book is the first to bring together, in a single volume, proponents of these exciting new developments in research on leadership and power.

A key perspective in the social categorization approach to leadership and power is provided by social identity theories. Broadly defined, that is theories that are grounded in the concept of social identity as a self-construal in terms of one's membership of social groups (e.g., Brewer, 1991; Brewer and Gardner, 1996; Hogg and Abrams, 1988; Tajfel and Turner, 1986; Turner, Hogg, Oakes, Reicher, and Wetherell, 1987). Because leadership is pre-eminently a group process (e.g., Chemers, 2001), an analysis in social identity terms is ideally suited to tackle issues of leadership and power.

Social identity theories were originally developed to understand intergroup relations (see e.g., Tajfel, 1982; Brewer and Brown, 1998). More recently, however, it has been emphasized that, because they explain how our group memberships guide our perceptions of self and others, our beliefs and attitudes, and our behavior in the context of salient group memberships, social identity theories are suited to understand self-definition, perceptions, attitudes, and behavior in all group contexts (e.g., Hogg, 1996). This has turned the attention of social identity researchers more towards group processes within small groups, and accordingly more towards issues that are of importance in organizational contexts (e.g., Haslam, 2001; Haslam, van Knippenberg, Platow, and Ellemers, in press; Hogg and Terry, 2000, 2001a). This refocus has included leadership and power.

Accordingly, from the mid-1990s, a number of social identity studies and analyses of leadership have been published (e.g., Duck and Fielding, 1999; Haslam and Platow, 2001; Turner and Haslam, 2001; Reicher and Hopkins, 1999). Part of what set the stage for this book, and what positioned us for the role of editors of this volume, is our own work in this field. For many years we have explored social identity processes in organizational contexts. For example, at the University of Queensland, one of the key activities of the Center for Research on Group Processes over the last 12 years has been precisely this integration – which recently produced an edited book (Hogg and Terry, 2001a) and an Academy of Management Review article (Hogg and Terry, 2000). We have run, in 1997 and 2000, workshops on social identity in organizational contexts, sponsored by the Kurt Lewin Institute in the Netherlands. We also ran a conference in Amsterdam in 2000 sponsored by the European Association of Experimental Social Psychology, which was published as a special issue of the journal *Group Processes and Intergroup Relations* (van Knippenberg and Hogg, 2001). This integration of social identity and organizational analyses has always had a strong emphasis on leadership processes. In addition, over the past eight years or so, outside of this organizational link, we have worked on and developed a social identity model of leadership (e.g., Hains, Hogg, and Duck, 1997; Hogg, 1996, 2001a, 2001b; Hogg, Hains, and Mason, 1998; Hogg and van Knippenberg, in press; Platow and van Knippenberg, 2001; van Knippenberg, van Knippenberg and van Dijk, 2000). This analysis very broadly states that in high salience groups with which people identify strongly, leadership effectiveness is significantly influenced by how prototypical of the group the leader is perceived to be by the members.

The social identity perspective may be an important perspective in the new approach to leadership and power, but it is by no means the only perspective. Approaches that are more rooted in the social cognition tradition, with its focus on information processing and impression formation, have made important contributions to our understanding of leadership and power. An important perspective in this tradition is leadership categorization theory developed by Lord and associates (e.g., Lord, Foti, and DeVader, 1984; Lord and Maher, 1991), which focuses on the social cognitive processes that underlie leadership perceptions. More recently, this approach has been expanded to include theories of self-construal and social identity (Lord and Brown, 2001; Lord et al., 1999), thus providing a strong basis for further integration of social identity theories and social cognitive information processing theories of leadership. From a similar social cognitive perspective, there has also been considerable development in research on social power that focuses on the way power differentials affect information processing, stereotyping, and prejudice (e.g., Fiske, 1993; Goodwin, Gubin, Fiske & Yzerbyt, 2000). Although not with such a clear social cognitive basis, work on role identities has also been well attuned to the category-based shared social schemas that underlie the likelihood that individuals with different demographic backgrounds will be able to successfully assume leadership positions (e.g., Eagly and Karau, 2002; Ridgeway, 2001).

Inspired by the burgeoning of this field and the multitude of perspectives that all share a common basis in theories of social categorization, social identity, and social roles, and by our own enthusiasm for, and involvement in, the social identity analysis of leadership, we decided to edit this volume. Feeling that such a volume was timely, our aim was to integrate all these perspectives and approaches in a single forum. We hope this book will provide both a state-of-the-art overview of this burgeoning field, and a focal point for further theoretical integration and future research agendas.

The Future

This book underscores a new revival of leadership research in social psychology – a revival that is growing in strength as new opportunities for research are recognized. There are at least three important new directions that emerge from the chapters in this volume.

All the chapters in this volume share a common basis in theories of social categorization, social identity, and social roles. At the same time, however, they are very diverse in emphasis and terminology, and in the work leading up to the present chapters it often is just as easy *not* to see the common ground shared by some analyses as it is to see the common ground shared by others. One of the things we hope to accomplish with this volume is to make the links and overlap between these different analyses more visible, thus placing firmly on the agenda for future research further integration of these approaches.

One important new direction is an exploration of the interplay of social identity analyses of leadership and organizational science theories of leadership effectiveness. A number of the chapters in this book have started to explore charismatic and transformational leadership and leader-member exchange – probably now the two dominant perspectives on leadership in the organizational sciences. This is an exciting development, because it opens up the possibility of integrating major perspectives on effective leadership from social psychology and from the organizational sciences that have so far largely led separate lives. The key to this integration seems to lie in the social identity processes that are highlighted in the present volume (e.g., De Cremer, Chapter 7; De Cremer and van Knippenberg, 2002; Haslam and Platow, 2001; Hogg et al., Chapter 3; Hogg and van Knippenberg, in press; Platow et al., Chapter 4; Lord and Brown, 2003; Lord et al., 1999; Lord and Hall, Chapter 5).

Another new direction is an examination of the ways social identities shape and are shaped by leaders' behavior (for example the chapters by Kramer, Reicher and Hopkins, and Reid and Ng). Within this perspective two key questions concern how leaders construct and communicate their leadership properties and their group prototypicality, and how leadership may be constrained by leaders' self-construal. These are important research questions that have so far been under-represented in research. Moreover, as is evident from these chapters, much of the research in this area has relied on analysis of case material. Expanding and extending the volume of research in this area and complementing the present analyses with quantitative and experimental studies would seem another important avenue for future research.

Acknowledgments

In closing this introductory section we would like to thank our contributors for being so cooperative and efficient in meeting our various requests in terms of timing and space considerations. They have been a wonderful group to work with. We would also like to express a special thanks to the team at Sage in London, particularly to Michael Carmichael and Zoë Elliott, for being so enthusiastic and supportive, and for providing wise practical advice. Finally, because Daan and Michael live on different sides of the globe, we have needed to travel extensively to meet to discuss and plan this project. Without financial support from various research bodies this would have been impossible. We would therefore like to acknowledge the Australian Research Council, the Kurt Lewin Institute, and the European Association of Experimental Social Psychology, for their support over the years of our collaboration.

Daan van Knippenberg
Amsterdam, June 2002
Michael Hogg
Bristol, June 2002

2 Leadership Effectiveness: Functional, Contructivist and Empirical Perspectives

MARTIN M. CHEMERS

Three Dialectics of Group Life

Naturally occurring groups – not ad hoc laboratory groups with no history and no future working on a task with no meaning; and not questionnaire-based scenarios that exist only in the manipulated imaginations of college sophomores, but real groups – exist for a purpose with meaning and consequences. Any attempt to understand leadership in naturally occurring groups must recognize that reality.

It is the thesis of this chapter that the performance demands placed on naturally occurring groups significantly affect the dynamics of those groups, and that appropriate research and theorizing on leadership and power must recognize the important role of performance in group life.

The purpose, goal, or task of naturally occurring groups usually arises from an environment that is external to the group. But the group also has an internal environment that must be managed in order to ensure that it is capable of dealing with its external purpose. The internal environment makes demands for order, predictability, meaning, inclusion, and identity. The external environment makes demands for attention, flexibility, responsiveness, and effectiveness. The demands of the internal and external environments are not always perfectly compatible. For example, the members of a group might feel most comfortable with a decision-making process that relies heavily on internal conformity to group traditions, even though a complex and fast changing environment requires innovative solutions. The dialectic divergence between internal and external demands creates one of the powerful tensions of group life.

A second dialectic anomaly of group life is that groups, while real entities with a common purpose, are made up of individuals. The individual members of groups bring their own personal, sometimes selfish, goals to group interaction, and those goals may be independent of, or contradictory to, the goals and needs of the group as a collective whole. For example, an individual member of a group might evaluate his/her contributions to the group and the appropriate reward for those contributions in a more positive manner than others might, creating internal conflict that lessens the group's ability to mobilize its collective resources most effectively. Resolving individual and collective interests is a second tension of group life.

A third distinction can be made between what might be thought of as the relatively objective versus the relatively subjective aspects of group and individual perception and knowledge. Members of a group have perceptions of the group's competence, status, or some other characteristic that may be more or less accurate. The relative importance of objective accuracy for the group will vary with the conditions of the group's situation. For example, it might be psychologically rewarding for the group members to evaluate their task-relevant, collective efficacy at an overly positive level. However, the inaccuracy of those perceptions would be very costly if it occurred in a situation that carried significant consequences, such as might be the case if a military unit unexpectedly engaged with a more powerful or better prepared foe.

These three potentially contradictory elements of groups – that they must respond to both internal and external environmental demands; that they must accommodate both individual and collective goals and interests; and that they must negotiate a balance between subjective and objective realities – create a challenge for theories of group effectiveness, leadership, and power. Different theoretical perspectives can be more or less attuned to one or the other pole of the dialectic dimensions of group life, but a complete and ultimately useful theory of leadership and group effectiveness must attend to the full spectrum. I turn now to a discussion of how these three dialectic perspectives play out in the analysis of the basic components of effective leadership.

Three Essential Components of Effective Leadership

Leadership is a process of social influence in which the leader enlists the talents and efforts of other group members, i.e., followers, in order to accomplish the group's chosen task. For some groups (e.g., a recreational club), the only goal may be the happiness and satisfaction of group members. Such groups are rare. Most groups exist for the purpose of accomplishing an assigned task.

Leadership success for task-focused groups can best be defined as the level of task performance sustained over the appropriate time period. This definition of success reflects the recognition that factors other than short-term productivity or performance, such as sustained levels of commitment and motivation of group members, are essential to group success in the long run.

Effective leadership has three essential components. First, the would-be leader must induce the other members of the group to regard that person as a credible and legitimate source of influence, i.e., as having a special status and responsibility in the activities of the group. Once a person has gained the legitimacy of leadership status, she or he must develop relationships with followers that motivate and enable them to act to attain collective goals. Finally, the leader must mobilize and direct the efforts of the group to make the most effective use of the combined resources of the group in task accomplishment.

Image management: establishing credibility and earning status

Status is a central concept in the study of leadership. Because leadership is a process of social influence, a potential leader's first necessity is to gain the credibility and authority to exert influence. Hollander (1958; Hollander and Julian, 1969) established that a leader's legitimacy flows from the perception that the leader is competent enough to help the group attain its goal and trustworthy enough to remain loyal to collective interests and objectives. The two factors – competency, rooted in the group's externally oriented goals, and trustworthiness, tied to the internal norms and values of the group – are the bases for judgments about the leader. An examination of the leadership literature reveals that theories about the source of a leader's influence diverge depending upon which perspective (internal or external) is most prominent.

The work of Lord and his associates (Lord and Maher, 1991; Lord and Smith, 1998; Chapter 5) provides a rich and comprehensive examination of the social-cognitive factors that affect perceptions of leadership. Lord, Foti, and de Vader (1984) established that observers possess implicit theories about what a good leader is and does, and these theories give rise to a set of stereotypical traits and behaviors which leaders are expected to exhibit. Individuals displaying the characteristics appropriate to a particular category of leaders (e.g., military, political, business, religious) are 'recognized' as leaders (Lord and Maher, 1991). Effective leaders are aware of this process and seek to present an image consistent with followers' and other observers' expectations. It should be noted that the stereotypical characteristics associated with task-focused leadership tend to be those that indicate task or goal relevant competence, such as decisiveness, insight, or coolness under pressure.

Another contributor to judgments of leadership suitability involves observers' inferences about positive or negative outcomes ostensibly associated with the leader's actions (Lord and Maher, 1991). Thus, leaders who can take credit for positive outcomes (e.g., an increase in company profits) and avoid responsibility for failures are likely to gain status and influence. In the case of both the prototypical traits to be recognized and the evidence of success to be inferred, the judgments of leadership are strongly influenced by the leader's ability to foster and promote the group's effective goal attainment.

Hogg and his associates (2001; Hains, Hogg, and Duck, 1997) have taken a very different perspective on how leaders establish legitimacy. From the standpoint of social identity theory (Tajfel and Turner, 1979), groups are seen as a vehicle for an individual to establish and maintain a distinct and positive personal identity. That identity is based in large part on the properties and characteristics of the groups of which the individual is a member. To maintain a clear and distinct identity, the individual must focus on the ways in which his or her group is different from and better than other groups. This categorization process leads to a strong need to characterize the in-group and out-group and results in a definition of each group on the basis of the prototypical character- istics of the group (Turner, 1985). Status in the group is determined by each individual's conformity with the representative characteristics of the group, i.e., by his or her prototypicality. (The social identity theorists use the term prototypicality to denote the *particularistic* normative attitudes and behaviors of the in-group. This causes some confusion, because Lord and his associates use the term 'prototype' to indicate the characteristics associated with the *universal* category of leader. Hogg uses the term 'stereotypicality' to denote universal characteristics. In deference to the distinguished editors of the current volume, I follow the practice of the social identity theorists here.)

Because leadership is based on status, Hogg (2001) maintains that leaders are those individuals who are most prototypical, i.e., in greatest conformity with the most central and representative characteristics of the group. At one level, this idea is quite consistent with Hollander's (1958) notion that one of the con- tributors to status is the leader's perceived trustworthiness, which is based on behavior that is in conformity with group norms. However, the similarity between the two theories is misleading. In Hollander's model, conformity was important, because it reassured group members that the influence afforded to the leader would be used for purposes consistent with group values and goals. For Hogg, prototypicality serves a different purpose.

By being prototypical, the individual becomes socially attractive. Other members, who themselves desire to be highly prototypical, want to interact with and be close to the most prototypical group members and are willing to accept influence from them. Rather than conformity being a vehicle for sanc- tioning the use of influence earned through evidence of task relevant compe- tence, conformity (i.e., prototypicality) becomes the basis for influence. Further, the leader's influence and authority are exaggerated, because when she or he encourages other group members to behave in prototypical ways which they were likely to do anyway, their resultant compliance appears as further evi- dence of the leader's power, influence and authority. The leader's ability to move the group towards some externally defined task is not a central feature in the social identity theory approach to leadership.

A number of studies have been conducted to test the social identity theory of leadership (Hain, Hogg and Duck, 1997; Fielding and Hogg, 1997; Hogg and van Knippenberg, in press; Chapter 3). These studies involve evaluations of real or potential group leaders and use three common variables; (a) the extent to which the leader is described as expressing attitudes consistent with the group prototype, (b) the extent to which the leader displays behavior consistent with the universal schema of an effective leader (Lord and Maher, 1991), and (c) the importance of group identity to the group member/rater. The studies are designed to test the hypothesis that strong group identification is associated with a preference for highly prototypical leaders. The results of these studies largely support the hypothesis revealing that increasing group identification is associated with an increase in the relative evaluation of the prototypical leader and a less positive evaluation of the schema consistent (i.e., task competent) leader.

The social identity leadership research appears to be in conflict with the earlier work on the perception of effective leadership (Hollander, 1958; Lord and Maher, 1991). The social identity findings emphasize the leader's prototypicality, while the earlier work emphasizes the leader's competence. In fact, I believe the two approaches to be complementary, rather than contradictory, and their relevant insights depend on whether one takes an externally focused, goal oriented perspective or an internally focused, personal perspective. The two approaches reflect two aspects of follower desires in groups (also see Chapter 5).

Followers want to feel included, supported, and reinforced by their group memberships. When such needs are aroused and made salient, a homogeneous group with common norms and values is comforting, and prototypical leaders are reassuring. To the extent that the members of a group are internally focused, that agenda will be sufficient for satisfaction and positive evaluation of a leader. However, when groups exist in a demanding environment in which the welfare of each group member is at least partially determined by the group's success in achieving some tangible goal, other leader characteristics become desirable. A leader who possesses and displays behaviors that are likely to move the group toward its goal and who achieves success will be highly valued by group members. A comprehensive view of leadership should take into account both the internally oriented needs of followers for inclusion and identity and the externally oriented needs of followers for goal attainment and success. The relative salience of each of these needs will help to determine the basis for evaluating leaders and assigning intra-group status.

However, status accrual and influence are part of a dynamic group process and involve more than simple judgments of prototypicality or competence. Our discussion of leader credibility and legitimacy accrual must attend to two other issues which are (1) the factors that bias and distort judgments of competence or prototypicality and (2) the way that such biases affect the dynamic struggle for status ascendancy in groups.

Observer perceptions of the degree to which a potential leader possesses characteristics indicative of competency, trustworthiness, and prototypicality are not objective judgments. Rather, such perceptions are heavily influenced by the biases, stereotypes, and expectations that the observer brings to every social encounter. Nowhere is this more clearly revealed than in the study of factors associated with judgments of women as leaders. Almost three decades ago, Schein (1975) found that the stereotypical traits associated with managers were much more similar to the gender stereotypes for men than for women, and that this difference made it far more difficult for women to be recognized as leaders or as appropriate for leadership roles. A comprehensive meta-analysis of the evaluation of male and female leaders by Eagly, Karau, and Makhijani (1995) documented that women leaders suffer from biased expectations particularly in settings where female leadership is highly non-traditional (e.g., organized sports) or when ratings are made by men who hold negative attitudes about female leadership. When biases are removed, the actual performance of male and female leaders in a variety of settings is quite similar (also see Chapter 7).

Lord and Maher (1991) suggest that biases against female leadership are strongest when objective evidence of competence is less available, i.e., before the leader has had a chance to serve in the role. Bias is reduced when observers, especially followers, have more information about the female leader's behavior and performance. Gender is not the only factor that biases perceptions of leadership potential, but it is quite illuminative in illustrating the tension between objective and subjective forces in group functioning. To the extent that leader competence is related to group success, biased judgments are a potential threat to the viability and success of the group.

Berger and his colleagues (Berger, Cohen, and Zelditch, 1972; Berger, Ridgeway, Fisek, and Norman, 1998) have addressed broadly the way in which status accrual is affected by the various characteristics that individuals bring to the group encounter. Characteristics such as gender, race, age, or occupation are associated with *status value*, because of the expectations they create among group members. Our cultural and social beliefs lead us to expect certain individuals to contribute more to the success of the group than would others. The expectation states create the initial hierarchies that influence participation, evaluation, and influence. It is very important to recognize, however, that while such judgments might be highly biased and unfair, they are based on sincere expectations of value to the group.

Ridgeway (2001; Chapter 6) makes the cogent point that group members have three sets of interests in goal-oriented groups. They have a cooperative interest in giving authority on the basis of expected contribution so as to maximize collective rewards. They have a competitive and selfish interest in gaining personal status to increase their personal share of rewards, both tangible and psychological. Finally, they have a collective interest in ensuring that status will be granted to others on the basis of their likely contributions to the maximization of collective benefits to be claimed. This last interest – to see that the most competent and valuable members of the group attain the highest status – will affect the eventual awarding of authority in dynamic, contested status struggles that often occur in groups.

Chan and Drasgow (2001) have shown that individuals vary in their desire or motivation to lead. The motivation to lead affects their attempts to participate in leadership roles and influences the judgments of others about their suitability for such roles. Ridgeway (2001) argues that as a group's interactions proceed, more and more information about each group member's characteristics (e.g., competencies) becomes available to all. In dominance struggles for the leadership role, group members may support the attempts to gain leadership status by competent members who initially entered the interaction process with lower status by virtue of their social characteristics (e.g. race, gender, occupation, etc.). To the extent that such processes play out in a way that elevates competent and trustworthy individuals into positions of status and influence, the group is likely to benefit.

From the foregoing analysis, we see that the process of status accrual in groups is framed by both internal and external factors, involves both selfish and collective interests, and is played out in ways that include both objective and subjective processes. Theory and research investigating the role of social influence in leadership, power, and group effectiveness should take all three of these dialectic perspectives into account.

Relationship development: building capacity and motivation

Once a leader has established a basis for influence, the next task is to motivate followers to contribute enthusiastically to the attainment of the group's goals and to help followers develop the capacity to make such contributions. Relationships that create competence and motivation involve effective coaching which is guided by sensitive and accurate judgment and delivered in a context of fairness.

Leaders alone do not accomplish the tasks of groups. So, to understand effective leadership, it is first necessary to recognize the characteristics of effective followership. The first such characteristic is ability, both real and perceived. Followers must, of course, have the knowledge and skills to carry out the tasks under their purview. That followers have the requisite competencies must be recognised by the leader, but also by the followers, because task-relevant self-efficacy (Bandura, 1997; Chemers, Watson, and May, 2000) is an essential feature of high performance.

Second, followers must feel the desire (i.e., motivation) to expend effort to perform at high levels. The most effective form of motivation arises from the tasks themselves and the opportunities for personal growth and gratification they afford to the follower (Hackman and Oldham, 1976). However, motivation must also be translated into long-term commitment to group and organizational goals in order to create a stable team that contributes at the necessary levels over time. In his definition of work team effectiveness, Hackman (1987) makes team viability a central concept. Viable teams are characterized by high levels of member satisfaction, participation in team activities, and willingness to continue to work together as a team – in a word, commitment. To build follower efficacy and to help followers recognize their own efficacy requires good coaching by the leader.

Coaching and guidance

Effective leaders provide subordinates with direction and support (i.e., coaching) that helps them to accomplish their goals. Leadership theories that are focused on subordinate motivation, such as path–goal theory (House and Mitchell, 1974) have shown that the form of coaching that is most effective depends on the situation and the specific needs and personality of the particular subordinate. Directive or instructive leader behavior may have its most positive effects when the subordinate is low in knowledge or experience or is confronted with a very difficult task. On the other hand, considerate, supportive leader behavior is most beneficial (i.e., will result in the highest levels of subordinate satisfaction and motivation) when an aversive job environment creates a need for sympathy or encouragement.

At the core of this analysis lie the characteristics of intrinsically motivating jobs, i.e., that through the requisite levels of autonomy and performance feedback, they provide the individual with maximal opportunities for contribution, meaningfulness, and personal growth and challenge (Hackman and Oldham, 1976). Leader behaviors that help to build that kind of task environment for subordinates can be maximally motivating.

Judgment

What is also implicit in this analysis is that each subordinate is a unique individual. One size does not fit all. Not all subordinates want direction, even when they are confused, and not all subordinates find the same situations to be threatening. For example, followers who have a strong need for personal growth and development are less likely to be threatened by a complex or difficult task and their need for autonomy make them less likely to respond positively to direction and control from their superiors.

A central component of transformational leadership (Bass, 1985) is 'individualized consideration,' which refers to leader behaviors that indicate a concern and understanding for each subordinate as an individual. An effective leader must be sensitive to a follower's situation, personality, and emotional state.

Thus, a leader functions in an attributional nexus, evaluating the information available about a subordinate's performance and behavior to understand the causes of performance which then, in turn, suggest the appropriate strategies for coaching and support. Studies of subordinate attributions by leaders (Green and Mitchell, 1979) reveal that judgments are guided by the traditional factors of distinctiveness, consistency, and consensus (Kelley, 1967), and susceptible to the same tendency to overemphasize the role of the actor (Jones and Nisbett, 1971) as are other forms of attribution. However, a particular aspect of the leader–follower relationship adds a powerful additional factor to this judgmental process. Leaders and followers are tied together in a relationship of 'reciprocal causality' (Brown, 1984). The performance of the follower reflects on the effectiveness of the leader, and the leader's actions have important implications for the follower's welfare. For example, a follower might perform poorly on a task, because the leader has failed to provide clear instructions or failed to structure the task properly. Leaders are often slow to recognize their own responsibility in subordinate failure. Excellent leaders must overcome the natural tendency toward self-serving ego defensiveness that can cloud their judgment and render their actions ineffective or even damaging.

To this point, our discussion of coaching, guidance, and motivation has been based on the implicit assumption of a transactional quid pro quo. Followers are motivated to expend effort, work diligently, and perform well if the situation provides them with opportunities that they find personally rewarding, either through tangible external rewards (e.g., pay and promotion) or less tangible, intrinsic rewards, such as growth and self-esteem. But leadership theorists of the past (e.g., Weber, 1947) and present (e.g., House, 1976; Bass, 1985) have argued that truly great leadership (i.e., leadership that transforms followers) requires that followers shift their motivational perspective from a self-interested concern for personal rewards to a commitment to achieve the collective mission. House and Shamir (1993) argue that leaders can accomplish that transformation by influencing followers to tie their personal satisfaction to the attainment of the group's goal. The capability of a leader to have that sort of influence is built on a foundation of trust between the leader and the follower. The basis of such trust is the follower's perception that the leader is honest and operates with justice and fairness.

Fairness

The leadership relationship, like all social relationships, is an exchange (Thibaut and Kelley, 1959). To be motivating and sustainable, the leader–follower exchange must be fair and equitable. Followers need to believe that they are being reasonably compensated for their efforts and loyalty.

Graen and his associates (Graen and Scandura, 1987) take the exchange notion further. Their research shows that subordinates who are in a highly satisfying exchange relationship with their superior – characterized by access to information, interesting assignments, and personal growth opportunities – are motivated to maintain the relationship by working hard, contributing to team success, and remaining loyal to the leader and the organization. Indeed, followers who feel fairly treated are likely to engage in 'organizational citizenship behaviors' which Organ (1990) defines as behaviors that are discretionary and not explicitly rewarded, but which can improve organizational functioning, i.e., the kinds of 'extra effort' contributions that distinguish successful from unsuccessful teams and organizations.

However, to understand fully what factors affect perceptions of leadership fairness and the implications of those perceptions for organizational functioning, we have to go beyond the limited focus on quid pro quo allocations of outcomes dealt with in theories of transactional exchange. We must turn to the broader and more important domain of procedural justice in organizations.

The earliest work on justice in organizations was focused on fairness in the distribution of outcomes (Adams, 1965), but it was soon recognized that perceptions of the fairness of the process by which decisions were made was equally important (Thibaut and Walker, 1975). (For comprehensive reviews of the empirical literature on procedural justice in organizations, see Cropanzano and Greenberg, 1997; or Lind and Tyler, 1988. Our focus here is on the more specific relationship between leadership and justice.)

Justice has been conceptualized in a variety of ways, including allowing subordinates input in decision-making, i.e., voice (Thibaut and Walker, 1975); consistency and the use of accurate and correctable information (Leventhal, 1980);

treating subordinates with respect and dignity (Tyler and Bies, 1990); and providing information and justification about decisions (Bies and Moag, 1986). Although these distinctions can be supported as separate, they are, in fact, moderately intercorrelated and their effects on various organizational outcomes are reasonably similar (Colquitt, Conlon, Wesson, Porter, and Ng, 2001). For our purposes it is fair to say that leaders who listen to followers, explain their decisions, and treat followers with respect, politeness, and dignity evoke high levels of trust and positive evaluations among those followers. Further, high levels of trust in a leader are associated with greater satisfaction with the leader, attachment to the team, and high performance (Dirks, 2000; Phillips, Douthitt, and Hyland, 2001; also see Chapters 8 and 9).

Cropanzano and Greenberg (1997) make the point that justice is socially constructed. That is, an act or decision is just if the parties involved believe it to be just. Nonetheless, the implications of justice perceptions are far reaching. People who believe their leaders, and by implication their organizations, to be fair are motivated to give extra effort, make long–term commitments, and to be open to leader influence. The process of shifting an individual's motivational orientation from self to collective interest depends on such trust and confidence in the fairness of leadership. Here again we see the dialectic interplay between subjective and objective aspects of leadership and between individual and collective aspects of group life.

To this point in our discussion, most of the key elements of leadership effectiveness have been rooted in perceptions and social constructions. Perceptions of competence, loyalty, and fairness can be divorced from an external reality, but when we turn to the third facet of effective leadership, resource deployment (i.e., the utilization of the group's energy, knowledge, and capacities for goal accomplishment), we abut a less malleable external environment.

Resource deployment: utilizing group process for goal attainment

When a leader has established legitimacy and built relationships that prepare, guide, and motivate followers, the success of the group in accomplishing its assigned task depends on how well the leader is able to make use of the capacities of the group. Successful deployment has two aspects.

The group needs to adopt task accomplishment strategies that are appropriate to task environment. One of the first great breakthroughs in leadership research was the recognition that task or organizational environments differed primarily in the degree to which information for decision-making was stable, clear, and unequivocal, versus dynamic, complex, and contestable (Fiedler, 1967; Lawrence and Lorsch, 1967). Groups or teams with well understood and orderly task environments benefited from leadership that emphasized clear direction, tight control, and relatively top-down decision-making strategies, while effective leadership in more equivocal task settings employed more participative and flexible leadership styles.

For example, an extensive body of research on Fiedler's contingency model (Ayman, Chemers, and Fiedler, 1998; Fiedler, 1967) has found that task-oriented leaders who tend to employ a directive leadership style have the most effective teams when they enjoy high levels of cooperation from followers and clear, structured tasks. Relationship-oriented leaders, whose leadership style is more focused on issues of team morale and who employ more participative decision-making, function best in the more ambiguous environments that are created when tasks are complex and unclear or followers are not totally supportive of the leader or committed to the group enterprise. Vroom and Yetton's (1973) normative decision model of leadership decision-making reaches similar conclusions.

When leaders employ decision styles that are appropriate to the task environment, attention to and processing of the most important and relevant information is enhanced. That is, directive styles provide for speed and efficiency in orderly and predictable environments, and participative, open decision environments allow for more information and for its creative integration, which is most useful when well understood solutions are not available. However, choosing the right strategy is only half the story in effective deployment. The other half concerns the ability of the leader to elicit and maintain team commitment in the face of the inevitable ups and downs, successes and setbacks of group life.

Recent research by Chemers and his associates (Chemers, Watson, and May, 2000; Watson, Chemers, and Preiser, 2001) has found that a leader's confidence in his or her ability to lead (i.e., leadership self-efficacy) and the collective efficacy of the team are critical components of team success over the long run. Chemers et al. (2000) found that leadership confidence among military cadets was strongly related to perceptions of leadership ability by instructors, ratings of leadership performance by superiors and peers, and to performance in military combat simulations. In a study of men's and women's college basketball teams, Watson et al. (2001) reported that teams led by captains high in leadership self-efficacy were characterized by more team collective efficacy (i.e., confidence in the team's ability to perform and win) at the beginning of the season, were able to maintain high collective efficacy throughout the season, and won more games during the season and in post-season competition than were teams led by less confident captains.

In a study of college basketball teams that focused on the role of followers' trust in their leader, Dirks (2001) found that trust was strongly related to team performance. Teams who reported high levels of trust in their coach early in the season excelled, and high team performance further reinforced and increased perceptions of trust. When leaders enjoy the trust of their followers, their influence is enhanced. This allows the leader's confidence and enthusiasm to bolster the collective efficacy of the team, providing the basis for high levels of effort and perseverance. Watson et al. (2001) reported that the relationship between the team's evaluation of the leader and the team's collective efficacy was strongest for teams that had amassed a poor performance record during the early part of the season. In other words, the leader may become most important when helping the group deal with adversity.

In these studies of college athletes or military units in battlefield simulations, success is not a social construction. Performance feedback comes clearly and unequivocally in the form of won and lost records or performance ratings by observers. While leaders can help to spin the implications of feedback and maintain team confidence, they cannot deny performance outcomes. Research paradigms that do not incorporate a realistic connection to a group goal miss the role that performance plays in leadership.

Some Conclusions

In this chapter, I have argued that effective leadership is based on three elements. Because leadership is, at center, a process of social influence, a potential leader must establish the credibility on which to base influence. The sources that contribute to the garnering of credibility and status are many and include possessing the traits associated with leadership effectiveness, espousing attitudes consistent with group prototypes, being associated with positive performance outcomes, and projecting a sense of personal efficacy.

Second, a leader must prepare followers to contribute to the attainment of the collective mission. That preparation involves providing the direction and guidance that allows followers to develop skills and confidence in a manner that is motivating. To provide the right level of guidance at the right time, a leader must be able to make accurate judgments about the follower's need for, and receptivity to, direction. Good judgments are based on sensitivity to both the follower's performance as well as a recognition of the leader's own responsibility for that performance. Also, it must be acknowledged that attempts to motivate and direct subordinates cannot be successful unless they take place in an atmosphere of fairness. Leaders who listen to the opinions and advice of followers, treat followers with politeness, respect, and dignity, and who explain the bases for their decisions, are likely to be seen as just and to increase trust and the capacity for influence.

Finally, leaders must foster the material and psychological resources of the group and deploy them for mission accomplishment. Effective deployment involves the choice of information processing, decision-making, and delegation strategies that match the nature of the group's mission-relevant environment. Orderly and predictable environments call for different strategies than do complex, poorly understood, and equivocal environments. Once the accurate information has been compiled and the correct decision has been reached the energies and motivations of group members must be deployed for maximum impact over the long run. A major component of that deployment is maintaining high levels of individual and collective efficacy that allow each group member and the team as a whole to act with enthusiasm and maintain focus and energy despite setbacks or difficulties.

These three elements of effective leadership can be researched and understood employing a variety of theoretical approaches and methodological techniques. A phenomenon as complex as leadership is more likely to yield its secrets to a multi-pronged attack. However, the study of group processes is one of the most complex endeavors in social psychology. The student of groups must recognise the contradictory elements of groups.

Groups are made up of individuals with particular interests. It is very useful to understand that individual perspective, but groups are also collectivities with common interests. To ignore the impact of those common interests reduces the utility of the theory. Likewise, although many goals and needs of individuals (e.g., for identity or inclusion) are played out in internal processes, groups are most often assembled for purposes that find realization in the external environment. Research designs that attempt to model internal group processes, but ignore external demands, cannot adequately reveal those processes. Finally, group processes are affected both by social constructions and more objective realities. Both of these influences are important.

High quality research that is likely to yield important findings over the long run must integrate the contradictory features of group life into a comprehensive research program. This certainly entails research in both the laboratory and the field, and across a range of types of groups and organizations. In the chapters included in this volume, such a range of approaches, theories, research strategies, and contexts is displayed. The thoughtful reader can gain considerable knowledge by comparing, contrasting, and integrating the multiple perspectives offered.

3 Leader–Member Relations and Social Identity

MICHAEL A. HOGG, ROBIN MARTIN, AND KAREN WEEDEN

The question we address in this chapter is a simple one. To be effective, should leaders, particularly leaders of relatively small groups such as work teams in organizations, treat their followers in a *depersonalized* manner as an undifferentiated mass of people who share membership in the same group? Or should leaders treat them in a *personalized* manner that acknowledges them as unique individuals who differ from other group members?

At first sight, a personalized leadership style might appear to be the most effective. Being recognized and treated by the leader as a unique individual is likely to be more rewarding than being treated merely as one of the crowd. Thus, a personalized leadership style should build strong and rewarding inter-personal leader–member bonds that allow the leader to lead easily and effectively. Indeed, there is a body of theory, called leader–member exchange (LMX) theory, and supporting data, that explicates this process (e.g., Graen and Uhl-Bien, 1995; Schriesheim, Castro, and Cogliser, 1999; Sparrowe and Liden, 1997).

In this chapter we would like to question this assumption and propose that other styles of leadership might be appropriate in different contexts. Under some circumstances, specifically where there is high group solidarity and members identify very strongly with the group, a depersonalized leader–member relations style may be preferable because it recognizes and affirms one's membership in the group and treats all members as equals. In this context, a personalized leadership style might be counter-productive as it could make group members feel uncomfortably isolated from the group with which they so strongly identify, and this would generate opposition to the leader. This analysis is consistent with the recent social identity analysis of leadership processes (e.g., Hogg, 2001a; Hogg, in press b; Hogg and van Knippenberg, 2003; also see Chapters 4 and 10).

In this chapter, we briefly describe LMX theory and the social identity theory of leadership. We explore and make predictions about the conditions under which a personalized or depersonalized leader-member relations style enhances leadership effectiveness, and describe two studies designed to examine these predictions and to extend the analysis. We close by outlining some conceptual developments that suggest directions for future research.

Defining Leadership

Research on the social psychology of leadership has a long and illustrious history. For example, it was an important focus of research in the small group dynamics tradition of social psychology (e.g., Shaw, 1981). Attempts to identify stable context-independent personality traits associated with effective leadership have only met with limited success (Stogdill, 1974). There is better support for the idea that people's leadership effectiveness varies from situation to situation (e.g., Carter and Nixon, 1949). Research has generally shown that leadership effectiveness is an interaction between leadership styles and situational demands. This perspective culminated in Fiedler's (1965) contingency theory, which suggested that leadership effectiveness is contingent upon the leader's style (i.e., person-oriented or task-oriented) and the favorability of the situation for the leader to influence group members.

The influence of social cognition on social psychology (Devine, Hamilton, and Ostrom, 1994) underpins a social perception perspective on leadership – *leader categorization theory* (e.g., Lord, 1985; Nye and Simonetta, 1996; Chapter 5). People have an array of different schemas of how leaders should behave in general or more specific situations – i.e., we have a repertoire of leader categories. Once we categorize someone as a leader, by virtue of behavioral cues, the associated schema generates further information about that person which encourages followers to let him or her lead effectively.

Another strand of leadership research highlights the role of followers in leadership processes, and focuses on *transactional leadership*. Effective leadership rests on the nature of the transactions between leaders and followers, in which followers allow leaders to lead (e.g., Bass 1990). For example, a leader who behaves as a good solid group member can gradually accrue idiosyncrasy credits, which can be spent later by acting as an innovative leader (Hollander, 1958; Hollander and Julian, 1970). This idea has been extended by research on *transformational leadership* that has become popular in organizational psychology (Bass, 1990, 1998; Bass and Avolio, 1993). Transformational leaders' transactions with followers are characterized by idealized behavior, inspirational motivation, intellectual stimulation, and individualized consideration, which motivate followers to work for group goals that transcend immediate self-interest. Transformational leaders are those who respond positively to change and who actively induce change. The notion of charisma plays a significant role in transformational leadership perspectives, but critics have worried that this may lead us back to early notions of personality and leadership (e.g., Haslam and Platow, 2001a).

Our own perspective is that leadership is quintessentially a group process. It identifies a relationship in which some people are able to influence others to embrace, as their own, new values, attitudes and goals, and to exert effort on behalf of, and in pursuit of, those values, attitudes and goals. The relationship is almost always played out within a group context – a small group like a team, a medium-sized group like an organization, or a large group like a nation. The values, attitudes, goals and behaviors that leaders inspire others to adopt and to follow, are ones that serve the group as a collective, and that define membership of the group. Thus, leaders are able to transform individual action into group action. Leadership is an essential feature of social groups; it is very difficult to think about groups without thinking about who leads or manages them, and about how well they are lead or managed. This characterization of leadership places a premium on the role of group membership and group life in the analysis of leadership; leadership is 'a process of social influence through which an individual enlists and mobilizes the aid of others in the attainment of a collective goal' (Chemers, 2001, p. 376).

Leader–Member Exchange (LMX) Theory

Theory

Leader–member exchange (LMX) theory (e.g., Graen and Uhl-Bien, 1995; Schriesheim, Castro, and Cogliser, 1999; Sparrowe and Liden, 1997) is a transactional leadership theory. The development of the theory was in reaction to the dominant view that leaders adopt the same leadership style with all group members, which had been implicitly assumed by behavioral and contingency models of leadership (the so called 'average leadership style' approach). The initial version of the LMX approach was proposed by Graen and his colleagues, called the vertical *dyad linkage model* (VDL) (Dansereau, Cashman and Graen, 1973; Graen, 1976; Graen and Cashman, 1975). The focus was on dyadic exchange relationships between the leader and specific subordinates. The quality of these relationships can vary widely, with initial versions of the theory suggesting that leaders form ingroup and outgroup relationships with their subordinates. More recent theorizing within the LMX area pays less attention to the in- versus outgroup status of these relationships but more to the *quality* of the exchanges. Low quality LMX relationships are ones where subordinates are disfavored by the leader and thus receive fewer valued resources. Leader–member exchanges simply adhere to the terms of the employment contract, with little attempt by the leader to develop or motivate the subordinate. In contrast, high quality LMX relationships are ones where subordinates are favored by the leader and thus receive many valued resources. Leader–member exchanges go beyond the formal employment contract, with managers showing influence and support, and giving the subordinate greater autonomy and responsibility. LMX theory predicts that effective leaders should develop high quality LMX relationships with their subordinates, because these should enhance subordinates' well-being and work performance.

Research

Research on LMX theory has shown that in organizations, managers tend to differentiate among their subordinates, and establish better LMX relationships with some subordinates than with others (Dansereau, Graen and Haga, 1975; Johnson and Graen, 1973; Vecchio, 1982). According to Liden and Graen (1980), over 90 per cent of managers vary greatly in the quality of the relationship they have with their subordinates. There is probably a practical reason for this. Managers have limited resources, with many demands upon their time, and therefore direct resources to a smaller number of their subordinates who take primary responsibility for helping with work-related issues. Differentiation in quality of relationships may be a functional strategy adopted by managers to achieve optimal performance when resources are limited or when there are many demands placed upon them (e.g., work complexity, managing many individuals).

Research has identified four main antecedents of different LMX relationships (Liden, Sparrowe and Wayne, 1997): member characteristics (e.g., performance, personality and upward influence behavior), leader characteristics (e.g., leader ability), interactional variables (e.g., demographic compatibility and similarity), and contextual variables (e.g., leader workload, high time pressure). LMX relationships have a number of important effects. Subordinates' ratings of their LMX relationships are positively related to job satisfaction (e.g., Major, Kozlowski, Chao and Gardner, 1995), well-being (e.g., Epitropaki and Martin, 1999), organizational commitment (e.g., Kinicki and Vecchio, 1994), and organizational citizenship behavior (Townsend, Phillips and Elkins, 2000). There is also longitudinal research that suggests that if leaders develop a *partnership*, rather than just an exchange relationship, with specific followers, there can be significant performance gains (e.g., Graen, Scandura and Graen, 1986; Scandura and Graen, 1984).

Critical commentary

Research on LMX underscores the importance of examining leader–subordinate relationships as a dynamic system of exchanges. Leaders can, and do, have very different quality relationships with their subordinates. Some subordinates are afforded privileges while others are excluded and marginalized in the workplace (Schriesheim, Castro, and Cogliser, 1999). Dansereau, Cashman and Graen (1973) actually, but from our perspective misleadingly, refer to high quality LMX relationships as ingroup exchanges, and low quality LMX relationships as outgroup exchanges. LMX theory and research has also been the target of some criticism (e.g., Dienesch and Liden, 1986). For example, the measurement of LMX is problematic (e.g., Keller and Dansereau, 2000), and some researchers have found that LMX fails to consistently predict important outcomes, such as performance (e.g., Vecchio, 1998).

From our own perspective we would like to highlight two key criticisms or limitations of LMX theory (also see Hogg and Martin, 2003). First, the majority of research on LMX is, quite explicitly, located at the dyadic level, with very little theorizing or empirical work examining LMX at the group level. One exception is Sparrowe and Liden's (1997) examination of LMX development from a social network perspective (also Wayne, Shore and Liden, 1997). Research and theory focus on the leader–subordinate relationship without acknowledging that each dyadic relationship occurs within a system of other relationships (Cogliser and Schriesheim 2000; Graen and Scandura, 1987; Schriesheim, Castro and Yammarino, 2000).

What is missed is the fact that a specific leader–member relationship is located within the context of other leader–member relationships, and indeed the entire network of member–member relationships. These other relationships will affect the member's perceptions of how other leader–member relations are structured and conducted. People make social comparisons to evaluate the nature of their own perceptions and relationships (e.g., Suls and Wheeler, 2000), and in a group these comparisons will overwhelmingly be made with fellow group members' leader–member relationships – the group provides the parameters for valid social comparisons. We can take this argument one stage further by noting that the social organization of many groups is not structured around isolated individuals but around a number of distinct subgroups. Social comparisons are therefore more likely to be intergroup than interpersonal comparisons. How does the leader relate to my subgroup in comparison with other subgroups? Intergroup comparisons have a quite different logic to interpersonal comparisons (see Hogg, 2000). They have the familiar characteristics of intergroup behavior – ingroup favoritism, ethnocentrism, outgroup denigration, and so forth. This will have far-reaching consequences for subordinates' relations to their leader and reaction to their work – a possibility that has not been explored by LMX research.

The second, and related, issue we wish to highlight concerns the process whereby subordinates evaluate their LMX relationship. LMX theory tends to assume that people simply evaluate their own LMX relationship in an absolute sense. In the light of research on social exchange processes (e.g., Kelley and Thibaut, 1978) this seems rather oversimplified. It is much more likely that subordinates evaluate the quality of their LMX relationship not only in the absolute sense (low vs high) but also with reference to their perception of other subordinates' LMX relationships. More broadly, evaluation of LMX relationships will be influenced by concerns about what is considered to be fair within the context of the organization. Notions of equity, prior LMX history, comparison with other LMX relationships and procedural justice, are all likely to play an important part in determining LMX quality (see Scandura, 1999).

These two critical points or limitations hinge on the same overarching issue. Leadership, and the nature of leader–subordinate relationships, needs to be understood in the context of a deeper and more textured analysis of group processes, intergroup behavior, and the nature of group membership. Leaders lead groups that furnish group members with a sense of identity, and this exists within a wider intergroup comparative context. Furthermore, differentiated leader–subordinate cliques within the group may establish powerful inter-group relations within the group. If perceived leader–member relations affect leadership effectiveness, then an understanding of such relations needs to recognize that the leader–member relationship does not exist in isolation from other interpersonal, inter-subgroup, and intergroup relationships. In addition, the notion of 'member' needs to address the member's self-concept. Is the member conceiving of self as an isolated individual, as an individual in relation to the leader, as a member of a subgroup, or as a member of the group as a whole (e.g., Brewer and Gardner, 1996; Hogg, 2001b)?

Social Identity Theory of Leadership

The social identity theory of leadership (e.g., Hogg, 2001a; Hogg, in press b; Hogg and van Knippenberg, 2003) is well placed to address some of the above concerns, because it explicitly attributes an influential role in leadership processes to group members' self-conception. It may matter quite significantly whether a member identifies strongly or not with the group that the leader leads.

Based on the social identity perspective (e.g., Hogg and Abrams, 1988; Tajfel and Turner, 1986; Turner, Hogg, Oakes, Reicher, and Wetherell, 1987; see recent overviews by Abrams and Hogg, 2001; Hogg, 2001c, 2002), the key idea is that the cognitive basis of leadership endorsement, and thus the ability of a leader to be effective, is transformed as a function of the extent to which group members identify with the group as an important aspect of their self-concept. Where a group is a relatively loose aggregate of individuals who do not derive a strong sense of social identity from the group, social perception is largely governed by idiosyncratic preferences and by personal relationships. Under these circumstances people use relatively general or more task-specific leadership schemas to determine their perceptions of leadership effectiveness (e.g., Lord, Foti, and DeVader, 1984). People who are perceived to match the relevant leadership schema are more likely to be endorsed as a 'leader' and to be able to lead effectively.

The basis of perception is quite different in more compact, cohesive groups, which are self-conceptually important. People identify strongly with these groups, and thus the basis of perception of self and others is firmly circum-scribed by group prototypicality – the extent to which the leader seems to match members' cognitive representation of the defining features of the group. Social categorization of self and fellow ingroup members depersonalizes per-ception, feelings, and behavior in terms of the contextually salient ingroup prototype. Self and others are not perceived as unique individuals, but rather are viewed through the lens of group prototypicality. Prototypical members embody the essence of the group and are the target of consensual group membership-based positive regard or liking – consensual social attraction (Hogg, 1993). Conformity processes in conjunction with consensual social attraction make prototypical members more influential. Under these circumstances people who are perceived to match the relevant ingroup prototype are more likely to be endorsed as leaders and to be able to lead effectively.

It should be noted that a recent approach to leader categorization theory is consistent with this social identity analysis (Chapter 5). Lord and his colleagues now view leadership categorization as a highly dynamic and context-dependent process, and propose that under conditions of high social identity salience the leadership schema may be construed in terms of the group prototype.

The social identity analysis of leadership generates a straightforward hypothesis. As people identify more strongly with a group, leadership endorsement, perceptions of leadership effectiveness, and actual leadership effectiveness, become increasingly influenced by how group prototypical the leader is perceived to be. Correspondingly, leadership schema congruence will decline in relative importance. This is precisely what was found in a series of four direct tests of this hypothesis – three laboratory experiments (Hains, Hogg, and Duck, 1997; Hogg, Hains, and Mason, 1998), and a field study (Fielding and Hogg, 1997). In the three experiments participants were provided with information about the group prototype, in the form of the group's position on a single attitude dimension, and information about where a randomly appointed leader's attitude fell on the same dimension. In this way it was possible to manipulate the group prototypicality of the leader and see how much influence prototypicality had on perceptions of leadership effectiveness as a function of a standard group salience manipulation. Further support for the role of prototypicality in leadership of high salience groups comes from a variety of studies that test the hypothesis in less direct ways or in different contexts (e.g., Duck and Fielding, 1999; Haslam and Platow, 2001b; Platow, Reid and Andrew, 1998; Platow and van Knippenberg, 2001; van Vugt and de Cremer, 1999).

There are a number of extensions and elaborations of the social identity theory of leadership. Because members of high salience groups are sharply focused on prototypicality, highly prototypical members are figural against the background of the group and tend to have their behavior internally attributed, via the fundamental attribution error (Ross, 1977), or correspondence bias (Gilbert and Malone, 1995). This process constructs a charismatic leadership personality for the leader that facilitates leadership. However, charisma is here the outcome of a group process not a stable personality trait that influences leadership effectiveness (cf. Haslam and Platow, 2001a).

Another extension identifies a paradox. Prototypical leaders are very much 'one of us', and yet are distanced from the rest of the group by virtue of their leadership role. This role differentiation can, under some circumstances, create a schism between leader(s) and followers that has many of the properties of hierarchical power-based intergroup relations where one group has the monopoly of status and power. In this way prototype-based leadership can be transformed into power-based leadership (see Hogg, 2001d; Hogg and Reid, 2001).

A third extension focuses on another paradox. Leaders should be group serving; they should favor the ingroup, show group commitment, and be procedurally fair (Haslam and Platow, 2001a, 2001b; Platow, Reid, and Andrew, 1998; Tyler, 1999; Chapter 8, Chapter 9). However, highly prototypical leaders' group membership credentials are not in question, whereas less prototypical leaders' credentials require confirmation. This means that there is actually less constraint on highly, than less highly, prototypical members to behave in ways that are overtly group oriented (Platow and van Knippenberg, 2001).

We do not elaborate here on these aspects of the social identity analysis of leadership (for more detail see Hogg and van Knippenberg, 2003). Instead, our focus is on leader–member relations and the relationship between the social identity analysis and the LMX analysis of the role of leader–member relations in leadership effectiveness.

Social Identity and Leader–Member Relations

The social identity analysis, as described above, focuses on perceptions of how prototypical the leader is, but also on the extent to which the leader behaves in a group-serving manner. Although not much is said about the sort of relationship the leader has with his or her followers, the analysis does have clear implications for leader–member relations.

The key idea is that as group membership becomes psychologically increasingly salient, people define and perceive themselves and others in terms of the group prototype rather than as unique individuals. People also treat one another in group terms, and inter-individual interactions are increasingly structured and governed by prototypical expectations. Relations among ingroup members become increasingly *depersonalized*, to the extent that people's relationship partners are largely interchangeable. Under these circumstances, leader–member relations will be depersonalized – the leader treating each member as prototypically equivalent to each other member.

Contrast this with a low salience group. Here, perceptions and behavior are not prototype based. People perceive and interact with each other in a much more idiosyncratic manner that recognizes unique features of self, other and the relationship. Relationships among group members are *personalized*, to the extent that people's relationship partners are largely *not* interchangeable. Under these circumstances, leader–member relations will be personalized – the leader treating each member quite differently to each other member.

Thus, as group membership becomes more salient, the basis of effective leadership changes from leadership schemas, personalized relations, idiosyncratic preferences and so forth, to group prototypicality, depersonalized relations, collective preferences, and so forth. The sorts of groups that mediate high salience include those that are high in entitativity (e.g., Hamilton and Sherman, 1996), high in cohesiveness (e.g., Hogg, 1993), under external threat (e.g., Ellemers, Spears, and Doosje, 1999), critically important to self-conception, and occupy minority status positions. An example would be an established organization confronting a hostile takeover, or a start-up company struggling to establish a niche in a competitive market. The sorts of groups that mediate low salience are ones in which there is a degree of membership diversity, and there is some disagreement on what the group stands for and what the prototype looks like. The group may not be highly cohesive, may not have high entitativity, may not feel under threat, and so forth. The group is more heterogeneous and the followers are more highly individuated.

Leaders of low salience groups would be expected to treat and relate to members in a personalized manner, because members conceive of themselves largely as unique individuals. If the leader were to treat them as interchangeable members of a collective, this would invite negative reaction from members that would not be conducive to effective leadership. Leaders of high salience groups would be expected to treat and relate to members in a depersonalized manner, because members conceive of themselves as group members, not unique individuals. If the leader were to treat them as unique individuals, this might appear procedurally and distributively unjust, and even as an attempt to sever depersonalized bonds among group members. It would invite negative reaction from members that would not be conducive to effective leadership.

Thus, in contrast to LMX theory, which argues that effective leadership rests on positive interpersonal relationships between the leader and specific followers, the social identity analysis of leadership argues that the leadership effectiveness of personalized or depersonalized leader–member relations depends on the psychological salience of the group to its members. A very simple prediction can be made. As group membership becomes more salient, leader–member relations will become less interpersonal and more depersonalized, and effective leadership will rest increasingly on depersonalized not personalized leader–member relations.

Two Studies

We have recently conducted a pair of preliminary studies to test these predictions about leader–member relations and leadership effectiveness in high and low salience groups.

Study 1

Hogg, Martin, Weeden and Epitropaki (2001, Study 1) analysed questionnaires returned by 439 respondents performing a range of jobs in seven UK service and manufacturing companies. The dependent variable was leadership effectiveness, which was measured by eight items from Bass and Avolio's (1997) Multi-factorial Leadership Questionnaire (MLQ). These items fall into three separate scales measuring different aspects of leadership: (1) leader satisfaction (2 items, r (439) = .76, $p < .001$) – for example, how frequently does the leader use methods of leadership which are satisfying?; (2) leader effectiveness (3 items, $\alpha = .80$) – for example, is the leader effective in meeting organization requirements?; and (3) motivation to exert extra effort on behalf of the group (3 items, $\alpha = .78$) – for example, does the leader 'get me to do more than I expected to do'?

There were two predictor variables. (1) A five-item scale measured the extent to which respondents felt that the company encouraged people to work in teams or not ($\alpha = .85$). The items asked how committed the company was to training people to work in teams, how much importance it placed on, and how much it encouraged, working in teams, and how much it organized people to work in teams and how much people actually worked as individuals or as team members. High scores approximate a high salience group and low scores a low salience group. (2) A two-item scale measured the extent to which the leader's style treated subordinates as unique individuals (personalized) or as one of the team (depersonalized) ($r = .44$, $p < .001$). The items asked respondents how frequently the leader 'treats me as an individual rather than just a member of a group' and 'considers me to have different needs, abilities, and aspirations from others'. High scores reflect an interpersonal leadership style, indicative of more personalized leader–member relations.

Stepwise regression revealed that after demographic variables had been removed at Step 1, perceived leader effectiveness and leader satisfaction were

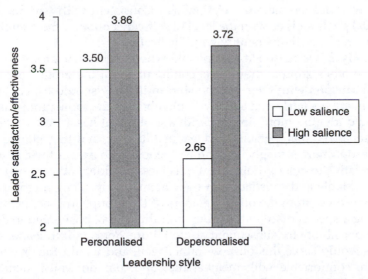

Figure 3.1 Hogg, Martin, Weeden, and Epitropaki (2001, Study 1): The interactive effect of group salience and leadership style on the composite measure (1–5 scale) of leader satisfaction and leader effectiveness – F (1,423) = 4.17, $p < .05$.

predicted by salience and by leadership style (beta > .33, $p < .0001$), and, most importantly, by the interaction of salience and style (beta = .09, $p < .05$ on leader effectiveness, and .08, $p < .05$ on leader satisfaction). The interaction generally supports predictions derived from the social identity model. For ease of presentation, we combined the effectiveness and satisfaction measures into a composite five-point leader satisfaction/effectiveness scale, dichotomized the predictor variables of salience and leadership style, and conducted a 2 (salience) × 2 (style) ANCOVA, with demographic variables as covariates, on the composite leadership scale. The two-way interaction was significant (F (1,423) = 4.17, $p < .05$), see Figure 3.1. As predicted, a personalized leadership style was considered more satisfying/effective than a depersonalized group-membership based style in low salience groups, and the effect disappeared in high salience groups. Put another way, as the group became more salient a depersonalized group-membership based leadership style became more satisfying/effective, whereas a personalized style was left largely unchanged.

Study 2

Our second study (Hogg, Martin, Weeden, and Epitropaki, 2001, Study 2) sought to extend and qualify the findings from Study 1. One of the points we have made about leader–member relations is that in high salience groups depersonalized relations are more identity consistent than personalized leader–member relations and thus support effective leadership, whereas the opposite is the case in low salience groups. An implication of this idea is that if the nature of leader–member relations is inconsistent with various group or individual goals and/or with the level of self-conception of the members, then members might well dis-identify with the group.

For Study 2, we reasoned that people who expect their group to do well, relative to other groups, should feel confident about the group, and comfortable and satisfied with their membership in it. They should expect leaders to treat all members fairly and equally as members of the same group, and therefore should identify more strongly with a group that has a leader who adopts a depersonalized than personalized leadership style, and they should endorse such a leader more strongly. In contrast, people who expect their group to do poorly, relative to other groups, should feel less confident about the group, and less comfortable and satisfied with their membership. They might try to distance themselves from the other members of the group, and see themselves as occupying a special place in the group and thus being positioned to deny personal responsibility for subsequent group failure. Personalized leader–member relations would serve this purpose rather well, and would thus make people feel more comfortable with membership, and, paradoxically, identify more strongly with the group. People should therefore identify more strongly with a group that has a leader who adopts a personalized rather than depersonalized leadership style, and they should endorse such a leader more strongly.

In summary, we predicted that personalized leader–member relations would be associated with stronger identification and leadership endorsement in groups that have low rather than high expectations of intergroup success, whereas depersonalized leader–member relations would be associated with stronger identification and leadership endorsement in groups that have high as opposed to low expectations of intergroup success. The key idea is that there is an interaction of leadership style or leader–member relations and group performance expectations that impacts identification, and identification in turn impacts leadership evaluations; identification mediates the impact of style and expectations on leadership evaluations.

This idea was tested by manipulating group success expectations (high vs low) and leadership style (personalized vs depersonalized) in a 2 × 2 laboratory experiment ($N = 68$) based on a computerized variant of the experimental paradigm devised by Hains, Hogg and Duck (1997) and Hogg, Hains and Mason (1998). The groups were relatively highly salient throughout the study. We manipulated and checked on expectations of group success in an intergroup competition, and whether the randomly appointed leader adopted a personalized or depersonalized leader–member relationship style – all done within the context of non-interactive decision-making groups of psychology students supposedly in competition with groups of business students.

Expectations of group success were manipulated by informing participants that psychology groups like theirs, generally performed better/worse than groups of business students. Thus there were relatively high or low expectations of intergroup success. Leadership style was manipulated via feedback ostensibly from the leader that he or she would develop a separate interpersonal relationship with each group member, and would interact with each of them as individuals rather than group members (personalized leadership style), or would develop a common relationship with all group members, and would interact with all of them as group members rather than individuals (depersonalized leadership style).

We measured the effects of these manipulations on four constructs: (1) Group identification (6 items, $\alpha = .92$) – items assessed commitment, happiness, liking, cohesiveness, identification, and self-prototypicality with regard to the group. (2) Leader effectiveness (6 items, $\alpha = .95$) – participants indicated how much they felt their leader would have the qualities, image and behavior of a leader, would be an effective leader, and would be a leader they had confidence in and who would represent the group well. (3) Leader satisfaction (6 items, $\alpha = .91$) – participants indicated their feelings for the leader in terms of liking, commitment, respect, and trust, and how happy they were and how much they identified with the leader. (4) Group performance (3 items, $\alpha = .87$) – participants indicated how well they felt their group would perform, how able their group was to perform the task, and to what extent their group would make decisions that were better than that of any other group.

As predicted participants in high expectation groups identified significantly more strongly with the group when the leader adopted a depersonalized rather than personalized leadership style, whereas participants in low expectation

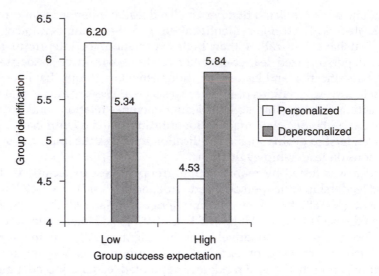

Figure 3.2   Hogg, Martin, Weeden, and Epitropaki (2001, Study 2): Interactive effect of group performance expectation and leadership style on group identification (1–9 scale) – $F(1,64) = 10.54$, $p < .01$

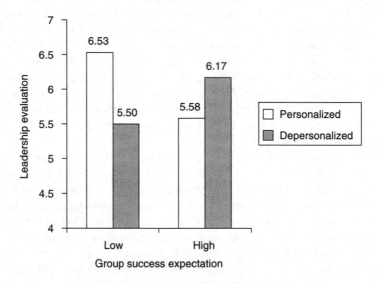

Figure 3.3   Hogg, Martin, Weeden, and Epitropaki (2001, Study 2): Interactive effect of group performance expectation and leadership style on the composite leadership evaluation measure. (1–9 scale) – $F(1,64) = 7.98$, $p < .01$

groups identified more strongly with the group when the leader adopted a personalized rather than depersonalized leadership style – $F(1,64) = 10.54$, $p < .01$ (see Figure 3.2). Another way to describe this is that participants with a leader who adopted a personalized leadership style identified with the group significantly more strongly when there were low rather than high expectations of group success. Also as predicted, this pattern of results emerged on the three leadership variables. Because variables were intercorrelated ($r > .55$) they were combined into a single leader evaluation measure. In high expectation groups, participants evaluated leadership more positively when the leader adopted a depersonalized rather than personalized leadership style, whereas in low expectation groups the reverse was true – $F (1,64) = 7.98$, $p < .01$ (see Figure 3.3). Another way to describe this is that participants with a leader who adopted a personalized leadership style evaluated that leader more favorably when there were low, rather than high, expectations of group success, and vice versa when the leader adopted a depersonalized leadership style. A mediation analysis confirmed that the interactive impact of expectation and style on leadership evaluation was fully mediated by identification.

Conclusions

The two studies reported here show that the relationship between leader–member relations and leadership effectiveness is not a mechanical one. It is not the case that personalized leader–member relations are always associated with effective leadership. The effect of leader–member relations on leadership effectiveness is influenced by group membership factors, in particular social identity. Personalized leader–member relations are associated with effective leadership only in low salience groups or groups that anticipate failure. In high salience groups or groups that anticipate success, depersonalized leader–member relations are more effective.

Summary, Extensions, and Concluding Comments

The aim of this chapter has been to explore an integration of LMX theory and the social identity analysis of leadership. We felt that LMX theory (e.g., Graen and Uhl-Bien, 1995) makes an important point – that effective leadership is strongly influenced by the sort of relationships a leader establishes with members of the group. However, we felt that LMX theory was limited, because it fails to distinguish between leader–member relationships that are based on idiosyncrasies of the member. We called these *personalized* leader–member relations, and those that are based on the fact that the member is simply a member of the group, we called *depersonalized* leader–member relations.

This sort of distinction is derived from the social identity analysis of group membership, self-conception, and group and intergroup phenomena. We described the social identity analysis of leadership (e.g., Hogg, 2001a; Hogg and van Knippenberg, 2003). The key point of this analysis is that as people identify more strongly with a group the entire process of leadership is increasingly based upon the extent to which followers perceive the leader as being more prototypical of the group than are other members. In such groups, prototypicality can assume overwhelming importance, even to the extent that other very important qualities for effective leadership can be underplayed or overlooked.

The implication of this analysis of leadership is that as people identify more strongly with a group, leader–member relations should become less personalized and more depersonalized, and that leader–member relations that conflict with the salient level of self-conception will be less effective than those that are consistent with it. We reported two studies designed to test this idea (Hogg, Martin, Weeden, and Epitropaki, 2001). The first study, a large survey of organizational leadership, provided some support for the idea. Among low group identifiers personalized leader–member relations were associated with more effective leadership than were depersonalized relations. Among high identifiers depersonalized relations became more important, to the extent that the leader effectiveness advantage of personalized relations disappeared. We are currently conducting a replication of this study in a different leadership context, and a laboratory analogue where the predictor variables are experimentally manipulated.

The second study was a laboratory experiment that textured the analysis somewhat; showing that expectations of intergroup success or failure set up different leader–member relations preferences. Depersonalized relations are preferred where group success is anticipated, and personalized relations where group failure is anticipated. Group identification was stronger where actual leader–member relations matched expectations than where a mismatch occurred, and identification mediated more positive leader effectiveness rating.

To conclude this chapter we would like to explore a future extension of our social identity analysis of leader–member relations. Thus far we have argued that in high salience groups with which members identify strongly, people prefer depersonalized leader–member relations, and that such relations treat all members equally as group members. In contrast, in lower salience groups with which members identify less strongly, people prefer personalized leader–member relations, and that such relations treat each member as an individual person who is different to other members.

The analysis of depersonalized leader–member relations in high salience groups can perhaps be qualified. According to the social identity perspective, and the social identity analysis of leadership, people in high salience groups are highly attuned to prototypicality – they exist in an environment in which perception, cognition, affect and behavior is governed by prototypicality. Prototypicality is the yardstick of group life, and being prototypical is highly valued – there is a valenced prototypicality gradient (e.g., Hogg, 1993). In these circumstances not only is the leader singled out as being most prototypical, but members will also differentiate among followers in terms of who is more, and who is less, prototypical – who is core and who is peripheral. Research shows that under these conditions marginal members can be downgraded and rejected as black sheep (e.g., Marques, Abrams, Páez, and Hogg, 2001).

It is thus quite possible that as far as leader–member relations go, members who consider themselves core would like to have a special relationship with the leader that recognizes their core membership (high prototypicality) status, and differentiates them from more peripheral members. They would be seeking circumscribed depersonalized leader–member relations, based upon *circumscribed depersonalization*. Presumably, peripheral members would rather be treated simply as group members – they would seek uncircumscribed depersonalized leader–member relations.

Thus, in low salience groups members prefer personalized leader–member relations and leaders who adopt these relations are more effective. In high salience groups members prefer depersonalized leader–member relations, and leaders who adopt these relations are more effective. However, in high salience groups where some members consider themselves to be core members who are more prototypical and who identify more strongly than peripheral members, these members prefer circumscribed depersonalized leader–member relations that recognize their special status within the group. Effective leaders would need to attune their leader–member relations to this fact. These ideas have yet to be fully elaborated, and to be tested empirically.

4 Leadership as the Outcome of Self-Categorization Processes

MICHAEL J. PLATOW, S. ALEXANDER HASLAM, MARGARET FODDY, AND DIANA M. GRACE

Reviews of theory and research on leaders and leadership inevitably produce long lists of personality and situational traits, definitions and sub-types, qualifications and statistical moderators, and categories and processes (e.g., Bass, 1990; Hollander, 1985). Interestingly, the lists are not confined to the scientific reviews, but seem also to appear in group members' minds in the form of leadership schemas and expectations (Conger and Kanungo, 1998; Lord, Foti, and De Vader, 1984; Chapter 5). What is the lesson from this body of work with which we can return to our groups as we seek an understanding of the essence of leadership? In our view, the lists – the variables examined, and *found to be associated with*, leaders and leadership – inform us about the specific groups and societies studied more than leaders and leadership in the abstract. The research tells us that leaders are as much as, and yet no more than, good group members (e.g., Fielding and Hogg, 1997). To this degree, we concur with Bass (1990) in his rejection of the 'supposed unknowable, elusive, mysterious nature of leadership' (p. 914). However, rather than informing us of specific roles within groups, the long lists celebrate the diversity of the groups to which we all belong, the groups that define us, shape us, and allow us to achieve our individual and collective goals. Leadership is an outcome of self-categorization processes (Haslam, 2001; Haslam and Platow, 2001b; Hogg, 2001; Chapter 3, Chapter 10).

A Theory of Group Life: Self-Categorization Theory

An understanding of group life via self-categorization processes is outlined in self-categorization theory (SCT; Turner, 1982; 1985; 1987). Acknowledging the reality of groups, while building on the psychological advances of social cognition research, SCT provides a process explanation of intragroup and intergroup relations, as well as individuals' and group members' sense of self and identity (e.g., Onorato and Turner, 2001). The theory rejects the view that uniformities in social behavior that emerge in group life are caused by idiosyncrasies and differences between individuals (Reynolds, Turner, Haslam, and Ryan, 2001; Turner and Onorato, 1999). Group life is assumed to be a qualitatively different enterprise to that of idiosyncratic individual behavior (following in the legacy of Tajfel's social identity theory, e.g., Tajfel, 1982; Tajfel and Turner, 1979).

This qualitative difference, however, represents a difference in outcome rather than process. The fundamental assumption in SCT is that people's cognitive representations of themselves take the form of self-categorizations, categorizations of themselves as interchangeable with others at some level of abstraction. These self-categories are conceptualized along a theoretical hierarchy of relative inclusiveness. At one theoretical extreme, self is categorized with no one else; this is a personal self-category (akin to personal identity; Turner, 1982) wherein individuals differentiate themselves from others on the basis of idiosyncratic personal traits. At the opposite theoretical extreme, self is categorized with all other humans. Between these two theoretical extremes lie all other ingroup–outgroup self-categories, such as self as a male, self as an American, or self as a psychologist. With these latter social self-categorizations (akin to social identity), idiosyncratic personal characteristics diminish in relative salience as group members perceive themselves to be relatively similar to fellow self-category members (i.e., ingroup members), while collectively being different from non-self-category members (i.e., outgroup members).

Thus, at any given time in any given context, people's self-representations can vary between those that are personal and those that represent some form of social self-categorization (Antaki, Condor, and Levine, 1996). It is the *outcomes* of these various self-categorizations that will be qualitatively different from each other, although the *process* leading to the adoption of one self-category or another remains identical. Following Bruner (1957), this process takes the form of a combination of perceiver readiness and cognitive fit (Oakes, 1987). Perceiver readiness includes people's motives, goals and, indeed, their relatively enduring levels of social identification (cf. Branscombe, Ellemers, Spears, and Doosje, 1999). Cognitive fit takes two forms, *comparative* and *normative* fit. With comparative fit, contextually determined similarities and differences between stimuli (e.g., self and others) are assessed, with categorizations following from relatively high levels of intra-class similarities and inter-class differences. With normative fit, the similarity-based classification is assessed with reference to expectations based on category content (i.e., the normative meaning of the categories), with categorizations likely to be inferred from normatively fitting classifications (see McGarty, 1999).

Once a particular self-categorization becomes cognitively salient – that is, once one self-category or another is adopted by a person as self-defining in a given context – a variety of social and psychological outcomes emerge. Probably the most widely studied outcomes include some form of ingroup-favoritism (e.g., prejudice and discrimination) and stereotyping (e.g., Oakes, Haslam and Turner, 1994; Turner and Giles, 1981). However, a variety of other outcomes of the self-categorization process have also been identified, including cooperation (Caporael, Dawes, Orbell, and Van de Kragt, 1989), helping (Platow et al., 1999), collective action (Reicher, 1987), and group cohesiveness (Hogg, 1992), to name a few (see Haslam, 2001 for a review). Of particular import to our current discussion are four specific outcomes examined within the SCT framework that are also included on the leadership lists to which we alluded earlier. It is the presence of these four outcomes – and possibly others yet unexamined – on leadership lists that provide us with the first evidence that leadership is an outcome of the self-categorization process rather than the idiosyncratic qualities of individuals.

Four Leadership Qualities:
Influence, Trust, Fairness, and Charisma

So what is leadership? What is the stuff of which leaders are made? Heading the list of leadership qualities, we find, first and foremost, that leaders are *influential*. Indeed, the ability to influence is often considered the defining quality of leadership (e.g., Bass, 1990; Haslam, 2001; Hollander, 1985; Turner, 1991). When the vision of some is not followed by the rest, no leadership can be said to obtain. But when group members identify a path for others to take, *and the path is taken*, then leadership has arisen (Haslam and Platow, 2001a; House, 1971). And it is only through the adoption of this path as their own that fellow group members become followers. Thus, whether by directive or by inspiration, leadership is all about influence (also see Chapter 10).

But for us to follow, we must also *trust* (e.g., Tyler and Degoey, 1996; Pillai, Schriesheim, and Williams, 1999). It is through our expectation that others will act in ways to benefit (or not harm) us, before we know the outcome of their behaviors (Foddy, Platow, and Yamagishi, 2001), that we are willing to submit ourselves to their visions. In this manner, followers' trust in leaders is registered as a second entry onto the list of leadership qualities (e.g., Hughes, Ginnett, and Curphy, 1999). A third leadership quality on the list is that of leader *fairness*. Simply put, when leaders are fair – or, at least, perceived to be fair – group members will follow (e.g., Hollander and Julian, 1970; Michener and Lawler, 1975; Tyler, Rasinski, and McGraw, 1985). Finally, the fourth leadership quality, associated primarily with transformational leadership (e.g., Bass, 1988; House, Woycke, and Fodor, 1988), is that of leader *charisma*. Charismatic leaders are said to have special gifts allowing them to invigorate and inspire followers to transcend their conventional practices in pursuit of new visions of future possibilities *in the absence of interpersonal exchange* (e.g., Bass, 1985; 1988).

These four leadership qualities – influence, trust, fairness, and charisma – are also relatively high in leader prototypicality (Lord et al., 1984). This suggests that these are qualities that ought to be associated with leaders, in light of group members' expectations, if the leaders are to be viewed as leaders by fellow group members (Cronshaw and Lord, 1987; Maurer and Lord, 1991).

Four Outcomes of Self-Categorization:
Influence, Trust, Fairness, and Charisma

As we noted above, each of the four leadership qualities of influence, trust, fairness, and charisma have also been observed to be *outcomes* of the self-categorization process. Ingroup members are influential and trusted; perceptions of fairness vary with leaders' actual behavior *and* the nature of the group context; and the more ingroup-like leaders are, the more charismatic fellow group members claim they are. We now consider the research into each of these phenomena.

Ingroup members are influential

A large literature now exists identifying the ingroup-based nature of social influence (e.g., Turner, 1991). Within SCT, it is ingroup members who are assumed to provide people with socially valid information, information worthy of attention and systematic processing. It is ingroup members, not outgroup members, to whom we will attend and ultimately by whom we will be persuaded.

Clear demonstrations of this point were provided by Abrams, Wetherell, Cochrane, Hogg, and Turner (1990). In one study, they employed the classic Sherif (1936) autokenetic social influence paradigm in which stationary pinpoints of light appear to move (as a visual illusion), and participants naive to the illusion estimate the distance of movement. Sherif observed clear convergence over a series of trials in the estimates among groups of participants about the distance of movement. If such social influence were group-based, however, then the presence of subgroups ought to affect estimate convergence. This is what Abrams et al. observed when they created two subgroups within the paradigm. If anything, estimate diverged between the subgroups. Participants did not conform to outgroup members' descriptions of reality, as it was only ingroup members who were understood to provide valid descriptions about reality. Note that we use 'reality' deliberately. It does not matter for our discussion of leadership that the light was not moving. Leaders direct group members' opinions, initiate group structure, and provide a vision for group members to follow (see Bass, 1990). *None* of these, however, necessarily has any greater basis in reality than the autokenetic visual illusion. What matters is that group members adopt as their own the opinions, structure, and visions of leaders *as if they were real*.

The ingroup nature of social influence is very robust, and has been observed in children as young as four years. Grace and David (2001), for example, asked boys and girls to watch a videotape of actors playing with various non-gender specific toys, engaging in specific actions, and reciting specific phrases. Depending on the experimental condition, the actors were either boys and girls, or same-sex children and adults. The child participants were then allowed to play with the same toys as they saw in the video. The basic question was, whom would the children follow? Consistent with an SCT analysis, children followed contextually salient ingroup members. When boys and girls were the actors, then the child participants followed the actions of the same-sex actor. When same-sex children and adults were the actors, then the child participants followed the children. As in the previously described research, the four-year-old children were influenced by fellow ingroup members.

At this point, we might ask whether ingroup influence is simply heuristic and, essentially, mindless public compliance, rather than systematic information processing leading to internalization (Chaiken, 1987; Kelman, 1958). Mackie, Worth, and Asuncion (1990; see also McGarty, Haslam, Hutchinson, and Turner, 1994) examined this question by presenting university students with communications containing strong or weak arguments from a university ingroup member or a university outgroup member. As expected, greater influence occurred in response to the ingroup communication than the outgroup communication. This occurred, however, primarily in response to strong messages; weak ingroup messages did not lead to social influence. Moreover, participants had better memory for the ingroup than the outgroup communication, suggesting more systematic processing of the former. Finally, the relative favorability of participants' thoughts about the communication significantly predicted the degree of social influence *only in response to an ingroup communication*. Participants' thoughts about the communication were unrelated to their attitudes in response to outgroup communications. These patterns are precisely what would be expected if ingroup-based social influence were caused by systematic processing and actual internalization.

Overall, the social influence research clearly shows that, for individuals to emerge as leaders within a group – that is, for individuals to influence others *without the use of some form of resource power* (e.g., rewards and punishments) – the individuals must be perceived to be members of an ingroup. Social influence is an outcome of shared self-categorization.

Ingroup Members are More Trusted than Outgroup Members

Trust is an inference about people's intentions and traits made when there is no structural assurance regarding their behavior (Yamagishi and Yamagishi, 1994). It represents the expectation of benevolent treatment from others in both dependent and interdependent situations (Foddy et al., 2001). Within SCT, trust is understood as an outcome of the self-categorization process rather than a personality trait or a cognitive bias (Turner, 1987).

To examine this view, Foddy et al. (2001) developed a paradigm in which participants are presented with two envelopes said to contain an unknown (to the participants) amount of money from $0 to $16. The task facing participants is simply to choose one of the two envelopes. Participants are further informed that two prior participants (called 'allocators') were each given $16, and were allowed to keep it all, or to give any portion or all of it away by placing it in the envelope. The key feature of the paradigm is that one allocator is described as an ingroup member, while the other is described as an outgroup member. In this manner, participants are confronted with two risky options, one from an ingroup member and one from an outgroup member. Systematic choice of one envelope or the other is a representation of trust, an expectation of benevolent treatment on the part of one allocator over the other.

In Foddy et al.'s (2001) first study, university participants were presented with this decision situation, and group membership was based on the university they attended. A full 87 per cent of participants chose the envelope from the ingroup member. In their second study, Foddy et al. (2001) varied the salient outgroup along a valence dimension implied by the group's stereotype. Participants' ingroup of psychology majors was contrasted with: (1) economics majors (who participants more negatively stereotyped than the ingroup), (2) engineering majors (stereotyped in a similarly valenced manner to the ingroup), and (3) nursing students (stereotyped more positively than ingroup). Thus, in a between-subjects design, each participant was confronted with a choice from an ingroup member and an outgroup member from a group that was stereotypically more negative, more positive, or equally valenced to the ingroup. In all cases, the majority of participants still chose the ingroup over the outgroup allocator. These data provide strong evidence of trust emanating from shared category membership rather than beliefs about generosity *per se*. Importantly, individual differences in trustingness were completely unrelated to choice of allocator in either of these first two experiments.

Notwithstanding their clarity, the above findings still leave unanswered the question of whether people trust their ingroup members because: (1) they expect to be treated well *as a fellow ingroup member,* or (2) they believe that ingroup members are dispositionally nice, and will treat all people well (including outgroup members). Either explanation is viable given Foddy et al.'s (2001) first two studies because all participants were told that both allocators knew the group membership of the participants (as recipients) ahead of time. If participants believed that the allocators were blind to their (i.e., the recipients') group membership, then these two explanations could be differentiated. Under this 'no knowledge' condition, if ingroup trust disappeared, then the first identity-based explanation above would appear to be correct; people would trust ingroup members because they expected favorable treatment as a fellow ingroup member. However, if ingroup trust were maintained, then the second dispositionally based explanation would appear more likely.

Foddy et al. (2001) conducted two more experiments invoking this 'no knowledge' context. Using the same intergroup university context as their first experiment, Foddy et al. now observed a near disappearance of ingroup trust. Only 56 per cent chose the envelope from their ingroup member. In a fourth study, modelled on Experiment 2 above, Foddy et al. observed a choice pattern consistent with stereotype content. Ingroup choices increased in the presence of a negatively stereotyped outgroup, but outgroup choices increased massively (actually reversing) in the presence of a positively stereotyped outgroup. In other words, people used stereotypic dispositional information as a basis for trust only when the person to be trusted could not be expected to be aware of the social identity they shared with the participant. These data clearly suggest that ingroup trust is based upon an expectation of favorable treatment from an ingroup member *as an ingroup member*. This conclusion is consistent with the leadership research of Duck and Fielding (1999). They showed that group members expect group-aligned leaders to favor members of their own group (i.e., the leaders' group) over members of other groups.

Of course, in most situations in which group members opt to place their trust in leaders (or not), the group members know how the leader has treated others in the past – the leader has some form of *reputation* on which people may base their trust. Foddy and Platow (2001) examined the role that reputation plays in trust. Using their trust paradigm, with allocator knowledge of the recipient's group membership, Foddy and Platow directly manipulated the reputation of the allocator. In one condition, the ingroup allocator was said to have been unfair toward an outgroup recipient in the past, but no information was provided about the outgroup allocator. If group membership were irrelevant, then participants were simply confronted with a human with a reputation of being unfair to another human, and this should lead them to choose the outgroup allocator. In another condition, the outgroup allocator was said to have been fair towards his or her fellow outgroup member. Again, if group membership were irrelevant, then participants were confronted with a human with a reputation of being fair to another human, and this again should lead participants to choose the outgroup allocator. In both conditions, however, the majority of participants chose the ingroup allocator, confirming once again that trust is the outcome of shared social self-categorization.

This series of studies clearly demonstrates that people are willing to place their fortunes specifically in the hands of fellow ingroup members, at least ingroup members who are aware of the shared category membership. Trust, like social influence, has its basis in shared self-categorizations.

Fairness perceptions vary with behavior and the group context

There is no question that fairness is an essential quality of leadership. Unfair leaders soon lose their following (e.g., Tyler and Lind, 1992; also see Chapters 8 and 9). Fairness, however, remains an elusive concept. This is not to say that formal rules of fairness do not exist; they do. Nor is it to say that these fairness rules are not employed; they are. But there are many fairness rules, each employed in different situations and often in ways that benefit individuals' and groups' own interests. It is, thus, easy for group members to perceive what might be unfair behavior as fair *given the right context*. Indeed, such differential fairness perceptions have been observed in a series of studies by Platow and his colleagues.

In their first observation of differential fairness perceptions (Platow, O'Connell, Shave, and Hanning, 1995), university students read about a scuffle between two people, both of whom subsequently required costly medical aid. Because of the cost, both were described as requesting financial assistance. A third, uninvolved person either: (1) gave both requesters an equal amount of money (i.e., both received $150), or (2) gave one person a lot of money ($300) and the other person nothing. Importantly, both requesters were described as holding jobs, and as having already received their medical aid; in this manner, there were no differences in need. When both requesters were described as people from the same community as the participants (i.e., ingroup members), then participants perceived the equal distribution as fair and the unequal distribution as unfair. This was no surprise, and was wholly consistent with equity theory (e.g., Walster, Berscheid, and Walster, 1976). However, when one requester was described as a fellow ingroup member (a student) and the other as an outgroup member (a police officer), participants' perceptions changed. Giving $300 to the student and nothing to the police officer was perceived by the student participants as very fair. In this manner, the perceived fairness of the *identical distributive behavior* changed as a function of the group context; favoring one ingroup member over another ingroup member was seen as unfair, but favoring an ingroup member over an outgroup member was seen as fair (see also Platow, Wenzel, and Nolan, 2003).

A second test of this effect was made specifically in the context of leader-endorsement research (Platow, Hoar, Reid, Harley, and Morrison, 1997). In this study, student participants read about a student leader distributing money either equally or unequally between two equally needy people for travel to a student-related conference. In two conditions, the two recipients were students (intragroup conditions); in the other two conditions, one recipient was a student and one was a government representative (intergroup conditions). As in the previous study, an unequal distribution between two students (i.e., ingroup members) was seen as unfair, while an equal distribution was seen as fair. This difference in fairness perceptions disappeared, however, in the intergroup conditions when the inequality favored the participants' ingroup member. Moreover, endorsement of the leader who made the distribution paralleled participants' fairness perceptions.

In a third examination of changes in fairness perceptions as a function of the social context (Platow et al., 1997), New Zealand participants read about a chief executive officer (CEO) of a regional health authority distributing time on a single kidney dialysis machine between two equally needy patients. In one condition, the CEO distributed the time equally between the two patients; in another, the CEO gave more time to one patient than the other. When the two patients were both described as life-long New Zealanders, participants perceived the equal distribution as fair and the unequal distribution as unfair *regardless of how much the two patients contributed to the social welfare system*. However, when one patient was a recent immigrant to New Zealand, then the New Zealand participants perceived an unequal distribution favoring the fellow New Zealander as more fair than an equal distribution between the two patients. Again, the meaning of fairness changed with changes in the group-based social context. Moreover, participants' leadership endorsements of the CEO again paralleled their fairness ratings. Thus, normatively fair (i.e., equal) leaders were not always supported over normatively unfair (i.e., unequal) leaders.

Finally, Platow, Reid, and Andrew (1998) examined whether perceptions of procedural fairness – as opposed to distributive fairness – would also be subject to changes in the group-based social context. In this study, a randomly chosen, anonymous leader of a laboratory-created group was given the opportunity to canvass the opinions of two other participants prior to the leader making a decision. In two intragroup conditions, the leader, the actual participants and the participants whose opinions were to be canvassed were all from the same group. In two intergroup conditions, the leader and the actual participants were in the same group, as was only one of the canvassed participants; the second participant to be canvassed was an outgroup member. As a manipulation of procedural fairness, the leader canvassed both participants' opinions (i.e., process control; Thibaut and Walker, 1975); as a manipulation of procedural *un*fairness, the leader canvassed only one participant's opinions. Results clearly followed the previous research. In the intragroup condition, the leader was perceived to be more fair (and received stronger endorsements) when he or she was procedurally fair rather than unfair. In the intergroup condition, however, this difference in fairness perceptions (and leadership endorsement) disappeared when the leader canvassed the ingroup member's opinions but not the outgroup member's opinions.

Two very important points emerge from this program of research. First, people's endorsements of their leaders will follow their perceptions of the leaders' fairness (Hollander and Julian, 1970; Michener and Lawler, 1975; Tyler, et al., 1985). However, those perceptions themselves vary as a function of the intragroup and intergroup context, and not necessarily as a function of abstract justice principles. In this manner, fairness, at least in the eyes of potential followers, is yet another outcome of the self-categorization process.

Being charismatic by being one of us

For us to offer an analysis of charismatic leadership not based on individual characteristics may lead readers to claim that we are pushing our analysis too far. Surely, of all of the leadership qualities, charisma is the one that is most personal; indeed, much of the received treatments of charisma understand it as a special gift held by the leader him- or herself. Even analyses of charismatic leadership that have shifted their focus to followers' normal attribution processes still list specific behaviors to be learned by potential leaders to make them more charismatic (e.g., Calder, 1977; Conger and Kanungo, 1998). However, even a cursory glance at historical figures informs us of the partisan nature of charismatic leadership. One would be hard-pressed, for example, to identify similarities in the behavior and personality of Adolf Hitler and Mohandas Gandhi, despite both having bold visions of the future and leading nations to follow those visions. Indeed, one may even question whether these men were charismatic at all depending on whether one aligns oneself with their cause or not.

Recently, Platow, van Knippenberg, Haslam, van Knippenberg, and Spears (2001) conducted an empirical test of the group-based nature of charismatic leadership. They did this through the simple manipulation of the relative ingroup prototypicality of the leader – a variable shown clearly in previous research to affect leadership perceptions (e.g., Hogg, Hains, and Mason, 1998; Platow and van Knippenberg, 2001). Specifically, student participants read about a fellow university student leader who was described as being either high or low on ingroup-like characteristics. The specific characteristics were never stated, but were left to be inferred by participants. As a second independent variable, Platow et al. varied the communications of the leader to fellow students. In one condition the leader invoked an exchange-based communication (i.e., 'Do something for me, so I can do something for you.'), and in the other the leader invoked a group-oriented communication ('Let's do something together … for *all* of us.'). Results showed that only relative ingroup-prototypicality affected the perceived charisma of the leader. Highly ingroup prototypical leaders were perceived to be more charismatic on questions from Bass' (1985) Multifactor Leadership Questionnaire (MLQ) than non-ingroup prototypical leaders, independent of the actual communication of the leaders. Leaders who were perceived as being 'like us' were also perceived *inter alia* to inspire loyalty, have a vision of the future, and have a sense of mission.

In a second study, Platow et al. (2001) manipulated relative ingroup prototypicality by directly manipulating the content of the description of the leader. In this case, the leader was described as being either high on characteristics pilot tested as being ingroup stereotypical, and low on characteristics pilot tested as being outgroup stereotypical, or vice versa. Manipulation checks confirmed this as a successful manipulation of relative ingroup prototypicality. Once again, ingroup prototypical leaders were perceived to be more charismatic on MLQ items than non-ingroup prototypical leaders. Certainly, attributions of charisma in this study were based on specific qualities the leader was described as having. However, these were not qualities that set the leader apart from fellow group members. Instead, attributions of charisma were derived from qualities the leader shared with the rest of his ingroup, and that differentiated that group from a relevant outgroup (cf. Tajfel and Turner, 1979).

These two charismatic leadership studies thus demonstrate that leaders' charisma is directly related to the degree to which they embody characteristics of the group of which they are a part. Being charismatic requires a leader to be one of 'us'.

The Story Thus Far

We have examined results from a variety of experiments showing how key features of leadership are the outcomes of self-categorization processes. The leadership qualities of influence, trust, fairness, and charisma are all products of shared group membership. It is in this manner that we argue that being a good leader means being a good group member. But is the story as simple as we have presented? We have only shown, for example, the effects of *being* a group member. However, leadership is not simply about being, it is also about doing. Leaders actively make decisions with implications for their group and the individuals in that group. Of course, these decisions often follow specific procedures entailing the distribution of valued outcomes. And these acts of doing we *have* considered. Leaders' procedural and distributive behaviors are often fundamental behaviors entrusted into the hands of leaders.

In our earlier analysis, we showed that the nature of leaders' distributive and procedural behavior is differentially interpreted as a function of *what* the leader does and the *context* in which the behavior is performed. Our point was to demonstrate the group-based nature of fairness, and its relationship to leadership endorsement. We did not ask *why* this happens, despite the answer having important implications for an understanding of 'leadership-as-doing' in addition to 'leadership-as-being'. From a social identity perspective (Tajfel and Turner, 1979), why this happens is straightforward. Distributive ingroup favoritism is a way in which the ingroup can be differentiated positively from relevant outgroups. Such positive differentiation provides an opportunity for social identity enhancement (Chin and McClintock 1993; Platow, Harley, Hunter, Hanning, Shave, and O'Connell, 1997). Intergroup equality (or 'even-handedness') and outgroup favoritism will, *ceteris paribus*, fail to achieve such social identity enhancement; in fact, under the right conditions (see Tajfel and Turner, 1979), outgroup favoritism may be seen as a form of social identity negation.

Armed with this understanding of the psychological meaning of distributive behavior, we can make further, more subtle group-based predictions about the qualities of leaders and their relationship to what they do in addition to who they are. In particular, we might reasonably expect that identity-enhancing leaders will be more influential and be seen to be more charismatic than intergroup even-handed and social identity-negating leaders *even if the leaders in all cases are ingroup members*.

Re-Examining fairness behavior: social identity enhancement vs social identity negation

Recall the study above in which a CEO of a New Zealand regional health authority distributed time on a single kidney dialysis machine to two equally needy patients (Platow et al., 1997). In an additional feature of the study, the CEO expressed an opinion about the use of memoranda for informing employees of hospital policies. After reading the scenario, participants were asked their own private opinions about the use of memoranda for such purposes. Results clearly showed that participants aligned their own private attitudes more closely with the fair than the unfair leader in the intragroup condition, but with the *unfair*, ingroup-favoring (i.e., ingroup enhancing) over the fair (i.e., even-handed) leader in the intergroup condition. Thus, although social influence emerges from shared ingroup membership, leaders' ability to influence is easily shaken if they behave in a manner that either: (1) fails to maintain the integrity of the ingroup by unnecessarily differentiating between group members (cf. Haslam et al., 1998), or (2) threatens the ingroup's status with respect to a relevant outgroup by failing to differentiate the ingroup from the outgroup.

Platow, Mills and Morrison (2000) demonstrated a similar effect with participants' preferences for modern paintings. In this study, a psychology-student experimenter distributed experimental tasks equally or unequally between either two psychology students, or between one psychology student and one dental student. Participants, who were also psychology students, were then shown a series of modern paintings supposedly by Paul Klee and Vasilij Kandinsky, and were asked to rate their liking of each painting. Prior to the ratings, but after the experimenter's distribution, the experimenter mentioned that he or she preferred Kandinsky over Klee. The data were very clear. Participants who self-categorized with the experimenter expressed a greater preference for paintings labelled 'Kandinsky' over those labelled 'Klee' (i.e., consistent with the experimenter's preference) when the experimenter showed intragroup fairness rather than intragroup unfairness. However, this pattern reversed when the experimenter made intergroup distributions, and the unfairness favored the ingroup over the outgroup. Lest the reader think this a trivial finding with respect to leadership, reflect back upon Hitler's infamous 1937 'Degenerate Art' exhibit. Here a leader renowned for his 'ingroup favoritism' displayed, among others, specifically Klee and Kandinsky paintings as 'degenerate art', with the clear goal of influencing Germans' artistic evaluations against them (and other artists; Barron, 1991). Of course, our simple laboratory experiment barely approximates the horrors of Hitler; however, we can observe a very simple psychological analogue of an ingroup-favoring leader effectively legislating taste.

In a third study, Haslam and Platow (2001) presented university students with a university student leader who had behaved in either an identity-enhancing, even-handed, or identity-negating manner between groups. In this study, participants' fairness ratings of both the even-handed (i.e., equal) and identity-enhancing (i.e., unequal, ingroup-favoring) leader were identical, and both were significantly higher than their fairness ratings of the identity-negating (i.e., unequal, outgroup-favoring) leader. After providing their ratings, participants were asked to generate arguments for or against novel proposals that the leader had put forward. Very few opposing arguments were generated, and there were no differences between the three distributive conditions. However, the number of arguments in favor of the leader's proposals was significantly greater in the identity-enhancing condition than in either the even-handed or identity-negating conditions. It was only the identity-enhancing leader who had the ability to influence fellow ingroup members to do the intellectual work necessary for his plan to be realized. Only where he had advanced the identity of the group was the group willing to work to advance his vision of the future.

In the last study we will discuss, Haslam et al. (2001) presented university students with a description of a university student leader. Across four independent conditions, the leader was said to have overseen one of four forms of organizational performance during his tenure as leader: an organizational downturn, a steady loss, a steady profit, or an organizational upturn. Replicating previous research (Meindl, 1993), participants attributed increasingly greater charisma to the leader across these four conditions (in the order presented). Importantly, however, Haslam et al. also introduced a manipulation in which the leader was seen to have been identity-enhancing, even-handed, or identity-negating in an intergroup context. Analyses clearly showed that the identity-enhancing behavior of the leader buffered him from the negative effects of overseeing an organizational down-turn. The leader was effectively able to maintain his charisma in the eyes of group members during an organizational down-turn *only if* he was simultaneously seen to be distributively ingroup favoring. In this manner, by behaving in what would otherwise be considered to be a normatively unfair manner, the leader's charisma was maintained.

Conclusion

We began this chapter by observing that qualities often attributed to leaders are actually outcomes of the self-categorization process. To support this, we demonstrated how the qualities of influence, trust, fairness and charisma are all produced by shared group membership. At the same time, we recognized that leadership is more than simply being, it is doing as well. We then reviewed research showing that engaging in identity-negating behaviors, for example, can actually undermine the production of several leadership qualities, even if the would-be leader is a fellow ingroup member. It is in this manner that we argue that, to be a good leader, one must be a good group member. Like other group processes (e.g., stereotyping, prejudice, cohesion, collective action), reducing leadership to a set of individual differences remains unsatisfactory. The immense leadership literature attests to this. As we noted in our introduction, that literature 'celebrates the diversity of groups' studied, but its conclusions are varied because authors have sought answers to their questions in a specific person or role.

At this point, the reader may be asking the question often posed to us: 'How does the self-categorization analysis allow me to seek out and choose the best person to appoint to a leadership position within my group or organization?' One answer is that psychometricians should develop inventories measuring the fit between specific group members and the group itself (cf. van Vianen, 2000), rather than qualities of individuals in the abstract. Unfortunately, however, the dynamic nature of groups means that even this method will fail as soon as the group context changes. As Sherif, Harvey, White, Hood, and Sherif

(1961), and more recently Turner and Haslam (2001) observed, the qualities leading to follower endorsement change as soon as the intergroup context changes. In one intergroup context, intelligence may be highly valued in a leader, but in another intergroup context, intelligence may not be valued at all. And, as we showed with fairness, the actual meaning of intelligence may very well change too given changes in the social context.

This observation leads to a second response to the statement: 'The self-categorization analysis doesn't help.' Insofar as the SCT analysis of leadership does not provide a list of stable qualities, traits, attributes or abilities that people in power should seek when appointing others to leadership roles, this second answer remains true. In this way, some may find no *practical* use in our analysis.

Of course, we do not doubt that psychologists *can* develop inventories to administer to individuals with the goal of predicting the future behavior of one or two individuals within a specific social context (e.g., an organization). But seeking individuals with specific traits and qualities, and appointing them to leadership positions represents only one approach to group life. The desire of managers and executive boards to appoint individuals to leadership positions is a *desire* and a *preference* only, not an inherent necessity. This desire represents a particular set of political values held by those who wish to pursue a particular form of social relation. By contrast, the SCT view that good leaders are good group members highlights how the placement of the appointment process in the hands of a few powerful people represents the imposition of the values of the powerful onto the lives of the powerless (cf. Haslam et al., 1998). It is precisely at this point that scientific realities expose political follies. Armed with the theoretical and empirical gains, the practical use of the SCT analysis of leadership is, thus, the *empowerment* of group members through the exposure of political decisions in the guise of impartiality, science, or simply the 'bottom line'.

The self-categorization analysis has shown us that the ability to influence, to hold the trust of others, to be seen as fair, and to be attributed with charisma, are all consequences of sharing group membership and actively promoting ingroup identification with potential followers. In this manner, to know what it is to lead, one must look to both the followers who are to be led and to the potential of the shared identity that any creative partnership between leaders and followers might forge.

5 Identity, Leadership Categorization, and Leadership Schema

ROBERT LORD AND ROSALIE HALL

Leadership, identity, and social power are dynamically intertwined in a process that unfolds as group members interact and establish a status structure. In the current chapter we highlight the role that leaders' and followers' cognitive structures play in this process, and the implications of current knowledge about the nature of mental representations of the self and others for understanding leadership and the use of power. In particular, we focus on the role of shifting identities as a means of explaining differences in leadership perceptions and effectiveness. At the core of our approach is a belief that the cognitive mechanisms that determine the thoughts and actions of both leaders and followers must share fundamental similarities.

A key concept that underlies much of this chapter is that of leadership perceptions. Leadership perceptions refer to an assessment made by observers, or by potential leaders themselves, that the target individual has both the qualities typical of leaders and the potential to exhibit leadership in a specific situation. Perceptions are important to leadership and organizational processes for several reasons. First, when one is perceived as a leader, the bases of social power are enhanced (Lord, 1977), and the latitude of discretion to change organizational processes is increased. Second, due to their greater power, people who are peceived as leaders have a greater potential impact on organizational processes and outcomes. This does not necessarily mean that the leader's actions will always result in higher organizational performance, simply that more extreme positive *or negative* outcomes can be produced. Third, leadership perceptions have a reciprocal relationship with performance. Higher performance enhances leadership perceptions; lower performance reduces leadership perceptions, so that over time ineffective leaders will eventually be restricted or replaced, although they may create substantial costs to the organization in the interim. Finally, because perceptions and effectiveness are not always congruent, it is important to understand the variety of ways that leaders can manage, or fail to manage, the way that they are perceived by others. Scientific knowledge about the leadership perception process can help avoid two undesirable situations: (1) potentially effective individuals who are not perceived as leaders, and therefore have minimal impact on the organization; and (2) ineffective leaders who nevertheless are successful at manipulating leadership perceptions as a means to retain power in the organization.

This chapter contains three major sections. We begin by describing our basic social–cognitive viewpoint on leadership, addressing the developmental and functional parallel between our views on leadership categorization and Hogg's views on the development of group identities. This section is followed by an integration of the social cognitive perspective with recent theorizing which focuses directly on the role of self-identities in leadership processes (Lord, Brown, and Freiberg, 1999). The concluding section moves from descriptions of existing theory and research, to their theoretical and practical implications, particularly for understanding the relation between self-identity, power and gender.

Leadership Perceptions and Categorization Theory

Our research on leadership perceptions and perceived social power over the past 25 years has been guided by two fundamental ideas. First, that leadership perceptions are jointly constructed through an emergent, dynamic process that involves the target, the perceiver, the task, and the organizational context. Second, that the core of this process is a categorization of the target by the perceiver in terms of an implicit theory of leadership. Leadership perceptions appear to operate much like many other implicit social perception processes, such as spontaneous trait inferences (Van Overwalle, Drenth, and Mausman, 1999), which guide social actions but often operate outside of conscious awareness. Our early work, which emphasized the prediction of leadership perceptions and perceived social power in terms of observable group behaviors (Lord, 1977), was modified to incorporate both social cognitive research on categorical structures (Lord, Foti and De Vader, 1984; Lord and Maher, 1991) and the recognition that affect is a critical component of leadership (Hall and Lord, 1995). Such work explains processes that are central to the emergence and maintenance of leadership.

More recent research has added two additional ideas of considerable importance. First, effective leaders must act in a flexible manner, modifying their behavior to match different task and social requirements (*Hall, Makiney, Marchioro, and Philips, 2002*; Hall, Workman, and Marchioro, 1998; Zaccaro, Foti, and Kenny, 1991). And second, both the underlying scripts which guide leader behavior, and the prototypes which guide social perceptions, must function in a manner that allows such flexibility. That is, scripts and prototypes themselves are flexible, rather than fixed, cognitive structures that are automatically constructed to meet specific contextual demands (Lord, Brown, Harvey, and Hall, 2001). We suggest this adjustment occurs through a process involving networks of cognitive units which respond to current internal and external constraints. In the next two sections, such reconstructive models of leadership prototypes are described, as well as their historical predecessors.

Early perspective: memory retrieval models of leadership prototypes

The integration of social and cognitive psychological developments in the 1970s provided many ideas that were useful in understanding leadership perceptions. The social–cognitive approach recognizes that social perceptions occur within the boundaries and through the processes imposed by human cognitive systems. A central idea borrowed from the social–cognitive paradigm is that perceivers are *active* contributors to the leadership perception process, rather than being passive responders to leader characteristics. For example, leadership perceptions depend upon the knowledge structures currently activated in perceivers, as well as potential characteristics of the leader. Another important idea was that similar principles are applied to the categorization of both social stimuli and inanimate objects. An important principle, popularized by Rosch (1978), was that categories are defined by sets of central features (prototypes), rather than by critical features that produce clear distinctions between category members and non-members. This emphasis on the importance of prototypes provided a basis for the development of leadership categorization theory.

Leadership categorization theory (Lord et al., 1984) maintains that leadership perceptions may be based on one of two processes. First, leadership can be *recognized* when the pattern of traits or behaviors associated with a potential leader matches a salient prototype used by perceivers. Good fit produces high leadership ratings, while poor fit produces lower ratings. In either case, once individuals are labeled as leaders, behavioral expectations and descriptions of past leadership behavior are highly dependent on the prototype used by perceivers. In addition, behaviors of successful leaders are described as more prototypical, while leaders who fail are described as less prototypical, even when their objective behavior is the same (see Lord and Maher, 1991 for a review of this literature).

Second, leadership can be *inferred* from events and outcomes that result in causal attributions to potential leaders. A large number of experimental studies illustrate this process by showing that bogus performance information affects leadership perceptions, with good performance resulting in high levels of attributed leadership and poor performance producing low levels of attributed leadership (see Lord and Maher, 1991). Interestingly, behavioral descriptions of leaders are also affected by experimentally manipulated performance information, suggesting that behavioral ratings are reconstructed based on leadership labels and category structures, rather than being veridically retrieved. Both inferential and recognition processes illustrate the important role of perceivers in helping to construct leadership perceptions, because it is the trait/behavior profile *as interpreted by perceivers* that ultimately produces leadership perceptions (and thus the behavioral ratings assigned to leaders).

Category prototypes have been viewed as central components of perceivers' implicit leadership theories, because prototype matching appears to be one determinant of leadership perceptions, and also because knowledge about a leader's performance, traits, and behaviors is assimilated with category prototypes. This assimilation is often so thorough that once categorization has occurred, unobserved, but category-consistent information is believed by perceivers to have actually been seen. Because category prototypes were originally thought to be fixed structures that were learned through experience, early research focused on articulating the content of the 'leader' category, as well as articulating its taxonomic structure.

The content of leadership categories

Lord et al. (1984) identified 27 characteristics that were highly prototypical of leaders, with the ten most prototypical being: dedicated, goal oriented, informed, charismatic, decisive, responsible, intelligent, determined, organized, and verbally skilled. In a very extensive study of implicit leadership theories, Offermann, Kennedy, and Wirtz (1994) found eight factors that were prototypical of leaders. The five which were most strongly associated with leadership were: dedication, intelligence, charisma, strength, and sensitivity. A meta-analytic review of traits associated with leadership emergence showed that traits of intelligence, masculinity and adjustment were strongly associated with leadership emergence in small groups (Lord, De Vader and Alliger, 1986). And, a study looking at the relationships of leader characteristics with stable perceiver components of leadership impressions, found consistent relationships over time and over perceivers with extroversion, dominance, flexibility, experience, and social influence (Hall et al., 2002). This substantial agreement on the content of leadership prototypes should not be interpreted as indicating that all leaders possess a few critical features, but rather it is more in line with the idea that there is an overlapping pattern of leadership features or a family resemblance structure.

There is also an obvious relation of many of the features associated with leadership to those associated with social power. This idea is shown graphically in Figure 5.1, which depicts a set of features (upper hexagon) with links that make it part of both a leader prototype and a set of relations with social power. For example, perceptions of another's task contribution and strength may be part of the basis for legitimate power; perceptions of intelligence relate to expert power; dominance may relate to coercive power; and flexibility and extroversion may relate to referent power. Figure 5.1 also shows that leadership perceptions and perceived social power may have reciprocal causal relationships, which is supported by the high correlation between these constructs (Lord, 1977).

The structure of leadership categories

Early work on the structure of leadership categories built on Rosch's (1978) theorizing. Taxonomic work by Lord et al. (1984) supported a hierarchical model of category structure. Consistent with Rosch's theory, they found support for a three-level hierarchy of superordinate, basic, and subordinate level categories.

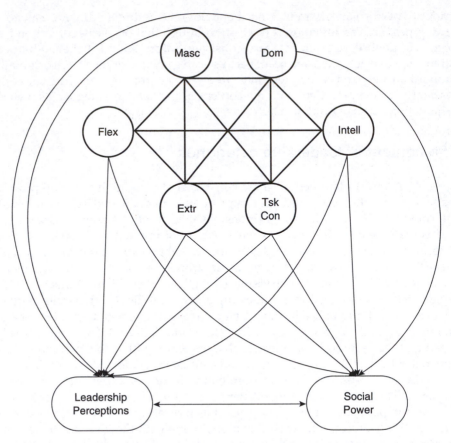

Figure 5.1   Pattern of leadership prototype activation in recurrent connectionist network influences perceptions of leadership and social power. Masc = Masculinity/Femininity; Dom = Dominance; Intell = Intelligence; Tsk Con = Task contribution; Extr = Extraversion; Flex = Behavioral Flexibility.

The superordinate category corresponded to the leader/non-leader distinction; the basic level corresponded to eleven different types of leaders that depended on organizational context (business, education, labor, finance, national politics, mass media, military, minority, religious, sports, and world politics); the subordinate level distinguished among leaders at higher and lower levels in the authority hierarchy. Considerable research suggested that social categories like leadership were learned through experience, and were defined by central features or prototypes rather than by critical features that distinguished all leaders from all non-leaders. For example, Matthews, Lord, and Walker (1990) interviewed children and adolescents in five different school levels (1, 3, 6, 9, and 12) to examine prototype development. They found that older students defined leadership in more elaborate and abstract terms, consistent with reliance on a prototype. In contrast, younger students defined leadership more simply and concretely, often focusing on a specific exemplar.

Implications of this work for understanding key issues in leadership perception

An important aspect of leadership categorization theory was that categorization or leadership perception was viewed as an on-line process which reflected implicit sense-making and offered ongoing guides to social situations, rather than being an explicit, reflective process. That is, leadership was experienced as group or organizational activities transpired, with leadership perceptions, behaviors, and outcomes simultaneously emerging through a dynamic, reciprocal causal process. When potential leaders were encountered, perceptually based, data-driven information regarding the perceptual target was thought to be integrated with top-down information regarding category prototypes that was retrieved from a perceiver's memory. Thus, both target and perceiver components contributed to social perceptions (Lord et al., 2001). This process was believed to be contingent on situationally cued definitions of leadership that were widely shared in both the United States and cross-culturally (Den Hartog, House, Hanges, Ruiz-Quintanilla, Dorfman, and associates, 1999, although there is considerable evidence of cross cultural variability as well (Den Hartog et al., 1999; Gerstner and Day, 1994).

Because cognitive structures or schemas appear to guide most social perception processes, leadership categorization theory integrates research on leadership perceptions with broader thinking about social perception processes. For example, by incorporating additional elements such as gender into thinking about the development of leadership categories, critically important developments in understanding the perceptions of women in management could be integrated with categorization theory. Biases against female leaders could be explained in part by the fact that there was much greater overlap between the attributes thought to be possessed by typical men and leaders, than there was between attributes possessed by typical women and leaders (Heilman, Block, Martell, and Simon, 1989). Thus, leadership categorization theory and the resulting attribution of qualities associated with leadership can help explain why females are less likely to emerge as leaders in small groups (Hall et al., 1998), providing a cognitively based explanation that is consistent with more sociological theories such as status theory (Ridgeway, Chapter 6) and gender role theory (Eagly, Chapter 7).

Contemporary perspective: reconstructive models of leadership prototypes

Memory-retrieval views of leadership categorization such as those previously discussed are based on a symbol storage metaphor, with memory viewed as analogous to a file drawer in which information is organized and preserved intact (Lord et al., 2001b). This symbolic-level view of leadership prototypes is consistent with social cognitive research which shows that prototypes are learned through extensive experience in a given context by a relatively slow process (Sherman and Klein, 1994). However, the leadership prototypes held by individuals may vary extensively across context (e.g., business versus military), hierarchical level (upper versus lower level management) (Lord et al., 1984), and target gender (Heilman et al., 1989). Analogous research shows that gender-related patterns of leadership emergence change with task type (Hall et al., 1998), implying that gender-related prototypes interact with task characteristics. In addition, results from group identity research strongly suggest that leadership prototypes change to be more consistent with desirable group characteristics as perceivers identify more with a group (Hogg, 2001; Chapter 3). While these results are not inherently inconsistent with the notion of fixed prototypes, the extreme context sensitivity of prototypes suggests that leadership categories, like other cognitive categories, may be generated on-the-fly (Barsalou, 1983) so as to conform to external and internal constraints from contexts, tasks, subordinates, or group identities.

Research showing that perceivers consider patterns of leadership characteristics which seem to influence perceptions in an interactive manner further suggests that leadership categorization is quite flexible (Smith and Foti, 1998). This Gestalt-like quality suggests that incremental changes in prototypes are likely to be less important for understanding changing perceptions than are context-based shifts in entire patterns of desired leadership qualities. Conceptions of prototypes based on retrieving fixed structures from memory have difficulty explaining such dynamic, and particularly, discontinuous changes in the application of leadership prototypes, and their corresponding discontinuous effects on leadership perceptions (Brown, Lord, Hanges, and Hall, 2002). Connectionist network models of leadership prototypes, also described as distributed neural network models, have the capacity to change in such a manner. Further, because connectionist networks operate in parallel, they can *reconstruct*, rather than simply retrieve, category prototypes in a manner that is consistent with situational constraints.

Neural network representations of prototypes

In brief, *connectionist networks* are systems of neuron-like processing units that integrate information from input sources and feed the resulting activation (or inhibition) on to connected output units. Meaning (e.g., a categorization) is carried in the resulting pattern of activation. In the case of leadership categories, units may reflect perceived characteristics of a target, such as relevant physical and psychological characteristics, as well as beliefs about which characteristics are indicative of leadership. Activation in neural networks occurs as a result of *positive constraints*, which occur when units fit together or are consistent. For example, when a target individual is perceived as being experienced and wise, those units would be mutually activated. Inhibition reflects *negative constraints*, which occur when units conflict (e.g., being naive yet wise). In connectionist networks, the amount of activation or inhibition transmitted from one unit to another depends on the weights connecting these units. Such weights are

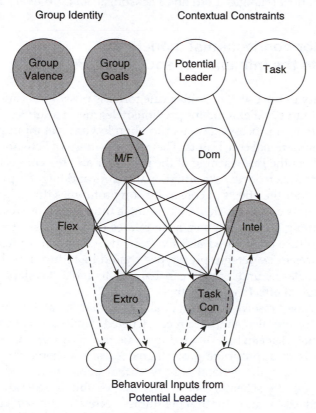

Figure 5.2   Group and contextual constraints on leadership prototype. Units with higher activation are indicated by shaded circles; top-down constraints on behavioral input are indicated by dashed lines.

learned over time through experience, and thereby incorporate the statistical regularities in observed leadership stimuli into perceptual schema.

One particular configuration of connectionist networks, called *recurrent networks*, allows all units at a particular level to influence each other. That is, all aspects of a leadership prototype can show mutual activation or inhibition. A recurrent network is shown in Figure 5.2, with a pattern of activation/inhibition depicted in the centre portion of the figure. Recurrent networks are particularly good at learning category prototypes (Smith and De Coster, 1998). Importantly, when activated by an input pattern – which may be a social stimulus like a potential leader – patterns of activation in recurrent networks are refined through dynamic adjustment processes so as to maximally agree with internal and external constraints. Thus, recurrent networks can not only construct prototypes on-the-fly, but importantly, they can do this subject to a number of constraints from culture, current tasks, target leaders, and follower's goals, identities, or affect (Hanges, Lord and Dickson, 2000; Lord et al., 2001).

Capacity for connectionist models to incorporate the influence of social factors

Such flexibility in the use of cognitive categories is possible because neural networks operate in parallel to adapt previously learned patterns of connections, by using them as a processing system to align lower-level input patterns with higher-level situational constraints. That is, the pattern of activation can simultaneously reflect the *past* learning of the perceiver and the connections of these units to constraints from *current* situational factors and target inputs. It is interesting to consider the effects of constraints on prototypes due to group context. These constraints cumulate, thereby priming a more and more restricted leader prototype among group members as identities develop, tasks become clearer, and group culture and shared affective tone develops. Put differently, individual differences in leadership prototypes should be reduced as these multiple constraints coalesce, and groups can be said to have developed a common 'mental model' of effective leadership.

We have argued elsewhere (Lord et al., 2001) that the scripts or schema that guide behavior are also similarly reconstructed, subject to constraints as just described. That idea can be extended to argue that as group identity develops, mental models of appropriate group behavior also become more commonly held. If one accepts the general argument that perceptions and behavior are guided by cognitive schema, then it may be possible to extend our cognitive process-based explanation for the constrained reconstruction of leadership prototypes to the reconstruction of cognitive schema in general. In such an extension, group identities would have a profound impact on the development of group mental models that guide both perceptions *and* behavior.

Identity and Leadership

Connectionist models of prototypes and schema, we believe, have the capacity to provide a general perspective that fits with a variety of other social and social cognitive theories of leadership that stress the importance of followers' identities. For example, Hogg's (2001) work indicates that individuals may emerge as leaders based on their fit with a group identity that develops over time. In addition, the identification of followers with their group may influence the basis on which the quality of their dyadic relationship with the leader is evaluated, thus influencing the extent of legitimacy leaders are perceived to possess (Tyler, 1997; Chapter 8). Finally, leaders may help subordinates construct appropriate identities, thereby affecting a variety of motivational processes (Shamir, House, and Arthur, 1993; Lord et al., 1999). In short, understanding individual and group identities is central to understanding effective leadership. In the following sections we take a more detailed look at each of these lines of research.

Group identities and leadership perceptions

Hogg (Hogg, 2001; van Knippenberg and Hogg, 2001) builds upon Tajfel and Turner's (1979) Social Identity Theory to develop the idea that membership in a group influences the social perception processes of followers, which in turn affect leader emergence and maintenance of power. In particular, he argues that in situations where group membership is salient, i.e., where members identify strongly with the group, a group prototype develops. Individual group members will vary in their match to this prototype. Group members who are more proto-typical will first appear to, and then actually come to, exert greater influence over other group members (van Knippenberg, van Knippenberg, and van Dijk, 2000). In part, this effect can be explained by a depersonalization process, in which a group member evaluates others not in terms of personally held values and stan-dards, but by reference to the socially constructed group prototype. Persons who closely match this prototype will be perceived by other group members as highly similar (to a collective 'us'), and similarity-based attraction and liking will typi-cally result. Prototypicality also may serve as a basis for the internal attribution of leadership qualities such as charisma to highly prototypical members. The leader's ability to gain and maintain power thus depends in part to the extent that he or she continues to be perceived as closely matching the group prototype. A leader may manipulate the situation to ensure that his or her prototypicality stays high, by employing such tactics as villifying an outgroup or sanctioning ingroup members who deviate from the prototype.

Among the key arguments made by Hogg and colleagues (Hogg, 2001; Platow and van Knippenberg, 2001) is that as group identity becomes stronger, the group prototype plays an increasingly strong role in determining leader-ship, relative to a normative leadership prototype such as those described in our section on memory retrieval models of leadership prototypes. The general point made in this argument is an extremely insightful observation that high-lights the important influence of group processes on leadership perceptions and effectiveness. And Hogg's perspective may be more compatible with our own than might initially appear to be the case. His perspective implies that the *content* of leadership prototypes changes so as to become more consistent with group norms as group members increasingly identify with a group. But noth-ing in it requires that the nature of leadership perception processes changes. We view group identity as one of many external constraints on the construction of a leadership prototype, whose content and structure is influenced by the fact that it emerges at a particular time and in a particular situation.

Figure 5.2 provided a graphic illustration of how group level constraints might influence prototype reconstruction. To make this rather abstract idea more concrete, consider the possibility that identification with a group makes achieving group goals more important and increases the positive valence associated with being a group member. Such developments may increase group norms for high task contributions and expressive behavior (extroversion), and these characteristics could also become more salient in leadership prototypes. This occurs because constraints from group norms to these neural units help activate 'task contributions' and 'extroversion' when prototypes are reconstructed.

Identification with leaders and social power

Tyler (1997) builds upon his extensive work in the psychology of justice perceptions, to explain the psychological factors influencing group members' willingness to voluntarily follow the rules set down by authorities. The willingness to give authorities the right to issue rules and expect obedience creates a basis of legitimate power for leaders. Tyler suggests that previously proposed, resource-based, instrumental models of legitimacy do not provide complete explanations. Such instrumental models explain legitimacy as the outcome of an exchange relationship in which inputs include characteristics of the leader such as competence and likely success, as well as resources which have been received in the past or are expected in the future. Thus, this model implies that people will grant greater legitimacy to groups and authorities from whom they have received, or anticipate receiving, greater resources.

Tyler (1997; Chapter 8), however, demonstrates that an *identification-based relational model* of legitimacy is at least equally important, and perhaps, more important, to understanding legitimacy. He suggests that group members trade acknowledgment of their status within the group, for deference to authority. A key psychological variable is thus the extent to which members feel that they are valued and respected by the group. Being treated well by authorities, in terms of classic relational justice concerns (Tyler and Lind, 1992), including neutrality, trustworthiness or benevolence, and respectful treatment, provides information that is especially important to the maintenance of group members' positive self-conceptions and esteem.

In six data sets spanning settings where the group was defined in terms of family, workplace, educational, and national/political membership, Tyler (1997) showed that the overall attribution of legitimacy depended more strongly on relational judgments of experiences with authorities, than on instrumental judgments (although both were relevant in all data sets). More detailed inspections of this relationship showed that as identity concerns became more salient, relational experiences increased in importance. Specifically, people were more influenced by relational concerns when the authority was an in-group member, when they drew a greater sense of self or identity from the group membership, and when they perceived that they shared more values with the authority.

A clear implication of this work for the literature on leadership categorization is that factors which influence the extent of identification with the group will impose a constraint on leadership perceptions. When identification is high, individual leader characteristics that convey competence and control over resources should drop in importance relevant to characteristics which signal the subordinates can expect respectful treatment from the leader. It is interesting to think back to the Ohio State studies (e.g., Fleishman and Harris, 1962; Yukl, 1971), with their basic distinction between two types of leader behaviors corresponding to Initiating Structure and Consideration, and to wonder if in part these were important behaviors because they signalled information related to workers' instrumental and relational concerns, respectively. As a set, studies using this approach were inconsistent in their findings about the importance of the two behavioral dimensions. Perhaps the differences are explainable in terms of the extent of member identification with the group across samples.

Leadership and the development of subordinate identities

Previous sections examined the effect of group identities on leadership perception and social power. However the direction of this relationship may also be reversed. Leadership can also be an important causal factor influencing subordinates' identities (Lord and Brown, 2004; Reicher and Hopkins, Chapter 15). This may happen in the shorter-run, as leaders temporarily influence the content of subordinates' working self-concept (WSC, Markus and Wurf, 1987), which is the currently activated portion of their overarching self structure. Leaders may also have more long-run effects as their repeated influences cause more permanent changes in follower prototypes and schemas.

Leader effects on working self-concept

Lord and colleagues (Lord et al., 1999; Lord and Brown, 2004) propose that subordinates' WSC mainly involves three types of components: *self-views*, which are an individual's perceived standing on attributes made salient by a particular context; *current goals*, which have a short-run duration and are narrowly focused; and *possible selves*, which have a long-term, future focus and provide much broader comparative standards. They maintain that leaders can affect subordinate motivation through their influence on these three aspects of subordinate identity.

Lord and Brown also propose that self-concepts can be defined at the independent (individual) level, or at two interdependent levels: relational and collective. A *collective identity* is defined in terms of group membership, a *relational identity* is based on one's dyadic relationships with specific others, and an *individual identity* emphasizes one's sense of uniqueness (Lord and Brown, 2003). Brewer (Brewer and Gardner, 1996) suggests that most people have developed elements of identities at each of these three levels, but one identity is more central because of individual differences in learning histories or because of situational factors that make one identity particularly salient. This salient identity would be incorporated in the WSC and would impact on subordinate's intrapersonal and interpersonal self-regulatory processes.

Lord and Brown further maintain that leadership and group processes work best when they are congruent with highly active identities of subordinates. Some evidence that level of identity does indeed affect important subordinate psychological processes comes from recent studies by Phillips (Phillips, 2000; Phillips and Hall, 2001) and Praslova and Hall (2002). Phillips demonstrated that the extent of identification with the organization mediated the relationship between employee perceptions of organizational support and commitment, and also that levels of the self acted as moderators of the strength of these relationships. Praslova and Hall (2002) studied a sample of Russian workers and found that a measure of collective self-concept positively predicted the extent to which they engaged in discretionary and altruistic behaviors, as rated by supervisors.

Lord and Brown view identity levels as being malleable; however, they do not discuss the possibility that self-structures, like leadership prototypes, could be reconstructed to fit situational constraints. One might expect, as Markus and Wurf (1987) suggested, that core aspects of the self are relatively stable across situational constraints, but many peripheral aspects could be made salient or suppressed by situational constraints, with organizational culture and leadership practices being fairly powerful constraining factors. Thus, the changing emphasis on individual, relational or collective self-structures shown in Figure 5.3 can be viewed as a transformation of the WSC as contextual constraints make specific identities more or less salient (shown by the shaded circles). As shown by the arrows connecting shaded circles, the salient identity can then constrain aspects of leadership prototypes. Note that we have also included an individual's core identity as being a potential situational constraint in this figure.

More permanent effects on identity development

It is tempting to merely assert that leaders can affect subordinate identities through the direct application of social power. However, recent descriptive evidence suggests that the effects of leaders on subordinate identity development are more subtle. For example, Ibarra suggests that subordinates develop identities through a social process in which they tentatively adopt a provisional identity, use it to generate identity-consistent behavior, then adjust this identity based on social feedback which may come from leaders or a more diffuse role set. This theory fits nicely with the Lord and Brown framework because this identity development process operates differently depending on the level of subordinates' identity as we show in Table 5.1.

Ibarra (1999) examined the development of new identities for management consultants and investment bankers who were in transitions to higher level

Input Sources

Identity Level   Core Self

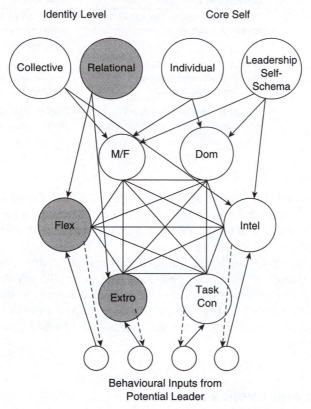

Behavioural Inputs from
Potential Leader

Figure 5.3   Identity level and core self-schema constraints on leadership prototype. Units with higher activation are indicated by shaded circles; top-down constraints on behavioral input are indicated by dashed lines.

roles. In her study, some individuals developed a provisional self that was based on their own individual values, which we believe would be most likely when individual level identities were salient; some imitated the qualities of a mentor with whom they had strong affective bonds, which should be most likely with salient relational level identities; while others developed a provisional self which was an amalgam of many individuals' styles, perhaps reflecting the development of a group prototype which Hogg's work has shown is critical to collective level identities.

Selecting or discarding provisional selves that have been considered also varied with identity level. Some participants used a true-to-self strategy to discarded provisional selves that prevented them from discovering their 'true' character and competence, a concern most relevant to individual level identities. Others relied on implicit, affectively based guidance from important role

Table 5.1   *Development and Evaluation of Provisional Selves as a Function of Identity Level*

Identity Level	Development	Evaluation
Individual	True-to-self strategy based on internal values	Based on provisional self inhibiting true character or competence
Relational	Holistic imitation of role model (mentor) with whom strong affective bonds existed	Informal guidance from role models with whom they identified
Collective	Selective imitation from many others to customize provisional self	Implicit and explicit reactions from broader role-set

models with whom they identified, which suggests a relational identity level. A third group used both implicit and explicit social feedback a broader role-set to gradually develop a personal identity that was consistent with a collective definition of effective consultants.

Ibarra's work nicely illustrates the idea that self-structures are constructed through both cognitive and social processes that vary with identity level. Her work can easily be incorporated into the general process we have shown in Figure 5.3 if one's core identity serves as a constraint on the development of provisional identities and on scripts used to test such identities through organizational behavior.

Integration and Application

We have explained that constraints on prototypes and behavioral schema can come from a number of sources such as leaders, group identities, core aspects of one's self-schema, tasks, gender or organizational culture. When consistent, these multiple constraints simplify leadership and influence by reducing uncertainty and providing less ambiguous cognitive schema to guide perceptions or behavior. When inconsistent, they can produce a changing basis for behavior or perceptions depending on the strength and consistency of various constraints. For example, new tasks may alter perceptions of needed behavior, temporarily changing both behavioral tendencies and the basis for social perceptions until the new task is completed. As we discuss elsewhere (Lord et al., 2001) these various constraints vary in the level of analysis that they suggest is appropriate for understanding perceptions, behavior or social power, with the most appropriate level being the one with the strongest and most consistent constraints. For example, the group level may be appropriate when there is consistency among members, but heterogeneity may weaken group level constraints making group level identities harder to develop and less likely to affect social processes. Tyler's (1997) work on legitimacy nicely illustrates this process.

Constraints can also vary in their salience. Gender, though consistent for an individual, may vary in salience depending on whether groups are homogeneous or heterogeneous with respect to gender. In mixed-gender groups, research on status theory (Ridgeway, Chapter 6) suggests that the salience of sex-related leadership expectations will be greater than in same-gender groups. Our perspective suggests that multiple prototypes – one constrained by typical male and one constrained by typical female characteristics – will compete as behavioral and perceptual guides in mixed gender groups. One resolution of this uncertainty for both actors and observers is to automatically integrate both diffuse and specific characteristics of perceivers into a social status evaluation, which then may operate as a hidden source of activation in connectionist networks, making a masculine prototype more accessible. Though a source of gender bias in leadership, such a process would also reduce perceptual and behavioral uncertainty.

We have suggested that constraints operating through neural networks can tune both perceptual prototypes and behavioral scripts to current contexts. However, it should also be realized that these schemas impact on different social processes. Scripts pertain to one's own behavior, and they are also primed by one's current goals. Their translation into actual behavior depends on meta-cognitive processes such as beliefs about one's ability or the likely social acceptance of leadership or influence. Thus, for females, stereotype threat, which may operate through internal metacognitive processes (Norris-Watts and Lord, 2001), can limit the generation of leadership behavior, while status factors may limit the perceived social acceptance of leadership behavior or influence.

Inconsistencies between behavioral and social processes can also arise from inconsistencies in underlying constraints. Consider the case of a female with a strong and consistent leadership self-schema who is a member of a mixed-sex group performing a masculine task (see Figure 5.3). Leadership scripts may be highly accessible for such an individual resulting in attempted leadership, but group members may not see leadership prototypes as fitting with a female, thus limiting the acceptance of her attempted leadership.

Conclusions

Though we have focused on gender and leadership biases to illustrate the applied implications of our social-cognitive perspective, the framework we have developed is more general. Individuals operating in social contexts must always operate as both perceivers and potential actors. They must also respond to many concurrent situational constraints. We suggested that these demands can be handled automatically and in parallel by connectionist neural networks that tune the regeneration of schema to one's current context. Thus, what we are proposing is a general, unified approach for understanding the cognitive underpinnings of social processes with relevance to issues such as skill development, behavioral flexibility, social attributions (e.g., leadership, power, or personality), or the potential conflict between individuals and groups.

6 Status Characteristics and Leadership

CECILIA L. RIDGEWAY

Leadership is inherently a group rather than individual phenomenon. It is widely understood as the process of social influence through which a group member 'enlists and mobilizes the aid of others in the attainment of a collective goal' (Chemers, 2001, p. 376). Thus, rather than the act of an individual, it is an emergent social response to a collective need, a response that develops out of the transactional relationships between a would be leader and others who share the collective goal (Bass, 1990; Chemers, 2001; Hollander, 1985). As I argue here, it is a consequence of the broader processes by which social hierarchies of prestige, influence, and power develop among people when they are oriented toward the accomplishment of a collective goal or task.

As recent approaches to leadership have shown, the relational dynamics out of which leadership emerges are framed and driven by the sociocognitive prototypes and schemas that group members use to conceptualize the group, leadership, and themselves in relation to these identities. Research in the tradition of social identity theory has shown, for instance, that the more prototypical a member is perceived to be in relation to the group's self conception, the more likely he or she is to emerge as the leader (Hogg, 2001; Chapter 3). Lord and colleagues (Lord, Brown, Harvey, 2001; Lord and Maher, 1991; Chapter 5) have demonstrated as well that people hold established social schemas of leaderlike behavior. When a group member's own behavior evokes these schemas in the minds of other members, they transform that member into a leader.

In this chapter, I argue that there is an additional set of widely shared social schemas that also powerfully shapes the emergence of leadership and the exercise of power in groups. These schemas too are widely shared cultural conceptions of significant social identities. These social identities, however, refer to the social categories to which people belong that carry *status value* in their society, such as gender, race, occupation, ethnicity, education, or age. A categorical social identity carries status value when cultural beliefs that are widely held in a society attach greater status worthiness and competence to people in one category of the identity (men, whites, professionals) than other categories of the identity (women, people of color, factory workers). Widely shared cultural conceptions of these identities transform the identities into *status characteristics* that affect how individuals are perceived and act in groups. As they do so, status characteristics systematically affect the likelihood that some categories of people will emerge as leaders compared to others (Berger, Fisek, Norman, and Zelditch, 1977; Berger and Zelditch, 1998; Ridgeway, 2001b; Webster and Foschi, 1988).

Like group prototypes and leadership schemas, status characteristics are taken for granted cultural tools that people use to frame their relationships with one another and organize collective, group efforts to achieve shared goals. Unlike these other sociocognitive schemas, however, status characteristics are an integral part of the organization of inequality in society. They are social representations of the important axes along which inequalities in power, prestige, and wealth are distributed within a society. Since the cultural beliefs that constitute status characteristics are broadly shared, different people coming together in interacting groups across diverse settings in a society draw on similar status characteristics to frame their relationships and help organize their groups. Consequently, to the extent that status characteristics shape the development of leadership in groups, they structure the inequality within each group in a manner that recapitulates and legitimates the larger structure of inequality in society (Berger, Ridgeway, Fisek, Norman, 1998). Status characteristics, then, show us the hand of social structure operating in the group dynamics of leadership.

To describe how status characteristics shape the emergence of leadership and the exercise of power in groups, I rely on expectation states theory and its variant, status characteristics theory (Berger et al., 1977; Berger and Zelditch, 1998). Expectation states theory is a sociological theory that has developed over several decades to account for the way that social hierarchies emerge in goal-oriented groups. It provides a detailed and well-documented account for the way these hierarchies are shaped by status characteristics (see Ridgeway, 2001b for a review).

I begin with a closer scrutiny of the cultural beliefs that constitute social identities as status characteristics. In particular, I consider the relationship of status beliefs to other sociocognitive schemas, such as group and leadership prototypes, that are also important for the leadership process. With a better understanding of status beliefs in hand, I turn to evidence about their effects on the behaviors, evaluations, and social hierarchies out of which leadership emerges. I then turn to the way status characteristics affect the exercise of authoritative power by a leader by affecting the leader's apparent legitimacy in that position.

Status Beliefs and Leadership

Status beliefs are shared cultural schema about the status position in society of categorical groups such as those based on gender, race, ethnicity, education, or occupation (Ridgeway and Erickson, 2000). In status beliefs, cultural assumptions about the evaluative ranking of one group compared to another are represented and legitimated by presumptions about differences in competence among people from those groups. Since a group identity is socially constructed as a status characteristic through widely held cultural beliefs, the identities that act as status characteristics vary from society to society and may change over historical periods (Berger et al., 1977). In the United States, gender (Wagner and Berger, 1997); race (Webster and Diskell, 1978), age (Freese and Cohen, 1973), occupation (Conway, Pizzamiglio, and Mount, 1996; Strodtbeck, James, and Hawkins, 1957), education (Moore, 1968) and physical attractiveness (Webster and Driskell, 1983) are among the social identities that function as status characteristics for most people.

When status beliefs develop about groups defined by a sociodemographic distinction such as race or occupation, they form an element in the social stereotypes of those groups. Status beliefs, however, add a distinctive, signature content to the stereotypes by associating greater social significance and competence, as well as specific positive and negative skills, with one category of the social distinction compared to others. In the US, for instance, gender stereotypes and racial stereotypes differ in many ways. However, both sets of stereotypes share a common status element in which one group (men, whites) is linked with greater social significance and competence than others (women, people of color) (see Webster and Foschi, 1988, for a review).

As sociocognitive schemas, status beliefs carry two sorts of implications that affect the relational dynamics out of which leadership emerges in goal-oriented groups. First, by associating greater general competence as well as specific skills with some categories of people compared to others, status beliefs potentially affect the perceived expertise different people could offer the group in a leadership position. Second, there is growing evidence that the status evaluation between categories of people contained in status beliefs carries with it an implied schema of leader–follower behavior (Berger, Ridgeway, and Zelditch, 2002). Conway, Pizzamiglio, and Mount (1996) have shown that when one group is perceived as higher status than another, observers attribute more agentic, instrumentally competent, and leaderlike behaviors to the higher status group and more reactive, expressive, and follower-like behaviors to the lower status group. Conway and colleagues demonstrate this effect with status-differentiated groups as different as gender, occupation (stockbroker vs file clerk), and hypothetical tribal groups.

Conway et al. (1996) speculate that people may have a general schema for status relations that describes a profile of proactive–reactive, leader–follower behaviors. Thus, the status beliefs that constitute a social identity as a status characteristic not only attach status value to it; in so doing, these beliefs simultaneously evoke a schema of leader–follower relations. Consequently, when status beliefs become salient in a goal-oriented group, these beliefs imply not only status and competence differences between the group members, but also a leader–follower relationship between them.

As the discussion above suggests, status beliefs combine elements of both group prototypes and leadership schemas. As elements of the stereotypes of categorical groups, status beliefs help define the prototype of those groups. For instance, images of men and professionals as more agentic and instrumentally competent and women and factory workers as more reactive and expressive are part of the sociocognitive prototypes of those groups that become salient for actors whenever those group identities are salient.

There are some interesting differences, however, between status beliefs and the typical group prototypes addressed by social identity theory approaches to leadership (Hogg, 2001). The group identities that status beliefs apply to are *categories* of people grouped by a principle of social distinction rather than typically *concrete groups* of people oriented around a collective goal such as those captured in group prototypes. Leadership, of course, occurs in real groups with a shared goal, not abstract categories of people. We should expect, then, that in real groups, members' prototypes of their concrete group and their salient status beliefs about their social characteristics may have separate, although sometimes interacting, effects on the emergence of leadership in the group.

Occasionally, the members of a concrete group will define themselves in terms of a shared, status valued categorical identity (i.e., a women's group) so that the effects of their status beliefs and group prototypes will converge. More often, the consensual prototype of an established real group, such as the military, that is dominated by a particular sociodemographic category of people (men) becomes imbued with the status valued stereotype of that category in addition to having its own quite distinctive elements (Boldry, Wood, and Kashy, 2001). As we shall see, the more closely aligned a particular status characteristic is with the prototype members hold for their group, the more powerful the impact of that status characteristic on the emergence of influence and leadership in that group.

Status beliefs are also distinctive in that they apply not to single groups, but to sets of two or more categorical groups that have been delineated by a given principle of social distinction or contrast. All social identities, of course, imply a contrast with an outgroup (Tajfel and Turner, 1986). The point, however, is that status beliefs describe group prototypes *in terms of* their evaluative relation to one another. Thus, status beliefs are sociocognitive schemas of metacategories (e.g., occupation) that contain within them two or more relationally defined prototypes of subgroups (e.g., agentic stockbrokers and reactive file clerks). In this way, status beliefs contain both within-group and intergroup elements and, as such, are more complex than a single in-group prototype.

There is a final, significant difference between status beliefs and the typical group prototype discussed in social identity theory approaches to leadership. Not only do status beliefs represent an evaluative relationship between subgroups of a metacategory, they turn on the fact that this evaluative relationship is *consensual* among the subgroups (Ridgeway, Boyle, Kuipers, and Robinson, 1998; Ridgeway and Erickson, 2000). In status beliefs, both subgroups agree that, in the eyes of 'most people', one particular subgroup is more respected and seen as more competent than the other subgroup. The evaluative structure of status beliefs differs from the competitive in-group favoritism that is most often a product of social identity processes. Certainly, those who are advantaged by a status belief may embrace the evaluative superiority attributed to their own subgroup more thoroughly than do those from the disadvantaged subgroup. Yet those from the status disadvantaged subgroup still concede, as a matter of social reality, that people from the other subgroup are commonly held to be higher status and more competent than people from their own group (Ridgeway and Erickson, 2000). Thus status beliefs represent what Jost and colleagues refer to as system justification beliefs more than beliefs about in-group favoritism (Jost and Banaji, 1994; Jost, Burgess, and Mosso, 2001).

Status, Expectations, and Leadership

Expectations and social hierarchies

Leadership in a group emerges jointly out of the assertive, goal-directed behaviors of a would-be leader and the group members' shared, socially constructed evaluation of that behavior. As recent approaches to leadership have shown, group members' evaluative reactions depend heavily on the sociocognitive schemas that the members use to judge the assertive actor (Hogg, 2001; Lord and Maher, 1991). Expectation states theory argues further that members' sociocognitive schemas not only shape their evaluative reactions, but drive their tendency to engage in assertive, goal-directed behaviors in a given group context.

Expectation states theory argues that, when a group of people are confronted by a shared task that they want to accomplish, they look for cues about how to act in the situation. To decide whether to speak up and offer task ideas or wait for others to speak first, to decide whether to hold their ground or back down in the face of disagreements, actors form *performance expectations* for themselves compared to others. Performance expectations, which are often unconscious assumptions, are guesses about the likely value of one group member's contributions to the task effort compared to another's (Berger et al., 1977).

Performance expectations are important for the development of leadership because, as expectations often do (Miller and Turnbull, 1986) they have self-fulfilling effects both on actors' goal-directed behaviors in the situation and on evaluations of those behaviors by self and others. The more positive the performance expectations an actor holds for another compared to herself: (1) the less likely the actor is to offer her own task suggestions, (2) the more likely she is to ask for the other's ideas, (3) the more positively she is likely to evaluate the others' contributions compared to her own, and, therefore, (4) the more likely she is to accept influence from the other by changing to agree with the other (Berger et al., 1977). Through these self-fulfilling effects, the theory argues, a social hierarchy quickly emerges among the group members in which expectation advantaged actors act more agentically and contribute more ideas, receive more positive attention and evaluations from others, and are more influential.

Members disadvantaged by performance expectations for themselves compared to others in the group, on the other hand, direct their attention towards others and are more reactive and deferential in their behavior.

Since leadership involves mobilizing group members to accomplish the group goal, it emerges out of this behavioral process of assertion and evaluation through which the group's influence and prestige hierarchy takes shape. The person who emerges at the top of the hierarchy is the leader whose ideas direct the group and to whom others in the group defer. Sometimes this leadership position is shared with one or two other high ranking members in the hierarchy who collectively make up the group's leadership clique. Expectation states theory argues that both the agentic behaviors of group members who become leaders and the positive responses to these behaviors by the rest of the group emerge together because both are driven by the members' shared performance expectations for each other. These expectations in turn, the theory argues, are shaped by group members' sociocognitive schemas, including status characteristics, that have become salient in the situation (Berger et al., 1977).

Status Characteristics and the Emergence of Leadership

When a status characteristic is effectively salient for group members as they seek to define one another through performance expectations, the characteristic provides the members with an immediate sociocognitive basis on which to proceed. Both the cultural presumptions about competence that the status characteristic carries and its associations with leader–follower behavior suggest higher performance expectations for those advantaged by the characteristic than those disadvantaged by it. Furthermore, since the cultural beliefs that constitute status characteristics are widely held, performance expectations based on salient status characteristics are likely to be implicitly shared by all the actors in the situation. The results of these expectations make some members seem apparently more competent and more appropriately and credibly leaderlike than other members simply based on their status characteristics.

To the extent that actors' performance expectations have been shaped by status characteristics, then, those advantaged by these characteristics tend to move the top of the hierarchy of influence and prestige out of which leadership emerges in goal-oriented groups. Those disadvantaged by these characteristics find themselves nearer the bottom. In this way, the status of the social categories to which actors belong in the larger society generalizes to their presumed competence, social standing, and acceptability as a leader in the group.

A distinctive claim of expectation states theory, however, is that the impact of status characteristics on actors' behaviors, evaluations, and emergence as leaders in goal-oriented groups may vary from imperceptible to substantial depending on the characteristic's salience in the situation and relevance to group goals (Berger et al., 1977). Since status beliefs form an element in the cultural stereotypes of particular categorical groups, they are implicitly primed whenever actors in a group categorize each other according to a status-valued group distinction such as gender or race (Fiske, 1998). The theory argues, however, that status characteristics (i.e., categorical identities with associated status beliefs) are only *effectively salient* for actors, that is sufficiently salient to measurably affect their behavior and evaluations, when the characteristics have diagnostic value for anticipating goal-related behaviors in the group (Ridgeway, 2001a).

Status characteristics are effectively salient under two general conditions, according to the theory (Berger et al., 1977). A status characteristic becomes effectively salient whenever it differentiates among the actors in the situation, such as race in a racially heterogeneous group. A status characteristic also becomes effectively salient for actors whenever it is culturally linked to the group goal, task, or setting, such as gender for a gender-typed task. Situations that meet this second condition are frequently ones where there is an established cultural prototype of the group that implies a particular social category of people as more prototypical, such as a sport that culturally implies men and, therefore, evokes the status characteristic of gender.

Once a status characteristic is effectively salient in a situation, the strength of its impact on behaviors, evaluations, and the emergence of leaders is proportional to the characteristic's presumed relevance to the group's goal or task. Note that these principles of salience and relevance suggest a distinct pattern of effects of status characteristics. Status characteristics that are effectively salient simply because they differentiate group members rather than are relevant to the task nevertheless shape expectations for competence and performance in the situation and, thus, opportunities for leadership. Yet the effects of such status characteristics are weaker than are those of status characteristics that are perceived as directly relevant to the task.

A substantial body of evidence supports expectation states theory's account of the impact of status characteristics on influence, prestige, and the emergence of leadership in goal-oriented groups. In a meta-analysis involving a variety of status characteristics including educational attainment, gender, race, and military rank, Driskell and Mullen (1990) found support for a central argument of the theory. Status characteristics do appear to affect group members' power and prestige behaviors (influence, task contributions, evaluations) indirectly through their performance expectations for one another rather than directly. A number of experiments have also demonstrated that, as the theory predicts, simple knowledge alone of another's status characteristics relative to one's own is sufficient to significantly affect willingness to accept influence from the other in task settings (for reviews, see Ridgeway, 2001b; Webster and Foschi, 1988). This occurs both when the status characteristic differentiates actors but is not initially task relevant (e.g., Webster and Driskell, 1978) and when it is task relevant (Webster, 1977).

There is also a good deal of support for the theory's argument that the strength and direction of a status characteristic's impact on influence, prestige, and the emergence of leadership depends on its relevance to the group's goal or task. One set of predictions that can be derived from this argument is the following. In a mixed sex group with a gender-neutral task, gender status will modestly advantage men over women in power and prestige since gender will be effectively salient but not directly task relevant. When such a group confronts a stereotypically masculine task, men's advantage over women in power and prestige will be greater because of gender's direct task relevance. Yet when a group like this deals with a feminine task, gender will be relevant but modestly advantage women over men in power and prestige (see Ridgeway, 2001a, for a discussion).

A number of studies confirm precisely this pattern of gender effects in mixed sex task groups. As the theory predicts, these patterns can be seen in members' power and prestige behaviors, the evaluations these behaviors elicit, and their likelihood of emerging as leaders (for reviews, see Aries, 1996; Ridgeway, 2001a). A study by Dovidio, Brown, Heltman, Ellyson, and Keating (1988) offers a particularly vivid demonstration for assertive power and prestige behaviors. Dovidio and his colleagues gave mixed sex dyads gender neutral, masculine, and feminine tasks to work on sequentially and recorded a variety of the participants' verbal and nonverbal power and prestige behaviors including speech initiations, time talking, and visual dominance. When the groups worked on a gender neutral task, men displayed moderately higher rates of these behaviors than their women partners. When the group shifted to a masculine task, this difference became exaggerated. Yet when the group shifted to a feminine task the hierarchy reversed and women displayed more assertive power and prestige behaviors than their male partners.

Leadership, of course, emerges not simply from assertive task behaviors, but from the evaluation of these task performances by other group members. As the theory predicts, a meta-analysis of evaluation studies found a modest overall tendency for the same task performance to be evaluated more positively when it was produced by a man rather than a woman (Swim, Borgida, Muruyama, and Meyers, 1989). This tendency was stronger when the task was culturally linked to men and tended to disappear when the task was linked to women.

Given these effects of gender status on the behaviors and evaluations out of which leadership emerges, we should expect a similar pattern for the emergence of men and women as leaders in mixed sex contexts. This is what Eagly and Karau's (1991) meta-analysis shows (also see Chapter 7). They found a moderate overall tendency for men rather than women to be selected as leaders in mixed sex settings. When leadership in the group was defined in more masculine terms as strictly task-oriented the tendency for men to emerge as leaders was stronger. When the task was culturally linked to women or leadership was conceived in social terms, men's advantage over women disappeared and there was a slight tendency for women to be selected as leaders.

If the impact of status characteristics on influence, prestige, and leadership in groups depends on the characteristics' salience and relevance in the situation, as the evidence indicates, then there are no status characteristics that advantage actors in all group settings. This is a significant implication of expectation states theory's account of status characteristics and leadership. Gender, for instance, is often referred to as a 'master status' that advantages men over women. Yet the theory predicts and the evidence confirms that while gender will advantage men over women to emerge as leaders in many mixed sex contexts, there are nevertheless some contexts where gender will disadvantage men for leadership compared to women who are otherwise similar to them. Further, the theory predicts that in same sex groups with gender-neutral tasks, gender status will not be effectively salient for the members and, as a result, men and women in such groups will display similar rates of task-related, leaderlike behaviors. Reviews of the evidence show support for this prediction as well (Ridgeway and Smith-Lovin, 1999).

Multiple Status Characteristics, Behavior, and Leadership

In many, perhaps most, work-oriented settings there are multiple status characteristics that simultaneously become effectively salient for group members and affect their expectations for one another. In addition to status characteristics made salient by their presumed relevance to the group context or goal, group members often differ on several status characteristics at once, such as gender, education, and occupational role in a diagnostic medical team made up of doctors, nurses, and nutritionists. The status and competence implications of some status characteristics that are salient in the situation may be inconsistent with the implications of others, as in an American legal team composed of a Harvard trained African-American lawyer and a state university trained white lawyer. The theory argues that in such situations, actors combine the positive and negative implications of all salient status information, each weighted by its relevance to the task to form aggregate performance expectations for themselves compared to each other group member (see Berger et al., 1977 for the precise form of this aggregating principle). Actors' behavior and evaluations, in turn, are based on these aggregated performance expectations.

A number of studies confirm that people in goal-oriented groups do form influence and prestige hierarchies as though they were combining status information as expectation states theory predicts (Berger, Norman, Balkwell and Smith, 1992; Webster and Driskell, 1978). An interesting implication of this combining principle is that if two people are differentiated by two inconsistent status characteristics, one of which is relevant to the task and one of which is not, then the person who is advantaged on the more relevant status characteristic will emerge as slightly more influential in the situation. Thus, in the example of the American legal team in the paragraph above, the Harvard trained African-American lawyer should emerge as the more influential of the pair.

As we have seen, when status characteristics are salient in a group setting, they evoke not only competence expectations but behavioral profiles of proactive versus reactive behavior that are played out through the enactment of the group hierarchy of influence and deference. Thus status characteristics generally drive actors' assertive or deferential behavior in the situation (Fisek, Berger, and Norman, 1991). But there are often some group members who are roughly equal in status characteristics. For these members, the patterns of behavioral interchange that they engage in may serve to further differentiate their standing in the group hierarchy. If they fall into a behavioral pattern where one such member agrees with or accepts influence from the other, their behavior will evoke for group members a cultural schema of leader–follower behavior, according to the theory. This, in turn, will raise performance expectations for the more influential actor compared to the less influential one and differentiate their standing in the group hierarchy (Fisek et al., 1991).

In fact, in addition to status characteristics, actors' performance expectations for one another can be affected by a number of other factors including their behavior in the situation, the distribution of valued rewards such as pay or office space, or an outside evaluation of success or failure at the task (see Ridgeway, 2001b). Generally, the implications of these additional factors combine, again weighted by their task relevance, with the effects of salient status characteristics to create the aggregate expectations that drive actors' standing in the group. As a result, status characteristics alone generally do not fully determine the outcome of the leadership process in actual, complex, multifactor groups. Instead, status characteristics act as systematic biases that subtly but pervasively favor the emergence of actors from status advantaged social categories as leaders without guaranteeing that outcome in every case.

Status and double standards for competence

Perhaps the most pervasive way that salient status characteristics affect the emergence of leadership is through performance expectations that embolden some to confidently assert themselves and others to react positively and deferentially to such assertions. Yet status characteristics also have another effect that underwrites the emergent leadership and the stability of a leader's authority. As Foschi (1989; 2000) argues, when a status characteristic such as gender or race is salient in a situation, it activates double standards for inferring an actor's ability from a performance of a given quality.

Such double standards have two effects. First, they mean that status-disadvantaged actors must produce objectively better performances than status-advantaged actors to be seen as having equally high ability at the task. Second, they modestly insulate status-advantaged actors from the perception of incompetence since high ability may be inferred from a less exceptional (although still good) objective performance. Studies have documented such double standard effects for both gender and race (white versus African-American), suggesting that they are indeed a status effect rather than a result of some other aspect of categorical stereotypes (Biernat and Kobrynowicz, 1997; Foschi, 1989; Foschi, 2000). Since the emergence of leadership in goal-oriented settings is usually predicated on, and legitimated by, perceptions of the leader as a person of high ability (e.g., Chemers, 2001), double standards play a significant role in advantaging actors from higher status social categories in the attainment of leadership.

Legitimacy and the Exercise of Authority

The effects of salient status characteristics on performance expectations, behavior, evaluations, and the inference of ability combine to make status-advantaged group members 'seem more the leader type' than status-disadvantaged members. The appearance of being more credibly leaderlike or, in other words, appearing more prototypical of widely shared leadership schemas, undergirds status-advantaged members' greater likelihood of emerging as group leaders. The same sense of being more credibly leaderlike also enhances a status-advantaged actor's appearance of *legitimacy* in a leadership position, once attained. As Zelditch concludes, based on a review of theory and evidence, legitimacy is the appearance of consensual support for the leader in a group that allows the leader to mobilize the resources necessary to ensure compliance with directives (Zelditch, 2001; Zelditch and Walker, 1984). Legitimacy, then, is central to a leader's effective exercise of power, particularly directive, coercive power that goes beyond simple persuasion (Chemers, 2001).

Expectation states theory points to two ways that salient status characteristics affect a leader's legitimacy in the group. The first is straightforward. If leadership is not just emergent, but also involves the attainment of a defined leader role (e.g., 'chair' or 'manager'), the role itself brings presumptions of competence that enhance performance expectations for the new leader and support legitimacy. However, the theory argues that the enhancing effects of the leader role will *combine with*, rather than eliminate the effects of the new leader's status characteristics. Consequently, lingering, status-based presumptions of lower competence for status-disadvantaged members make them appear slightly less competent in their leader role compared to similar status-advantaged leaders. Evidence supports this prediction with regard to gender, which is the status characteristic that has been most widely studied in relation to leadership (Heilman, Block, and Martell, 1995).

There is more to legitimacy, however, than the perception of task competence. Expectation states theory argues that status characteristics also affect legitimacy directly by affecting group members' sense that an actor is the type of person who 'should' or 'should not' be leader (Berger et al., 1998; Ridgeway and Berger, 1986). The status beliefs that transform an identity into a status-characteristic contain an essential hierarchical element that associates greater status worthiness and leaderlike attributes with people in one social category compared to another. When a person from a salient, status-advantaged category takes on the leader role in a group, that person enacts and confirms the hierarchical assumptions of a taken for granted status belief. Because of the status belief, people expect leadership from status-advantaged actors, and expect that others, who presumably share the belief, also expect such leadership. The presumption that others also expect such leadership makes it seem normative in the situation so that when it occurs, people treat it as 'right' by acting deferentially towards it. Their deferential reactions, in turn, create the appearance of consensual support for the leader that invests the leader with legitimacy and enhances the leader's power (Berger et al., 1998).

On the other hand, when a person from a salient, but status-disadvantaged category becomes leader, it violates the central, hierarchical structure of group members' status beliefs about the category. Those status beliefs imply that a person like that 'should not' be leader in a group like this. Consequently, the same expectation process that causes people to defer to a status-advantaged actor's leadership leads group members to resist a status-disadvantaged person in that role. Such resistance undercuts legitimacy and reduces the leader's power to ensure compliance with directives. Resistance is likely to be especially evident when a status-disadvantaged leader attempts to wield more coercive, directive power. As with behavior, evaluations, and the emergence of leadership, expectation states theory predicts that the strength and direction of the impact of salient status characteristics on a leader's legitimacy depends on the characteristics' relevance to the group's goals and setting (Berger et al., 1998).

A number of studies of women's leadership in mixed sex contexts support this analysis. These studies show that when women attempt to exercize authority outside of traditional female domains, particularly over men, they often encounter resistive, 'backlash' reactions that undercut them (see Rudman and Glick, 2001 for a review). In a meta-analysis of the evaluation of male and female leaders, Eagly, Makhjani, and Klonsky (1992) found that when women leaders directly asserted their authority by acting in a directive, autocratic style, they were particularly likely to be devalued compared to male leaders who acted this way.

There is evidence as well that such resistive reactions are indeed status-based, rather than a unique consequence of gender stereotypes. Ridgeway, Johnson, and Diekema (1994) examined reactions to directive behavior by actors who were advantaged by status distinctions other than gender – specifically, age and educational attainment. In their study, confederates in same-sex dyads who were more skilled at the task than their partner, but younger and less educated, were resisted when they engaged in highly directive behavior and gained less influence from such behavior than age and educationally advantaged confederates. The resistance the age and educationally disadvantaged confederates encountered was not due to perceptions of them as less competent and, therefore, influential, since these results controlled for confederates' influence levels before they initiated their directive behavior. It appears, then, that the legitimizing or delegitimizing effects of status characteristics on leaders' power and authority are not unique to gender.

As the above discussion suggests, status beliefs legitimize leadership for actors from advantaged social categories by adding an appearance of consent that, in turn, increases the leader's power in the situation. On the other hand, these beliefs also bind followers from status-disadvantaged categories together in an apparently cooperative relation with the status advantaged leader by legitimizing the leader's right to exercise power. Both of these effects are a consequence of the consensual nature of the evaluative structure of status beliefs. Through their effects on a leader's legitimacy in a group organized in accord with status beliefs, these beliefs mitigate against competitive splits between leaders and followers. Yet status beliefs achieve this cooperative unity at the expense of people from status-disadvantaged social categories.

Conclusion

I have argued that leadership should be understood as an emergent consequence of the broader process by which people organize social hierarchies when confronting a collective goal or task. While many factors affect such hierarchies, the status characteristics of the members are particularly pervasive and insidious in their effects. Widely shared status beliefs that transform social distinctions like gender, race, or ethnicity into status characteristics in a given society act as sociocognitive schemas that systematically bias the development of social hierarchies and the emergence and exercize of leadership. When status characteristics are salient in a situation, because they either differentiate the group members or are culturally linked to the group goal, they bias performance expectations, behavior, evaluations, influence, the inference of ability from performance, selection as leader, the appearance of legitimacy, and the ability to exercize power and receive compliance, all in favor of status-advantaged actors and against status-disadvantaged actors.

The biasing effects of status characteristics at any given point in the processes by which leadership emerges and is exercized are often subtle, but the effects accumulate. For individuals, the result is that the playing field on which leadership is attained and effectively exercized is systematically tilted in favor of actors from certain social categories compared to others. Yet, because status beliefs are taken for granted cultural knowledge held by both advantaged and disadvantaged actors, the effects of these beliefs on expectations, behavior, and evaluations are mostly unconscious and appear in that way to be consensual. As a result, the systematic tilts in the playing field for leadership are insidiously difficult for actors to perceive and resist.

At the societal level, the accumulating effects of status characteristics on leadership in groups has another effect. It causes multiple groups over diverse settings to develop leadership hierarchies that recapitulate the structure of inequality in a society by representing certain categories of people as more leaderlike, effective, and competent than others. Through their effects on leadership in groups, widely shared status beliefs in a society reconfirm and justify the social distinction that are the axes around which inequality in a society are organized.

7 Few Women at the Top: How Role Incongruity Produces Prejudice and the Glass Ceiling

ALICE H. EAGLY

When Frank Rich wrote his reflections about the consequences of the terrorist attack of September 11 in an essay titled 'The Father Figure' that appeared in the *New York Times Magazine,* he described the people of America as searching for a father: 'When a nation is under siege, it wants someone to tell us what to do, to protect us from bullies, to tell us that everything's OK, and that it's safe to go home now' (Rich, 2001, p. 23). In Rich's analysis, the source of this protection and comfort is a father, not a mother or a parent but a father who leads, a dad who takes care of everyone, including mom. Mayor Giuliani of New York became this father figure and before long was the Man of the Year for *Time Magazine* and the entire nation. For Americans, Giuliani symbolized an ideal sort of leadership – taking charge in a crisis and inspiring commitment and patriotism from New Yorkers and many other Americans. Rich's portrayal of this longing for a resolute and protective father illustrates the decisive edge that men generally possess in gaining powerful leadership roles, performing well in them, and maintaining themselves in them over time.

This male advantage appears in aggregate data as well. Consider, for example, data from a Gallup Poll question asking respondents in the United States if they would prefer a man or a woman as their boss. A clear preference for male bosses over female bosses has been present for respondents of both sexes at all time points from 1953 to 2000, and this same preference for male bosses appeared in all 22 of the nations that the Gallup organization surveyed in 1995 (Simmons, 2001).

Putting men rather than women in charge of the most consequential activities is not a subtle trend, but a profound divide whereby women are generally barred from elite leadership positions. In the hierarchical structures of governments and large organizations, the proportion of women thus decreases at higher levels, until at the highest level women are extremely unusual. This patriarchal system in which men hold far more power than women is hardly rare in world societies. Many anthropologists have pointed out that it is disproportionately men who monopolize political leadership in non-industrial societies (Whyte, 1978), and some even claim that male dominance of public leadership is a cultural universal (e.g., Brown, 1991).

Even in postindustrial societies, leadership at the highest levels has remained an overwhelmingly male prerogative in corporate, political, military, and other sectors of society. Although women have gained considerable access to supervisory and middle management positions, they remain scarce as elite leaders and top executives. Consider, for example, that in the United States, women comprise only 4 per cent of the five highest-earning officers in Fortune 500 companies and 1 per cent of the chief executive officers (Catalyst, 2000, 2002). In addition, women are a mere 13 per cent of senators, 14 per cent of congressional representatives, and 10 per cent of state governors (Center for the American Woman and Politics, 2001). Other nations also have small proportions of women in most high positions (Adler and Izraeli, 1994).

Why do women continue to be rare in elite leadership positions, even in nations in which women have high levels of labor-force participation? This chapter offers an explanation that differs from traditional explanations that focused on the idea that a lack of qualified women created a 'pipeline problem'. This well-worn pipeline rationale assumes that women are less likely than men to have the requisite education, training, and leadership experience for high-level positions. Underlying women's lesser qualifications might be their acceptance of a disproportionate share of domestic responsibilities, which may make it difficult to assume very demanding and time-consuming occupational roles. Also, authors influenced by evolutionary psychology have argued for sex differences in evolved dispositions whereby women are endowed with fewer of the traits and motivations that are necessary to attain high-level positions and achieve success in them (e.g., Browne, 1998). Regardless of the vestiges of the sex-typed division between domestic labor and wage labor and any relevant inborn psychological sex differences, many social indicators suggest a rapid shift in postindustrial societies toward greater gender equality in education and labor-force participation. For example, in the United States, women make up 47 per cent of all workers (US Bureau of Labor Statistics, 2002) and 45 per cent of those in executive, administrative, and managerial occupations (US Bureau of Labor Statistics, 2001). And in the United States and many industrialized countries, women now attain university degrees at higher rates than men (United Nations Development Programme, 2001).

The presence of large numbers of educated women who are not only employed but already occupying positions as managers and administrators raises serious doubts about claims that there are few appropriately qualified women who are available to accept higher-level leadership roles. Therefore, it is sensible to consider other causes as the main source of women's near-exclusion from elite leadership roles. In this chapter, I consider prejudice as a principal cause of women's rarity in major leadership positions.

The idea that a barrier of prejudice and discrimination excludes women from higher-level leadership positions is not new. Public discussion has centred for years on the idea of a 'glass ceiling' of discriminatory barriers that prevent women and minorities from ascending past a certain level in organizations. After the term 'glass ceiling' was introduced in 1986 in the *Wall Street Journal* (The corporate woman, 1986), it spread rapidly among journalists and other writers and soon became a part of the culture. This metaphor caught on because it captured the essence of the explanations for the exclusion of women from high-level leadership that had begun to take shape in many people's minds. The term thus labeled prejudicial barriers in a way that recognized both their increasing subtlety and continuing strength.

Despite the extensive public discourse on the glass ceiling, social scientists have been slow to develop a systematic analysis of the contours of prejudice against female leaders. Understanding of such prejudice can explicate the sense in which women and minorities face a glass ceiling, although in this chapter I develop only the implications for prejudice directed toward women. To illuminate its psychological dynamics, it is necessary to come to a new understanding of what prejudice is in general. Breaking away from the classic approaches, Eagly and Karau (2002) proposed a role congruity theory of prejudice toward female leaders.

Role Congruity Theory: How Gender Roles and Leader Roles Produce Two Types of Prejudice

Prejudice toward female leaders is one instance of more general social psychological processes that can produce unfair disadvantage for a group of people. At its core, prejudice consists of differential evaluation of people on a basis that is not fair or legitimate. As Allport (1954) noted, prejudice occurs when people are placed at some disadvantage that is not warranted by their individual actions or qualifications. Prejudice is a common outcome when social perceivers react to others on the basis of their group membership. Information about group membership allows people to infer others' attributes based on assumptions about the attributes that are typical of members of their group. Social perceivers tend to ascribe these attributes to group members, regardless of whether their individual characteristics correspond to the attributes assumed to be common in their group.

In general, prejudice arises from the relations that people perceive between the characteristics of members of a social group and the requirements of the social roles that group members occupy or aspire to occupy (Eagly, in press). A potential for prejudice exists when social perceivers hold a stereotype about the group that is incongruent with the attributes that they think are required for success in certain classes of social roles. When a group member and an incongruent social role become joined in the mind of a perceiver, this inconsistency lowers the evaluation of the group member as an actual or potential occupant of the role. The group member is thought to be less than fully qualified for the role because of the assumption that members of his or her social group do not have the qualifications that are requisite for the role.

As Eagly and Karau (2002) argued, the principle of role incongruity is critical to understanding prejudice toward female leaders because this prejudice follows from the inconsistency that people often perceive between the characteristics typical of women and the requirements of leader roles, as Heilman (1983) also argued. In perceivers' minds, women tend not to match the requirements of high-level leadership roles and thus tend to be excluded, regardless of their individual qualifications. To explain these ideas in more detail, I review consensual beliefs about men and women and consider the typical degree of congruity between these beliefs and leader roles. Then I argue that this analysis implies two distinct forms of prejudice toward women as occupants or potential occupants of leadership roles and review relevant empirical evidence.

At the outset, it is helpful to understand that this analysis departs from social identity analyses of leadership that assume that members of groups desire to represent their own prototypical characteristics in their leaders (e.g., Hogg, 2001). From a social identity perspective, 'prototypical members are more likely to emerge as leaders, and more prototypical leaders will be perceived to be more effective leaders' (Hogg, 2001, p. 191). Instead, group members who are identified with their groups seek leaders who are prototypical, not of themselves, but of their shared ideas about the attributes of good leaders. If people share the prototype of leaders as fathers, for example, they seek men with appropriately paternal attributes, but not women. Thus, even in small groups studied in laboratory and field settings, men, more than women, emerged as group leaders even though women tended to emerge as better liked and as social facilitators (Eagly and Karau, 1991). Moreover, several social scientists have noted the natural-setting phenomenon of the 'glass escalator' (Williams, 1992), defined as men's marked success in rising to leadership in female-dominated organizations, professions, and industries (e.g., Maume, 1999; Williams, 1995). When leadership is defined in masculine terms, the leaders who emerge are disproportionately men, regardless of the sex composition of the group, and consequently leaders are very often non-prototypical of group members' own identities.

The approach of this chapter also diverges from classic theories that treat prejudice as arising from holding an unfavorable stereotype and consequently a negative attitude toward a social group (e.g., Allport, 1954). From that perspective, women's under-representation as leaders would be ascribed to a negative stereotype and attitude toward women in general. However, such a context-free theory cannot explain why women are discriminated against in some roles but not in others. Moreover, research on evaluations of women and men as social groups challenges this traditional approach with evidence that women are *not* regarded as less good than men in the sense of overall evaluation, even though they are perceived as inferior to men in power and status (see Eagly and Mladinic, 1994; Langford and MacKinnon, 2000).

Gender roles: expectations about the actual and ideal behavior of women and men

How can the preference for male leaders be explained? The first component of an explanation is an understanding of how people think about women and men. Gender roles comprise people's beliefs about women and men. Because social roles are socially shared expectations that apply to persons who occupy a certain social position or are members of a particular social category, gender roles are consensual beliefs about the attributes of women and men. These beliefs comprise two kinds of expectations, or norms: *descriptive norms*, which are consensual expectations about what members of a social group actually do, and *injunctive norms*, which are consensual expectations about what group members ought to do or ideally would do (Cialdini and Trost, 1998). The term *gender role* thus refers to the collection of descriptive and injunctive expectations associated with women and men. Other researchers have used different labels for this distinction between descriptive and injunctive expectations, including descriptive and prescriptive stereotypes (e.g., Burgess and Borgida, 1999; Fiske and Stevens, 1993). However, in analyzing leadership, role terminology is convenient because roles, not stereotypes, are the building blocks of the organizations within which leadership takes place.

People derive their beliefs about social groups from observing their typical behaviors, which occur within the context of their social roles (Eagly, 1987; Eagly, Wood, and Diekman, 2000). The descriptive aspect of gender roles thus originates in perceivers' correspondent inferences from the observed behavior of men and women to their personal qualities – that is, from the activities that men and women commonly perform in their typical social roles to the personal qualities that are apparently required to undertake these activities. Gender roles, or stereotypes, thus follow from observations of people in sex-typical social roles – especially men's more common occupancy of breadwinner and high-status roles and women's more common occupancy of homemaker and lower-status roles (e.g., Conway, Pizzamiglio, and Mount, 1996; Eagly and Steffen, 1984).

Both the descriptive and injunctive aspects of gender roles are well documented. Descriptively people thus believe that the sexes have somewhat divergent traits and behaviors (e.g., Diekman and Eagly, 2000; Newport, 2001). The majority of these beliefs pertain to *communal* and *agentic* attributes. Communal characteristics, which are ascribed more strongly to women, describe primarily a concern with the welfare of other people – for example, affectionate, helpful, kind, sympathetic, interpersonally sensitive, nurturing, and gentle. In contrast, agentic characteristics, which are ascribed more strongly to men, describe primarily an assertive, controlling, and confident tendency – for example, aggressive, ambitious, dominant, forceful, independent, self-sufficient, self-confident, and prone to act as a leader. Although people's ideas about the sexes also encompass beliefs about physical characteristics, typical roles, cognitive abilities, attitudes, specific skills, and emotional dispositions (Cejka and Eagly, 1999; Deaux and Lewis, 1984; Eckes, 1994), it is the communal and agentic aspects of these beliefs that are especially important to the study of leadership.

Gender roles also embrace injunctive norms about male and female behavior. People thus especially approve of communal qualities in women and agentic qualities in men. Evidence of the prescriptive aspects of these beliefs has emerged from several types of research. For example, these preferences are apparent in: (1) the beliefs that people hold about ideal women and men (e.g.,

Spence and Helmreich, 1978), (2) the beliefs that women and men hold about their ideal selves (W. Wood, Christensen, Hebl, and Rothgerber, 1997), and (3) the attitudes and prescriptive beliefs that people hold about the roles and responsibilities of women and men (e.g., Glick and Fiske, 1996).

Gender roles have pervasive effects. Their descriptive aspects – that is, stereotypes about women and men – are easily and automatically activated (e.g., Blair and Banaji, 1996). In addition, encoding processes advantage information that matches gender-stereotypic expectations (von Hippel, Sekaquaptewa, and Vargas, 1995), and spontaneous tacit inferences fill in unspecified details of male and female social behavior to be consistent with these expectations (Dunning and Sherman, 1997). The activation of beliefs about women and men by gender-related cues thus tends to influence people to perceive women as communal but not very agentic and men as agentic but not very communal.

Congruity of gender roles and leadership roles

Prejudice against female leaders arises because of the incongruity between the predominantly communal qualities that perceivers associate with women and the predominantly agentic qualities that they believe are required to succeed as a leader. Beliefs about leaders and women thus tend to be dissimilar, and beliefs about leaders and men tend to be similar.

In Schein's (2001) many empirical demonstrations of the masculine construal of leadership, respondents gave their impressions of either women, men, or successful middle managers. Successful middle managers were perceived as considerably more similar to men than women on a group of primarily agentic characteristics such as competitive, self-confident, objective, aggressive, ambitious, and able to lead. Many researchers have replicated Schein's findings in the United States and other nations.

The dissimilarity of beliefs about leaders and women would not be important if expectations based on gender faded away in organizational settings. However, these beliefs remain influential. Observing an individual as an occupant or potential occupant of a leader role places two sets of expectations in competition – those based on gender and those based on leadership. Gender roles continue to convey meaning about leaders, albeit in conjunction with organizational roles (e.g., Ridgeway, 1997). Because gender roles are highly accessible – that is, activated by gender-related cues in virtually all situations – their impact is maintained in group and organizational settings. Therefore, in thinking about women as leaders, people would combine two divergent sets of expectations – those about leaders and those about women, whereas in thinking about men as leaders, people would combine largely redundant expectations. Suggestive of this blending of gender and leader roles in thinking about female leaders are demonstrations that male managers rated 'women managers' as more agentic and less communal than 'women in general' but not as close as 'men managers' to a group identified as 'successful middle managers' (e.g., Heilman, Block, Martell, and Simon, 1989).

Paradoxically, becoming prototypical of desirable leadership in a group or organization does not protect women from prejudiced evaluations. Instead, perceiving a female leader as very similar to her male counterparts may produce disadvantage because such women can be perceived as undesirably masculine (see also Heilman, 2001). This disadvantage thus arises from the injunctive norms associated with the female gender role, by which niceness, kindness, and friendliness are especially valued in women. Women who are effective leaders tend to violate standards for their gender because they manifest male-stereotypic, agentic attributes and can fail to sufficiently manifest female-stereotypic, communal attributes. These gender-role violations can lower evaluations of women in leadership roles.

A woman who fulfills a leader role may thus elicit negative reactions, even while she may also receive some positive evaluation for her competence as a leader. For example, Heilman, Block, and Martell (1995) found that, even when researchers described female managers as successful, participants regarded these women as more hostile and less rational than successful male managers. Well known are the negative epithets often applied to powerful women in business settings, such as 'dragon lady' and 'battle axe' (Tannen, 1994).

To the extent that a woman who fulfills a leader role elicits a mix of positive and negative reactions – that is, an ambivalent attitude – reactions to her would tend to be inconsistent across time and situations (see Jonas, Broemer, and Diehl, 2000). As found in research on attitudinal ambivalence, reactions may polarize by becoming very negative or even sometimes very positive – depending on the particulars of the judgment context. This negativity often emerges, for example, when a powerful women takes tough or unpopular actions, even when they are required by her role (see Atwater, Carey, and Waldman, 2001; Sinclair and Kunda, 2000).

Two forms of prejudice toward female leaders

A major proposition of Eagly and Karau's (2002) role congruity theory is that prejudice toward female leaders and potential leaders takes two forms: (1) less favorable evaluation of women's (than men's) potential for leadership because leadership ability is more stereotypic of men than women and (2) less favorable evaluation of the actual leadership behavior of women than men because such behavior is perceived as less desirable in women than men. As I have explained, the first type of prejudice stems from the descriptive norms of gender roles – that is, the activation of descriptive beliefs about women's characteristics and the consequent ascription of female-stereotypic qualities to them, which are unlike the qualities expected or desired in leaders. In general, women do not fit the prototype of leadership that is shared among members of an organization, especially when high-level or very powerful roles are considered. The second type of prejudice stems from the injunctive norms of gender roles – that is, the activation of beliefs about how women ought to behave. Women who break through the glass ceiling to occupy leadership roles are in danger of biased evaluations stemming from their nonconformity to the cultural definitions of femininity. If female leaders thus violate prescriptive beliefs about women by fulfilling the agentic requirements of leader roles and failing to exhibit the communal, supportive behaviors preferred in women, they can be negatively evaluated for these violations, even while they may also receive some positive evaluation for their competent fulfillment of the leader role.

The role incongruity analysis thus portrays women in leadership roles as facing two sorts of dangers – being too feminine or too masculine. Threats to these women thus come from two directions: conforming closely to their gender role would produce a failure to meet the requirements of their leader role, and conforming closely to their leader role would produce a failure to meet the requirements of their gender role.

This analysis thus makes the glass ceiling understandable. Prejudicial evaluations create barriers to women's achievement of leadership roles and vulnerability to lack of success in these roles. In other words, these two forms of prejudice produce: (1) lesser access of women than men to leadership roles, and (2) more obstacles for women to overcome in becoming successful in these roles. The lesser access would follow from the tendency to ascribe less leadership ability to women, and the obstacles to success could follow from this aspect of prejudice as well as from people's preference that women do not behave in ways that are typical of leaders.

Women would not always be targets of prejudice in relation to leadership roles because various conditions would moderate these prejudices. Because the first form of prejudice follows from incongruity between the descriptive content of the female gender role and a leadership role, prejudice would be lessened or absent to the extent this incongruity is weak or absent. If some roles in middle management, for example, or in certain functional areas of organizations place a premium on socially skilled behavior, incongruity with the female gender role would lessen. In addition, because the second form of prejudice follows from incongruity between a leader's behavior and the injunctive content of the female gender role, various moderators would affect this form of prejudice. Specifically, the more agentically a leader role is defined or the more completely women fulfill its agentic requirements, the more likely such women are to elicit unfavorable evaluation because their behavior deviates from the injunctive norms of the female gender role.

In principle, role incongruity could sometimes produce prejudice against male leaders. The key condition for this outcome would be that a leader role has descriptive and injunctive content that is predominantly feminine. However, because leadership is generically masculine, such leader roles are rare. Therefore, ordinarily women but not men are vulnerable to role incongruity prejudice in relation to leadership.

Support for role incongruity analysis

To what extent has research substantiated this role incongruity analysis? Eagly and Karau's (2002) review of leadership research revealed a consistent pattern of supportive findings in diverse research paradigms that included true experiments, quasi-experiments, organizational studies, and studies analyzing aggregate social statistics such as wages. These paradigms range from those that have excellent internal validity but less external validity to those that have excellent external validity but less internal validity.

Several types of research have confirmed the hypothesis that women have lesser access to leadership roles than men. For example, most studies of actual wages and promotion supported the claim of discrimination against women in general and female managers in particular, albeit on a decreasing basis over the years (see review by Jacobsen, 1998). Experiments that obtained evaluations of female and male job applicants who were experimentally equated supported the narrower claim of prejudice as a disadvantage for women in relation to male sex-typed positions, which would include most leadership roles (see meta-analysis by Davison and Burke, 2000). Other studies showed that women usually have to meet a higher standard to be judged as very competent and possessing leadership ability, and that agentic behavior tends not to produce as much liking or influence for women as men, without special circumstances (e.g., adding communal behavior to an agentic repertoire; see review by Carli, 2001). Research in addition has demonstrated that it is generally less likely that women emerge as leaders in groups, especially if the group's task is not particularly demanding of interpersonal skill or is otherwise relatively masculine (Eagly and Karau, 1991).

Research also has substantiated the prediction that there are more obstacles for women to overcome in becoming successful in leadership roles (Eagly and Karau, 2002). Specifically, studies of leaders' effectiveness showed consistent role congruity effects, such that leaders performed more effectively when the leader role that they occupied was congruent with their gender role (see meta-analysis by Eagly, Karau, and Makhijani, 1995). Women suffered diminished outcomes in roles given especially masculine definitions, and men suffered somewhat poor outcomes in roles given more feminine definitions. More definitive support emerged in an experimental research paradigm that removed possible differences in the leadership behavior of women and men by equating this behavior (see meta-analysis by Eagly, Makhijani, and Klonsky 1992). These studies can make a stronger case that it is prejudice and not other factors that produce disadvantage for women in leadership roles. In these studies, women fared slightly less well than men overall. More important, just as in studies of leaders' effectiveness, women fared less well than men when leader roles were male-dominated or given especially masculine definitions and when men served as evaluators.

Also lending plausibility to the role incongruity theory of prejudice are the particulars of sex discrimination cases that have been brought to trial. Burgess and Borgida (1999) provided an insightful analysis of the relation of gender roles to such cases, the most famous of which is *Price Waterhouse vs. Hopkins*. This case pertained to Ann Hopkins, a woman who approached her work at a large accounting firm with a forthright, agentic style (Fiske, Bersoff, Borgida, Deaux, and Heilman, 1991). Although her task competence was widely acknowledged, she was denied partnership essentially on the basis of her nonconformity to the female gender role. Thus, the Supreme Court of the United States said in rendering its decision on the case: 'It takes no special training to discern sex stereotyping in a description of an aggressive female employee as requiring "a course at charm school". Nor…does it require expertise in psychology to know that, if an employee's flawed "interpersonal skills" can be corrected by a soft-hued suit or a new shade of lipstick, perhaps it is the employee's sex and not her interpersonal skills that has drawn the criticism' (Price Waterhouse vs. Hopkins, 1989, p. 1793). The reactions to Hopkins are part of a pattern of prejudice by which women in male-dominated roles are at risk for discrimination, particularly if they heighten role incongruity by enacting their role in an agentic style.

The Rise of Female Leaders

Despite role incongruity prejudice, women are rising into elite leadership roles around the world. Although the pace of change may be slow, there is discernible acceleration. As Adler (1999) pointed out, 26 of the 42 women who have ever served as presidents or prime ministers of nations came into office since 1990, and a continuing tally beyond Adler's review yields 12 additional women in these roles (de Zárate, 2002). Although large business organizations have been very slow to accept women in elite executive roles, Adler's list of female business leaders contained 18 women from various nations who led companies with revenues over $1 billion or banks with assets over $1 billion. Female executives such as Charlotte Beers, Carleton Fiorina, Andrea Jung, Marjorie Scardino, Martha Stewart, and Linda Wachner appear frequently on the business pages of major newspapers. It is thus unmistakable that women are rising, not merely into lower and midlevel managerial roles but into leadership roles at the tops of organizations and governments.

What changes have enabled at least some women to rise into leadership roles that women have very rarely occupied in other historical periods? Consistent with the role incongruity theory of prejudice, I explain and then discuss three reasons for women's increasing presence in leadership roles at the highest levels: specifically, (1) women have changed their personal attributes in a masculine direction toward greater consistency with common definitions of leader roles, (2) leader roles have changed in a direction that incorporates a greater measure of feminine qualities, and (3) women leaders have found ways to lead that finesse the still remaining incongruity between leader roles and the female gender role.

Masculine changes in women

As women shift a large portion of their time from domestic labor to paid labor, they assume the personal characteristics required to succeed in these new roles (Eagly et al., 2000). Women's decreased child care obligations and increased entry into paid employment are associated with a redefinition of the patterns of behavior that are appropriate to women. Social perceivers thus believe that women are becoming more masculine, particularly in agentic attributes, and will continue to change in this direction (Diekman and Eagly, 2000). Moreover, it is not surprising that research tracking sex differences across recent time periods suggests that psychological attributes and related behaviors of women have actually changed in concert with their entry into formerly male-dominated roles.

Research conducted primarily in the United States has documented the erosion of sex differences in numerous psychological tendencies over various time periods beginning as early as the 1930s and extending to the present: (1) the value that women place on job attributes such as freedom, challenge, leadership, prestige, and power has increased to be more similar to that of men (Konrad, Ritchie, Lieb, and Corrigall, 2000), (2) the career aspirations of female university students have become more similar to those of male students (Astin, Parrott, Korn, and Sax, 1997), (3) the amount of risky behavior in which women engage has become more similar to that of men (Byrnes, Miller, and Schafer, 1999), (4) the tendency for men rather than women to emerge as leaders in small groups has become smaller (Eagly and Karau, 1991), (5) women's self-reports of assertiveness, dominance, and masculinity have increased to become more similar to men's (Twenge, 1997, 2001), and (6) the tendency for men and boys to score higher than women or girls on tests of mathematics and science has declined (Hedges and Nowell, 1995; US Department of Education, 2000). Such findings suggest some convergence in the psychological attributes of women and men in traditionally masculine domains.

Feminine changes in leadership roles

The advice on what constitutes good leadership offered by management consultants and organizational experts has for some years construed management in terms that are more congenial to the female gender role than traditional views. These managerial experts have emphasized democratic relationships, participatory decision-making, delegation, and team-based leadership skills that are consistent with the communal characteristics typically ascribed to women (e.g., Garvin, 1993; Juran, 1988). These new themes reflect organizational environments marked by greatly accelerated technological growth, increasing workforce diversity, and a weakening of geopolitical boundaries. According to many organizational analysts (e.g., Lipman-Blumen, 1996) leaders need to seek new modes of managing in such environments.

The implications that these contemporary trends in management have for women's participation in leadership roles emerged in Fondas's (1997) analysis of the gender-stereotypic themes prevalent in expert opinion on desirable modes of management. In a textual analysis of mass-market books exemplifying contemporary advice on management, Fondas showed that much of this advice features traditionally feminine, communal attributes. Similarly, Cleveland, Stockdale, and Murphy (2000) noted that the female-stereotypic themes of empowering and enabling subordinates and communicating and listening effectively are prevalent in the advice of managerial experts. To the extent that organizations shift toward the democratic and participatory views advocated by many contemporary scholars, the role incongruity that underlies prejudice toward female leaders would moderate.

Finessing role incongruity with competent, androgynous leadership style

The analysis that I have offered might suggest that problems of role incongruity for female leaders are largely a thing of the past and that therefore women should have no special worries about presenting themselves as leaders and potential leaders. After all, if women have become more masculine and leader roles more feminine, a comfortably androgynous middle ground may have been reached where the characteristics ascribed to women match leadership roles as well as those ascribed to men. This resolution is not near at hand, however, because masculine changes in women's behavior still meet with some resistance. Moreover, consistent with traditional contingency theories of leadership (see House and Aditya, 1997), effective leadership in some situations no doubt requires an authoritative, directive approach. Because gender roles have injunctive aspects, women tend to receive negative reactions if they behave in a clearly authoritative, agentic manner, especially if this style entails exerting control and dominance over others (Carli, 2001; Eagly et al., 1992). When female leaders do not temper the agentic behaviors required by a leader role with sufficient displays of female-typical communal behaviors, they tended to incur a backlash whereby they are passed over for hiring and promotion (Burgess and Borgida, 1999; Heilman, 2001; Rudman and Glick, 1999).

Some evidence of the continuing potential for women to face role incongruity as leaders and potential leaders emerged in Schein's (2001) research on perceptions of the managerial role. Schein's newer studies have shown that in the United States, although not in several other nations (United Kingdom, Germany, Japan, China), female managers and students of management generally have shifted toward a more androgynous view of managerial roles as requiring communal qualities as well as agentic ones. This shift thus corresponds to much of the advice offered by management consultants and organizational experts (Fondas, 1997). However, this change in concepts of good management was not apparent in the beliefs expressed by male managers and students of management. This greater conservatism of men places serious limits on the redefinition of management, especially given men's greater power in most organizations.

Easing this dilemma requires that women in leader roles behave competently while reassuring others that they to some degree conform to expectations concerning appropriate female behavior. Many writers have thus commented on the fine line that female leaders must walk to avoid negative evaluations. For example, Morrison et al. (1987, p. 87) noted the 'narrow band of acceptable behavior' allowed for women leaders – behaviors that are somewhat feminine but not too feminine and somewhat masculine but not too masculine. Therefore, as suggested by several studies (e.g., Hall and Friedman, 1999; Moskowitz, Suh, and Desaulniers, 1994) as well as the Eagly and Johnson (1990) meta-analysis on leadership style, many women in managerial positions manifest language and communication styles that are somewhat more collaborative and less hierarchical than those of their male counterparts – that is, a repertoire of behaviors that is somewhat consistent with the communal requirements of the female gender role. The disapproving and uncooperative reactions that women receive when they proceed in an assertive and directive manner may dissipate at least partially when women complement their agentic repertoire with communal behaviors that are consistent with the female gender role, as long as these behaviors do not violate the relevant leadership role.

A tendency for female leaders to discover ways of leading that ease role incongruity appears in recent reviews of the transformational, transactional, and laissez-faire styles of women and men (Eagly and Johannesen-Schmidt, 2001; Eagly, Johannesen-Schmidt, and van Engen, 2003). Research on these aspects of leadership style was initially inspired by Burns's (1978) delineation of a type of leadership that he labeled *transformational*. Such leaders set especially high standards for behavior and establish themselves as role models by gaining the trust and confidence of their followers. They state future goals, develop plans to achieve these goals, and innovate, even when the organization that they lead is generally successful. By mentoring and empowering their followers, such leaders encourage them to contribute more capably to their organization. Researchers have generally contrasted this transformational style with a *transactional* style that emphazises management in the traditional sense of clarifying subordinate responsibilities, monitoring their work, and rewarding them for meeting objectives and correcting them for failing to meet objectives (Bass, 1998). In addition, researchers sometimes distinguished a *laissez-faire* leadership style that is marked by a general failure to take responsibility for managing. A substantial body of research has shown that transformational leadership and one component of transactional leadership (contingent reward) show positive relations to leaders' effectiveness, whereas the other aspects of transactional leadership and laissez-faire leadership show negative or null relations (Lowe, Kroeck, and Sivasubramaniam, 1996).

As Yoder (2001) also argued, transformational leadership may be especially advantageous for women, although it is an effective style for men as well as women. The reason that this style may be a special asset for women is that it encompasses some behaviors that are consistent with the female gender role's demand for caring, supportive, and considerate behaviors. Especially communal are the individualized consideration behaviors, which are marked by developing and mentoring followers and attending to their individual needs. Other aspects of transformational leadership do not seem to be aligned with the gender role of either sex (e.g., demonstrating attributes that instill respect and pride by association with a leader). Few, if any, transformational behaviors have distinctively masculine connotations.

If transformational behaviors allow some resolution of women's role incongruity because they are consistent with the female gender role (or at least not inconsistent with it) yet highly appropriate for leaders, transformational leadership might be somewhat more common in women than men who occupy leadership roles. Eagly et al. (2002) obtained such trends in a meta-analysis of 45 studies that compared the leadership styles of male and female managers.

In general, female leaders were more transformational than male leaders and also engaged in more of the contingent reward behaviors that are one component of transactional leadership. Although fewer studies had investigated the other aspects of transactional leadership and laissez-faire leadership, male leaders were generally more likely to manifest these styles. These differences between male and female leaders were small, but their implications for female leadership are nonetheless favorable because all of the aspects of style on which women exceeded men have positive relations to leaders' effectiveness and all of the aspects on which men exceeded women have negative or null relations to effectiveness. Although there may be other causes for the sex differences observed in transformational leadership (see Eagly et al., 2002), this transformational repertoire may help resolve some of the incongruity between the demands of leadership roles and the female gender role and therefore allow women to excel as leaders. Moreover, these findings suggest that organizations may enhance their chances for success by giving women leadership responsibility.

Conclusion

This chapter began with a portrayal of the role incongruity dilemmas that women face as leaders and potential leaders. These dilemmas arise because people choose leaders who match their construals of good leaders, which are typically more masculine than feminine. Women, perceived as unlike leaders, often face a glass ceiling that excludes them from leadership, especially at the highest levels.

Despite these barriers, women are rising to claim more leadership roles, even at the highest levels of governments and large organizations. Women's increasing masculinity and leader roles' increasing femininity may lie behind this easing of discriminatory barriers. However, in the short run, female leaders and potential leaders generally have to deal with some lingering role incongruity. Female leaders' legitimacy problems that are rooted in the incongruity of leader roles and the female gender role may be at least partially eased by their careful balancing of masculine and feminine behavior by leading with a transformational style or otherwise adding communal elements to behavior. Still, it is possible that some relatively communal behaviors might compromise women's advancement to higher-level positions in some contexts because such behaviors may appear to be less powerful or confident than those of their male counterparts. Nonetheless, given the analysis of this chapter, the appearance of female leaders in greater numbers than in the past and their success in these roles portend increasing representation of women in leadership roles in the future.

Author Note

The writing of this chapter was supported by National Science Foundation Grant SBR-9729449. I thank Mary Johannesen-Schmidt, Shannon Kelly, and Esther Lopez Zafra for comments on a draft of the chapter.

8 Justice, Identity, and Leadership

TOM R. TYLER

Leadership involves the possession of qualities that lead the people in groups to *want* to follow the leader's directives, either because they feel obligated to do so, or because they desire to do so. In other words, leadership is a characteristic that is conferred upon a leader by followers. It involves the ability of a leader to engage the active, voluntary, and willing cooperation of their followers. Leadership is, therefore, a process of influence that 'depends more on persuasion than on coercion' (Hollander, 1978, pp. 1–2). This discussion of *process based leadership* focuses on the ability of the leader to gain voluntary cooperation from others in the group ('followers') in pursuit of group goals. It draws upon prior examinations of the antecedents of cooperation by group members (Tyler, 1999; Tyler and Blader, 2000; Tyler and Lind, 1992). This work links the qualities of leaders and their leadership behavior to their ability to obtain cooperative behaviors from followers. Those leadership qualities are outlined within the 'relational' framework of leadership criterion in the *relational model of authority* (Tyler and Lind, 1992), and are linked to cooperative behavior in the *group engagement model* (Tyler and Blader, 2000).

Cooperative behavior

Leaders seek to gain two types of behavior from their followers. The first is rule-following behavior – i.e. 'compliance with the rules'. For leaders to be effective, they must be able to motivate their followers to follow group rules. Members of the group must limit their behavior in response to guidelines prohibiting or limiting engagement in behaviors that harm the group. This type of behavior – 'limiting' behavior – is studied in the literature on social regulation, and is the focus of a considerable body of research in the area of law and in studies of the exercise of legal authority (Tyler, 1990).

The second type of behavior is follower effort on behalf of the group. Such behavior involves proactively working in ways that promote the group's goals. A student needs to study and work hard to learn the material in their classes (proactive efforts to engage in desirable behavior), in addition to not cheating on tests or having someone write their terms papers for them (limiting

	Rule following (limiting behaviors that harm the group)	Working on behalf of the group (promoting behaviors that advance group goals)
Mandatory	Compliance with leaders, rules, decisions	In-role behavior
Discretionary	Deference to leaders, rules, decisions	Extra-role behavior

Figure 8.1   A behavioral typology of cooperation

undesirable behavior). Similarly, an employee needs to work hard at their job, in addition to not stealing office supplies. Understanding how leaders can motivate these proactive behaviors to promote group goals is the focus of much of the writing within the fields of organizational psychology and organizational behavior (Tyler and Blader, 2000; Chapter 9).

Together with Steve Blader, I have recently proposed and tested in a work setting the *group engagement model* (Tyler and Blader, 2000). That model explores the mechanisms through which leaders can motivate the members of groups, organizations or societies to both limit their undesirable behavior and to increase their involvement in desirable behaviors that promote group goals. This model encompasses both rule following and proactive engagement in-group tasks within a single conceptual framework.

In addition, the *group engagement model* makes a distinction between two forms of each behavior: mandatory and discretionary (see Tyler and Blader, 2000). Mandatory behaviors are those that are required by one's role or by group rules. Discretionary behaviors are not formally required. For example, employees can do their jobs well or poorly. This is referred to as in-role behavior. They can also engage in actions not required by their role, often referred to as extra-role behaviors. When we combine these two distinctions, we end up with the four type of behavior shown in Figure 8.1.

Motivations for Cooperation

The task of the leader is to engage members of the group in the four types of cooperative behavior outlined in Figure 8.1. There are two basic ways in which leaders might try to shape the motivation of the people in their group. These approaches seek to engage the two central sources of human motivation. These two types of motivation for social behavior in groups were first identified and articulated by Kurt Lewin in his field theory model of human motivation (Gold, 1999), which views behavior as a function of the person and the environment (Behavior = f (person, environment)).

First, from this perspective, leaders might alter motivation by shaping the situation in which their followers are making rational behavioral decisions, either by creating incentives to reward desired behaviors, by punishing or threatening to punish those who engage in undesired behaviors, or by using both strategies. This type of motivation has already been discussed in the context of the deterrence or social control models for gaining compliance. Environmental motivational force reflects the incentives and risks that exist in the immediate environment, so tapping that motivation involves changing the nature of the situation. These environmental contingencies influence people's motivation because one core motivation underlying people's behavior is the desire to gain rewards and avoid punishments.

I have already discussed the influence of environmental forces on motivation, and noted that control over environments does allow leaders to shape followers' behaviors to some degree. Of course, leaders can never completely control the environment. For example, criminal behavior is not only shaped by sanction risk. It is also shaped by whether a person is able to get a job, and has an alternative way to make a living, as well as by whether inviting criminal opportunities exist. Nonetheless, as already noted, the aspects of the environment that the leader can control do shape behavior and this provides an opportunity for leaders to shape the motivations of the people in the group.

Second, leaders might try to create or activate attitudes and values that would lead group members to voluntarily engage in desired types of behavior. The personal motivational force reflects the internal motivations that shape the behavioral direction that a person brings into a given setting – the things that the person wants to do or feels that they ought to do.

Attitudes and Cooperation

One type of internal motivation develops from attitudes – the things that a person wants to do. There are two types of attitude of particular relevance here. The first is intrinsic motivation. People like or enjoy certain types of activities and do those activities because of their intrinsic interest. People may like playing baseball, entertaining friends, or cleaning up their yard. These activities are rewarding in and of themselves, and people engage in them for internal reasons, not for external reward. Similarly, employees may like their jobs, family members may enjoy doing housework, and college professors may enjoy teaching introductory psychology.

A second type of attitude shaping cooperation is loyalty or commitment to the group or organization. People in groups come to identify with those groups, and to care about the well being of the group and its members. In fact, two of the key findings of social identity theory (Hogg and Abrams, 1988) are that: (1) people in groups come to identify with those groups, merging their sense of themselves with the identity of the group and (2) that once people identify with organizations, they put the welfare of the group above their own welfare. For example, when group members are given the choice of maximizing personal or group outcomes, they maximize group outcomes (Hogg and Abrams, 1988). So, acting in ways that benefit the group becomes an internal motivation, and people act in these ways without the expectation of personal reward.

So, intrinsic motivation and commitment to the group are two types of internal motivations that lead people to act on behalf of groups. In each case, people act in cooperative ways, without the need for incentives or sanctioning. Groups gain from such internally motivated behavior because the group, its authorities and its institutions, do not need to deploy group resources for resource-based motivational strategies. Instead, the members of the group act in cooperative ways due to their own internal motivations.

Clearly supportive attitudes are important and valuable for groups, organizations, and societies. The question is how leaders might create and sustain these motivations. The clearest case is that of commitment to the group. Leaders play an important role in creating and sustaining a group with which members can identify and to which they become loyal and committed. This feeling of group identification encourages cooperation on behalf of the group because people merge their sense of themselves in the group and the welfare of the group becomes indistinguishable from their personal welfare. The literature in social psychology describes identification with the group as superordinate identification, and notes a variety of ways that such superordinate identification can be developed and sustained. Gaertner and Dovidio (2000), discuss this issue in the context of their 'common ingroup identity model'. They suggest that a range of factors can shape the strength of people's awareness of group boundaries as well as the degree to which people identify with their own group.

It is also clear that situational factors shape the development of people's intrinsic motivation. In particular, the use of incentives or sanctions to promote desired behavior diminishes or 'crowds out' intrinsic motivation (Deci, 1980; Frey, 1997). This suggests that the use of these basic instrumental strategies, while having the immediate effect of promoting desired cooperative behavior, also has the effect of undermining other motivations for that behavior. In the long-term the use of incentive or sanction-based strategies of motivation may diminish cooperation.

Values and Cooperative Behavior

A second type of internal motivation is that of social values, and reflects the influence of people's sense of responsibility and obligation on their cooperative behavior. Values are people's feelings about what is right and proper – what they 'ought' to do. Values motivate people to cooperate by refraining from engaging in undesirable behaviors. People with values that support the group, for example, feel it is wrong to steal office supplies, to take long lunches, and to otherwise break work rules. Similarly, in society more generally, supportive values lead people to follow the law by not using drugs, not robbing banks, and not murdering their neighbors.

There are two basic types of values that are potentially relevant to people's degree of cooperation in groups. One social value is legitimacy – the feeling of obligation to obey the rules, authorities, and institutions of a group. A group leader who has legitimacy can issue directives and the people in the group will follow them because they feel that the leader is entitled to be obeyed. Again, people are self-regulatory. They follow the directives of the leader because they feel that it is their personal responsibility to do so. Hence, the leader does not have to deploy incentive or sanctioning systems in order to gain cooperative behavior from group members.

The value of having legitimacy is that people voluntarily defer to authority. Tyler (1990) found that the legitimacy of laws had a direct influence on whether or not people followed those laws in their everyday lives. Further, that influence was a more important influence on behavior than was the influence of the likelihood of being caught and punished for rule-breaking behavior and was 'voluntary' in character. Tyler and Blader (2000) found similar results in work organizations in the case of work rules. Those who viewed work rules and managerial authorities as legitimate were more willing to follow those rules. Again, the influence of legitimacy was greater than the influence of sanctioning possibilities. Legitimacy had an especially strong influence on voluntary rule-following behavior (deference to rules) in comparison to the influence of risk assessments. As was true with morality, legitimacy shaped cooperative behavior.

Another set of values are those linked to personal morality. Personal model values are internal representations of conscience that tell people which social behaviors are right or wrong to engage in within social contexts. Following moral rules is self-directed in that when people violate moral rules they feel guilt, an aversive emotional state (Hoffman, 2000). Consequently, people follow moral rules for internal motivational reasons, distinct from the contingencies in the environment.

Morality is an important force shaping people's compliance with rules (Robinson and Darley, 1995; Tyler, 1990). In fact, in the context of ordinary people's relationships with the law, morality has a greater influence on people's behavior than does the threat of being caught and punished for wrongdoing (Tyler, 1990). As a consequence, if the people in a group feel that it is morally wrong to break group rules, the level of rule-breaking behavior will diminish considerably. Leaders benefit from creating and sustaining a moral climate in which it is viewed as morally wrong to break group rules.

Despite the value of morality as a motivator of rule-following behavior, from the perspective of leaders morality is a double-edged sword. If people's morality supports the group and group authorities, the group gains a powerful motivational force supporting group rules. However, if the moral values of the members of a group are linked to a different moral code, that difference undermines the leader of a group, since group members are internally motivated to deviate from group rules (Kelman and Hamilton, 1989; Levi, 1997).

Efforts to stimulate cooperation by appealing to attitudes and values are more effective ways to encourage cooperation than are approaches that rely on the use of incentives or sanctions to achieve the same objectives. These approaches are found to be more influential in stimulating cooperation than are incentive or sanction-based systems. Further, they have the advantage of being self-motivating. When acting in response to their attitudes people are responding to their own feelings about what they like and want to do. So, people are motivated to engage in cooperative acts without focusing on the rewards for such actions. When responding to their values people are focusing on their own sense of what is right, and their behavior is self-regulating.

The important role of attitudes and values in stimulating cooperation suggests the importance of creating a supportive culture or value climate within a group. Leaders need to stimulate intrinsic interest in group roles, identification with the group, and the development of moral values and feelings that group authorities are legitimate. Such a culture can then be drawn upon when authorities are seeking to motivate cooperative behavior within a group.

Because of the motivational power of legitimacy, leaders, who represent the group, are in a unique position of being able to call upon the members of the group to engage in behaviors that involve risks and sacrifices in the name of the group. Such legitimate authority is typically associated with formal leaders and authorities. While it can be developed by informal leaders in spontaneous and temporary groups, legitimacy is not easily acquired, nor are people especially willing to forgo personal gains in deference to the directives of others. The unique ability of authorities to use legitimacy as a motivational force leadership is likely to be most important when a situation calls for restraint on the part of group members – in particular the willing deference to group rules. Such motivation is different from the willingness to make personal sacrifices for the group that may flow from attitudes of commitment and loyalty, and may lead to volunteerism.

Cooperative Behavior in Work Settings

The factors shaping cooperation in the arena of work organizations can be studied by examining the results of a study of 404 employees interviewed about their behavior in their work organization (see Tyler and Blader, 2000, for a detailed discussion of the results of this study). One reason that people might participate in and cooperate with groups is to gain the resources associated with group membership. Traditional explanations of people's choices among possible behaviors they might engage in within groups or organizations; their decisions about whether or not to stay or leave a group or organization; their decisions about the extent to which they will enact organizational roles; and their decisions about the degree to which they will follow rules all suggest that these decisions are shaped by estimates of gain and loss (as defined within social exchange theory, see Thibaut and Kelley, 1959). In particular, social exchange theories emphasize people's comparison of the expected utility of alternative courses of action. People are predicted to seek to join and stay within the group that they think will offer them the greatest short and long-term rewards.

Social exchange theory suggests that people's orientation toward organizations reflects their views about the favorability of the exchange of effort and resources between themselves and that organization. If people feel that they are receiving favorable resources from the organization, they stay within it, performing their organizational roles and following organizational rules.

Gain/loss arguments have also been used by a variety of social psychologists as possible explanations for the motivations underlying people's willingness to help others in groups. The willingness to help others has been linked to the perceived benefits and costs of helping (Latane and Darley, 1970; Piliavin, Piliavin and Rodin, 1975), while cooperation within groups has been linked to estimates of the likelihood that others will reciprocate such cooperative behavior (Komorita and Parks, 1994; Tyler and Kramer, 1996; Williamson, 1993; Rousseau, 1995). Expectancy theory similarly links work motivation to expected payoffs (Vroom, 1964), as does goal-setting theory (Locke and Latham, 1990). An example of the application of social exchange theory to behavior within groups and organizations is provided by the work of Rusbult on the investment model (Rusbult and Van Lange, 1996).

Making use of the distinction between mandatory and discretionary behavior, it is possible to focus directly on voluntary deference to authority (Tyler, 1990, only examines mandated behavior – i.e., compliance). When we make this distinction, we find that both the risks associated with rule breaking and the legitimacy of organizational rules influence whether employees defer to organizational rules. Of these two factors, legitimacy is more important. It explains 21 per cent of the variance in deference to rules beyond what can be explained by risk judgments. In contrast, risk judgments explain 1 per cent of the variance in deference to organizational rules beyond that which can be explained by legitimacy. The key factor shaping deference to rules, in other words, is the legitimacy of those rules. Hence, like legal authorities, managerial authorities need legitimacy to effectively manage the rule-related behavior of employees.

The advantage of studying the work environment is that it allows the full range of the group engagement model to be tested. When such a test is conducted, using the sample of employees already outlined, the results shown in Figure 8.2 are obtained (this figure is taken from Tyler and Blader, 2000, p. 191, and a fuller description of the study is provided there).

Several arguments are supported by the results shown in Figure 8.2. First, they suggest that it is important to distinguish between external and internal sources of motivation. Internal sources of motivation – attitudes and values – are

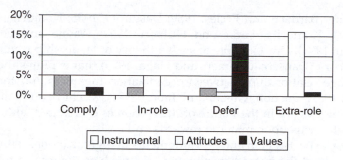

Figure 8.2   The influence of instrumental judgments, attitudes, and values on cooperation (entries are the unique contribution of each factor to explaining the behavior)

especially important in shaping discretionary behavior. Further, attitudes are central to proactive behavior, in the form of extra-role behavior, while values are the key antecedent of deference to organizational rules. Hence, attitudes and values both have an important influence on discretionary cooperative behavior, but the nature of their influence differs greatly depending upon which type of cooperative behavior is being considered.

These findings suggest that leaders gain a great deal when they can appeal to attitudes and values among their followers. The existence of those attitudes and values provides a motivating force for discretionary behavior of two types: deference to rules and extra-role behavior. The question, to be addressed later in this discussion, is how such attitudes and values can be activated. In other words, what leadership or management practices lead to cooperative behavior among group members?

The Antecedents of Effective Leadership

As I have noted, many theories of leadership argue that leaders exercise influence through their control of incentives and sanctions. This approach to leadership is central to many models of leadership. The literature on motivations for following leaders often argues that leader–follower relations depend on the exchange of rewards. According to this perspective, if leaders make good decisions that lead to success and to the gain of resources for group members, followers respond by obeying the directives of their leaders (Levine and Moreland, 1995). For example, some studies of leaders emphasize the importance of their task competence (Hollander and Julian, 1978; Ridgeway, 1981), suggesting that people will follow those leaders that they feel can solve group problems in a way that will lead to personal gain for group members.

Similarly, transactional theories of leadership suggest that leader–follower relations depend on the resources received from leaders in the past or expected in the future (Bardach and Eccles, 1989; Dasgupta, 1988; Komorita, Chan and Parks, 1993; Komorita, Parks and Hulbert, 1992; Wayne and Ferris, 1990; Williamson, 1993). One example of such a theory of leadership is vertical dyad linkage theory (Dansereau, Graen, and Haga, 1975) that explores the nature of the exchange relationships between organization members and their leaders (Chemers, 1987; Duchon, Green, and Taber, 1986; Vecchio and Gobdel, 1984). Such exchanges vary in the nature of the resources exchanged, although theories typically focus upon material rewards and costs.

Of course, expected gain and loss judgments in organizational settings are not only made about the immediate situation. People have long-term relationships with groups and they make long-term judgments about the expected costs and benefits of group membership. In the context of ongoing groups, these more long-term judgments of expected rewards/costs guide people's behavior within their group. In making such long-term judgments about what types of behavior will be rewarding, people evaluate the overall quality of the outcomes they are receiving from the group, across situations, relative to their available alternatives, as well as by judging the degree to which they have already invested resources in the group. An example of the application of long-term resource-based approaches to the study of behavior in groups is provided by the investment model (Rusbult and Van Lange, 1996), which studies the factors shaping people's decisions to leave or remain within groups (their 'loyalty' to the group).

All of these models support the argument already outlined in suggesting that leaders shape the motivations and behaviors of followers via their control of incentives and sanctions. Hence, they all argue for the role, at least in the short-term, of expectations of gain and loss.

Justice models

In contrast to these outcome models, Tyler and Blader (2000) argue that effective leadership is based on the judgment by followers that a leader is exercising authority through fair procedures – the procedural justice based model of authority dynamics that I earlier labeled the relational model of authority (Tyler and Lind, 1992).

Tyler (1990) found that the legitimacy of social regulatory leaders is rooted in judgments about the justice of their decision-making procedures. Tyler explored the influence of different aspects of personal experience with police officers and judges on judgments about the legitimacy of legal authority. That study showed that the primary aspect of experience shaping people's views about legitimacy was their evaluation of the fairness of the procedures used by the authority involved. In addition, a second study of legal authority, which examined the basis of the legitimacy of the United States Supreme Court, found that institutional legitimacy is linked to evaluations of the fairness of Court decision-making procedures. In other words, irrespective of whether we consider personal experiences or institutional level evaluations, the roots of legitimacy lie in procedural justice.

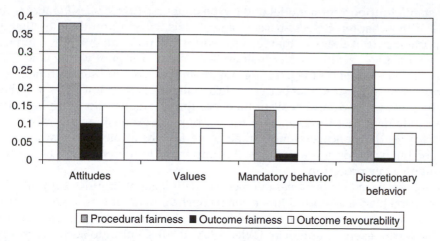

Figure 8.3   The influence of outcome favourability, outcome fairness, and procedural fairness on attitudes, values, and cooperative behavior (beta weights showing independent influence)

More recent work extended this analysis to the area of work organizations, using the previously outlined sample of employees (Tyler and Blader, 2000). That study compared the influence of general evaluations of the fairness of organizational procedures to the influence of general evaluations of the favorability and fairness of the outcomes of those procedures. It explored the influence of these three factors on attitudes, values, and mandatory and discretionary decision-making procedures. The results are shown in Figure 8.3, which is drawn from Tyler and Blader (2000, p. 193). The results suggest several conclusions. First, procedural justice is the key antecedent of attitudes and values. Second, procedural justice is the key antecedent of discretionary behavior. Taken together, these findings support our argument that procedural justice is the key to promoting discretionary behavior. In this case, however, discretionary behavior is not only deference to rules; it also involves extra-role behavior.

These findings suggest that leadership rests upon the judgments of followers that the leader is making decisions using fair procedures. When followers believe that this is true, their intrinsic job motivation, their commitment to the organization, and their view that the organization's rules are legitimate and ought to be obeyed all increase. As we have already noted, these internal motivations are the key to discretionary behavior. As we would expect, in such a situation, we find a direct influence of procedural justice on discretionary behavior (also see Chapter 9).

What is a fair procedure?

If, as I am suggesting here, the roots of effective leadership lie in leading via the use of procedures that people will experience as fair, then we have substantial support for a model of the type of *process-based leadership* that is the title of this chapter. Process-based leadership is based upon the idea that an important part of the way that leaders lead is by motivating group members to act on their attitudes and values, leading to self-motivating and self-regulating behavior on the part of group members. The findings outlined here support the suggestion that both people's willingness to follow rules and their willingness to work on behalf of their groups or organizations are linked to their judgment that the leaders of their group are exercising authority using procedures that followers understand to be fair. To implement a strategy of leadership based on these findings, it is important to understand what people mean by a fair procedure.

Research based on personal interactions with legal authorities suggests that procedural justice is a multidimensional construct with at least eight independent factors shaping overall judgments about the fairness of the methods used by leaders to exercise authority (Tyler, 1988, 1990). Central to such procedural justice evaluations are evaluations of the neutrality of decision-making procedures, the degree to which leaders treat followers with dignity and respect, and the extent to which followers think that leaders are trustworthy and benevolent (Tyler and Lind, 1992).

We examined the antecedents of procedural justice in work settings, using our previously described sample of employees (Tyler and Blader, 2000). To conduct that analysis we drew upon a new conceptualization of the potential antecedents of procedural justice that identifies four potential antecedents of procedural justice: the fairness of the decision-making procedures; the quality of the treatment that people receive from group leaders; the fairness of the outcomes received; and the favorability of the outcomes received from the organization and its leaders. This model is referred to as the *two component model of procedural justice* because it divides the antecedents of justice into two basic components (see Blader and Tyler, 2000). The more complex four component model of procedural justice, which distinguishes among sources of information about these issues, will not be discussed here.

The results of the previously outlined analysis suggest that there are two key antecedents of procedural justice evaluations (Tyler and Blader, 2000). Those are judgments about the quality of decision-making and about the quality of the treatment that followers receive from leaders. In other words, both of the components of procedural justice expected to matter make important independent contributions of judgments about the fairness of procedures. And, both of these components are more important than are judgments about outcome favorability or outcome fairness.

It is similarly possible to examine the influence of these elements on the attitudes, values, and behaviors already outlined. To conduct such an analysis we created two summary indices reflecting orientation toward limiting behavior (summarising legitimacy, compliance, and deference) and orientation toward promoting behavior (summarizing commitment, in-role behavior, extra-role behavior). We then examined the influence of the four elements of organizations on these two key motivational indices.

The results suggest that both the quality of decision-making and the quality of treatment are central elements of procedures (Tyler and Blader, 2000). The quality of decision-making is the most important factor encouraging limiting behaviors, like following workplace rules, while quality of treatment is the key to motivating behaviors such as engaging in non-required work for the group. In contrast, the influence of outcome judgments on either limiting or promoting behavior is minor.

If leaders want people to be willing to self-regulate, to voluntarily work for the group, and to voluntarily defer from engaging in personally rewarding behaviors that break organizational rules, they need to make clear that they are making their decisions in fair ways. They do so by making clear that their decisions are made neutrally, based upon objective facts and without bias or favoritism.

If leaders want people to be motivated in working on behalf of the group, and to engage in voluntary behaviors that promote the organization's welfare, then they should communicate clearly that they respect the members of their group and their rights. They do so by treating people with dignity and respect.

Of the findings outlined, the most striking is the central role of the quality of treatment that people receive on their views about the fairness of procedures, and on their willingness to engage behaviorally in groups and organizations. This is especially true when we are exploring people's orientation toward promoting behavior, such as in-role or extra-role behavior in work organizations. When people feel valued as people, they actively involve themselves in activities that benefit their group, organization, or society.

Implications

Leaders are typically trained in the specialized knowledge and skills that they need to attain technical competence in their field. This set of skills allows them to make decisions that are of high quality, when evaluated against objective criteria. The equation of leadership to technical competence and expertise is widespread, and flows from the certification of authorities through training programs that emphasize technical skills.

The findings outlined here show that the quality of the decision-making that people experience when dealing with leaders is important. It plays an especially important role in shaping people's willingness to follow social rules. However, the quality of the treatment that people receive is the key antecedent of their willingness to engage themselves proactively in tasks that help the group. Hence, the ability to make decisions well is only one element of effective leadership.

One implication of this finding is that people judge leaders using a broad set of criteria, only some of which involve their competence. In addition to making decisions through appropriate and reasonable procedures, authorities also have to be concerned about how they treat the people with whom they are dealing.

These findings suggest that leaders need to focus on a two-pronged approach to *process-based leadership*. The first prong involves fair decision-making. People are sensitive to a variety of issues about decision-making, including whether or not the decision maker is unbiased and neutral; uses facts and objective information; and treats people consistently. The second prong involves the quality of people's treatment during the decision-making process. People are sensitive to whether or not they are treated with dignity and respect; whether their rights are acknowledged; and whether their needs and concerns are considered.

Interestingly, both of the prongs of *process-based leadership* that I have outlined are distinct from the favorability or the fairness of people's outcomes. In each case, people's reactions to the actions of their leaders are linked to the manner in which those leaders behave, rather than to the outcomes of their behavior. Hence, the ability of leaders to motivate their followers is rooted largely in their process by which they lead, rather than in the outcomes they deliver.

This finding is consistent with the findings that emerge in studies of trust in authorities (see Tyler and Degoey, 1996). In such studies trust in authorities is divided into two distinct elements: trust in the competence of authorities to solve problems and deliver favorable outcomes and trust in the benevolence and caring of leaders. When that division is made, trust in motives (benevolence, caring) is found to be the key antecedent of the willingness to accept the decision of leaders. Again, it is not the outcomes that leaders can or do deliver that shapes people's responses to those leaders.

What Psychological Processes Underlie Leadership?

The findings outlined make clear that people care about the fairness of leadership practices. However, they do not address the question of why people care about procedural justice. To understand that question, we need to examine two social psychological models that define the connection between people and the group to which they belong.

One model is the social exchange model. That model is quite consistent with the instrumental or exchange-based theories of leadership already outlined in this discussion. These models argue that people involve themselves in groups, organizations, and societies to gain desired resources for themselves. They evaluate groups and leaders by assessing the level of resources they obtain from the group and its leaders, both intrinsically and relative to other possible groups. These models are instrumental in character in the sense that they view people's connection to leaders as being linked to judgments about the nature and quality of the resources people receive from leaders. People join and cooperate with groups when they feel that their commitments to those groups lead to desired resources.

A second model is identity based. This model suggests that people want to belong to groups because being connected to others is a core human characteristic

(Hogg and Abrams, 1988). One function that membership in groups serves that helps to explain why people want to be connected to groups is helping people to define themselves and assess their self-worth. People use the groups to which they belong to help define themselves (Hogg and Abrams, 1988). They further use the status of the groups to which they belong to help assess their self-worth. This identity model suggests that people are motivated to join groups for identity reasons, and are motivated to cooperate with groups when doing so can create, enhance, or maintain a favorable sense of self-worth and self-esteem.

The relational model argues that the reason that people view the quality of their treatment by leaders as so important is that those actions communicate identity-relevant information to group members. In other words, it suggests that it is the person's identity that is influenced by procedural justice, and that identity shapes cooperation. As a key representative of the group, the leader's actions tell people whether they are accepted within the group and have secure group status. This message is especially relevant to those who may be marginal in some way, and more uncertain about their status. However, even the founder's son may have occasional doubts about the certainty of his status. Everyone uses the quality of their treatment and the fairness of decision-making procedures, 'relational' criterion (Tyler and Lind, 1992), to make status evaluations.

The key question is whether either one or both of these models is the mediator of procedural justice effects. Tyler and Blader (2000) address this question using a causal model. That model examines whether the relationship between procedural justice and cooperative behavior is mediated by resources judgments,

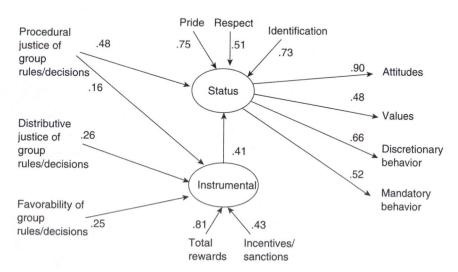

Figure 8.4   Status influences on cooperation

identity judgments, or neither form of judgment. The results are shown in Figure 8.4. They suggest that the impact of procedural justice on cooperative behavior is mediated by identity judgments. Resource judgments have no direct influence on cooperation.

Interestingly, resource judgments have an indirect influence on cooperation because they influence identity judgments. To some degree, people identify strongly with groups because they receive favorable resources from them. So, resources are not irrelevant to cooperation. However, people also identify with groups because they think those groups are fairly managed. It is here that leaders have the opportunity to engage in *process-based leadership*. By acting fairly the leader can encourage people within their group to be proud of group membership, to feel respected by the group, and to merge their sense of self in the group. These identity-based effects directly encourage cooperation with the group.

9 A Relational Perspective on Leadership and Cooperation: Why it Matters to Care and Be Fair

DAVID DE CREMER

We all still very much recall the tragic terror attack that took place September 11th, 2001, at the World Trade Center (WTC) in New York. This act of violence put the whole world in sorrow. However, if we were to point out one positive thing emerging from this disaster, it may well be the fact that people felt a strong sense of belonging, and consequently were very much willing to voluntarily cooperate with one another. In this process, Mayor Rudolph Giuliani played an important role. By means of his active and influential approach to this disaster he was able to promote this feeling of belonging and emergence of pro-social behavior even more. The interesting fact is that his leadership did not make use of instrumental means by focusing on 'what is in it for you' (i.e., an outcome-based focus), but more on the existence of communal relationships in which the value of social bonds and affect-based relationships were emphasized (i.e., a relational-based focus).

One of the implications that can be derived from this example is that relation-based leadership may be a useful, and sometimes a necessary, tool to foster cooperation in situations in which personal and collective interests are at odds. That is, helping others in this tragedy is costly at the personal level, but at the level of society or community it is beneficial. The major aim of the present chapter is to discuss and illustrate *how* and *why* leadership can be used to promote cooperation. More specifically, in this chapter, I will develop a model claiming that, in promoting cooperation, leaders should not solely focus on outcome concerns, but also on relational means like promoting belongingness particularly if their followers have a high need to belong. It will be argued that such a need-based focus (i.e., belongingness) may be effective to motivate people to transform personal goals to the level of the group, consequently enhancing cooperation. In doing this, two specific relational leadership qualities will be examined: a leader's procedural fairness and a leader's ability to communicate concern for others (also see Chapter 8).

The Issue of Cooperation

Group members are often confronted with the dilemma of either serving one's own personal interests or serving the group's interests. This points to the fact that different conflicting motives are often apparent in interdependent group contexts. These interdependence situations in which personal and collective interests are at odds are referred to as *mixed-motive situations* (for reviews see Komorita and Parks, 1994). More specifically, in such situations the essence of the social conflict is that pursuing the personal interest may yield the individual decision-maker the highest outcomes, but, if each individual attempts to maximize his or her self-interest, the collective outcome will be lower than if each individual attempts to further the collective interest.

For example, within organizations it is often valued that its members devote extra time, energy and effort to interdependent tasks and actions that benefit the organization as a whole. In other words, to coordinate activities in interdependent relations, successful cooperation by the individuals involved is required (e.g., Smith, Carroll, and Ashford, 1995). Despite the immense importance of cooperation to yield high organizational performance, it is often observed that cooperative contributions to the group remain relatively limited. More specifically, often people do not go above and beyond the job description or do not invest energy and time in team projects, because it yields only immediate costs and no immediate gains. However, if all organizational or group members act in this way, team projects will fail and the welfare of the individual, group or organization will not be served.

As cooperation is of huge importance to the viability of groups (e.g., organizations), it cannot be denied that one of the major functions of leadership is to promote, or at least sustain, cooperation. Indeed, definitions of leadership as a group feature, make its relationship to cooperation very clear, as 'leadership involves persuading other people to set aside for a period of time their individual concerns and to pursue a common goal that is important for the responsibilities and welfare of a group' (Hogan, Curphy, and Hogan, 1994, p. 493).

Because leadership clearly represents an important aspect of group life (Chapter 2), it is necessary to examine which specific group processes may underlie a leader's influence on cooperation. Because a leader's influence is only successful if subordinates perceive the leader to be credible and capable of serving their needs (e.g., Chemers, 2001), one important aspect to look at is the type of motives underlying cooperation and to see how leadership can exert influence contingent on those motives.

Leadership, Motives, and Cooperation

Based on traditional theories like game theory (e.g., Luce and Raiffa, 1957) and social exchange (e.g., Blau, 1964), research on cooperation (including the social dilemma domain) has started from the assumption that people are basically self-interested, emphasizing the importance of motives like greed and free-riding on the contributions of others as dominating in the mind of decision-makers in social dilemmas (e.g., Wilke, 1991). This belief is also exemplified nicely in the myth of self-interest, which states that people have developed a stereotype that people's actions are generally guided by self-interested concerns; an assumption which is likely to reinforce a self-fulfilling prophecy (Miller, 1999). This focus on pursuing self-interest at any cost has influenced research on the relationship between leadership effectiveness and cooperation significantly.

Indeed, this self-interest or instrumental-based approach is reflected very much in the use of coordination and leadership systems based on changing the outcome or incentive structure in complex and uncertain situations. For example, like the use of sanctioning and/or leadership systems in which cooperation is rewarded and non-cooperation punished (e.g., McCusker and Carnevale, 1995; Van Vugt and De Cremer, 1999; Yamagishi, 1986) – as can be seen in many organizations using surveillance systems (Tenbrunsel and Messick, 1999); or, the adoption of autocratic leaders taking decisions on behalf of the group, particularly when groups are inefficient or inequality in outcomes exists (e.g., De Cremer, 2000; Messick et al., 1983; Samuelson and Messick, 1986). However, leader systems as these are hardly viable, because they are perceived as undesirable in terms of emotional and productivity consequences (e.g., Tenbrunsel and Messick, 1999), are likely to undermine communal trust in others (Mulder, Wilke, Van Dijk, and De Cremer, 2002), are too infringing on people's freedom, and too expensive (Hollander, 1985; Rutte and Wilke, 1985). In addition, such coordination mechanisms (i.e., sanctioning) may also be inadequate, as contingencies cannot always be properly planned for (Katz, 1964).

To avoid such negative consequences of leadership-based systems, in the context of cooperation, it seems necessary, in addition to instrumental means, to focus also on psychological mechanisms that motivate people to internalize the value of cooperation, or, in other words, to foster group-oriented motivations. This psychological outcome may be more easily achieved when use is made of a more need-based monitoring and leadership system. One specific need that is strongly related to a group-oriented focus is the 'need to belong' (Baumeister and Leary, 1995). When deciding to cooperate or not, people do not only care about their personal outcomes (i.e., *instrumental or outcome concerns*), but also weigh their decision as a function of how pleasant and viable they consider the within-group relations to be (i.e., *relational concerns*; Tyler and Dawes, 1993; Van Vugt and De Cremer, 1999), as this communicates a certain inclusiveness in the group (De Cremer, 2002a).

Thus, leadership aimed at promoting cooperation has to serve both group maintenance and outcome-related functions to reveal an optimal level of cooperation. In a similar vein, the leadership literature broadly distinguishes between relation-oriented leaders and task-oriented leaders, which both are fulfilling instrumental or socio-emotional functions (Yukl, 1998). One way of serving this group maintenance function is to make group members feel included by creating positive and constructive intragroup relationships. More specifically, in order to promote cooperation, leadership is also assumed to convey relational information that indicates the quality of the within-group relationships, as this type of information can then be used to assess the fulfillment of the need to belong. In the following paragraph, I will discuss why the fulfillment of this fundamental need is so important.

Belongingness Needs, Intrinsic Motivation and Cooperation

Entering new relationships or social situations brings with it a degree of uncertainty about the position one takes within those relationships. As a result, people may be rather uncertain about their self-definition in that specific situation or relationship (Hogg and Mullin, 1999). Such uncertainty is considered as aversive because the self can be regarded as the central and organizing principle of one's thinking, feeling and actions. In line with this, I argue that in order to promote cooperation, leadership should be able to reduce uncertainty about people's feelings of group belongingness (e.g., De Cremer and van Dijk, 2002; De Cremer and Van Vugt, 1999). As Hogg and Mullin (1999, p. 256) argue: 'belonging is a critical social motive that is satisfied by membership of social categories of all sizes, but it is a motive that is tied to an underlying need for [self] certainty' (brackets added). Furthermore, meeting this need to belong may trigger a motivational process in which group members will perceive both group and personal interests as interchangeable, thereby positively influencing an intrinsic motivation to cooperate. This is in line with Deci and Ryan's comment that 'intrinsic motivation will be facilitated by conditions that conduce toward psychological need (*e.g., belongingness*) satisfaction' (2000, p. 233; brackets added).

Taken together, this line of argument suggests that individuals may have different reasons for claiming membership in a specific group. That is, based on their personal agendas, people may claim group membership, because they perceive identification as a means to fulfill their need to belong. Such analysis is in line with recent thinking on social identification that suggests that social identities might serve different functions such as belongingness needs (see Deaux, 1996; Deaux, Reid, Mizrahi, and Cotting, 1999).

Since belongingness is considered to be an existing function of group membership, recent research on the effects of social identification on cooperation can be interpreted as supportive of the earlier mentioned assumption that serving belongingness needs facilitates cooperation. In a line of research, De Cremer and his colleagues (De Cremer and Van Dijk, 2002; De Cremer and Van Vugt, 1999), showed that strong feelings of group affiliation promoted cooperation primarily because people's motives were transformed from the personal to the collective or group, that is, reinforcing group identification motivated people to incorporate the goals of the group in their self. De Cremer and Van Vugt (1999; Study 3) invited participants to the laboratory to play a public good dilemma game. Participants were given an endowment of 300 pence at the start of the session, and were free to contribute any amount of it to establish the common good. It was explained that the total amount contributed by the group would be multiplied by two and then would be split equally among all members regardless of their contribution. Level of identification was manipulated by telling participants (who were all Southampton University students) in the high group identification condition that the decisions of groups of SU students would be compared to the decisions made by students of a rival university in southern England. In the low group identification condition, they were told that the individual decisions of each student would be compared.

Finally, at the start of this experiment, participants' social value orientation was assessed (see Van Lange, Otten, De Bruin, and Joireman, 1997 for specific details about the measurement). Social value orientation is a stable individual difference variable, which refers to the value people assign to their personal welfare versus the collective welfare (De Cremer and van Lange, 2001). The results of this study revealed an interaction showing that reinforcing identification with the group motivated pro-selfs to contribute more, whereas pro-socials were not affected by this manipulation. This finding suggests that enhancing feelings of belongingness motivates people to internalize group values and, in turn, to increase levels of cooperation (i.e., a goal-transformation process from the personal to the group level). In line with this assumption, I argue that relation-based leadership is expected to fulfill belongingness needs to activate a similar process of goal-transformation.

Leadership and The Importance of Need to Belong: A Relational Equilibrium Model

In this chapter, the argument is made that, in addition to instrumental concerns, also relational concerns will determine a leader's ability to promote cooperation. The communication of such relational information is important as it can satisfy belongingness needs, which, in turn, leads to a transformation of motives. Of course, the extent to which these relational concerns – as communicated by leadership – will determine cooperation may not be the same across people. This assumption is in line with Erez and Earley's (1993) remark that a leader's effectiveness will be rather low if followers do not recognize themselves in the values and norms a leader advocates. More specifically, in the present chapter, it is argued that relation-based leadership will reveal more effect when people have a need to explore their relationships with others (including authorities), to see whether or not these communicate inclusiveness. In other words, when people experience uncertainty about themselves in terms of belonging to the group, community or society as a whole, leadership communicating relational information to satisfy this need will be most important.

Such an argument is closely linked to Baumeister and Leary's (1995) assumption that cognitive, emotional, and behavioral consequences emerging from a need to belong will be stronger if levels of belongingness fall below threshold. Under those circumstances, people will be monitoring for social inclusiveness and acceptance information that will increase their belongingness. This framework also fits well with research on paranoid cognition showing that people who are newcomers in a group or organization, and for whom uncertainty about their intragroup status is high, are much more receptive toward remarks from and relational information communicated by others (Kramer, 1994). Finally, Tyler and Smith (1999) have also argued that relational information communicating one's position within the group (e.g., respect) influences motives and behaviors most when people's reputational social self (i.e., a focus on the self as an inclusive member of a group or not) is activated.

Taken together, if people have a need to belong, leadership communicating relational information, like respect and fair treatment, should reveal strong effects, as it will reduce self-uncertainty in terms of belongingness. Consequently, feeling more included by means of relational leadership should motivate people to incorporate the group into one's self-concept, thereby leading to a transformation of motives, and, hence, cooperation (see the earlier discussed effect of belongingness [as a function of group identification] on cooperation

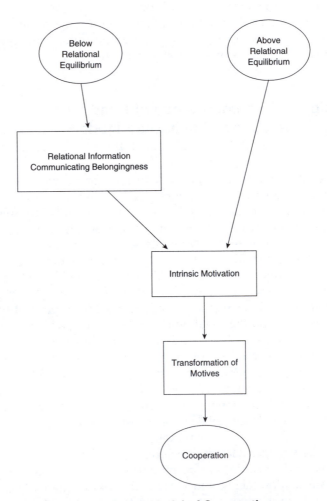

Figure 9.1   A Relational Equilibrium Model of Cooperation

and intrinsic motivation, De Cremer and Van Vugt, 1999; De Cremer and van Dijk, 2002). However, people who do not experience such strong belongingness needs, should be influenced less by relational leadership, as their need to belong is fulfilled and intrinsic motivation to cooperate is already high. This line of reasoning fits well within the framework of the Relational Equilibrium Model (REM) of justice (De Cremer, in press; 2002c, see Figure 9.1). This model assumes that the extent to which people's reactions are influenced by means of relational information depends on people's general need to belong and the position one takes within the relationship or group at hand (i.e., the latter being belongingness needs instigated by the situation). In more formal terms, responsiveness toward relational information is expected to be a function of: (1) an equilibrium or base rate that indicates the influence of this information, independent of people's belongingness need, (2) people's need to belong, and (3) the belongingness information communicated by the group or relationship at hand. If people's need to belong and situational belongingness increases then relational information will matter more.[1]

Some direct evidence for this model has recently been found in leaderless situations. In a line of studies, De Cremer (2002c) showed that group members with a strong need to belong were more responsive toward respect information (a relational aspect of procedural information, see Tyler, 1999), and this information reduced feelings of self-uncertainty. In addition, De Cremer (2002a) demonstrated that belongingness needs as induced by the situation (i.e., being a peripheral vs core group member) influenced how people's cooperation level was affected by the degree of respect communicated by the group. Thus, these findings indicate that wanting to belong goes together with feelings of uncertainty about themselves in that specific group, and one way to reduce this is to attend more carefully to information communicating a degree of acceptance and inclusiveness. In this chapter, some studies will be reviewed illustrating how leadership may communicate such relational information and, in turn, promote cooperation.

Procedural Fairness: Why it Matters to Be Fair

One possible source of relational leadership may be derived from the procedural fairness literature (Tyler and Lind, 1992). Indeed, Tyler and Dawes (1993) suggested that the procedural fairness and the cooperation literature have in common their focus on both relational and instrumental concerns. More specifically, relational models of justice (e.g., Tyler and Lind, 1992) assume that people do not only care about the resources that groups supply to people, but also consider the importance of the group in defining people's self worth. Thus, the viability and enjoyability of within-group relationships is believed to influence significantly one's self-conception and consequently one's motivation to act in favor of the group (e.g., Tyler and Blader, 2000; Tyler and Smith, 1999). One of the means by which such relational information can be communicated is the fairness of procedures enacted by the group authority. If a leader uses fair procedures (e.g., allowing voice in the decision-process or not; cf. Folger, 1977), people will feel treated in a respectful and considerate manner. As a result, people will feel valued by the group and will incorporate the group into their self-definition, thereby enhancing group identification and subsequently motivating them to engage in positive group behavior (Tyler and Smith, 1999; Chapter 8).

In the context of cooperation, some empirical evidence exists in support of this relational model of fairness (e.g., Tyler and Blader, 2000; Tyler and Degoey, 1995). For example, Tyler and Degoey (1995) provided evidence that the fairness of procedures enacted by the authority significantly influenced citizens' willingness to restrain their water use during a water shortage. Also, Tyler, Degoey and Smith (1996) showed in four correlational studies that relational judgments about authorities influenced significantly people's level of commitment and identification with the group, and these feelings, in turn, mediated group-oriented behavior. Finally, Tyler (1999) illustrated, in an organizational setting, that both respect and pride (reflecting aspects of people's identification with the organization) were influenced most by procedural fairness and that these identity aspects were important determinants of organizational oriented behavior (i.e., following the rules, helping the group and staying within the group). Although this evidence is compelling it has several disadvantages. First, all designs were correlational; therefore, not allowing us to draw causal conclusions. Second, only one study (Tyler and Degoey, 1995) addressed a situation in which the decision-makers felt interdependent. Third, these studies made use of a rather broad definition of cooperation including aspects like following rules, and organizational citizenship behavior.

To examine whether procedural fairness communicates important relational information, consequently promoting feelings of belongingness, and, hence, cooperation in interdependent settings, an experimental social dilemma study with an appointed group leader was conducted (De Cremer and Van den Bos, 2001, Experiment 2). Procedural fairness was manipulated by providing, or not providing, participants with an opportunity to voice their opinions in decision-making processes. This 'voice' manipulation (Folger, 1977) is the most commonly used manipulation of procedural fairness in experimental studies. In addition, to see whether such relational or belongingness information has more effect on those with a focus on the quality of relationships, we measured participants' level of interdependent self-construal (ISC). People with a high ISC feel more interdependent to one another and therefore express a stronger desire to examine the quality of their relationships with others than those low in ISC (Heine, Lehman, Markus, and Kitayama, 1999). In other words, because of their need to belong, those high in ISC should be more attentive and responsive toward relational information communicating belongingness than those low in ISC.

Participants were informed that they and three other participants would form an organizational board of a company called MINDVISION. They were told that this board would make important decisions with respect to the welfare of the company (e.g., hiring people, making financial decisions etc.). To facilitate these decisions, it was decided that each board would need a director. After this director was appointed, the board had to hire a new middle-line manager. At this moment, half of the participants were told that the board director had decided not to ask anyone's opinion regarding this hiring decision (i.e., he would be the only one to make the decision), whereas the other half was told that the board director wanted to know their opinion about who to hire. After this, participants were told that MINDVISION had designed a new investment plan and that all members of the organizational board had to make a financial decision. Each board member was given 40 000 Dutch Guilders (DFL), and told that the board as a whole would invest more than 80 000 DFL. The total amount invested would be multiplied by two and then divided among all board members. However, how this amount would be divided depended on the board leader who did or did not provide voice in an earlier instance (motivating participants to use inferences of the procedural fairness information to base their decision on). Finally, participants made a decision.

The most important finding was that procedural fairness exerted significant influence on investments among those high in ISC, but not among those low in ISC. Moreover, a mediational analysis showed that this interaction effect on cooperation was explained by participants' sense of group identification (indicating a sense of belongingness). That is, it appeared to be that those high in ISC cooperated more when voice was provided because they felt more included in the group. All in all, these findings do suggest that leaders communicating relational information by acting fairly influences cooperation, particularly among those followers who are in need of such relational information.

Conclusion

The above findings demonstrate that relational information (De Cremer, 2002a, 2002c; De Cremer and Van den Bos, 2001), as communicated by a group leader or the group as a whole, is used by decision-makers as one of their reference points to decide to engage in cooperation or not. This relational influence, however, appears to be stronger among those followers with a focus on relationships and belongingness. With people who are motivated to examine the quality of their relationships with others (which communicate important belongingness information), relational leadership has a stronger effect to produce positive behavioral outcomes like cooperation.

Perceived Charisma and Commitment: Why It Matters To Care

Another way of satisfying members' need to belong may be that leaders convey information to them that they truly care about the group's welfare, and that they may be willing to go an extra mile as well. One leadership feature related to communicating such caring message is perceived charisma. A notable illustration of this leadership skill is US former president Bill Clinton; for many the prime example of a charismatic leader. In his speeches and actions, Clinton was always able to clearly convey the message, 'I can feel your pain' and 'I am willing to do something about it' (*USA Today*, 2001). His ability to connect to the people in such a charismatic way created, among his followers, a sense of belongingness and a willingness to work for the nation (also see Chapter 4).

Charismatic leadership is proposed to appeal to group members' motives, aspirations, and preferences, and to motivate people to go beyond self-interest (House and Baetz, 1979). One way to do this is that charismatic leaders make public demonstrations of their dedication to the cause, and in doing this, they communicate clearly that they are willing to engage in significant personal sacrifice and danger (Jacobsen and House, 2001). Thus, they show courage and dedication to the interests of the collective. Through such sacrificing and courageous projects, charismatic leadership is believed to bolster a sense of group belongingness, and thus to shift group members' focus from self-interest to collective interest (Conger and Kanungo, 1987; Shamir, House, and Arthur, 1993).

Following from recent research (e.g., Yorges, Weiss, and Strickland, 1999), an important facet of charismatic leadership is *self-sacrifice*. Sacrifice by the leader indicates that he or she is willing to engage in risky behavior to serve the goals and mission of the group or organization (Shamir et al., 1993). Moreover, if a leader is perceived to be sacrificing, perceptions of trust are enhanced (Conger and Kanungo, 1987), which is an element necessary to promote cooperation (e.g., De Cremer, Snyder, and Dewitte, 2001).

In a first test of the notion that caring leadership (by means of self-sacrifice) is able to take subordinates beyond self-interest, De Cremer (2002b) utilized a public good dilemma setting in which a leader was appointed who either was self-sacrificing (this leader worked hard for the benefits of the group, which, in turn, influenced negatively his own interests) or benefiting (i.e., this leader clearly searched for extra personal benefits and would take extra money from the group bonus for himself). Participants were members of groups representing a company called MINDVISION. One group member was appointed as the group leader, and was asked to select a scenario that described best his or her own management style. The type of scenario chosen constituted the leadership style manipulation. In the self-sacrifice condition (i.e., caring leadership), the scenario expressed a deep concern with the company's welfare (i.e., the leader would be willing to work very hard). In the benefiting scenario (i.e., non-caring leadership), it was clear that the leader was most motivated to gain personal, rather than group, benefits. After this information, participants were informed about the financial situation of MINDVISION, and a similar public good dilemma as in De Cremer and Van den Bos (2001) was introduced. Results indicated that the leader in the self-sacrificing condition was perceived as more charismatic than the one in the benefiting condition. Most importantly, however, the results revealed an interaction showing that caring leaders (who were high in perceived charisma) increased group member cooperation, but, only among individuals with a pro-self orientation, and not among those who were dispositionally inclined to maximize joint outcomes (i.e., pro-social orientation). This finding supports the assertion that leaders perceived as caring might promote cooperation because they motivate others to pursue the group or organizational interest. In a laboratory-based public good dilemma study, De Cremer and van Knippenberg (2002) demonstrated that this perceived charisma effect was mediated by people's feeling of belongingness. Appointing a caring leader, by means of self-sacrifice, installed a feeling of belongingness among participants, consequently increasing intrinsic motivation to work for the group.

In these studies, caring leadership was manipulated by means of self-sacrifice; a feature indicating that the group leader was committed to the group and its welfare. As such, an essential feature of caring leadership seems to be the leader's dedication and commitment to their own group (characteristics which form leader's charisma as well; Jacobsen and House, 2001). This signal of commitment, in turn, seems to motivate group members to transcend their self-interests and to work for the group by cooperating. De Cremer and Van Vugt (2002) tested the impact of leader's commitment information on cooperation – as a means of caring leadership – directly by providing groups of participants with the average group commitment score (on measures earlier assessed in the study) of the group leader. Their results revealed that this commitment information affected level of contributions in an experimental public good dilemma, but mainly among participants who identified more strongly with their group. This finding is again in line with the REM of justice (De Cremer, in press). That is, those people who identify with a group or organization will care most about the way they are treated (Lind, 2001). As a result, particularly strong group identifiers will be most worried about the quality of relationship they have with their group representative, and from such a perspective, leader's group commitment may be a useful means to assess this quality. In other words, in such a context, strong group identifiers will have a strong need to evaluate the extent to which they actually belong to the group, in which they value group membership.

Conclusion

These findings suggest that communicating concerns for the group and its members by means of self-sacrifice and exhibited commitment on behalf of the group (in addition to respect and procedural fairness) are indeed effective to establish effective relational leadership. Although this observation does not imply that all these relational elements have to be combined to reveal effective leadership (e.g., De Cremer and van Knippenberg (2002), showed that procedurally fair leaders do not need to be charismatic to engender cooperation and vice versa). Also, in line with the REM, such a relation-based leadership style seems most effective when people are in need for evaluating the quality of their relationships with authority or leader to establish or confirm belongingness.

However, contrary to De Cremer and Van Vugt's (2002) group commitment study, the design of the described charisma studies did not include a manipulation of such belongingness needs. Future research is needed to examine in more detail whether charismatic leaders are most effective among those who have a strong need to belong. Recent evidence by Ehrhart and Klein (2001) suggests that this may be the case. Their research showed that individuals differ in their responses to identical leadership behaviors, and that, as a consequence, effectiveness of charismatic leadership depends, at least in part, on followers' need fulfillment. In a similar vein, Conger and Kanungo (1988) have also argued that the effectiveness of charismatic leadership may well depend on their ability to show sensitivity to followers' needs.

Summary and Conclusions

The main purpose of this chapter was to illustrate the importance of relational concerns in leadership effectiveness to promote cooperation. It was argued that, in addition to outcome concerns, people expect leaders to convey important relational information indicating the degree to which one is accepted and included in the group or collective that the authority represents. Moreover, these relational concerns would be most prominent among people who have a strong need to belong. Two types of relation-based leadership styles were identified: leader's fairness and leader's charisma.

The specific type of leader's fairness that was discussed in this chapter is procedural fairness (Lind and Tyler, 1988). Literature on the effects of procedural fairness has repeatedly pointed out that fairness of procedures has both 'outcome' and 'relational' components (Lind, 2001; Tyler and Dawes, 1993). Indeed, earlier studies have shown that receiving voice influences people's fairness judgments and subsequent actions, primarily because people may feel a sense of control over their outcomes (Thibaut and Walker, 1975), or because they feel respected and as such accepted as fully fledged group members (Tyler and Lind, 1992). With respect to the relational-based leadership style advocated in this chapter, the latter reason of feeling included and/or accepted as a core group member (when fair procedures are used), constitutes an important feature of relational leadership. As argued earlier, fulfilling belongingness needs may lead to heightened intrinsic motivation (Deci and Ryan, 2000), resulting in a greater willingness to cooperate and to work for the group's welfare (De Cremer and Van Vugt, 1999). As leadership is all about influence, it it is important to examine how leadership can influence and promote feelings of belongingness and group membership.

As I have shown in this chapter, leader's procedural fairness seems to be one way of achieving such belongingness, as fair procedures communicate acceptance and respect by the leader and the group as a whole. In addition, receiving respect and fair treatment facilitates cooperative interactions, consequently promoting the group's welfare (De Cremer, in press, a; Tyler and Blader, 2000). This effect of procedural fairness on cooperation is also mentioned explicitly in fairness heuristic theory (Lind, 2001). More specifically, fairness heuristic theory suggests that, during their interactions with authorities and leaders, people use their impressions of fairness as a guide (as this communicates trustworthiness on behalf of the group leader), and this heuristic use of fairness may motivate people to incorporate the group's interest to their self-concept. As Lind (2001) puts it: 'The essence of fairness heuristic processes is that fair treatment leads to a shift from responding to social situations in terms of immediate self-interest, which might be termed the individual mode, to responding to social situations as a member of the larger social entity, which might be termed the group mode ... people in group mode are primarily concerned with what is good for the group and what they can do to reach group goals' (p. 67).

Relational leadership also involves establishing relationships with followers based on a dedication and commitment to the group's interests (i.e., an image of a caring leader), as witnessed among many charismatic leaders (Jacobsen and House, 2001). This argument thus suggests that charismatic leadership is not solely a personality issue, but, maybe even more so, a relationship between a leader and his/her followers (see Ehrhart and Klein, 2001). Communicating to followers that one cares about the group and its members, is likely to facilitate interaction and promote a sense of group belongingness. One of the key behaviors in House's (1977) and Shamir et al.'s (1993) charismatic leadership theories is indeed emphasizing belongingness or a collective identity. Therefore, it follows that caring leaders (with characteristics as perceived charisma and commitment) may be able to increase intrinsic motivation, and consequently group-oriented behavior.

A final point made in this chapter is that the effectiveness of procedurally fair and caring leaders (who seem to work on people's feelings of belongingness), is a function of people's need to explore the quality of their relationships with the group and its leader to assess their degree of belongingness. Thus, both fair and caring leaders may be most effective in increasing cooperation among those who are in need of belongingness information. In a certain way, this relational equilibrium analysis – as described in the present chapter – is also in line with the 'naïve' moral philosopher image of the individual as judge of political objects (Tyler, 1984). This image implies that people, who are regarded as the judges, base their evaluation of authorities and procedures on a specific sense of fairness. In a similar vein, people's reactions to procedures enacted by leaders may vary as a function of their position in terms of the relational equilibrium (i.e., a specific sense of belongingness). Or, in other words, leadership fairness judgments and behavioral reactions may be responses based on belongingness needs and therefore will be subject to the position of the judge in terms of the relational equilibrium.

A potentially interesting relationship that emerges from the present discussion is the possible link between procedural fairness and perceived charisma. In essence, the effectiveness of both leadership features is considered to be explained, at least in part, by a common focus on influencing collective identification or group belongingness (see also, House, 1977; Shamir et al., 1993; Yukl, 1999). Reviewing the existing charismatic leadership theories, such a relationship may not be so surprising. Indeed, Yukl (1999) even argues that core transformational behaviors (with leader's charisma as an important aspect; Conger and Kanungo, 1988), among other things, include empowerment. More specifically, in his review article, Yukl (1999) explicitly refers to empowerment as 'providing significant voice ... to followers' (p. 290). Furthermore, in a newly developed transformational leadership questionnaire by Alimo-Metcalfe and Alban-Metcalfe (2001), empowerment is treated as one of the nine important factors constituting transformational leadership. To summarize, recent leadership research thus seems to suggest that procedural fairness and charismatic leadership may share common features, and, as such, may reveal similar consequences. In line with this assumption, a recent study by Pillai, Schriesheim and Williams (1999), indeed demonstrated that the effect of transformational leadership on pro-social organizational behavior (e.g., helping colleagues etc.) was significantly related to perceptions of procedural justice. More specifically, transformational leaders enhanced employees' perceptions of procedural fairness and trust, and consequently pro-social actions.

In conclusion, in this chapter I have tried to make clear that effective leadership cannot only be understood in terms of instrumental or economic exchanges, but, even more so, from the perspective that leaders can help followers in defining themselves as belonging to a social entity or group (cf. Hogg, 2001; Chapter 3). In this way, leadership is perceived as a quality of relationships that helps to contribute to people's personal outcomes, but, in addition to this, to their sense of belongingness. This helping in terms of belongingness needs, may, of course, be a function of followers' personal agendas as they are shaped by their position relative to the earlier defined relational equilibrium. Helping followers to achieve fulfillment of their belongingness needs reveals positive consequences from the perspective of the group, like commitment and cooperation.

Note

1 According to the REM, cooperation will not be influenced as a function of relational leadership among those with a strong need to belong, however, if their membership in the group at hand is likely to be neglected in the near future. That is, motivational theories argue that the link between satisfying belongingness needs and intrinsic motivation is a fundamental psychological process that is valid across situations. In addition, Baumeister and Leary (1995) argue that the need to belong is a universal and innate motivation to seek out the quality of the relationships one has with others. Thus, following these assumptions, the respectful and fair treatment should nearly always affect those with strong belongingness needs. However, the REM suggests that if one feels that his/her future membership is at stake, relational information as a function of belongingness needs will not reveal any influence. For example, De Cremer (2002d) demonstrated in an experimental field study that respect influenced organizational citizenship behavior among those with a high general need to belong, but only when employees were certain that they would not be fired. Those employees working in the departments that would have a high chance of being fired did not react toward variations in respect as a function of belongingness need.

Author Note

Preparation of this chapter was supported by a fellowship of the Netherlands Organization for Scientific Research (NWO, grant no. 016.005.019).

Part of this chapter was written while the author was a visiting scholar at New York University. The author wishes to acknowledge the important contribution of Mark van Vugt in developing the framework that distinguishes between instrumental and noninstrumental concerns in social dilemma settings.

10 Leadership, Identity and Influence: Relational Concerns in the Use of Influence Tactics

BARBARA VAN KNIPPENBERG
AND DAAN VAN KNIPPENBERG

The study of leadership and the study of influence are closely intertwined: the two topics are often discussed concurrently in handbooks and review articles and they are frequently treated as more or less similar or related concepts in empirical studies. Some researchers make an even stronger link between leadership and influence. They claim that the use of influence is the essence of leadership (e.g., Yukl, 1998). After all, leaders need to guide, structure, mobilize, facilitate, envision, and define identity, foster harmonious relations, and enhance performance (in organizations or other groups), and they can only do so by exercising influence. How leaders exercise influence is therefore a core question for students of leadership.

In this chapter, we use theoretical insights in identity processes to present a framework to understand the choice and effectiveness of leaders' influence attempts. Building on prior development of taxonomies of influence tactics in organizations, and empirical work on the antecedents and consequences of the use of different tactics, we outline how relational and collective identity processes affect the use of influence tactics. Central to this analysis are the relational concerns associated with relational and collective self-construal, and the leader's role as representative of the group's identity. First, however, we briefly overview research on the categories, and use, of influence tactics.

A Brief Review of Research on Influence Tactics

Categories of influence tactics

Influence tactics are ways in which power can be used to get something done. Influence tactics are proactive, behavioral actions that are taken to change the attitudes, beliefs or behaviors of individuals (Barry and Shapiro, 1992; Kipnis, 1984; Yukl, 1998). The source of influence may be leaders, but does not necessarily have to be. Thus, research on influence tactics is not limited to the study of influence attempts by leaders, but also incorporates studies of proactive influence attempts in general. Researchers have tried to classify the ways in which influence can be exerted, and have proposed a number of somewhat similar taxonomies of influence tactics (Kipnis and Schmidt, 1988; Kipnis, Schmidt, and Wilkinson, 1980; Schriesheim and Hinkin, 1990; Yukl and Falbe, 1990; Yukl and Tracy, 1992). Of these taxonomies, perhaps that described by Yukl and his colleagues (e.g., Yukl, Kim, and Falbe, 1996; Yukl and Tracy, 1992) is the most extensively used.

The most commonly recognized influence tactics include rational persuasion (use of logical arguments, information and factual evidence), inspirational appeals (arousing enthusiasm by appealing to ideals, values or aspirations), consultation (involving the target in the process of making, or planning how to implement, a decision, policy or change), ingratiation (using flattery, praise or helpful behavior prior to presenting a request), personal appeals (appealing to feelings of friendship or loyalty when asking for something), exchange (offering the exchange of material or immaterial goods in reply), coalition (aiming to seek compliance by seeking or claiming support from superiors or peers), legitimating tactics (claiming authority or the right to make a request, or referring to its congruence with existing policies, rules or traditions), and pressure or assertiveness (intimidating the target by using demands, threats or persistent reminders).

Determinants and consequences of the use of influence tactics

Research studying the antecedents and consequences of the use of various influence tactics has shown that different patterns of influence behavior are associated with different outcomes for the influencing agent. In general, frequent use of assertiveness as an influence tactic is not a good way to obtain favorable performance evaluations from supervisors. Moreover, frequent users of assertive, forceful tactics earn less and report higher job tension (Kipnis and Schmidt, 1988). Other studies indicate that different influence tactics have different effects on the target's task commitment (Brennan, Miller, and Seltzer, 1993; Xin and Tsui, 1996; Yukl et al., 1996; Yukl and Tracy, 1992). Overall, the use of rationality, inspirational appeals, and consultation tactics are most likely to be effective and to lead to target commitment. The use of tactics like pressure, coalition, legitimating tactics, or sanctions (i.e., threatening, or carrying out, administrative compulsory measures) is considered to evoke reactance and resistance in the target. Although the use of these tactics can be effective in eliciting compliance, commitment is seldom secured.

The tactics that have these less desirable side effects, are generally the tactics that fall at the *hard* end of what has been called the *strength dimension* of influence tactics (Bruins, 1997; Falbo and Peplau, 1980; Farmer, Maslyn, Fedor, and Goodman, 1997; van Knippenberg, van Knippenberg, Blaauw, and Vermunt, 1999). This dimensions refers to 'the extent to which using particular influence tactics takes control over the situation and the target, and does not allow the target any latitude in choosing whether to comply' (Tepper, Brown, and Hunt, 1993, p. 1906). Hard tactics are relatively unfriendly and socially undesirable (Raven, 1992; van Knippenberg, 1999; Yukl and Tracy, 1992). They are tactics that are relatively controlling and coercive (e.g., pressure, legitimating tactics, coalition). *Soft* influence tactics fall at the other end of the strength dimension. They include tactics like ingratiation, inspirational appeals, consultation, and rationality (Farmer et al., 1997; van Knippenberg, van Knippenberg et al., 1999; Yukl, Falbe, and Youn, 1993).

Although specific soft tactics and specific hard tactics can be clearly distinguished from one another in terms of the behaviors involved, the soft–hard dimension clearly recognizes systematic differences in the amount of freedom that the target is allowed in choosing whether or not to comply. The distinction between hard and soft tactics mirrors differences in forcefulness of influence tactics. The unfriendliness and social undesirability of hard tactics is likely to be the cause of their less frequent use relative to tactics that do not have these negative connotations (Rule, Bisanz, and Kohn, 1985; van Knippenberg and Steensma, 2003; van Knippenberg, van Eijbergen, and Wilke, 1999; Yukl, Guinan, and Sottolano, 1995). After all, the use of hard influence tactics is likely to place more strain on the relationship between influencing agent and target than the use of soft tactics. Moreover, other research has shown that whenever forceful and unfriendly tactics are employed, they are likely to be preceded by the use of less forceful tactics, like ingratiation, consultation, rationality, and inspirational appeals (Yukl et al., 1993). In other words, the negative aspects of coercive tactics contribute to their being a last resort (Rule et al., 1985).

There also appears to be a growing interest in the determinants of the use of influence tactics. Several studies (Erez, Rim, and Keider, 1986; Kipnis et al., 1980; Xin and Tsui, 1996; Yukl and Falbe, 1990; Yukl et al., 1993; Yukl and Tracy, 1992) focused on the question of whether the direction of influence affects the use of influence tactics. These studies revealed, for instance, that rational persuasion is used more frequently in upward influence attempts (superior targets) than in downward (subordinate targets) or lateral (peer targets) ones, personal appeal and coalition tactics are used most often in lateral influence attempts, and the remaining tactics are used more frequently in downward influence attempts than in upward ones. Other studies show that people scoring high on Machiavellianism use tactics such as deceit, ingratiation, and assertiveness more often than low Machiavellians (Falbo, 1977; Farmer et al., 1997; Grams and Rogers, 1990; Vecchio and Sussmann, 1991).

Differential use of tactics has also been found for various objectives of influence attempts (Buss, Gomes, Higgins, and Lauterbach, 1987; Erez et al., 1986; Kipnis et al., 1980; Yukl et al., 1995), for people varying in self-esteem (e.g., Raven, 1992), for people varying in status (Stahelski and Paynton, 1995), for people varying in competence (van Knippenberg, 1999; van Knippenberg, van

Eijbergen et al., 1999), for people varying in whether they use a transactional or transformational leadership style (Deluga and Souza, 1991), for people varying in level of education (Farmer et al., 1997), and for ingroup versus outgroup targets (Bruins, 1997).

Finally, a line of research on cultural differences in the use of influence tactics is emerging (Fu and Yukl, 2000; Hirokawa and Miyahara, 1986; Xin and Tsui, 1996), showing for instance that the use of gifts, coalition tactics and upward appeals is rated more effective by Chinese managers than by American managers. This list of consequences and determinants of the use of influence tactics is not exhaustive, but it does cover the main themes in research on influence tactics.

Levels of Self Representation and Influence Tactics

Although research on influence tactics has uncovered a number of relationships between the use of specific tactics and other variables, research has typically fallen short of providing explanations for these relationships (e.g., Steensma, 1995). We believe that an important step towards a theoretical framework to understand the use and effects of influence tactics can be made by focusing on the nature of the relationship between influencing agent and influencing target. Because most dyadic (e.g., leader–subordinate) and within-group (e.g., leader–workunit) relationships in organizations are at least to a certain extent cooperative in nature, our discussion concentrates on relationships that are in principle cooperative. However, we realize that relationships may sometimes be competitive, and that competitive interdependence is likely to influence the use and effects of influence tactics (van Knippenberg, van Knippenberg, and Wilke, 2001). Nonetheless, in this chapter we focus on how the nature of cooperative relationships may affect the choice and effect of different ways of wielding influence.

Surprisingly, there has been little explicit attention to the consequences of the fact that the use of influence tactics takes place in a relationship with (an) other person(s) (van Knippenberg et al., 2001). For instance, most of the research on influence tactics takes place in interpersonal contexts, but ignores the question of how elements of this relationship may shape the choice and effect of the use of influence tactics. Research on the use of influence tactics in the context of the group, the work unit, or team is almost completely absent. Hence, there is little insight into how the use of influence tactics is affected by the social–cognitive processes associated with group membership. To properly understand the use and effects of influence tactics, we need a theoretical framework that can account for influence tactics in both interpersonal and intragroup situations. One such framework is provided by theories of social identity and self-construal (e.g., Brewer and Gardner, 1996; Hogg and Abrams, 1988; Tajfel and Turner, 1986; Turner, Hogg, Oakes, Reicher, and Wetherell, 1987).

Levels of self-construal

One of the central aspects of an individual's relationship with others is the individual's self-definition in the relationship (Aron, Aron, Tudor, and Nelson, 1991; Brewer and Gardner, 1996; Markus and Kitayama, 1991; Turner et al., 1987). The individual may conceive of self in personal terms, independent from the other party in the relationship, or may construe the self in more relational terms, in a sense including the other party in the self. Such self-construals (i.e., self-identities, self-representations, self-definitions) function as templates for the development of cognitive, affective, and behavioral responses. The main distinction between forms of self-construal is between self-construal in personal and in social terms.

The personal form of self-construal is activated when an individual's sense of unique identity, differentiated from others, is the basis of self-definition (the *personal self*). At this level, motivations have a primarily egoistic character. When the self is socially construed, self-definition is derived from an individual's feeling of attachment to one or more others. This *social self* may be differentiated into an interpersonal and a collective level of self-definition (Brewer and Gardner, 1996; Lord, Brown, and Freiberg, 1999), depending on whether the feelings of attachment are more or less personalized. At the interpersonal level of the social self, an individual defines his or her self in terms of roles that specify their relationships with significant others (the *relational self*). The social connection with the significant other is a personalized tie of affection. Exemplary interpersonal identities are derived from close dyadic connections, such as the subordinate–leader, the husband–wife, or the brother–sister relationship. At this level, mutual benefits and the other's welfare become more salient. At the group level of the social self, self-definition comes from identification with larger collectives (the *collective self*). The social connection with larger collectives is a more impersonal bond of attachment. For the collective self, the basic social motivation is to strive for collective welfare and group enhancement.

Different levels of self-representation co-exist within the same individual, but may be more or less salient contingent on situational, individual, or cultural differences. As outlined in theories of social identity and self-categorization (Brewer, 1991; Hogg and Abrams, 1988; Tajfel and Turner, 1986; Turner et al., 1987), contextual factors like the presence of relevant comparison outgroups and the relative size of the group or organization may affect the salience of group membership, and thus the salience of the collective self. Similarly, factors that affect social identification with a group (identification may be conceptualized as the readiness for collective self-construal), such as group or organizational status (Ashforth and Mael, 1989), may affect people's level of self-construal.

In addition to situational factors, there are individual differences in the level at which individuals are prone to define the self (Triandis, 1989; Wagner and Moch, 1986) and in the propensity to identify with groups and organizations (James and Cropanzano, 1994; Mael and Ashforth, 1995). Finally, where people fall on the cultural dimension of individualism, collectivism (Hofstede, 1980), has a direct influence on self-construal. In collectivist cultures, the relational and collective level of self-representation tend to be more salient than in more individualist cultures (Markus and Kitayama, 1991; Triandis, 1989).

In view of abundant evidence that self-construal is a core aspect of interpersonal and individual–group relationships, affecting both attitudes and behavior (e.g., Brewer and Gardner, 1996; Markus and Kitayama, 1991; Turner et al., 1987), and the fact that influence tactics are always used in relation to one or more others, an obvious question is how self-construal affects the use and effects of influence tactics. The remainder of this chapter explores this question, first focusing on the relational self and then on the collective self. For simplicity, we discuss the relational self in interpersonal relationships and the collective self in individual–group relationships, even though the collective self may be salient in interpersonal encounters (i.e., individuals approaching each other in terms of their group membership) or the relational self may be salient in intragroup interactions (i.e., interpersonal relationships being salient in a group context). The theoretical framework we present is evolving, and therefore some aspects await more direct empirical tests. However, we hope to show how this framework has the potential to clarify the role of self-construal in influence and leadership.

The relational self: relational concerns and the use of influence tactics

As interpersonal relationships become closer, the representation of the self shifts from an individuated self-concept, in which the self is differentiated from the other, to a self-construal where the other is part of the extended self (Aron et al., 1991; Brewer and Gardner, 1996). As a consequence of this shift from personal to relational self, the other's needs and desires become more important, and fostering a harmonious relationship becomes an important motive. The relational self has most often been investigated in intimate relationships such as those between parent and child, lovers, or best friends.

Recently, relational self-construal has also been viewed in organizational relationships, such as that between supervisor and subordinate (Lord et al., 1999). In Chapter 3 of this book, for instance, Hogg, Martin and Weeden reconcile LMX-theory with the social identity approach to leadership (see also Graen and Scandura, 1987; Hogg and Martin, in press). The interpersonal level of self-construal is considered to be especially relevant for leadership research, because leaders are vital links between an employee and the organization and the relationship with the supervisor often colors work-related attitudes and perceptions (Gerstner and Day, 1997). Just as in intimate relationships, in organization-based relationships too a shift from the personal to the relational level of self-representation should be accompanied by an increased concern with relational considerations such as fostering interpersonal harmony. As a consequence, the use of influence tactics should become more contingent on relational concerns the more the relational self rather than the personal self is salient. Because, as discussed above, hard tactics typically place more strain on the relationship between influencing agent and target than soft tactics, the more the influencing agent's self-construal shifts from the personal to the relational level, the more the influencing agent should favor soft over hard tactics.

Van Knippenberg and Steensma (2003) tested this proposition in a laboratory experiment, and the results of this study indeed suggest that a shift from the personal to the relational level of self-representation affects the use of influence tactics. At the start of the study, participants were led to believe that they had higher task competency than their future partner (who was in reality simulated by a computer program) in an individual estimation task. The dyadic coopera-tive estimation task that would follow, closely resembled the individual task. However, in this dyadic cooperative estimation task one person per dyad (i.e., our participants) would not only have the opportunity to affect task perfor-mance by giving personal estimates, but would also be given the opportunity to influence the co-worker. Participants in the *hard influence tactic* condition were told that they had the opportunity to coerce an estimation out of the other: the other would be forced to do as the participant decided. Participants in the *soft influence tactic* condition were told they had the opportunity to give advice to the other person about the estimates, but that the other person was free to follow or disregard the advice.

Before participants started on this dyadic task, they were informed about yet another task that was to follow after the dyadic task. Participants in the *no future interaction* condition were told that the next task would again be an indi-vidual task: the participant would thus have nothing to do with the other person in what was to follow. In contrast, participants who did expect a *future interaction* were informed that the next task would be performed with the same partner again. This explicitly forced participants to focus on the relationship that they had with the other. By placing participants in a context that either stressed the upcoming individuality or the continuing relationship with the other, the manipulation thus either made the individual level or the relational level the more salient level of self-representation.

Participants now started the dyadic estimation task, and were given the opportunity on 12 separate occasions to wield influence, and thus use a hard or soft influence tactic, depending on condition. The main dependent variable was the number of times the participant used the opportunity to employ influence.

Results (see Figure 10.1) suggest that a shift from the personal to the rela-tional level of self-representation indeed leads to a preference for soft over hard influence tactics. By inducing an expectation of future interaction, the relational connection between the leader or influencing agent and target was made salient, which may have prompted relational concerns and thus motivated potential agents to uphold a good relationship with the target. Because the use of influence does not necessarily foster harmonious relationships, a lower fre-quency of influence was found when the salient level of self-representation was shifted towards the relational level ($M_{future} = 4.84$ vs $M_{no\ future} = 6.39$; $F(1, 40) = 4.20$, $p < .05$). In addition, because the use of hard influence tactics is

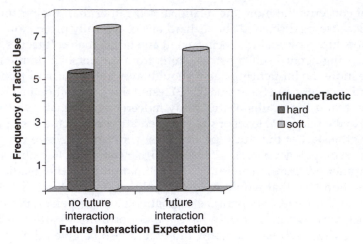

Figure 10.1   Future interaction expectation and the use of hard and soft influence tactics, adapted from van Knippenberg and Steensma (2003)

particularly likely to strain the relationship between agent and target, the shift towards a relational level of self-representation led to a lower frequency of hard tactics ($M_{hard} = 3.33$ vs $M_{soft} = 6.23$; $F(1, 40) = 4.42$, $p < .05$).

Presumably, the salient relationship between leader and target made the quality of the relationship important and the display of behavior that might endanger this relationship less attractive. Moreover, because participants were led to believe that they were more competent than their partner, the results suggest that relational considerations can prevail above direct task considerations. After all, individuals with relatively high task competence may be inclined to wield influence because they expect that their potential task contributions will have higher utility than those of others will (cf. van Knippenberg et al., 2001). Apparently, the desire to maintain a positive relationship with the target makes leaders less willing to employ influence, even though this could have been beneficial for task performance.

Another study, a survey, also aimed to investigate the role of the existing relationship between the influencing agent and the target of influence in the choice of using hard and soft influence tactics (van Knippenberg, van Knippenberg et al., 1999). Self-definition at the relational level is considered to be related to attraction or liking, which develops out of two people's personal traits and the degree of match between their individual identities (Brewer and Gardner, 1996; Hogg, 1992). Moreover, the stronger the interconnectedness of self and other in the relationship, the more the other is included in representations of the self (Aron and Aron, 1997; Aron and Fraley, 1999). Liking, then, should induce a preference for cooperative, socially acceptable behavior (the way that the self likes to be treated also).

Indeed, the data (van Knippenberg, van Knippenberg et al., 1999) showed that the more the influencing agent liked the target, the relatively less often he or she used hard tactics (cf. Kipnis, 1976). The difference between the correlation of the use of hard tactics with perceived likeability ($r = -.24$, $p < .05$) and the correlation of the use of soft tactics with perceived likeability ($r = -.04$, ns) was significant by t-test for dependent rs ($t(99) = 2.38$, $p < .001$). Similarly, Farmer et al. (1997) reasoned that when the dyadic leader–follower relationship is characterized by mutual liking, trust, and respect, (high on LMX, or in-groupness), the use of hard influence tactics is less likely. They found partial support for this prediction.

Of course, relational concerns may not only be rooted in identity processes, but may also be instigated by more direct pragmatic considerations. People may, for instance, rely on outcomes that are contingent on the quality of the relationship. Using tactics that may degrade the relationship with the other (i.e., hard tactics) can therefore sometimes be a luxury that one cannot afford (van Knippenberg, van Knippenberg et al., 1999). The conclusion should therefore not be that the threshold for using hard tactics is low when the personal self is salient, but rather that salience of the relational self rather than the personal self adds yet another threshold to the use of hard influence tactics.

Although there is no direct evidence from research in influence tactics, studies in social influence suggest that relational as opposed to personal self-construal renders individuals more open to the other's influence attempts. The influence process Kelman (1958) labeled 'identification', and the power base that French and Raven (1959) labeled 'reference' (i.e., influence based on a sense of oneness with the influencing agent) seems to reflect influence grounded in relational self-construal. Studies of group-based influence suggest that targets of influence attempts are more open to the agent's influence when agent and target have a shared social identity (for reviews, see e.g., Turner, 1991; D. van Knippenberg, 1999). More direct evidence for this proposition from research on influence tactics would be welcome though.

The research described above corroborates our proposition that a shift from the personal towards the relational level of identity affects the use of hard and soft influence tactics. Relational concerns occupy a more central place in a leader's or influencing agent's decision to use hard and soft influence tactics when the self is construed in relational rather than personal terms. In the following section we elaborate on the question of what happens to the use of influence tactics when the level of self-representation is at the group or collective level.

The collective self: relational concerns and the role of group prototypicality

At the collective level, self-definition comes from identification with social groups, using the group prototype as a basis for comparison (Tajfel and Turner, 1986; Turner et al., 1987). Self-construal at the relational level blurs the distinction between self and other. Self-construal at the collective level blurs the distinction between self and group, and turns the group into part of the self (Smith and Henry, 1996; Tropp and Wright, 2001). We propose that if the level of self representation shifts from the personal level towards the collective level, the use of influence tactics reflects the transformation of the group into part of the self, just as a shift from personal to relational self-construal is reflected in the use of influence tactics. Like the relational self that is motivated to foster relationships with significant others, the collective self is motivated to foster harmonious relationships with the group (members). Thus, the display of behavior that might endanger this relationship is again less attractive. In sum, we propose that when the collective self becomes salient, a leader/influencing agent will use fewer hard as compared to soft influence tactics, because hard influence tactics are particularly likely to strain the relation between the leader/influencing agent and the group.

The study that probably comes closest to providing a test of our proposition that leaders/influencing agents are less likely to use hard tactics the more the collective rather than the personal self is salient is a study by Bruins (1997). Bruins studied the use of hard and soft influence tactics towards ingroup targets, outgroup targets and unrelated individuals. Of these three target types, agents by definition only share a social identity with ingroup members, and thus we may assume that the collective self (i.e., in the sense of a shared identity between agent and target) was more likely to be salient when faced with an ingroup target than an outgroup targets or unrelated individuals. Bruins found that influencing agents only had a definite preference for soft over hard tactics when they attempted to influence ingroup targets. Moreover, influencing agents used hard tactics less often and soft tactics more often towards ingroup targets than towards unrelated individuals and outgroup targets. Bruins furthermore found that agents had a stronger desire to be liked by the target when the target was an ingroup member than an outgroup member or an unrelated individual. In addition, the desire to be liked mediated the effect of target of influence on preferences for influence tactics. Hence, the results of Bruins's study seem to corroborate our proposition that the use of influence tactics becomes more contingent on relational concerns when the collective self rather than the personal self is salient and that, as a consequence, leaders are less likely to use hard tactics.

There is, however, one important aspect in which the influence process in the collective context distinguishes itself clearly from the influence process in the interpersonal context, and that is the role of *group member prototypicality*. Prototypical group members represent the group's standards, values, and norms, and they reflect what members of the ingroup have in common and what sets them apart from relevant outgroups (Turner et al., 1987). In other words, group member prototypicality reflects the extent to which group members are representative of the collective self. This is an important point where the collective self may be differentiated from the relational self. In interpersonal relationships, it makes little sense to distinguish between more prototypical and less prototypical partners in the relationship. In a group context, however, where more than two individuals are involved, it is possible to distinguish between individuals that are more and less representative of the collective.

As outlined in self-categorization theory (Turner et al., 1987), group member prototypicality plays an important role in group-based influence. As group membership becomes more salient (i.e., self-construal shifts more to the collective self), group member influence is more contingent on the extent to which the group member is prototypical of the group (Hogg, 2001; Turner, 1991; van Knippenberg, 2000). More prototypical group members are more liked as group members (Hogg, 2001), more influential (van Knippenberg, Lossie, and Wilke, 1994), and more likely to emerge as a leader (Fielding and Hogg, 1997; cf. van Knippenberg, van Knippenberg, and van Dijk, 2000). In addition, the extent to which an established or appointed leader matches the group's prototype has also been shown to influence leadership effectiveness or endorsement (Hains, Hogg, and Duck, 1997; Platow and van Knippenberg, 2001). There thus is ample evidence that leaders who are more representative of the collective self are more effective.

Theoretical considerations as well as empirical findings suggest that prototypicality and behavior interact in various ways. More prototypical group members have a tendency to behave differently from less prototypical group members, and behavior displayed by prototypical group members is interpreted and evaluated differently from behavior displayed by non-prototypical group members. It has been suggested that because prototypical group members represent what the group stands for, their status as a group member is assured. The group belongingness of more peripheral group members is not so obvious. As a consequence, non-prototypical members may feel the need to assert their group membership by displaying group-oriented behavior (Bruins, 1997; Noel, Wann, and Branscombe, 1995; Platow and van Knippenberg, 2001; van Knippenberg et al., 2000). Indeed, non-prototypical members may actually need to engage in more group-oriented behavior than prototypical members in order to be accepted or endorsed as leaders by their fellow group members (Platow and van Knippenberg, 2001).

A study that focuses explicitly on the use of influence tactics in studying the proposed interaction between prototypicality and behavior was conducted by Noel et al., (1995). They found that peripheral members, as compared to prototypical members, advocated more use of coercive tactics in dealings with outgroup members, especially when they had to discuss their responses with fellow ingroup members (i.e., when their opinion on hard tactic use could be used to present themselves favorably to the ingroup).

A survey by van Knippenberg and van Knippenberg (2000) is, as far as we know, the only study that focused explicitly on the importance of leader prototypicality in the effects of use of influence tactics. They hypothesized that because subordinates will accept a wider range of behavior from more prototypical leaders than from less prototypical leaders (Platow and van Knippenberg, 2001), the influence of leaders' choice of influence tactics on the quality of the relationship between leader and subordinate will be smaller the more prototypical the leader is. The survey was carried out in organizations providing business-to-business services, such as cleaning, catering, surveillance, temping, etc. The members of 69 different teams were asked to assess the use of influence tactics of their supervisors, the quality of the relationship with their supervisor (i.e., LMX; Graen and Scandura, 1987), and the prototypicality of the team leader.

The results showed that the quality of the relationship between leaders and subordinates was better the more prototypical the team leader ($r = .32$, $p < .01$). Moreover, van Knippenberg and van Knippenberg found that the frequency by which leaders used soft influence tactics improved the leader–follower relationship for prototypical leaders much more than for less prototypical leaders (e.g., inspirational appeal, $\beta = .30$, $t(64) = 2.51$, $p < .015$; rationality, $\beta = .36$, $t(64) = 3.12$, $p < .005$; ingratiation, $\beta = .42$, $t(64) = 3.71$, $p < .001$). Even more interesting was the finding that whereas the frequency of the use of hard influence tactics slightly lessened the quality of the relationship between less prototypical leader and subordinate, it actually *improved* the quality of the relationship between prototypical leader and subordinate (e.g., legitimating tactics, $\beta = .31$, $t(64) = 2.67$, $p < .01$; pressure, $\beta = .37$, $t(63) = 2.27$, $p < .005$; see Figures 10.2a and 10.2b for a synopsis of our results). Thus, prototypical leaders apparently have more freedom in how they act, than non-prototypical leaders have. Presumably, the group context and the apparent group-mindedness of highly prototypical leaders change the negative connotation associated with the use of hard influence tactics into a more neutral or positive one. After all, the perception of distinction between self (in this case the group leader) and group is most obviously blurred for people representing what the group stands for (i.e., a prototypical leader is maximally representative of the collective identity). Therefore, group members will expect that the motive to attend to collective welfare is especially likely to be present in high prototypical leaders: when these leaders use hard tactics it must be because they think that this is in the group's best interest. Hence, the use of these hard tactics does not result in a deterioration of the relationship (as is usually the case), and it may even enhance the quality of the relation (i.e., because the leader actively exerts him or herself for the group).

According to the social identity theory of leadership (Hogg, 2001; Hogg and van Knippenberg, in press; Chapters 3 and 4), leadership perceptions, evaluations, and endorsement become increasingly influenced by prototypicality as people identify more strongly with the focal group (i.e., when the collective self is salient). This implies that the interactive effect of leader prototypicality and leader tactic use described in the previous section, is more pronounced for people who identify stronger with their group. We recently tested this assumption in a laboratory experiment (van Knippenberg and van Knippenberg, 2001) in which we measured the degree to which participants identified with the group, and investigated the effects of prototypicality and use of influence tactics on the relationship between agent and target for high and low identifiers. Results showed that for non-prototypical leaders the use of hard influence tactics led to a more negative perception of the quality of the relationship between agent and target then the use of soft influence tactics did, while this effect was less strong for prototypical leaders. However, we found this effect for high identifiers only, supporting the proposition that leader prototypicality is especially important as people identify more strongly with the focal group.

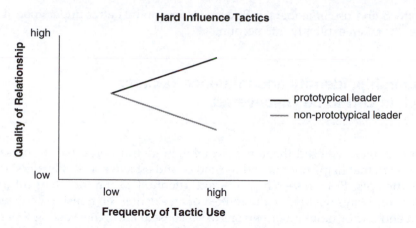

Figure 10.2a **Prototypical and non-prototypical leaders' use of hard influence tactics and the quality of the relationship between leader and subordinate, adapted from van Knippenberg and van Knippenberg (2000)**

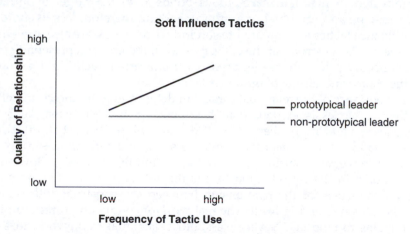

Figure 10.2b **Prototypical and non-prototypical leaders' use of soft influence tactics and the quality of the relationship between leader and subordinate, adapted from van Knippenberg and van Knippenberg (2001)**

To summarize, we propose that the collective self, being motivated to promote pleasant relations with fellow group members, will be relatively reluctant to use hard influence tactics. In addition, we argue that representativeness can be considered a key characteristics of the influence processes associated with the collective self. Leader prototypicality largely determines the influence process in groups, and thus also affects the perception of leaders' use of influence tactics. In general, we conclude that whenever the influence behavior takes place in a group context and the collective level of self construal is salient, the effects and use of leaders' influence tactics can be better understood if this context is taken explicitly into account.

Leadership, Identity and Influence Tactics: Much is Left to be Discovered

In this chapter, we used theoretical insights in identity processes to present a framework that helps understand the choice and effectiveness of leaders' influence attempts. Prior research paid scant attention to the idea that influence tactics are always wielded in the context of an existing relationship between an agent and one or more other persons. As a consequence, the existing literature gave little insight into how the use of influence tactics may be affected by the social–cognitive processes associated with dyadic interaction and group membership. Building on work that concentrates on the context-dependency of the self-concept, we argued that both the relational self and the collective self are motivated to maintain harmonious bonds with the target of influence (which may be an individual or a group), and are therefore less likely to use hard influence tactics as compared to soft influence tactics. We also argued that when the self is construed at the collective level, the group representativeness of the collective self of the leader becomes an important factor in determining both the choice and effects of influence tactics.

The importance of the relational context in determining the choice and effects of influence tactics is evident (van Knippenberg and Steensma, 2003; van Knippenberg, van Knippenberg et al., 1999; van Knippenberg et al., 2001), as is the importance of self-construal in interpersonal and individual–group relationships (Brewer and Gardner, 1996; Sedikides and Brewer, 2001). However, as already noted in the introduction to our theoretical analysis, the amount of empirical evidence for the relationship between self-construal and influence tactics is still small and indirect. The real work of conducting direct empirical tests remains to be done. Nevertheless, our conceptual framework does provide an interpretative foundation to build on.

In this chapter, we have focused on the relationship between self-representations and the choice and effects of influence tactics. We specifically focused on the effects of leader prototypicality and hard and soft tactic use on perceptions of the target of influence. In future research, it may be worthwhile to also involve the agents' own perception in the study of choice and effect of influence tactics and investigate whether agents' perceptions vary with their level of self-representation.

Level of self-representation may, for instance, affect people's assessment of effectiveness of their own tactic use. Pfeffer and Cialdini (1998) studied determinants of the illusion of influence. Illusion of influence refers to a belief that one has influence when one in fact has not, or to the tendency to overestimate one's control over behaviors and outcomes. In general, individuals like to think of themselves as being influential, because such self-perception enhances self-evaluation. Pfeffer and Cialdini argue that when the self-enhancement motivation is emphasized, the tendency to see oneself as being influential is increased. They state that this may also imply that the illusion of influence is magnified when personal rather than relational self-construal is dominant (i.e., the self-enhancement motive is especially prominent when independent self-construal is dominant). Consequently, a leader who feels strongly connected to a certain target of influence or leaders who feel highly involved in the group's functioning may be less prone to the illusion that their use of influence tactics are effective than are less attached leaders. Or, in other words, the personal self, as opposed to the social self (i.e., both the relational and the collective self), may feel more influential after tactic use than he or she in reality is. In turn, this misconception may hamper leader follow-up behavior, lessen leader endorsement and, in the end, diminish leader effectiveness.

Author Note

Netherlands organization for scientific research (NWO) is gratefully acknowledged for funding this project (MAGW-grant 490–01–200).

11 Power and Prejudice: A Social–Cognitive Perspective on Power and Leadership

STEPHANIE A. GOODWIN

We need look no further than the recent Enron scandal in the United States to see that powerful leaders can make decisions for self-gain that have substantial negative consequences for their subordinates. In the paper-shuffle to hide debt and promote company stock, Enron leaders accrued millions at the expense of those who depended on them for their livelihoods. Employees at Enron lost not only jobs, management's handling of employee retirement funds eradicated the life-savings of many employees. Regardless of whether Enron's leaders ultimately are held accountable for their behaviors, it is generally agreed that Enron's leaders acted in self-serving and unethical ways.

Enron's leaders are neither the exception nor the rule when it comes to the question of power and corruption. Social scientists pondering leaders' use and abuse of power have concluded there is no shortage of evidence that powerful leaders abuse subordinates (for review see Lee-Chai and Bargh, 2001). Documented abuses of power range from mild (e.g., teasing) to extreme (e.g., genocide). Whether people in power can behave badly seems obvious: yes, they can. *When* and *how* power leads to unscrupulous behavior, however, is less clear.

The present analysis adopts a social cognitive perspective on power. Although early social psychologists recognized the importance of power as a social phenomenon (Cartwright, 1959), it is only recently that we have begun to examine power's consequences for social judgment, emotion, and behavior. How do powerful people think about their subordinates, and with what consequences for subordinates' outcomes? Understanding when and how power holders' judgment processes go awry can inform our understanding of when they may stray from ethical behavior.

The present chapter reviews the social psychological literature on power and social judgment with an eye toward leadership and social identity. Consistent with research throughout the field, much, but not all, of this research focuses on the cognitive processes (e.g., stereotype use) that may bias reactions to (e.g., evaluation) and behaviors toward (e.g., task assignments) subordinates. The picture of power emerging from this literature suggests that powerful leaders are vulnerable to biases and errors when evaluating their subordinates. The theories discussed below identify several potential benefits of bias for those who hold power. In particular, biased perceptions of subordinates may serve to protect the powerful, maintaining their relative status within a power hierarchy. Importantly, these biases need not be inevitable; the research to date suggests limits on power holders' biased tendencies.

In keeping with the focus on individual leadership, the focus here is on individual power, as opposed to group level power. The discussion begins with a primer on impression processes and stereotyping geared toward the uninitiated reader. After defining key concepts and theories of social power, I review the literature regarding power's effects on social judgment processes versus outcomes (also see Chapter 12). The chapter closes with an eye toward avenues for future research.

Impression Formation and Stereotypes

Impression formation – the process of perceiving, evaluating, and forming descriptive judgments of others – is a fundamental component of social life. Whenever we encounter another person with whom we have more than incidental contact we likely engage in some form of judgment process. Our impressions of others are contingent upon our relation to those individuals and the nature of reactions required by the situation (Fiske, 1998). The person we pass walking down the street may require no reaction whatsoever whereas the person seeking our employment necessitates some reaction, perhaps even significant attention and deliberation. Assuming a reaction is required, whence does it arise?

Theorists generally agree upon four basic stages of impression formation: *categorization, activation* of category-relevant information, *interpretation* of available information, and *judgment* (for reviews see Bodenhausen and Macrae, 1998; Fiske, 1998). When we first encounter others, perceptions of physical (e.g., body shape) and contextual (e.g., clothing) cues promote categorization of that individual into specific social groups (e.g., gender, race/ethnicity, age). Our initial categorization, typically a spontaneous process occurring outside of conscious awareness, can have significant downstream consequences. Mental representations related to the category may become cognitively primed (i.e., increase in cognitive accessibility). Because these representations reflect cultural beliefs as well as experience with group members, they often include group stereotypes. *Stereotypes* are generalized beliefs about the traits (e.g., friendly, smart) or behaviors (e.g., likes to dance) presumed to characterize members of a group (Hamilton and Sherman, 1994). Note, although some stereotypes emerge from kernels of truth (e.g., some Texans are friendly), group generalizations may not apply to individual group members (e.g., some Texans are not friendly). When group stereotypes are applied to individual judgments, judgment errors are more likely.

Stereotype activation can influence judgment both directly and indirectly (Pierce and Brewer, 2002). Perceivers may infer directly that individual members of a social group have stereotypic traits (i.e., projective stereotyping). For example, stereotypes of nurturing women might lead to inferences that a specific woman is nurturing, even in the absence of supporting evidence. Other times, stereotype activation guides attention to and interpretation of available information (i.e., interpretive stereotyping). For example, stereotypes that women are poor at mathematics may lead perceivers to notice an individual woman's failure on a maths task and to interpret it as especially diagnostic of her underlying ability. In contrast, stereotypes of men as especially good at math may lead perceivers *not* to notice an individual man's failure on a math task, or to interpret the behavior as a non-diagnostic fluke. Stereotypes thus can shape the interpretation of information, leading to construals that fit group stereotypes rather than individual characteristics. Stereotypic inferences and interpretations, of course, can lead to erroneous judgments.

Whether people form stereotypic impressions is a function of motivation and cognitive ability to evaluate others more accurately (Fiske and Neuberg, 1990; Fiske, Lin, and Neuberg, 1999; Neuberg, 1989). As perceivers become increasingly motivated to form accurate impressions, their impression processes are characterized by greater attention, especially attention to stereotype-inconsistent information. Attending to stereotype-inconsistent information affords an opportunity to form an idiosyncratic – i.e., individuated – impression that more accurately matches an individual's traits.

Social categorization, the first step in the impression process, is of particular importance to our discussion of identity, leadership, and power. As several identity theories argue (e.g., Social Identity Theory, Tajfel and Turner, 1986; Self-Categorization Theory, Turner, 1987), categorization is influenced by one's own identities. People are motivated to notice what is similar/dissimilar to their own social identities, responding more favourably to people categorized as members of own (in-groups) versus other groups (out-groups). Leaders' social identities, therefore, surely matter when it comes to perceptions of subordinates. Identities that are important to the self, for example, will influence categorization (for review see Brewer and Brown, 1998). Leaders who are strongly identified with their racial/ethnic groups, for example, may be predisposed to viewing subordinates in terms of these categories. Similarly, identification with leadership roles may promote hierarchical categorization of others (e.g., 'us management' versus 'them employees'). Situational factors (e.g., group homogeneity) also figure in the categorization process (e.g., Biernat and Vescio, 1993; Wittenbrink, Judd, and Park, 2001). If, for example, the upper echelons of leadership are filled with individuals who share group identities (e.g., white males in the US), this context can promote categorization of subordinates as a function of out-group distinction (e.g., black females). Thus, self and situation may influence leaders' categorizations of subordinates.

The Keys to Power and Leadership

Perhaps the most problematic issue facing the scholar of power lies in pinning down the construct itself. Defining power has proven slippery at best, completely elusive at worst. Within the social psychological tradition, definitions of power have varied widely, driven largely by the questions of interest to a given researcher (for reviews see Fiske, 1993; Keltner, Gruenfeld, and Anderson, in press). For example, in their classic analysis of the bases of power, French and Raven (1959) defined power as social influence, the ability to alter the beliefs, attitudes, or behaviors of others.

Recent theorists assert that such broad definitions of power problematically confound power with related but discrete phenomena (e.g., status and prestige; Deprét and Fiske, 2000; Fiske, 1993; Keltner et al., 2003). Instead, current theories draw heavily from interdependence theories (Thibaut and Kelly, 1959), defining social power as *asymmetric control over another's desired outcomes*. These outcomes may be tangible (e.g., economic outcomes) or intangible (e.g., approval). The key to this definition of power is simply one's relative control. Whereas subordinates are contingent upon the powerful, they lack reciprocal levels of control over resources valued by the powerful. This definition emphasizes the relational aspect of power and unconfounds power from its common correlates.

Leadership, in contrast, is defined broadly as social influence – the ability to alter the beliefs, feelings, or behaviors of others (Smith, 1995). Within this definitional framework, powerful people may or may not be in leadership positions. However, leadership frequently implies power. Politicians, corporate executives, and grade school teachers share in common their occupation of leadership roles characterized by control over others' outcomes.

Given the fact that leaders typically have power, biases in their judgments can be problematic for at least three reasons. First, biased judgments (e.g., stereotyping) may promote decisions that lead to the mistreatment of individual, or groups of, subordinates. When the powerful control important resources, their judgments can have real and important consequences (e.g., promotions, livelihood, health, etc.; Goodwin, Operario, and Fiske, 1998). Second, biased judgments can lead the powerful to feel justified in their mistreatment of others. Across history, inaccurate evaluations (e.g., stereotyping, dehumanization) of relatively powerless social group members have served to justify a host of injustices, ranging from institutionalized pay disparities, to discrimination in education, to slavery and genocide (for further discussion see Sidanius and Pratto, 1999). Finally, individual injustices occur in a larger social context and serve to maintain macro-level group disparities. Aggregate bias is a function of individual decisions. When the powerful are biased, their judgments maintain status-quo differences between social groups (e.g., race, ethnicity, gender, sexual orientation, class) within societies. Such disparities are themselves unethical. In sum, understanding if and when powerful leaders are prone to stereotyping and social judgment errors is important because these judgments have consequences for individuals as well as groups.

Power theories

Although the social psychological study of power can best be described as occurring in fits and starts, several theories have emerged that address social judgment in whole or in part. Three theories are especially relevant to our discussion of social judgment: Power as Control (Fiske, 1993; Goodwin, Gubin, Fiske, and Yzerbyt, 2001), Power as Threat (Georgesen, 2001), and Power, Approach, and Inhibition (Keltner et al., 2003).

Power as Control (PAC)

Fiske's (1993) Power as Control theory is perhaps most central to our discussion because this theory focuses uniquely on power's consequences for social judgment. The model is predicated on impression formation theories that argue accurate impressions require both motivation and cognitive resources to attend to others (Brewer, 1988; Fiske and Neuberg, 1990; Fiske, Lin, and Neuberg, 1999); attending to idiosyncratic target information is a necessary, albeit not sufficient, requirement for accurate impression formation. According to the PAC model, powerful perceivers may be vulnerable to judgment biases because they: (1) need not be accurate, (2) may not want to be accurate, and (3) may be unable to be accurate when forming impressions of subordinates.

First, powerful perceivers' lack of (inter)dependence likely reduces motivation to form accurate impressions. A large body of research demonstrates greater individuation – impressions based on idiosyncratic target information – and reduced stereotyping under mutual interdependence (e.g., Fiske and Neuberg, 1990; Ruscher and Fiske, 1990). Second, to the degree that people seeking power are likely to be interpersonally dominant, the powerful may not want to be accurate. People high in dominance may stereotype or derogate subordinates to justify and protect their power. Third, the hierarchical nature of most power structures typically implies more subordinates than power-holders. If the powerful must attend to multiple subordinates, resulting limits on cognitive resources may reduce judgment accuracy.

In sum, the PAC model argues that power can alter both the motivation and the cognitive resources needed to form accurate, individuated impressions of subordinates. Failing to attend to information that individuates targets from their social groups, the powerful are left to rely on their prior expectations and stereotypes, a process defined as stereotyping *by default*. Stereotyping by default is an effortless impression strategy, characterized by inattention to expectancy-disconfirming information and reliance on prior knowledge and beliefs.

In an extension of the PAC theory, Goodwin et al. (2000) argued that powerful perceivers might engage in a more motivated form of social bias, stereotyping subordinates *by design*, as well as by default. Drawing from social judgeability theory (Leyens, Yzerbyt, and Schadron, 1992), they argued that the powerful often must make decisions that conform to social expectations about how to judge. These expectations may preclude snap judgments or imply accountability to others. When people are held accountable for their judgments, they tend to engage in more effortful information processing strategies (e.g., Tetlock, 1999). If so, one would expect the powerful to be less vulnerable to stereotyping subordinates.

Yet, social expectations regarding how people achieve power may further encourage stereotyping subordinates. Specifically, the powerful may be motivated to rely on stereotypes because of increased confidence in their own (presumably) expert beliefs, including their stereotypes. Finally, the powerful are likely motivated to minimize the risks to their power roles; loss of power is psychologically aversive. Stereotyping subordinates justifies individual and group power differentials (Fein and Spencer, 1997; Jost and Banaji, 1994). Together, these factors are hypothesized to create a tension between motives to think carefully about subordinates and motives to stereotype them. According to the theory, powerful perceivers may satisfy both types of motives by engaging in effortful yet stereotype-based impression strategies. These strategies are characterized by relatively high overall attention to subordinates, with attention focused on expectancy-confirming subordinate information. As a result, impressions of subordinates are predicted to be both stereotypic and resistant to change.

Of particular relevance to our discussion of leadership, the PAC model suggests that powerful leaders may benefit by stereotyping their subordinates in at least two ways. First, stereotyping subordinates justifies one's relative power over others. In societies where egalitarian values are held in high regard, such justifications may be especially important to the powerful leader. Second, stereotyping subordinates can reduce perceived threats to one's role, a point elaborated by the next theory under consideration.

Power as Threat (PAT)

Georgesen's (2001) Power as Threat theory focuses similarly on power-holders' evaluations of subordinates. As the name implies, however, the PAT approach delineates the role of threat in predicting negative reactions to subordinates.

According to this theory, occupying positions of power typically implies some form of threat. Academic tenure aside, few power roles are absolutely secure and stable over time. Hence, the powerful are likely to notice and respond to potential role threats. When threats become salient, the powerful may be motivated to make biased judgments not only of subordinates, but also of themselves.

Importantly, PAT theory differentiates threats to self-concept from threats to one's power position. Threats to self-concept are predicted to produce biased evaluations of self. Self-enhancing evaluations can reduce threats to self-esteem (e.g., Tesser and Moore, 1990). Positional threats, however, are presumed to elicit subordinate derogation. Derogation and negative evaluation of subordinates can reduce fears that a given subordinate poses a legitimate threat. Obviously, reducing such threats is in the leaders' self-interests.

Note here that, unlike the PAC model, the emphasis in the PAT model is on the evaluative nature of judgment. The focus is, therefore, on judgment outcomes, as opposed to the judgment process per se. Whereas the PAC model is concerned with what is going on in powerful leaders' minds, the PAT model is primarily concerned with what leaders say and do regarding subordinates.

Power, Approach and Inhibition (PAI)

Most recently, Keltner et al. (2003) have proposed a broad framework for understanding power's consequences for affect, cognition, and behavior. Drawing from Higgin's (1997) theory of promotion and prevention, these authors argue that power differentially activates approach versus inhibition systems. According to this theory, increased power activates an approach-related system, whereas lack of power activates an inhibition system.

Regarding social judgment, these different systems are presumed to produce biases consistent with both the PAC and PAT models. Powerful perceivers are presumed to be concerned with achieving rewards. In turn, they are predicted to engage in less deliberative judgment processes, relying more on stereotypes, and thinking of subordinates as a means to an end. These processes are hypothesized to increase the potential that the powerful will derogate subordinates and treat them unethically.

In contrast, powerless perceivers are presumed to be more concerned with understanding and predicting their situation, including their superiors. In turn, the powerless are predicted to engage in more deliberative judgment processes, forming more accurate impressions of the powerful, and thinking of themselves as a means to power-holders' ends. As a consequence, the powerless are predicted to inhibit their own responses more, bending to the expectations of the powerful.

Synthesizing the theories

At the heart of each of these theories is a common assumption that power can bias judgment. Yet these theories are distinct, most obviously in their level of analysis regarding social judgment. Keltner et al.'s (2003) theory is a general explanation of power's effects on a broad array of social phenomena. In comparison, the PAC model proposed by Fiske (1993) and later expanded by Goodwin et al. (2000) focuses specifically on power's effects on judgment, in particular on impression formation processes. These theorists are concerned with whether and how power promotes stereotypic judgments. The assumption here is that stereotyping leads to inaccurate evaluations, increasing the potential for discrimination in the distribution of subordinate outcomes. Finally, Georgesen's (2001) PAT approach focuses more narrowly on the role of (perceived) situational threats in producing judgment biases. This aspect of the model is compatible with issues of threat reduction identified by the extended PAC model. Despite differences in focus, both PAC and PAT argue that biased judgments reduce perceived threats to power. In the PAT model the bias of interest is subordinate derogation whereas the PAC model emphasizes subordinate stereotyping.

In sum, each of the theories reviewed above predicts that increased power promotes rather than reduces biased judgments of subordinates. In contrast, the powerless are hypothesized to be more accurate when judging superiors. Also of note, each theory recognizes that power's hypothesized deleterious effects are likely qualified by both individual (e.g., attitudes, individual differences) and situational (e.g., type of power, institutional judgment norms, accountability) factors.[1] Both the PAC and PAI models argue, for example, that individual differences in interpersonal dominance ought to moderate power's effects.

Power's consequences

Given the theoretical consensus that increased power promotes bias, one must ask whether empirical evidence supports these claims. As alluded earlier, research on power and judgment is still in an early period of development. Consequently, relatively few studies have addressed these issues directly. What follows is an overview of these studies, differentiating judgment processes (e.g., attention) from judgment outcomes (e.g., evaluation).

Judgment processes and power

Attention to subordinates

Empirical tests support the hypothesis that power promotes biased attention processes. First, increased individual power corresponds with increased attention to stereotypic information and lack of attention to counter-stereotypic information. For example, Goodwin et al. (2000, Study 1) asked students to play the role of personnel directors and evaluate applicants for high-school internships. When participants were led to believe their decisions would affect applicants' outcomes, they attended more to information stereotypically consistent with applicants' alleged ethnicity. In contrast, participants lacking decision power attended more to information that was inconsistent with the applicants' ethnicity. Attention to inconsistent information, as mentioned above, is linked in prior research to greater individuation of impression targets.

These attention patterns were replicated in two additional studies, including a study in which participants evaluated multiple targets across different power roles (Goodwin et al., 2000; Study 3). Participants volunteered for a study of task allocation in working groups, forming impressions of three different targets with whom they would later (allegedly) interact in different power roles: powerful task distributors, powerless task receivers, and power-irrelevant task observers. This round-robin design allowed a full test of the stereotyping by default and design hypotheses. In this study, power was operationalized as control over distributing desired tasks. Attention to target information – gender stereotypic or counter-stereotypic – was recorded via computer and served as the primary dependent variable.

As predicted, both powerful and powerless perceivers engaged in effortful attention strategies during impression formation. When evaluating either superiors or subordinates, perceivers paid significantly more attention than when they evaluated power-irrelevant targets. Despite similarities in overall effort, however, powerful perceivers differed from their powerless counterparts with regard to the focus of their attention. When perceivers evaluated subordinates, attention patterns were consistent with stereotyping subordinates by default; the powerful paid significantly less attention to counter-stereotypic information as compared to perceivers who were powerless. Moreover, powerful perceivers increased attention to stereotypic information relative to perceivers who were powerless, or those evaluating power-irrelevant observers. This increase in attention to stereotypic information is consistent with the extended PAC model's stereotyping by design hypothesis. Powerless perceivers, in contrast, paid significantly more attention to counter-stereotypic information relative to the powerful or those evaluating the power-irrelevant. This pattern is consistent with individuating attention strategies observed in previous impression formation research.

It is important to note that these effects were moderated by perceived responsibility. Goodwin et al. (2000; Study 1) primed half of the participants to think about responsibility toward others by asking these participants to complete the Humanitarian/Egalitarian Values Scale (Katz and Hass, 1988) prior to the impression task. Perceivers made to feel responsible by being reminded of egalitarian norms showed no attention bias as a function of power.

Research examining the effects of power legitimacy on attention to target information provide further evidence of judgment biases under increased power (Rodriguez-Bailon, Moya, and Yzerbyt, 2000). Adopting the round-robin design of Goodwin et al.'s Study 3 (2000), these researchers manipulated whether perceivers believed their power roles had been achieved legitimately (via personal competency) or illegitimately (via random assignment). Perceivers with illegitimate power were more likely to attend to negative stereotypic information. These effects are consistent with the threat reduction arguments posited by the PAT and PAC models. When the powerful perceive a threat to their roles, in this case a threat originating from illegitimate status, they attend to negative stereotypic information that could further justify subordinates' positions.

In sum, greater power appears to correspond with attention to stereotypic information and relative inattention to counter-stereotypic information. Reduced power reverses these effects, producing greater attention to counter-stereotypic and therefore potentially individuating information. These effects were qualified by situational factors, including the relative emphasis on responsibility norms and potential role threat.

Memory for subordinate information

To date, only one set of studies has examined whether individual power influences memory for subordinate information (Overbeck and Park, 2001). In these studies, participants play powerful (e.g., professor, judge) or powerless (e.g., student, attorney) roles while interacting via computer. Across studies, participants exchanged e-mails with targets in complementary power roles; this aspect of the study allowed for the controlled presentation of alleged target information. Subsequent memory for individual target information was measured via cued and un-cued recall. Overall, recall was much higher for participants in powerful roles. In addition, analyses of cued-recall tasks indicated fewer between-target recall errors when participants played powerful roles as compared to participants playing powerless roles.

On the surface, these results challenge the hypothesis that increased power produces judgment processing biases. After all, better recall for individuals ought to indicate more accurate impression formation, less stereotyping, etc. However, two aspects of the experimental design cloud this interpretation: the nature of the power manipulation, and the absence of stereotype measures.

First, power was not operationalized as outcome control in this study. Rather, college students played roles that typically involve power, never believing they actually controlled target outcomes or vice versa. It is possible that these results speak more to perceivers' schemas about power roles, rather than the experience of power per se. Dijksterhuis and van Knippenberg (1998) have demonstrated that simply priming the concept of *professor* increases performance on intellectual tasks. In the studies reviewed here, power roles were confounded with expectations of relative intelligence; conventional wisdom states that professors/judges are relatively more intelligent than their student/attorney counterparts. Hence, the recall advantage associated with greater power in these studies may result from priming intelligence in the absence of actual outcome control. It is possible that role expectations (e.g., intelligence) moderate the effects of actual outcome control, but studies to date have not addressed this possibility.

Second, measures of individuation in these studies addressed neither group categories nor stereotypes. These studies involved no express manipulation of group membership. Interestingly, however, target gender was implied by target names, a factor not considered in the analyses. This design issue makes it difficult to assess whether the results reveal an absence of intergroup bias. It is possible, for example, that perceivers in the professor role used gender to encode target information, whereas perceivers in the student role did not. If so, one could speculate that the differential use of group labels to encode target information could account for the observed memory differences across roles.

With regard to potential moderators of these effects, the data suggest that contextual norms play a role. When perceivers were directed to focus on organizational as compared to interpersonal concerns within the power relationship (Overbeck and Park, 2001; Study 3), perceivers playing powerful roles no longer displayed superior recall for individual information in cued-recall tasks.

In sum, initial data suggest a memory advantage for subordinate information under increased power, but design limitations preclude strong statements to this regard. Future tests incorporating clearer power manipulations and stereotype measures are warranted to better interpret these effects.

Information seeking

Results from a recent study suggest that power may alter the type of information one seeks about subordinates (Butz, Vescio, and Snyder, 2002). In this study, male and female participants were assigned to lead female subordinates in a task setting. Leaders believed they would control subordinates' outcomes via task assignments later in the study. Leaders were initially primed to think of their roles as either authoritarian or egalitarian in nature before they were given an opportunity to ask questions about, and provide help to, their subordinates. When leaders were primed to see their roles in more egalitarian terms, they sought more positive information and provided more help to their subordinates than their authoritarian-primed counterparts.

Importantly, this initial study lacks a control group to assess baseline effects of power in absence of contextual frame. Nevertheless, these data suggest important limitations of research designs that adopt the traditional 'canned information' paradigm, presenting participants with highly controlled, and typically equally balanced sets of target information (for discussion, see Johnston and Macrae, 1994). The attention and memory patterns described above might well be qualified by the less than naturalistic research designs that provide information rather than measure information seeking. Also of note, these data further suggest the importance of egalitarian norms in moderating power's negative effects; powerful participants in the present study – like those in the Goodwin et al. study reviewed above – engaged in less biased judgment processes when reminded of egalitarian norms.

Judgment outcomes

Within the literature on power and judgment, one may differentiate two types of judgment outcomes: stereotyping, and derogation. Although both outcomes may co-occur, they are not necessarily confounded. For example, stereotypes about women as nurturing are positively valenced, often leading to globally positive evaluations of women (e.g., Eagly and Mladinic, 1989). Nevertheless, these positive stereotype dimensions are undervalued relative to male stereotypes (e.g., intelligence) and likely to produce negative evaluations on some measures. It is important, therefore, to distinguish measures of stereotype from measures of derogation and general evaluation.

Subordinate stereotyping

Do powerful perceivers' evaluations reflect greater stereotyping of subordinates? The answer appears to be mixed. In the first three studies reported by Goodwin et al. (2000), power did not produce greater stereotyping of subordinates on traditional rating measures. However, the study's design – specifically, the equal presentation of stereotypic and counter-stereotypic information – may account for these null effects. Encountering large amounts of counter-stereotypic information typically reduces stereotyping, all else being equal. In the real world, it is unusual to encounter such a mixture of information about any one individual. To address this possibility, Goodwin et al. (2000; Study 4) adopted an idiosyncratic impression measure (Fiske, Neuberg, Beattie, and Milberg, 1987) to better assess the effects of power on stereotype use. In this design, participants first rated the valence of several different trait characteristics. Participants were subsequently assigned to power roles (control versus dependence to win a cash prize) and reviewed information about targets in complementary roles. Gender stereotypic and counter-stereotypic traits, drawn from the previously rated lists of traits, were presented as target information. Participants' subsequent ratings revealed a predicted effect of power on stereotyping. Powerful perceivers relied more on stereotypic information when evaluating subordinates than vice versa.

Derogation

With regard to subordinate derogation, the literature seems rather clear: powerful people are more likely to derogate others. Meta-analysis of relevant studies revealed a strong link between power and derogation (Georgesen and Harris, 1998). As power increased, so did negative evaluations of others. Importantly, direct empirical tests of the power-derogation link further support these findings (Georgesen and Harris, 2000). Participants in this research were assigned to perceiver and target roles and completed a dyadic problem-solving task. Half of the participants in each role were subsequently assigned to be either aware or unaware that the participant in the perceiver role would control target outcomes. Following the problem-solving task, participants rated themselves and their task partners. As predicted, perceivers who were aware of having power *rated their target partners more negatively* compared to perceivers in other conditions. Consistent with the PAT model, powerful perceivers also *rated themselves more positively* when they were aware they had power. These effects were moderated by individual differences in interpersonal dominance. High dominance perceivers were especially likely to derogate their subordinates.

Additional support for the power-derogation link can be found in studies of teasing among high versus low status individuals (Keltner, Capps, Kring, Young, and Heerey, 2001). Fraternity members with higher status were more likely to engage in hostile teasing of low-status fraternity members. One could argue that high-status individuals in these settings likely occupy positions of relative power over lower-status members. Adopting this assumption, these aggressive teasing behaviors may serve to justify and maintain higher-status members' relative power.

Summary

Despite a relatively sparse empirical base, evidence is accruing that power does indeed bias social judgment (also see Chapter 12). Importantly, power appears to bias both judgment processes (attention, information seeking) and outcomes (stereotype use, derogation). Several factors appear to moderate these patterns of effects. With regard to individual differences, interpersonal dominance seems to play a logical role in the magnitude of power's deleterious judgment effects. Greater interpersonal dominance magnifies power's negative effects. Contextual factors are similarly important. When situational norms suggest egalitarian values or responsibility, power has fewer negative consequences for social judgment.

Queries and quandaries: looking back and ahead

Although initial evidence supports the primary theses of contemporary theories, there is obviously much to be done when it comes to the study of power and social judgment. Five areas warrant discussion here: untested assumptions, resolving (potential) contradictions among research findings, links between process and outcomes, the role of power correlates, and institutional norms.

Untested assumptions

Across the three major theories reviewed here, several assumptions remain untested. For example, the PAC argument posits that power increases judgment confidence, an assumption based, in turn, on additional assumptions about social norms regarding who achieves power and why. Do powerful people experience heightened confidence in their judgments? If so, is this effect limited to particular types of judgments or is it a more general phenomena, as might be suggested by the PAI perspective on power and action? The PAT argument similarly rests on untested assumptions about the importance of threat to people in powerful positions. To what degree are powerful people sensitive to role threats? Do different types of threats (e.g., interpersonal versus intergroup) have different judgment consequences? Likewise, are powerful people motivated to reduce *any* threat, or are some threats more likely to promote negative judgment? Finally, the PAI argument, the most global approach among the three, has yet to be tested directly. Do powerful people adopt an action orientation? If so, is this orientation responsible for the observed effects on judgment or is it epiphenomenal?

Potential contradictions

With regard to potential contradictions in the research findings, the studies of memory reviewed above raise potential challenges to the argument that, all else being equal, power promotes bias. Assuming these effects replicate with improved research designs, it will be important to reconcile these effects with the attention effects observed in other research. Limitations of these findings aside, they highlight the need to consider moderators and mediators of the power-bias relationship. The PAI model provides an interesting framework that may help to resolve these inconsistencies in the future.

Missing links

A third issue raised by this collection of research is the absence of demonstrated links between many of the phenomena. First among the missing links is the lack of a clear relationship between biases in judgment processes and judgment outcomes. Such links have been demonstrated in other research, but have yet to be replicated in studies of power. Although these results may be due to artefacts of the research designs (e.g., equal presentation of stereotypic versus counter-stereotypic target information), it is important to demonstrate whether processing biases promote outcome biases. That is, we need a clearer understanding of what these processing biases represent. The information-seeking paradigm reported above is a promising avenue for demonstrating such a link.

A second missing link can be found in the many different types of judgment outcome measures. Specifically, when does power correspond to stereotyping versus derogating subordinates? When does power produce both? To understand the abuse of power, we need to better differentiate these types of outcomes, both theoretically and operationally. Although these two outcomes are likely related, they warrant distinction.

Finally, researchers have yet to link power's judgment biases to behavioral responses toward subordinates. Hence, future studies should incorporate measures of both evaluative judgments and behaviors toward subordinates to better assess the relationship between judgment and discrimination. The data to date speak of the potential for the powerful to discriminate, but they do not directly assess such outcomes.

Power correlates

The redefinition of power as outcome control has had an important impact on the study of this construct; clarifying the concept has enabled researchers to operationalize power while ruling out many common correlates. However, researchers need to keep in mind that power's correlates may be important for understanding how power influences judgment. Issues such as legitimacy, role status, and the sources of one's power remain important topics for future research. Any one of these factors could qualify the baseline effects of power. Future studies should include orthogonal manipulations of power and its correlates. For example, the early evidence on threat suggests that power legitimacy plays an important role in producing threat. Assessing the differential effects of legitimacy on power holders' judgments could lead to interesting hypotheses about when powerful perceivers might discriminate against subordinates to reduce threat.

Institutional contexts

Powerful leaders typically operate within institutional contexts. As institutional norms vary, so might the tendency for powerful leaders to abuse their power. Current investigations of power have yet to address directly how institutional norms may qualify the effects of power on judgment. Perhaps the closest indication of such effects lies in the research that has manipulated the salience of egalitarian norms; power's negative effects are reduced in these situations. However, egalitarian norms are only a small piece of the normative puzzle. Levels of accountability, institutional practices regarding the evaluation of subordinates and their value within the institution are additional factors that merit attention.

Power: For Better or Worse?

The weight of the evidence to date suggests that power has negative consequences for social judgment. Because the powerful, by definition, control others' outcomes, it is important for us to consider the depth and breadth of these effects. In so doing, we may be able to better understand past transgressions, such as the Enron scandal, and prevent future ones. Observers, for example, who question how Enron's leaders could justify their behaviors may gain insight from research on power and judgment. Applying theories of power and judgment, one might argue that stereotyping and derogating subordinates could have played a role at Enron. Specifically, if Enron's leaders viewed themselves favorably but derogated their subordinates, acts of greed may have seemed justified.

It is equally important for us to consider, however, those times when power does *not* lead to abuse and corruption. The focus of this chapter has been on the deleterious consequences of power on social judgment. One might ask 'Why the fascination with the negative?' After all, many powerful people engage in positive, self-sacrificing behaviors (e.g., Mother Theresa). Why not study the positive consequences of power? The early evidence of moderating factors alludes to the importance of studying such phenomena. If we are to identify remedies for power's negative consequences, we need a balanced understanding of both the negative and the positive consequences of power. In our striving to understand power, our progress will be enhanced if we set aside our own prejudices against power and recognize those factors that promote the responsible use of power as well as its abuse.

Note

1 This point is often overlooked in discussions of the PAC model.

12 Power, Social Categorization, and Social Motives in Negotiation: Implications for Management and Organizational Leadership

CARSTEN K.W. DE DREU
AND GERBEN A. VAN KLEEF

A prince should therefore have no other aim or thought, nor take up any other thing for his study but war and its organization and discipline, for that is the only art that is necessary to one who commands.

Niccolo Machiavelli, The Prince

In their classical work on the social psychology of organizations, Katz and Kahn (1978) observed that '... every aspect of organizational life that creates order and coordination of effort must overcome tendencies to action, and in that fact lies the potentiality for conflict' (p. 617). Indeed, based on 20 years of consulting and research experience, Pondy (1992) has concluded that organizations are inherently competitive and conflict-ridden, and Thomas (1992) reported that managers spend, on average, 20 per cent of their time managing conflicts between themselves and others. One way of dealing with conflict between leaders and followers, is through joint decision making and negotiation. In negotiation, managers directly communicate with the opponent in order to settle their conflict by mutual give and take (Pruitt, 1981). Often, negotiation is the preferred mode because it is the least costly, the least risky, and the most likely to lead to long-lasting agreements that satisfy all parties involved (Pruitt and Carnevale, 1993).

Negotiation between managers and their subordinates constitutes a special case for two reasons. First, managers usually have more power than their subordinates, begging the question how power differences affect negotiation processes and outcomes. Second, managers and subordinates are in an ongoing relationship that defines the self and shapes one's social identity, and thereby affects their cognition, motivation and behavior, including work motivation and performance (van Knippenberg, 2000). Supervisors categorize their subordinates as members of various social categories. Such social categorization may be based on cohort (e.g., the 'old crew' and the 'newcomers'), on gender or ethnic background, on educational background, and so on (Brewer, 1979). As specified in Leader–Member Exchange Theory (e.g., Graen and Uhl-Bien, 1995; Chapter 3), supervisors may categorize themselves as members of one social category, and not the other, and thereby develop affinity with some followers more than others.

According to the basic principles of self-categorization theory (Turner et al., 1987) and social identity theory (Tajfel and Turner, 1986), such self-categorization results in tendencies to favor (members of) the ingroup both cognitively and behaviorally, and to ignore or derogate (members of) the outgroup. When supervisors and subordinates categorize themselves as members of the same social category they are likely to adopt and seek *pro-social goals*, while they are likely to adopt *selfish goals* when they categorize themselves as members of different, opposing social categories (De Dreu, Weingart, and Kwon, 2000). This begs the question of how social categorization and concomitant social motives affect negotiation processes and outcomes between powerful leaders and their less powerful followers.

In the current chapter, we review research on negotiation processes and outcomes with a special emphasis on the role of power, social categorization, and social motivation. We discuss implications for management and organizational leadership. Consistent with Power-Dependency Theory (Bacharach and Lawler, 1981; Molm, Peterson and Takahashi, 1999), power is defined as the ability to influence others to do things they would not do otherwise. Thus, power is seen as structural potential, and it is explicitly distinguished from behavioral power use such as launching an attack, providing a reward, uttering a threat, or making a promise. Power as structural potential may derive from a variety of 'power bases' (French and Raven, 1958) such as the position one assumes within a group or organization, or the possibility to affect others through coercion, rewards, and expertise (Lee and Tiedens, 2001; Podsakoff and Schriescheim, 1985). Regardless of the specific power base(s) involved, it is the mutual dependence of actors that provides the structural basis for their power. In exchange relations such as negotiations between two individuals A and B, B's dependence on A increases with the value of benefits A can give B, and it decreases with B's access to alternative sources for those benefits.

Negotiation research has been concerned primarily with the extent to which one can provide the opponent with rewards and punishments, but some studies have also considered the influence of the availability of alternatives. In recent work, power has been operationalized as the extent to which one is central or peripheral in the group in which the negotiation takes place. In the current chapter we will review these studies. We have organized the chapter in four sections. First we introduce and discuss prototypical research on the influence of own and opponent's power on distributive and integrative negotiation. Second, we introduce in more detail the concept of social motives, and discuss research examining the interactions between power and social motives on negotiation processes and outcomes. Third, we review research concerning the influence of negotiator's power on information processing and search. We conclude this chapter with an overview of the main conclusions, and highlight some avenues for future research.

Power in Distributive and Integrative Negotiation

Many negotiation situations are mixed-motive with integrative potential. That is, parties' interests are neither completely opposed nor completely compatible, allowing agreements that satisfy both parties' aspirations to a greater extent than a simple, fifty–fifty compromise (Pruitt, 1981). This is nicely illustrated in the famous example of two sisters who quarrel about an orange. After some discussion, the sisters decide to compromise and split the orange in two equal parts. One sister squeezes her part, drinks the juice and throws the peel away. The other sister squeezes her part as well, but throws away the juice and uses the peel in a cake she is baking. Obviously, both would have been better off had they given all the juice to the first, and the whole peel to the second sister.

The two sisters in this example are not an exception. In international affairs, business transactions, and interpersonal exchange, individuals often fail to realize the integrative potential and instead reach an impasse or settle for a sub-optimal, fifty–fifty compromise (Rubin, Pruitt, and Kim, 1994). This is unfortunate because integrative agreements use available resources in an optimal way, produce satisfaction among the negotiators, strengthen the relationship between the negotiators, and reduce the probability of future conflict (Beersma and De Dreu, 2002; Rubin et al., 1994).

To defend and promote their own interests (e.g., how much of the orange do you get) individuals engage in distributive negotiation. They employ contentious behaviors such as placing demands, committing themselves to particular positions, advancing arguments about why the other should give in, strategically withdrawing from the negotiation table, and using threats and bluffs. To foster settlement (who gets what part of the orange) individuals engage in integrative negotiation. They employ cooperative tactics such as making and reciprocating concessions, seeking and giving information about preferences and priorities, adopting a problem-solving approach, and trying to build a positive negotiation climate (Pruitt, 1981).

Negotiation research and theory considering power and distributive behavior has flourished in social psychology, sociology, and the political sciences. Various strands of theorizing within these scientific disciplines have focused primarily on the link between coercive capability and punitive action, level of demand and concession-making. Perhaps the most prominent and most studied theoretical approach is *conflict spiral theory* (Deutsch, 1973). It assumes that individuals in conflict, in the final analysis, rely on their own strength only, and that the single best way to guarantee security is to use one's own threat capacity, and to attack and destroy one's opponents' coercive capabilities (Jervis, 1976). This produces a security-dilemma in that each individual party seeks expansion of his or her own coercive capabilities so as to deter other, potentially opposing individuals. However, because the other, potentially opposing individuals think and act along similar lines, each individual will find reason to expand their own coercive capabilities in the other individual's actions. In organizations we often see processes related to this security-dilemma. Employees who desire to acquire power, authority and control are likely to build the relationships necessary to get it (Burt, Jannotta and Mahoney, 1998), and this may trigger similar actions in colleagues observing such behavior (e.g., Bruins and Wilke, 1993; Krackhardt, 1990; Pfeffer, 1998).

The security-dilemma not only triggers strategic behavior among employees, it also produces coercive action. Jervis (1976, p. 64), a political scientist, observed that: ' ... the drive for security will also produce aggressive actions if the state either requires a very high sense of security or feels menaced by the very presence of other states.' This observation parallels social–psychological research and theory which argues that more coercive capability is associated with more punitive action (Bacharach and Lawler, 1981; Deutsch, 1973; Jervis, 1992). Punitive action is used to deter the opponent from employing coercive capability, and it is used to gain and maintain relative advantage vis-à-vis the opponent. Because using power often depletes power resources it subsequently increases the need to gather additional power, resulting in an ongoing process of gathering and using coercive power to secure and defend oneself against others inside or outside one's organization.

On the basis of the conflict spiral perspective, it can be argued that when the focal negotiator has high rather than low levels of coercive capability, he or she experiences greater control over the negotiation, feels entitled to greater profits, and sets higher aspirations. High rather than low aspirations result in high demands and small concessions (e.g., Siegel and Fouraker, 1960; Yukl, 1974), and more coercive capability induces more threats being uttered, and higher demands being placed.

A study by De Dreu (1995) showed negotiators with less punitive capability than their opponent made relatively small concessions, and placed relatively high demands. Perhaps to avoid looking weak, and to prevent one's relative disadvantage to become even worse, negotiators are tempted to make smaller concessions when their opponent's coercive power is high rather than low. Taken together, findings suggest that negotiations become more hostile and aggressive when there is a power asymmetry rather than power balance – powerful negotiators behave competitively because they feel entitled to a relatively large share, and the powerless negotiators behave competitively to avoid looking weak and to defend themselves as well as possible.

That power asymmetry produces hostile negotiations is consistent with several pieces of evidence in the political sciences (Bueno de Mesquita, 1981; Jervis, 1976), and in social psychology (e.g., Deutsch, 1973). De Dreu (1995) was one of

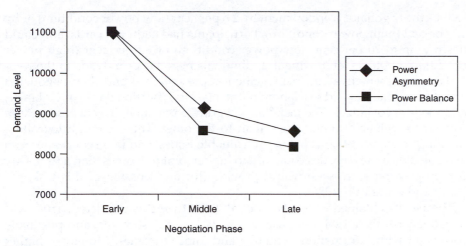

Figure 12.1   Negotiator demands as a function of power asymmetry.

the first to manipulate the negotiator's own and his opponent's coercive capability independently, and thus to provide a clear-cut test of this hypothesis. Findings are summarized in Figure 12.1, which shows that power asymmetry results in higher overall demands, and smaller concessions. Both are indicative of a power struggle.

Power struggle hinders integrative negotiation. Earlier, we described integrative negotiation as the behavior oriented towards increasing the joint utility (i.e., creating value) to be distributed among the parties. Critical in integrative negotiation is *interpersonal trust* – a state involving confident positive expectations about another's motives with respect to oneself in situations entailing risk (Lewicki and Bunker, 1995). Trust is vital, because without it negotiators are reluctant to share information about their preferences and priorities, and without an open and accurate exchange of such information, integrative potential goes unnoticed and negotiators forgo integrative agreements (Pruitt, 1981).

Punitive capability undermines interpersonal trust (Pruitt, 1981). When coercive capability is high rather than low, parties fear one another, which implies low trust, or they behave aggressively, which undermines trust. De Dreu, Giebels and Van de Vliert (1998) tested hypotheses about the effects of punitive capability on trust, information exchange, and integrative agreements. They looked at situations in which both negotiators are equally in power, and they varied whether parties had low or high punitive capability. Punitive capability was manipulated by giving each negotiator an endowment that was vulnerable to attack by the opponent – by flashing a red card the opponent could reduce the negotiator's endowment by 2.5 per cent (low power condition) or by 10 per cent (high power condition). Participants had eight red cards, and could destroy up to 20 per cent (low power condition) or 80 per cent (high power condition) of others' endowment. Individuals negotiated in dyads in the roles of labor-representative and management-representative, and they negotiated about four issues related to a labor-contract (salary, vacation days, annual raise, and medical coverage). The task had integrative potential, in that some issues were more valuable to one party than to the other. Thus, through logrolling (making small concessions on highly valuable issues, and large concessions on less valuable issues) parties could attain higher joint outcomes than a fifty–fifty compromise on each issue would provide (for a discussion of this task, see Pruitt and Carnevale, 1993).

The results obtained by De Dreu et al. (1998) were as predicted. Trust was negatively correlated with the use of threats and punishments, and positively correlated with information exchange and joint outcomes. Moreover, higher levels of punitive capability produced more punitive action, and a greater exchange of threats. Thus, De Dreu et al. concluded that 'these data support our idea that high rather than low levels of punitive capability ... lead to trust-undermining behavior in negotiation' (p. 413). In a second experiment, they showed that trust was negatively related to conflict-avoidance which, in turn, was negatively related to joint outcomes and integrative agreements.

Other studies that speak to the influence of power were conducted by Kim (1997) and Beersma and De Dreu (2002). Kim examined how the temporary presence or absence of high or low power members in a three-person negotiation group would affect integrative agreements. Groups were composed of a high, a medium, and a low power member. During the negotiation either the high or the low power member left the negotiation table temporarily. Results showed that groups in which the low power party left achieved *less* integrative agreements than groups in which either the high power party left, or in which no party left whatsoever. Beersma and De Dreu examined three-person groups that negotiated in a structure that made majority coalitions likely or not. Their results showed that groups achieved less integrative agreements when majority coalitions were likely to emerge, especially when the group did not need the third group member to ratify the agreement (i.e., majority decided, rather than unanimity).

The studies by Kim (1997) and Beersma and De Dreu (2002) strongly suggest that the low power party is important for integrative agreements to be achieved. When the low power party can be excluded from the agreement, or when the low power party temporarily leaves the negotiation table, less integrative agreements are reached. Kim advanced two more or less related explanations for this counter-intuitive pattern. First, because low power negotiators cannot rely on their power to secure good outcomes for themselves, they may simply exert more effort to develop integrative agreements that satisfy their opponents' interests as well as their own. Second, it may be that the presence of low power parties increases integrative complexity in the group. Research on minority influence has shown repeatedly that individuals become less rigid and more creative in their thinking when they are confronted with deviant perspectives forwarded by not too powerful others (for a review, see Nemeth and Staw, 1989). Thus, perhaps the presence and the active contribution of low power members make the group more creative and oriented towards problem-solving, ultimately leading to integrative agreements of high joint value.

Taken together, the research reviewed thus far paints a rather grim picture. Findings indicate that power preponderance tends to escalate the conflict – negotiators place tougher demands, make smaller concessions, and are more likely to use threats and coercive capability to get their way when there is a power difference rather than a power balance. Further, power undermines trust, increases suspicion, and reduces the quality of the negotiated agreement. As Giebels, De Dreu and Van de Vliert (2000, p. 268) conclude: 'the party lacking [power] may be primarily responsible for expanding the resource pie by disclosing more information about own preferences and priorities than the party with [power], who might … [use] this extra information to attain a greater share of the pie.'

Social Categorization and Social Motives

The main conclusion from the review thus far is that power asymmetries induce a power struggle and aggressive negotiation behavior, and that power undermines trust. That power undermines trust and, thereby, reduces the likelihood of reaching integrative agreements points to the critical role of social categorization processes and concomitant social motives – the negotiator's preference for a particular outcome-distribution between him or herself and the opponent (McClintock, 1977). Although an infinite number of social motives can be distinguished, a useful distinction is often made between a selfish and a pro-social motivation. Negotiators with a selfish motivation try to maximize their own outcomes, and they have no, or negative, regard for the outcomes obtained by their opponent. Individuals with a *selfish motive* tend to see the negotiation as a competitive game in which power and personal success are key. In contrast, negotiators with a *pro-social motive* try to maximize both their own and others' outcomes. Negotiators with a pro-social motive tend to see the negotiation as a collaborative game in which fairness, harmony and joint welfare are key.

As mentioned at the outset, social categorization provides an important basis for social motives. A prototypical example is the study by Kramer, Pommerenke, and Newton (1993) in which students engaged in a negotiation simulation with what they thought was a student from the same MBA program (ingroup condition), or someone from an MBA program from a competing school (outgroup condition). Results revealed more cooperative exchange in the ingroup condition than in the outgroup condition, an effect that is very consistent with the basic principles of self-categorization theory (Turner, 1987) and social identity theory (Tajfel and Turner, 1986).

Social motives not only derive from social categorization processes. Research has shown that social motives may be rooted in individual differences in social value orientations (McClintock, 1977; Van Lange and Kuhlman, 1994). For example, De Dreu and Van Lange (1995) found that individuals with a pro-social value orientation made more concessions and perceived their opponent as more fair and trustworthy than did negotiators with a selfish value orientation. In a study involving employees from several large manufacturing firms, Nauta, De Dreu, and Van der Vaart (2002) found that employees with a pro-social value orientation valued the goals and interests from partners in other departments more than employees with a selfish value orientation. Pro-social employees were also more likely to adopt a problem-solving approach to negotiations with employees from other departments.

Perhaps more in line with the great number of studies in the area of self-categorization and social identity processes (for reviews, see Hogg, 2001), social motives may be cued externally, by instructions from superiors, reinforcement schemes, or social relationships (e.g., De Dreu and McCusker, 1997; Sattler and Kerr, 1991). For example, Deutsch (1958) used instructions to induce pro-social and egoistic motives. In the pro-social motive condition, participants were instructed to be concerned about the other's feelings and welfare, and to see the other as 'partner'. In the selfish motive condition, participants were instructed to disregard the other and to do as well for themselves as possible. Other research used monetary incentives to induce social motives. Participants in pro-social motive conditions were told that payment depended on how they did *as a dyad*, while participants in the selfish motive conditions were told that payment depended on how they did *personally* (see, e.g., Deutsch, 1973). Social motive can also be manipulated indirectly by having negotiators anticipate future interaction with their opponent or not (Ben-Yoav and Pruitt, 1984), by emphasizing shared or unshared group membership (Kramer et al., 1993), or by having them negotiate with a friend versus a stranger (Fry, Firestone and Williams, 1983).

In a meta-analytical review of the studies on social motivation in integrative negotiation, De Dreu et al. (2000) contrasted effects on joint outcomes of: (1) individual differences (mainly social value orientation), (2) incentives, (3) instructions, and (4) implicit cues likely to trigger social categorization processes (group membership, future interaction, friend vs stranger). All four categories yielded positive and significant effect sizes, indicating that pro-social negotiators achieved higher joint outcomes than selfish negotiators. Importantly, De Dreu et al. found no significant differences in effect sizes between the four classes. This suggests that the various ways of manipulating or measuring social motives in negotiation are *functionally equivalent* – they may have different roots, but similar effects.

The important role of social categorization processes and concomitant social motives in relation to power has been demonstrated by Tjosvold (1985). Students became managers with either high or low power, and were led to believe that their goals were cooperatively, individualistically, or competitively, linked to those of their subordinates. Results showed that social motives affect how superiors use their power to interact with their subordinates. When a pro-social rather than an egotistic motive prevailed, high and low power managers interacted constructively, responded to requests for assistance, and developed positive relationships with their subordinates.

Tripp (1993) examined negotiators' reward allocation behavior as a function of the goal to maximize their own outcomes versus the goal to appear fair, and whether the negotiator had more or equal power. The critical dependent variable in this study was the distributive inequality – a positive (negative) score indicating that the negotiator got more (less) than his or her opponent. Results revealed an interaction between power distribution and goal, showing that negotiators with equal power as their opponent got about the same outcome as their opponent regardless of their goal. But when negotiators had a power advantage, they allocated more to themselves than to their opponent when they had the goal to maximize personal outcomes and they allocated *less* to themselves when they had the goal of appearing fair. Thus, powerful negotiators who strive to look fair allocate more resources to their subordinates than they should based on distributive justice principles – they over-stretch a little and benefit their subordinate to their own disadvantage.

In their review of this and other work, Lee and Tiedens (2001) conclude that high power individuals may be quite decent people:

> High power individuals are also more likely than low power individuals to interact constructively with the subordinate, restate the task in a helpful way, respond to requests for help, as well as seek help when needed ... Overall, high power individuals are more likely to be characterized as sensitive, socially adept, popular, supportive, trustworthy, helpful, and likable ... High power people are more likely to go out of their way to compliment others ... cooperate with others, ..., be altruistic and giving ... try to get others into a good mood ..., and build relationships and trust... (2001, p. 63).

While the review by Lee and Tiedens (2001) related to power in general, Giebels, De Dreu, and Van de Vliert (1998, 2000) studied the interactions between social motives and power in integrative negotiation. In their experiments, power was manipulated by reducing or not reducing the negotiator's dependence on the opponent by giving or not giving him or her an exit option – the possibility to leave the negotiation and start negotiations with someone else, with perhaps better outcomes. For example, Giebels et al. (2000) examined integrative negotiation as a function of none, one, or both dyad members having an exit option (having versus not having an exit option makes one less dependent on the opponent, and thus more powerful). In addition, they manipulated social motives by telling dyad members to see each other as opponents (selfish motivation), or as partners (pro-social motivation). Results showed that dyads with a one-sided exit option engaged in less exchange of information, had less of a problem-solving approach, and obtained less integrative agreements than did dyads with either two-sided or no exit options. This effect occurred only, however, in the case of selfish motivation, and not when negotiators had a pro-social motivation. Figure 12.2 summarizes the results from Giebels et al. (2000).

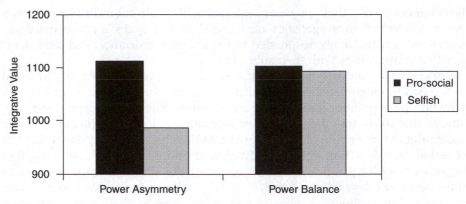

Figure 12.2 Intergrativeness of negotiated agreement as a function of social motivation and power asymmetry.

The findings obtained by Giebels et al. (2000) are important because they show that social motives play a critical role in determining whether, and how, power affects negotiation processes and outcomes. The findings indicate that the inevitable power asymmetry between managers and their subordinates does not necessarily lead to a contentious exchange geared towards lose-lose agreements. When a pro-social motivation is activated, the negative effects of a power asymmetry are mitigated and constructive negotiation with high joint outcomes is the result.

Power and Information Processing

Power not only influences strategic choice such as demand level and the use of threats. It also drives the processing of information about other people (e.g., Fiske, 1992; Chapter 11). The idea is that when people depend on others they may seek to (re)gain control over their own outcomes by paying close attention to the powerful other so as to be able to accurately predict and anticipate the other's intentions and behaviors. Erber and Fiske (1984) argued that when people's outcomes depend on others, they are motivated to be able to control and predict the other person's behavior. In two studies, they showed that outcome dependency produced a heightened attention to information that was inconsistent with the perceiver's expectations of the other person. In a similar vein, Neuberg and Fiske (1987) showed that outcome dependency increases the tendency to rely on individual attributes rather than stereotypes when forming impressions about others, and they also showed that accuracy motivation mediated the effects of outcome dependency on impression formation. Finally, Goodwin, Gubin, Fiske and Yzerbyt (2000) showed that power increased decision-makers' attention to stereotypic attributes, and decreased attention to counter-stereotypic attributes. Also, these authors showed that, relative to powerless perceivers, powerful perceivers' impressions were less based on target's traits, supporting the attention results (see also, Goodwin, Chapter 11).

Power and information search in negotiation

While the research by Fiske and colleagues greatly illuminates our understanding of the socio-cognitive consequences of having a power advantage or disadvantage, it remains unclear whether these processes generalize to the context of negotiation with its relatively conflict-laden character and its great incentive on truly understanding one's opponent. Granted, Ruscher and Fiske (1990; Vonk, 1999) argued and showed that these processes apply to cooperative as well as to competitive settings, but this work does not speak to the influence of differences in power and dependency in a negotiation setting. Thus, it cannot be excluded beforehand that in negotiation settings people individuate their opponent regardless of the power position they have. In addition, and perhaps more importantly, the work on power, dependency, and impression formation has not been extended to include information search strategies. That is, we do not know whether the effects of power remain confined to encoding and retrieval processes or extend to information search strategies as well.

In a series of experiments, De Dreu and Van Kleef (2002) examined the influence of power on negotiators' information search strategies. They argued that information gathering behavior in negotiation often takes place by asking one's opponent questions. People ask questions to test their pre-existing cognitive structures, and questions can be diagnostic or leading. Diagnostic questions can often be answered with a simple yes or no and provide direct evidence for or against the pre-existing cognitive structure. Leading questions, in contrast, are likely to yield answers that are perceived as consistent with the pre-existing cognitive structure, regardless of whether this structure is correct or not (Snyder, 1992). Diagnostic questions allow the individual to develop a more accurate impression of the opposing negotiator than do leading questions (e.g., Biesanz, Neuberg, Smith, Asher, and Judice, 2001).

Based on the work by Fiske and colleagues discussed above, it was predicted that, compared to high power negotiators, those with a power disadvantage should be more inclined to ask diagnostic rather than leading questions. De Dreu (raw data) tested this prediction by having negotiators with more or less power than their opponent select, from a prewritten list, questions they would like to ask their opponent. The list contained diagnostic and leading questions. It contained ten diagnostic questions and ten leading questions. Examples of diagnostic questions used are 'Have you negotiated before?,' and 'Do you see yourself as a skilled negotiator?' Examples of leading question used are 'How did you perform in other negotiations you've conducted?' and 'What makes you a skilled negotiator?' Leading and diagnostic questions were about the same topics and used, as much as possible, the same words and terminology.

This reduced the possibility that the distinction between leading and diagnostic questions was confounded with some unknown third variable. A pre-test with 15 students who rated the leading and diagnostic questions used in the experiment in terms of comprehensibility, competitiveness, and friendliness revealed no significant differences between leading and diagnostic questions.

Results are presented in Figure 12.3. As can be seen, negotiators with a low power position had a much stronger preference for diagnostic questions than negotiators with a high power position. In subsequent research, De Dreu and Van Kleef (2002) replicated this finding when participants generated their own questions. An important qualification found in this subsequent research was that the pattern presented in Figure 12.3 was found only when the opponent was believed to be competitive. When the opponent was believed to be cooperative, no differences between low and high power negotiators were observed, and no preference for a particular type of question was found. Thus, as in other research, it seems that motivational goals moderate the effects of power.

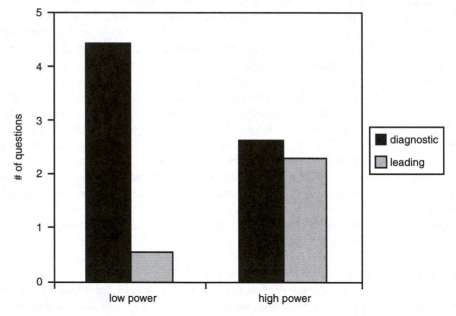

Figure 12.3   Number of diagnostic and leading questions asked by negotiators with more or less power than their counterpart.

Power and biased perceptions of negotiation behavior

Humans have the unique ability to reflect on themselves and to develop self-perceptions that are of stunning complexity. One of the key findings of over 80 years of research is that humans are essentially egocentric in their orientation towards others and that evaluations of the self are positively biased (Greenwald, 1980). For example, there is abundant evidence that people tend to interpret behaviors, events and outcomes in ways that have favorable implications for the self (Taylor and Brown, 1988). People take credit for success and they deny responsibility for failure (Ross and Sicoly, 1979). People are more likely to ascribe positive personality traits to themselves than to others, whereas negative traits are seen as more descriptive of others than of the self (Brown, 1990). For instance, people evaluate themselves as fairer, more moral, and more honest than the average other (e.g., Messick, Bloom, Boldizar and Samuelson, 1985). In sum, people reconstruct their past, present and future so that the self appears more favorable than it actually is (Greenwald, 1980).

The tendency to view oneself as more positive and less negative than others is present in conflict and negotiation settings as well and has important behavioral consequences. For example, Thompson and Loewenstein (1992) showed that students negotiating a labor dispute displayed self-serving assessments of what neutral third parties would see as fair wages. Also, the greater the self-servingness of these assessments, the longer temporary impasses lasted. De Dreu, Nauta, and Van de Vliert (1995) showed that professional negotiators view their own negotiation behavior as more constructive and less destructive than both the average other negotiator and their immediate opponent. This study further showed that higher levels of self-serving bias were associated with a reduced likelihood of settlement, less integrative negotiation, and greater probability of future conflict.

Nauta, de Vries, and Wijngaard (2001) examined whether power differences between departments in 11 manufacturing organizations were associated with biased perceptions of own negotiation behavior. Through questionnaires they obtained employees' assessments of negotiation behavior performed by their own department (sales or planning) and the other department (planning or sales). Results confirmed that sales departments were seen as the more powerful department, while planning departments were seen as less powerful. Moreover, results revealed a self-serving bias similar to the one found earlier by De Dreu et al. (1995): employees reported that they engaged in more problem solving and in less contending than negotiators from the other department. Most importantly, however, it appeared that powerful negotiators viewed their own contending behavior as similar to that of their low power counterparts, while powerless negotiators viewed their powerful opponents to engage in more contending than they did.

The results obtained by Nauta et al. (2001) indicate that powerful negotiators may be more prone to a self-serving bias than powerless negotiators, a conclusion that fits well with the general idea about information processing forwarded by Fiske (1992): powerless negotiators engage in effortful and systematic processing of information. As a result, they ask more diagnostic questions, develop more accurate perceptions of their opponent and, finally, they are less subject to self-serving bias.

Power and the self fulfilling prophecy

Various authors have speculated that some information search strategies may result in sub-optimal negotiation processes and outcomes (e.g., Rubin et al., 1994). De Dreu and Van Kleef (2002; Exp. 3) conducted an experiment to further understanding of the consequences of information search (i.e., asking diagnostic or leading questions), and the moderating influence of power. In general, leading questions are more likely to induce a self-fulfilling prophecy than are diagnostic questions (for a review, see Snyder, 1992). In negotiation, a self-fulfilling prophecy means that individuals respond with low demands when they are asked questions about their cooperative goals and intentions, and with high demands when they are asked questions about their competitive goals and intentions. Because leading questions are more likely to induce a self-fulfilling prophecy, this effect may be stronger when questions are leading rather than diagnostic.

De Dreu and Van Kleef (2002) reasoned that this pattern should be stronger when negotiators have low rather than high power. Low power negotiators are motivated to pay close attention to their powerful opponent, and to please him or her, while those with high power are more likely to operate on the basis of their own instead of the opponent's wishes and demands. Accordingly, lower demands are expected when negotiators have low rather than high power, but especially when their opponent asks leading rather than diagnostic questions about cooperative rather than competitive goals and intentions. They tested this prediction in an experiment where participants with low or high power negotiated with a (pre-programmed) opponent who asked leading or diagnostic questions about cooperation or competition.

Results showed that demand level of high power negotiators is not influenced by the low power opponent's questions. Demands by low power negotiators are, however, lower when the high power opponent asked about cooperation rather than competition, especially when questions were leading rather than diagnostic. These data suggest that low power negotiators are more susceptible to the self-fulfilling prophecy than are high power negotiators.

Conclusions

In this chapter we have reviewed research on power in negotiation. Our review suggests several conclusions about the influence of power, and several avenues for future research. The first conclusion is that power preponderance in negotiation is detrimental and should be avoided. Negotiators place tougher demands, make smaller concessions, and are more likely to use threats and coercive capability to get their way when there is a power difference rather than a power balance. Furthermore, power undermines trust, increases suspicion, and reduces the likelihood of integrative agreements that provide all parties involved with good value.

The second conclusion is that negotiators with a power disadvantage have a critical role in the negotiation process that is often underestimated. Low power parties engage in more integrative negotiation; they may reduce rigidity of thought and stimulate divergent thinking; they engage in more systematic and less biased information processing and search; and their information search strategies are unlikely to lead themselves and their (high power) opponents into a self-fulfilling prophecy. These positive and constructive contributions to the negotiation process do not necessarily pay off, however, as the high power negotiators may claim the lion-share of the value created by their low power opponents.

The third conclusion is about the negotiator with relative high power. While powerful negotiators are often depicted as utterly egotistic, greedy, and untrustworthy individuals, research evidence suggests otherwise. Recall Lee and Tiedens (2001) who wrote that 'high power individuals are more likely to be characterized as sensitive, socially adept, popular, supportive, trustworthy, helpful, and likable ... High power people are more likely to go out of their way to compliment others ... cooperate with others, ..., be altruistic and giving ..., try to get others into a good mood ... and build relationships and trust...' (p. 63). Indeed, our review of the negotiation literature suggested a similar pattern, albeit under very specific circumstances – when a pro-social motive has been made salient, and not when selfish goals prevail. Thus, managers and organizational leaders are likely to negotiate constructively with their subordinates when they categorize themselves as part of the same social category and have a pro-social motivation. When they see each other as part of a different social category and when they are selfishly motivated, however, they are most likely to use their powerful position to do well for themselves, perhaps even at the expense of their low power subordinate.

Pfeffer (1998) noted that negotiation is among the basic skills managers and leaders need to function effectively. This review points to a barrier to effective functioning that is inherent in every relationship between managers and their subordinates. That is, managers have more power than subordinates, and power asymmetries are likely to lead to contentious exchanges, undermined trust, and collectively poor outcomes. Fortunately, however, the research reviewed here also points to a variable that is under the control of managers and organizational leaders – when parties have a pro-social rather than selfish motivation, the negative consequences of power asymmetries are reduced, and negotiations develop more constructively, allowing all parties involved to realize their aspirations. One determinant of the social motives managers and leaders adopt is how they categorize themselves and their subordinate. When the subordinates are seen as being part of the ingroup, constructive negotiation processes may be expected and the result will often be an integrative agreement that serves the manager as well as the subordinate. When the subordinate is categorized as part of the outgroup, more hostile attitudes develop and cognitive and motivational processes conspire against constructive negotiation, and poor outcomes, especially for the low power subordinate, are the likely result.

Acknowledgments

Preparation of this chapter has been facilitated and financially supported by grants from the Netherlands Organization for Scientific Research (NWO 560-271-011; NWO 560-31-006) and the Royal Netherlands Academy of Sciences, awarded to Carsten K.W. De Dreu. We thank the editors for their constructive comments on a previous version of this chapter.

13 Aberrations of Power: Leadership in Totalist Groups

ROBERT S. BARON, KEVIN
CRAWLEY, AND DIANA PAULINA

Few phenomena provoke more interest in the concept of leadership than the power exerted by leaders in totalist groups. Whether we consider such cult behavior as mass marriages, mass suicides, or voluntary castrations, the power of such leaders to induce their members to ignore logic, self-interest and the entreaties of family members is undeniable. This chapter offers a number of suggestions regarding the basis of such power using three groups as highly typical examples of cult indoctrination. In such groups, members exhibit remarkable levels of obedience to authority following a period of systematic and intense indoctrination. It is this feature that marks the totalist group in our view (Baron, 2000). These case study descriptions will provide us with a vehicle for considering the factors that contribute to the unique nature of leadership in totalist groups.

Relevant Theories of Leadership

French and Raven's power model

One defining aspect of leadership in totalist groups is the unilateral power of the group leader. Checks and balances of power are rarely present in totalist groups. Indeed, purges frequently remove anyone who might challenge the leader's power (e.g., Davis, 1984; Ofshe, 1980). Thus, French and Raven's (1959) model is quite relevant to our discussion given the multidimensional nature of leader power in such groups (Forsyth, 1999). Typically such leaders are adept at controlling most dimensions of power identified by this model. Public humiliation and corporal punishment (i.e., coercive power) is common. These leaders generally have high reward power, controlling most of the financial, social and sexual resources of the group (e.g., Reavis, 1998). The expert-informational power of such leaders is high due to such factors as education, status as seer-guru or media-based reputation. In the three groups we spotlight, informational and coercive power was amplified by encouraging mutual spying among group members (e.g. Layton, 1998). Thus, these leaders could appear omniscient regarding member actions and feelings; an 'ability' Jim Jones (see p. 239) liked to display by revealing embarrassing facts about unfortunate followers at group meetings.

Formal acknowledgement of totalist leaders either by church ordination or media recognition, helps establish the legitimate power of these individuals. Finally, such leaders have a great deal of referent power. They are deeply admired by their followers who view them with profound reverence. One reflection of multidimensional and unilateral power enjoyed by totalist leaders is their ability to maintain group loyalty despite moving the group through various transformations. The People's Temple, originally a fundamentalist Christian Church, evolved into a socialist 'movement' complete with an armed security force, a media specialist, and so on. (Maaga, 1998). Synanon, initially a drug treatment program, emerged after several years as a religious movement (Gerstel, 1982).

A social identity model of leadership

The social identity view of leadership (e.g. Hogg, 2001: Hogg, et al. 1998; Chapters 3 and 4) also offers a perspective that seems quite relevant to totalist groups. Hogg (2001) describes leadership that is conferred upon those individuals who most closely adhere to prototypic group norms. Such norms tend to be displaced away from outgroup positions in an attempt to emphasize ingroup similarity while at the same time maximizing how the ingroup differs from salient outgroups. This form of leadership emergence is thought to occur when group identification and group salience is high (Hogg, 2001). Totalist groups clearly qualify. In totalist groups, members draw on their affiliation as a primary source of self-definition (e.g., Hoffer, 1951). Moreover, in such groups, the salience of one's group membership is kept extremely high by such means as physical separation, distinctive group dress, jargon, and so on.

According to the social identity perspective (Hogg and van Knippenberg, in press), leaders emerge in such settings because 'prototypic individuals' are viewed as models and are accorded high sociometric status thereby enhancing their persuasive power. These leaders are imbued by their followers with charismatic traits, due to the fundamental attributional error of seeing individuals as the causes of action. This last phenomenon is well represented in totalist groups in which leaders are literally deified by the membership. Hogg recognizes, however, that leaders who receive such adulation will often be accorded a status that marks them as 'different'. If so, they will increasingly have to maintain control of the group by relying on coercive or reward power as they will forgo their status as in-group prototypes. Hogg (2001) suggests that this pattern of leadership is particularly likely to characterize cults in their later stages.

Tranformation theory

Theories emphasizing the charismatic features of leaders (see House and Shamir, 1993) are highly relevant to totalist groups. A modern example of this category, Bass's theory of transformational leadership (e.g. Bass, 1998), combines a transactional perspective (focusing on exchange relationships between leaders and followers) with a charismatic approach. The transactional aspect of this model is that leaders receive power and status in return for facilitating the goal attainment of followers. According to this model, if the leader also has certain charismatic traits, she/he should be particularly adept at convincing followers to work for common goals, while ignoring their own vested interests. Bass argues that such a leader is well suited to evoking change or 'transformation' in groups, particularly change motivated by needs for self-actualization.

Some charismatic elements mentioned by Bass include: (1) intellectual stimulation (offering creative solutions and encouraging innovation in others), (2) individualized reaction to member needs and abilities, and (3) the ability to inspire and motivate followers. Effective transformational leaders should be innovative, should actively reward correct action (as opposed to punishing incorrect behavior), and, most crucially, should offer the group some transcendent purpose, mission or messianic goal. Bass (1998), like Hogg (2001), recognizes that members of the group may exaggerate the positive features of such leaders by amplifying their perceived charisma. Effective transformational leaders, however, will, in fact, manifest the three charismatic elements listed above.

From a transactional (or exchange) perspective, totalist groups provide members with a sense of mission, purpose, belonging, and the benefit of not having to agonize over various life decisions (which are dictated by the group's norms). The group in turn imbues the leader with exaggerated positive attributes, extreme power, as well as privilege, gladly tolerating the leader's violation of particular aspects of group doctrine. Thus, a surprisingly high number of totalist leaders have had erotic and material perks that were strictly forbidden to others (e.g., Davis, 1984; Kelley, 1995). Moreover, in accordance with this theoretical perspective, leaders in such groups invariably offer members a messianic purpose that most frequently requires members to override their immediate self-interest in lieu of some self-actualizing and transcendent common group goal (Baron, 2000; Hoffer, 1951).

From a charismatic perspective, leaders in totalist groups typically are confident decision-makers, accomplished speakers and imaginative at generating messianic group goals. As such, they generally qualify as 'stimulating and inspiring' (e.g., Weightman, 1983; Ofshe, 1980). However, in several key respects, leaders in totalist groups deviate from the charismatic pattern that Bass considers to be defining features for transformational leadership. Bass assumes such leaders encourage group member innovation, do not prematurely criticize ideas that contradict group policy, act in an unselfish and morally correct fashion and use a contingent reward system that justly rewards individuals based on their efforts and investments. Such leaders also depict an optimistic future. In contrast, Bass describes pseudo-transformational leaders who, while having many of the trappings of the transformational leader, cater to their own self-interest, rely on manipulation, fear, threat, and punishment to maintain control and seem to be governed by warped moral principles (Bass, 1998). It appears that leadership in totalist groups nicely illustrates this pattern of pseudo-transformational leadership. Thus, in such groups, leaders do not consistently use 'contingent' rewards to compensate followers on a basis that is commensurate with their contributions, tend to punish transgressions more than they reward correct behavior, and do not rise above self-interest. The case studies we consider below explore these themes.

The Effects of Intense Indoctrination on Leadership in Totalist Groups

Several key factors elevate the power of leaders in such 'high demand' groups. One such factor is that the identity-related benefits provided by group membership (Hogg, in press) are particularly gratifying for group members. As a result, members find themselves unusually dependent upon the group (i.e., the leader), for guidance, self-esteem and a sense of purpose, etc. A second factor involves the impact that totalist groups have on the attentional capacity of group members and how this in turn causes and maintains attitude change in such groups (Baron, 2000).

Numerous writers have noted that several social psychological processes appear crucial in triggering the attitude and value change that occurs in totalist groups. These include such processes as conformity dynamics, stereotyping of non-group members, group polarization, biased and incomplete message processing, and cognitive dissonance mechanisms that stem from inducing escalating commitments from group members (Pratkanis and Aronson, 2000, Schein, Schneier and Barker, 1961; Singer, 1995). Various writers have also commented on the stress and capacity-draining activity associated with group indoctrination and membership (e.g., Baron, 2000; Sargant, 1957). Sleep deprivation is extremely common in totalist groups with long work days and heavily regimented activity being an almost universal feature (Pratkanis and Aronson, 2000). Emotional arousal is frequently manipulated in such groups; such arousal is thought itself to deplete attentional capacity (Eysenck, 1977).

Baron (1986, 2000) has argued that such stress and capacity depletion heightens the various social psychological processes alluded to above (see also Bodenhousen, 1993). Several studies indicate that fear and arousal decrease the likelihood that individuals will notice and react to logical flaws in a persuasive message while elevating the tendency of individuals to be influenced by superficial aspects of a message such as the reactions of the audience, or the presumed credentials of the speaker (e.g., Baron, Inman, Kao and Logan, 1992; Sanbonmatsu and Kardis, 1988). Similarly, fear has been shown to elevate stereotyping (Baron et al., 1992; Keinan et al., 2000), compliance (Dolinski and

Nawrat, 1998), conformity (Darley, 1966), and cognitive dissonance generated attitude change (Pittman, 1975).

Given that life in totalist groups often entails emotional manipulations, sleep deprivation, high levels of regimented and required activity, and inadequate nutrition, there is ample reason to assume that attentional capacity is compromised in such groups, thereby heightening group members' susceptibility to a variety of persuasion manipulations. It is likely that such stress and the attentional depletion it causes, will also affect leadership dynamics in such groups. This argument is based on several key assumptions. The first is that low capacity increases the power differential between members and leader regarding expert and informational power. If stress does lower attentional capacity (or even if it just decreases confidence in one's capacity) one is rendered more dependent on a confident, informed, and well-credentialed leader to provide interpretations of events, as well as pre-packaged solutions and decisions.

The second assumption is that the stress of indoctrination lowers the self-confidence and self-efficacy of group members. Numerous reports support this view (e.g., Singer, 1995). Thus, a common indoctrination feature within totalist groups are recurrent instances where individuals must submit to detailed criticism, confession and other acts of mortification (e.g., Baron, 2000; Hinkle and Wolff, 1956). Moreover, members in totalist groups are often placed in the position of having to adjust to unusual group norms while trying to master an unfamiliar and complex doctrine or skill set, be it political, quasi-scientific or religious. This confusion, coupled with criticism of the individual member from within the group, is sufficient to shake the confidence of all but the most self-resilient (Lifton, 1961). Such attacks on self-efficacy and self-esteem make identification with the group very attractive. It has been assumed for some time that group identification is a very effective means of bolstering self-esteem or of 'escaping' from an inadequate self (Hoffer, 1951). It follows that the more inadequate one feels about oneself, the greater the allure of a totalist group.

A related idea is that these attacks on the member's confidence and self-efficacy, render the member more dependent on the group (in cults this means the group leader) for guidance, interpretation, explanation and normative control over activity and choices. As Hogg (2001) points out, one benefit of committed group membership and identification is that group norms reduce uncertainty regarding what to think, feel and do. Hogg (in press) extends this logic by arguing that people who experience uncertainty regarding their self-concept should be particularly attracted to distinctive groups characterized by unique, clear norms that produce high group entitativity – a common feature of totalist groups. Thus, uncertainty is viewed as a factor that heightens normative power. Interestingly, normative control has been found to be particularly strong in cases in which group members' task confidence is low (Bond and Smith, 1996) and the salience of group membership is very high (Abrams et al., 1990), as is the case in totalist groups. Indeed, recent research indicates that the more one conforms to the dictates of such highly salient, confident and self-referential groups, the better one feels about oneself (Pool et al., 1998) and the more confident one feels about the decision (Baron et al., 1996).

Thus, cult leaders have access to a double-edged sword. They use various techniques to assault the members' individual sense of self-adequacy while at the same time offering the group's messianic purpose as a means of transcending these feelings of doubt, meaninglessness, and low self-worth. In accord with this view, Galanter (1989) reported that established members of totalist groups report lower levels of neurotic distress than neophyte members. Thus, group identification offers members more than just the simple social benefits of affiliation and acceptance. It provides a means of alleviating anxiety, reducing decisional conflict and elevating feelings of uniqueness and self-worth. In summary, the low attentional capacity engendered by the features of life in many totalist groups not only heightens the impact of persuasive manipulations, but it elevates the power and allure of those in a position of leadership. This will be evident in the discussion we present below of leadership within three totalist groups.

The People's Temple

Background

Jim Jones founded the People's Temple in Indianapolis in 1955. By 1965, he had moved the church with about 70 followers to the San Francisco Bay Area where most lived in a communal compound (Maaga, 1998). From its earliest days, Jones's ministry combined elements of fundamentalist Christianity (e.g., faith healing) with progressive positions on racial and economic issues (Maaga, 1998). As a result, by 1967 Jones was a politically connected and well-known public figure in Bay Area politics. In California, he began to exert wide control over the personal decisions of those in his congregation. Monies and property were donated to the Temple, parents complied with Jones's direction that they allow their children to be raised by other parishioners, and married couples discontinued living together if so ordered (e.g., Layton, 1998; Weightman, 1983). Church meetings often became forums for public criticism of parishioners which were punctuated with physical and psychological discipline (Layton, 1998). Jones regularly engaged in extramarital heterosexual and homosexual liaisons with group members. (Maaga, 1998; Layton, 1998).

In the period from 1976–77, Jones had almost all members of the Peoples Temple move to the jungle compound that was Jonestown, Guyana. In Guyana, Jones showed increasing evidence of paranoid ideation, depression, and bizarre behavior (Layton, 1998). Group members regularly worked 12-hour days at arduous tasks on a protein deficient diet. Workdays were followed by prolonged group meetings after which loudspeakers would broadcast Jones's harangues long into the night. The group's commitment to 'revolutionary suicide' was discussed and practised in several all night sessions. This 'practice' turned into reality when Jones ordered a group suicide shortly after his security personnel assassinated visiting Congressman Leo Ryan. Over 900 individuals perished. Audio tapes made that night indicated that there was high initial group commitment for this action (*Weekly Edition*, January 23, 1999).

Theoretical Analysis of the People's Temple

Social identity theory

In accord with the social identity view of leadership (Hogg, 2001), group salience in the People's Temple was quite high, as were levels of group identification. There is little doubt that Jones's attitudes on everything from religion to socialism were admired, and almost by definition viewed as prototypically normative by the group. A key feature of Temple norms involved disparaging views of various out-groups (fascists, CIA, etc.). This all echoes social identity theory's emphasis on ingroup members maximizing their differences from outgroups. Over time Jones redefined the social identity of the group. This entailed gradually changing which positions, attitudes and behaviors were deemed prototypical for group members – a strategy identified by Hogg (2001) as a tactic used by leaders to maintain their position as prototypic individuals. This tactic is presumed to rely on the fact that by changing the group prototype, the leader assures that he, more than anyone else, continues to best embody this prototypic standard.

However, Jones was never viewed as a prototypic group member of the People's Temple by his followers. From the outset he was viewed as unique and superior. Nor did his leadership emerge because his attitudes and behaviors happened to coincide with the group's protoyptic norms. Rather, Jones established what the norms would be by dint of his own opinions. In addition, while group members undoubtedly inflated Jones's exceptional characteristics, his charisma was not just a function of this attributional bias. Rather it stemmed from exceptional skill at public speaking, identifying meaningful goals (e.g., racial equality), and his supreme confidence. It is true that Jones used increasing degrees of coercive control over time, but this seems primarily due to his psychological deterioration (Layton, 1998) rather than to his gradually being perceived as a 'non-group' member.

Transformational theory

Bass's (1998) construct of pseudo-transformational leadership provides a better description of leadership within the People's Temple. Members certainly derived a number of the psychological benefits we mention above from their group affiliation while Jones certainly accrued multiple benefits as well. Thus, both Jones and his followers could be viewed as being in the type of exchange relationship emphasized by a transactional approach. Jones also captured a good many of the charismatic features stressed by Bass, such as inspirational leadership (messianic goals, dynamic style, etc.), individual consideration of group members' needs and abilities, and an innovative, self-actualizing agenda for group members. On the other hand, Jones was intolerant of dissent, reveled in public criticism of members, was highly manipulative and deceptive relating to members (healings were staged, clairvoyant abilities faked, etc.), and clearly emphasized his own self-interest and privileges when governing the group. In addition, his own moral sense appeared twisted and abnormal. Jones would seem to be a prime exemple of the pseudo-transformational leader. This form of leadership is thought to be both ineffective and a source of stress for group members. It is not hard to make this case when considering the history and sad demise of this group.

Synanon

Background

Synanon was a residential drug treatment group founded in California by Chuck Dederich, in 1958. Synanon's treatment was based on the 'Game', a confrontational group session during which participants critically considered the defences and illusions that sustained their substance abuse. Within months, Synanon claimed to be an effective means of controlling not only alcoholism but drug addiction too. Between 1958 and 1968, the group processed over 5,000 individuals (Gerstel, 1982).

The purported success of this program as a treatment for drug addiction was based primarily on unsubstantiated reports in the press (Ofshe, 1980). While it is likely that members did remain drug-free and sober while in residence (given the no-nonsense, confrontational Synanon approach), there is little formal documentation that Synanon provided a successful cure for individuals who moved to non-resident status (Ofshe, 1980). In time, such graduation ceased to be a goal of the organisation. Its fame as a successful drug program led to donations, grants and expansion that permitted it to open businesses staffed by (unpaid) Synanon members (Gerstel, 1982). By 1967, Synanon had over 800 members in various residence facilities and had begun to admit non-addicted individuals from the community. The Game was offered as a powerful, albeit traumatic, means of self-exploration. Obviously it also served as a blunt instrument of punishment and control.

In 1968, Dederich formally re-conceptualized Synanon as a communal living experiment open to all. Entry required attending 'boot camp' complete with sleep loss, vigorous exercise and other humiliating initiation activities. Game 'marathons' lasting over 24 hours became common at this point. (Gerstel, 1984). By 1975 Dederich had declared Synanon to be a religion, renounced his vows of poverty, allocated himself a substantial salary, and established a luxury residence for himself and his entourage. Dederich could broadcast at will to all Synanon locations and used this communication system, 'the wire', to humiliate any Synanon member who displeased him (e.g., Gerstel, 1984).

Promiscuous sexual activity at Synanon had long been tolerated and, by 1977, was actively encouraged as a means of establishing 'mutual love' among group members (Gerstel, 1984). Dederich's power was reflected in the effectiveness of this edict even among married members as well as his success encouraging abortion and vasectomies for group members (Ofshe, 1980). By the mid 1970s, the group had abandoned non-violence and formed armed security details designed to 'protect' the group from outsiders as well as to discipline unruly members – particularly resistant adolescents. By 1975, these security personnel had engaged in physical attacks on local neighbors, the beating of an ex-Synanon member, and a case in which an 'enemy' attorney was bitten by a rattlesnake placed in his mailbox – a crime that eventually resulted in Dederich's accepting a plea bargain of five years' probation (Gerstel, 1984). Synanon then lost a series of lawsuits stemming from the physical assaults made by the group. The IRS revoked their tax-exempt status in 1986. Synanon was formally disbanded in 1991, and in 1997 Chuck Dederich died of heart and lung failure in California where he was living in a trailer park (Yee, 1997).

Theoretical analyses of Synanon

Social identity theory

In accord with a social identity view, group salience in Synanon was high given the residential nature of membership. Similarly, given the initiation ordeals, it is safe to assume that among those who chose to remain, group commitment and identification were very high (Baron, 2001; Pratkanis and Aronson, 2000). Moreover, the intense mortification process entailed in Gaming, recurrently encountered by both neophytes and veterans, was specifically designed to challenge members' feelings of esteem and self-efficacy – conditions we have emphasized earlier as facilitating conditions for group identification. Given that Dederich lived among the other members, participated in Games on a weekly basis, and for years did not take obvious material advantage of his leadership position, one could argue that he was viewed as a prototypic group member. Thus, Dederich was deeply admired within the group and his opinions on a wide range of issues (from sexual promiscuity to the need for brutal mutual criticism) defined normative opinion and behavior within the group. In addition, Dederich took positions that differentiated him from those outside the group on a number of issues (e.g., private property, promiscuity). Thus, conforming to his 'prototypic' opinions helped establish the distinction between Synanon members and those outside the group. In short, in several respects, Dederich's leadership style corresponds to that outlined by social identity theory.

However, as above, Dederich did not emerge as a leader because his attitudes and behaviors happened to correspond to prototypic group norms. Rather, as creator of the group, such norms were defined by whichever opinions and actions he favored. This fact does not correspond to the analysis offered by Hogg (2001). In addition, while there is little doubt that Dederich's leadership stemmed in part from his prototypic status as Hogg's analysis maintains, it is clear that his aura of charisma was due to his abilities as a speaker, manager, and innovator, over and above any attributional bias on the part of his membership. On the other hand, Hogg's suggestion that leaders come to rely more on coercive and reward power as they begin to distance themselves from the group is congruent with the fact that Dederich expanded his use of physical discipline as he adopted luxurious privileges not available to others. In short, the social identity perspective corresponds in some but not all respects to the leadership history within Synanon.

Transformational theory

One can also make a reasonable case that Dederich's leadership pattern represents the pseudo-transformational style alluded to by Bass (1998). Group members stood to gain any one of several transactional benefits, including a life free of drug addiction and crime (in the cases of drug addict members). Dederich offered inspirational leadership, a transcendent purpose, and individual consideration of group members. However, Dederich had little toleration of dissent, was an expert in humiliation and criticism of his followers, focused on punishing transgressions (as opposed to rewarding correct behavior), and was manipulative and Machiavellian in dealing with the group. Thus, Bass's conception of pseudo-transformational leadership provides a close description of Dederich's leadership style within Synanon.

The Children of God

History

David Berg founded the Children of God (COG) in 1967 in California, employing an anti-establishment, fundamentalist Christian message to recruit young adults. Berg transformed this group in a matter of 13 years from a fundamentalist sect to an international charismatic group that sanctioned promiscuous sexual behavior and religious prostitution. This activity funded a luxurious lifestyle for Berg and his inner circle (Davis, 1984; Charity Frauds Bureau Report, 1974). Berg was a man of voracious sexual appetites. In addition to three marriages and numerous affairs, he conducted incestuous relations with his children – a fact verified in his writings, the 'MO Letters' (Berg, 1976; Davis, 1984).

Local businesses and churches were originally called upon to 'provision' the group as a means of combating drug use among the young. Many recruits did, in fact, give up sex, drugs, and alcohol to become involved with COG in its early years (Davis, 1984). Berg urged members to 'forsake all' as a test of their faith (Berg, 1976). This commandment provided the basis for having members donate all their material possessions to Berg's sect. The group gained nation-wide media attention by 1969 after initiating prayer demonstrations at public events complete with biblical robes, wooden staffs, etc. (Davis, 1984).

By 1970 the group was located at a rural compound in Texas where recruitment techniques became systematized. The initial recruitment of an individual usually entailed depriving them of sleep with revolving indoctrination teams, and making certain that the recruit was never left alone nor given time to reflect quietly on issues. The recruit was continuously badgered regarding commitment to Jesus, the need to 'forsake all', etc. Once recruits signed a 'revolutionary sheet' donating their goods to the group, they began a minimum of three months' disciple training (Charity Frauds Bureau Report, 1974). This involved heavily regimented 18-hour days with religious broadcasts frequently played all night. Each recruit was continually squired by a committed member (Davis, 1984). Each new recruit was given a new name to symbolize their spiritual rebirth. Following the 'forsake all' doctrine, members were expected to break all ties with their old lives, especially friends and family – with the exception of writing to parents for funds. Time was spent in menial work and memorizing biblical verse, etc. All members, were expected to keep diaries listing accomplishments, evil thoughts, etc. These items were revealed in group meetings where public confessions were encouraged (Davis, 1984, 1973). In less than two years, the group grew from 200 to almost 2,000 members. By 1974, the group had over 100 enclaves in various countries (Charity Frauds Bureau Report, 1974).

From 1970 until his death in 1994, Berg was rarely seen by his followers as he took up residence in various locations from Europe to the South Pacific. To manage the group and its activities, he began, in the early 1970s, to communicate with the group via the 'MO letters'; a series of diatribes in 'bible-speak' that ranged in topic from direct prophecies from God to attacks on particular individuals. By mid-1971 the parents and friends of group members formed Free-COG, an anti-cult organization. Such groups provided the COG with necessary outgroups that could be vilified in MO letters. Defectors were threatened with harsh penalties. Berg preached that those who left the group would give birth to deformed children – a belief generally accepted within the group.

The evolution of the Children of God into a sex cult began in 1971. Originally the COG had a very puritanical position regarding sex (Davis, 1984). In mid-1971, Berg used a biblical quote to argue that 'all things were lawful' for any who were true and faithful Christians. Rank and file members learned of the sexual implications of this policy gradually so as to not shock them. Over time the formerly chaste and sexually segregated members of the group began to experiment with sex. By 1974, the sexual promiscuity in the group escalated to the practice of 'flirty fishing', i.e., using sexual behavior to recruit new members and to raise funds (Davis, 1984). Berg lived abroad until his death in 1994. The Children of God are still active and now refer to themselves as The Family (www.thefamily.org).

Theoretical analyses of the Children of God

Social identity theory

Both group salience and group identification within the Children of God were very high. The fact that members were generally accompanied by a buddy or partner when not in the group compound, the use of group jargon (e.g., flirty fishing, forsaking all, etc.) and the communal living arrangements of the group made group membership almost constantly salient. Given the sacrifices made by group members in terms of forsaking material goods and past relationships, members strongly identified with the COG and used it as a key source of self-identification. Berg's beliefs as expressed in the 'MO letters' defined what was normative within the group. Berg seemed quite distinct from the rank and file membership. In Berg's case this separateness stemmed from his age, his ministerial status, and his 'ability' as prophet. Indeed, after four or five years, he was rarely seen by members. As group founder, Berg's leadership did not emerge because his views happened to coincide with protoypic group norms. Rather, Berg took pains to mold the views of his members, albeit gradually, to match his own so that they became prototypic via manipulation. He apparently did not come to rely more on coercive or reward-based power as he grew more distant and distinct from his membership. In this respect his behavior does not confirm the suggestions made by Hogg regarding such issues. However, the evolution of group doctrine from literal biblical interpretation to doomsday prophesy, and eventually to sexual adventurism, does represent the type of change in prototypic position alluded to by a social identity perspective as a means of maintaining power.

Tranformational theory

Berg's leadership behavior provides numerous matches to Bass's description of the psuedo-transformational style. In terms of transaction, membership in the COG provided young recruits with the option of rebellion with a purpose. Serious young Christians were provided with an opportunity for establishing, beyond a doubt, their commitment to Jesus. Confused and alienated teenagers were offered structure, discipline, a sense of importance and meaning, and feelings of acceptance and belonging (Davis, 1984). In terms of messianic elements,

Berg offered innovative ideas and an inspiring message. However, in accord with the pseudo-transformational style, his reactions and behavior were not easily customized to reflect the individual desires and abilities of members, nor could he offer highly contingent reinforcement. He did not ignore his own self-interest, used reactive (punishment-based) control, was highly intolerant of dissent or of member innovation, and could hardly be called a person whose moral sense was impeccable. Rather than an optimistic approach, he relied on fear-based manipulations to redirect norms and behavior within his fiefdom. In short, there exists reasonable correspondence between Berg's leadership style and the pseudo-transformational style described by Bass (1998).

Alteration of Goals and Policy as a Leadership Tactic in Totalist Groups: Group Life as Drama

One distinctive feature marking the groups we have discussed is that all three seemed to be in a state of evolutionary flux – a characteristic marking many totalist groups (Hoffer, 1951; Sargant, 1957). In such groups, leaders commonly change the group doctrine and even group definition. One possible interpretation of this change is that it represents a tactic used by leaders to remain 'one step ahead' of the membership in terms of being a prototypic group member (Hogg, 2001). One fact that is congruent with this view is that these norms tend to change so that they define positions that heighten the distinction between the ingroup and salient outgroups – a key process according to a social identity perspective. This was certainly true in the three groups examined in this chapter, and also tends to be true in other totalist groups (Kelly, 1995).

An equally plausible interpretation of such induced change is that it creates a sense of mystery regarding group doctrine. Such mystery would maintain the leader's status as expert and necessary interpreter of that doctrine. A related reason leaders may encourage or generate such change is that it fosters feelings of excitement, growth and challenge thereby holding the interest of group members. This idea suggests that attraction to such groups is, in part, a function of the drama and excitement it provides for members. This 'drama' interpretation has some similarity with the transformational perspective in that such excitement would heighten the extent to which the leader was seen as an inspirational and innovative, leader, i.e., as a source of such drama and diversion.

However, theories of leadership and group process have heretofore not emphasized the notion that drama-based excitement is a benefit that is often provided by group life. In addition to serving this diversion function, a change in group doctrine provides leaders with a 'loyalty test' that can be applied to the followers; by instituting change, the leader can discern who is committed enough to embrace whatever transformation of group purpose and group values is introduced. Such tests can be used to discern who should be rewarded, trusted, punished, banished, or manipulated. This assures that those remaining closest to power will be likely to comply with the leader's interpretations and commands. Finally, inducing changes in doctrine, goals, etc. provides the leader with a means of eliciting a series of 'escalating commitments' from followers. Repetitive, and costly personal transformations represent an effective means of creating cognitive dissonance among disciples, thereby heightening members' loyalty and commitment to the group and its leader (Baron, 2000; Pratkanis and Aronson, 2000).

Summary and conclusions

We have considered three groups that have certain superficial differences but a number of disturbing commonalties. First, transformational change is a theme common to these three groups. A second common feature is that Bass's description of pseudo-tranformational leadership, provides a reasonable fit to these three case histories, especially given the nature of the morally questionable, self-centred and manipulative charismatic style adopted by these leaders. Third, all three groups exposed members to stressful and attention depleting procedures including overwork, sleep deprivation, regimentation, and various emotional manipulations. This is a common feature of indoctrination in most totalist groups (Baron, 2000). We feel this not only leads to inadequate and superficial scrutiny of group doctrine, but also heightens the members' reliance on the leader as a source of decision making and interpretation. A fourth commonality is that these leaders showed little tolerance for opinion deviates or member innovation. Individuals who persisted in such behavior found themselves the object of humiliation, and/or physical discipline. As several writers have noted, the existence of such deviates does serve a function for the organization in that the group's reaction marks the boundary of acceptable behavior and serves as an object lesson to other members regarding the consequences of norm violation (e.g., Hogg, 2001).

Fifth, the three leaders availed themselves of various material and erotic privileges that separated them from the rank and file membership. While this does not invariably occur in totalist groups (The Heavens Gate group is one exception), it is a common pattern (Pratkanis and Aronson, 2000). This separation is enhanced by the adulation directed at such leaders. The result is that the leader and close associates occupy a higher caste than the membership. These facts suggest that such leaders are not seen as just another group member, albeit prototypical. Hogg argues that such separateness eliminates the leader's prototypic status thereby forcing her/him to utilize coercive power over time. This did tend to occur in the People's Temple, and to some extent in Synanon, as well. Note however, that according to most accounts, there was relatively little overt defiance to control in Jonestown (Layton, 1998). It seems that Jones's use of coercive methods had more to do with his own mental deterioration than it did with the need to maintain control over the followers. It is important to note while we are considering this topic, that, although David Berg set himself well apart from the followers in the Children of God sect, he generally did not rely upon overtly coercive control tactics.

It would seem that leadership emergence, at least in the Peoples Temple and the Children of God, was not due to Jim Jones and David Berg happening to possess attitudes or traits that matched some prototypic standard. Instead, these leaders proactively specified for the group, who the outgroups would be and what ingroup norms would consist of. Although the loyalty and sacrifice exhibited by group members seems attributable to their intense social identification with the group, leadership seems, in these two groups, to be based more on power dynamics and charismatic features than on the members' admiration of individuals who happen to adhere most to prototypic norms. Our feeling is that this charismatic view of leader emergence will provide a good description and account of leadership in many totalist groups. Our reasoning here is that such groups are most frequently the 'creations' of single innovative leaders who are able to recruit followers based on the allure of their style and message. As such, the leader does not 'emerge' from an existing group of individuals on the basis of matching a prototypic standard. Rather, the group exists because of the leader's charisma and his or her skill at recruitment. In such 'boutique' groups, leadership is not 'decided upon' but rather is presented as a fait accompli. As a result, we feel the social identity view of leadership does not provide a particularly good explanation for leadership emergence in the totalist groups with which we are familiar. The social identity view may have more application in cases in which leadership passes from an original leader to a second or third generation of leaders. In addition, the extent to which the leader matches the group prototype may play a crucial role in leadership *maintenance* in that such a match almost certainly contributes to the leader's attraction and social power (Hogg, 2000).

We offer these observations with an obvious caveat. The case history descriptions we discuss above cannot constitute strong verification for any view. Problems of restricted sample size, and selective sampling forces us to offer our discussion more as illustrations than as findings. We feel however, that given the extreme and costly behavior evoked in totalist groups, even a descriptive consideration of such groups is provocative and worthwhile.

14 The Imperatives of Identity: The Role of Identity in Leader Judgment and Decision Making

RODERICK M. KRAMER

> We all need to be ready for those moments when our leadership is on the line and the fate or fortune of others depends on what we do. Perhaps only a few people will be touched by the decisions that we make at such critical moments; perhaps many will. But either way, we need to be prepared if we are to seize the opportunity.
>
> Michael Useem (1997, p. 3)

> Decision makers can violate a logic of consequence and be considered stupid or naïve, but if they violate the moral obligations of identity, they will be condemned as lacking in elementary virtue.
>
> James G. March (1994, p. 65)

Leaders are expected to make decisions. A swift and sure decisiveness may even be regarded as one of the *sine qua non*s of the true leader. Such, at least, seems to be one conclusion that readily emerges from even a cursory survey of the voluminous literature that characterizes leadership in terms of bold decisions rendered in moments of great crisis or opportunity (e.g., Janis, 1989; Useem, 1998). Few individuals have expressed this intimate linkage between leadership and decision making so clearly or with such authority as Theodore Roosevelt. 'It is not the critic who counts,' he suggested, 'nor the man who points out how the strong man stumbles, or where the doer of deeds could have done better.' Rather, he goes on to suggest,

> The credit belongs to the man who is actually in the arena, whose face is marred by dust and sweat and blood; who strives valiantly; who errs, and comes short again and again ... who knows the great enthusiasms, the great devotions ... who at the best knows in the end the triumphs of high achievement and who at the worst, if he fails, at least fails while daring greatly, so that his place shall never be with those cold and timid souls who know neither victory nor defeat.
>
> (quoted in Nixon, 1982, p. 345)

As Roosevelt's observations remind us, leadership is – in the words of Lyndon Johnson – not for 'timid souls or trembling spirits' (quoted in Gruber, 1991). We expect leaders to make decisions. We expect great leaders to make great ones.

Recognizing this intimate connection between leadership and decision making, social scientists have afforded considerable attention to explicating the psychological, social, and structural determinants of leader decision making. Their efforts reflect a variety of conceptual approaches and theoretical leanings. Some scholars, for example, have focused on the effects of power and politics on leader decision making (e.g., Neustadt, 1990; Pfeffer, 1992). Others have examined how leaders' advisory systems affect the quality of their decision-making (e.g., Burke and Greenstein, 1989; George, 1980; Janis, 1983). Still other researchers have explored the effects of various accountability regimes (Tetlock, 1992) and forms of institutional embeddedness (Allison, 1971) on leader decision making.

Each of these important theoretical perspectives has cast a useful light on the intimate linkage between effective leadership and decisive judgment. None alone, however, completely illuminates every facet of this complex relationship. In that spirit, the present chapter explores one neglected aspect of the leader decision making process. Specifically, I examine how leader identity affects the decision-making process. I define leaders' identities in terms of the self-categorization processes they use to define who they are and how they construe their leadership role. Using this definition as a starting point, I examine in this chapter the role such identities play in shaping how leaders make sense of the decisions they face. Specifically, I argue that leaders' identities influence how they weigh the anticipated consequences of their actions and inactions when in a leadership role.

One implication of this view that identity and decision are intimately connected in a leader's mind is that decisions have important identity-relevant consequences for leaders. Specifically, decisions can constitute identity-enhancing opportunities when they enable leaders to craft, sustain and project valued or desired identities through their decisions. At the same time, decisions can constitute identity-threatening predicaments when their consequences call into question or undermine a leader's valued or desired identities.

To advance this general argument, I first elaborate in more detail how leaders' identities might be characterized, drawing on insights and findings from social identity theory. Social identity theory, I suggest, provides a rich and generative framework for thinking about the relationship between how leaders think about themselves and the decisions they face. I next provide a general overview of previous social psychological theory and research on the relationship between social identity and decision making. Using these previous ideas and empirical findings as a conceptual foundation, I then present a brief overview of some preliminary findings from an ongoing archival study of presidential identity and decision making. Specifically, I present some findings from an analysis of the decisions made by President Lyndon Baines Johnson with respect to Vietnam. The analysis of these historic decisions, I argue, is useful in developing a better understanding of how identity-related concerns influence leader judgment and decision making. In particular, these decisions demonstrate some of the cognitive processes leaders engage in when trying to make sense of decisions that constitute severe perceived identity-threatening predicaments. I conclude the chapter by considering some of the implications of an identity-based perspective on leader decision-making.

Social Identity Theory: A Brief Overview

Because this analysis approaches leader decision-making from the perspective of social identity theory, it may be helpful to offer a few preliminary remarks about the basics of that theory. The fundamental idea of social identity theory, as summarized by Hogg and Terry (2001b) is that, 'a social category (e.g., nationality, political affiliation, organization, work group) within which one falls, and to which one feels one belongs, provides a definition of who one is in terms of the defining characteristics of the category' (p. 3). This category-based 'self-definition,' they go on to note, thus becomes 'a part of the self-concept' (p. 3). According to this functional view of the role self-categorization plays in the construction of a viable and enduring sense of self, our 'self-conception reflects self-categorization, the cognitive grouping of the self as identical to some class of stimuli and in contrast to some other class of stimuli' (Turner and Onorato, 1999, p. 21).

Research by social psychologists over the past several decades has provided considerable insight into the antecedents and consequences of social identities (see Hogg and Abrams, 1988 for a comprehensive overview). Several major conclusions from that body of research have particular relevance to the argument I aim to develop in this chapter. First, research has shown that individuals' social identities are complex, highly differentiated psychological constructs (Brewer and Pickett, 1999). This complexity derives, at least in part, from the obvious fact that people belong to multiple social categories. Because people simultaneously enjoy membership in numerous social categories, they can categorize themselves ('self-categorize') in a variety of different ways. Thus, the answer we give to even the seemingly fundamental question, 'Who are we *really*?' can be answered by us in myriad ways depending on the particular self-categorization we employ at the moment.

A second important conclusion emerging from research on social identity is that some social identities matter more to us than others. In other words, some identities will be viewed as more central to our self-concept, while others will be perceived as more peripheral in defining who we think we are. For example, for some individuals, their 'core' social identity may be defined largely in terms of their professional identities (what they 'do' for a living). Such individuals are likely to self-categorize primarily in terms of the work they do (e.g., being a social psychologist) rather than some other dimension (e.g., being a proud father of two children). For other people, their professional identities may carry little psychological freight in terms of influencing how they think about themselves or what they value. For these individuals, the salaried work they engage in merely helps them 'pay the bills', while they pursue some passion (e.g., acting or documentary film-making) that more centrally defines who they are and how they like to think about themselves (e.g., as an aspiring actor or independent film-maker). For such individuals, self-categorization as an 'aspiring actor' or 'film-maker' would dominate 'waiter'. Research on social identity suggests that most people care a great deal about their central or 'core' social identities. Thus, and not surprisingly, they are motivated to affirm such identities when possible, and they are motivated to protect and defend them when necessary (e.g., Elsbach and Kramer, 1996).

Research on social identity also documents the fact that the salience of any particular social identity – whether it is core or peripheral to the individual – can vary widely across social situations. In this sense, social identity is responsive to contextual 'cues' in the individual's ambient social environment. These cues influence or 'trigger' which particular social identity – out of all of the many potentially available social identities – is likely to be figure and which will be ground. This 'plasticity' of social identity reflects, it should be emphasized, not only our passive response to situational cues that trigger or invoke particular identities, but also our proactive (intentional, calculated, or strategic) efforts to construct and affirm particular identities in our actions with others (e.g., Elsbach and Kramer, 1996; Swann, 1987).

Another important facet of this identity construction and maintenance process depends, of course, on the particular construals (identity attributions) others make about us and our actions. These construals encompass how they categorize us (their categorizations of us), including whether they accept or repudiate our core identity aspirations and claims in a given situation. In this sense, our social identities are crafted or forged, at least in part, in the crucible of interpersonal experience. Therefore, our social identities are not autistic achievements, but rather must be thought of as negotiated products (Swann, 1987).

These basic research findings and conceptual conclusions from social identity theory and research, I argue next, provide useful building blocks for developing the concept of leader identity.

Conceptualizing Leader Identity

Within the past few years, there has been increasing interest by researchers in organizational identities as important forms of social identity. This interest reflects the convergence of two streams of scholarly activity. Within the field of organizational behavior, organizational theorists have viewed social identity theory as a powerful conceptual platform from which to view a variety of important organizational phenomena (see, for instance, Ashforth and Mael, 1989; Elsbach and Kramer, 1996). Within social psychology, leading social identity theorists have recognized that organizational identities constitute important and largely neglected forms of social identity (see, for instance, Hogg and Terry, 2001a).

Few, if any, organizational identities are as central or salient to organizational members as that of organizational leader. The leader is rightly regarded, in many respects, as the focal identity within any organization in so far as he/she has the power to direct organizational events and is generally the locus (and focus) of organizational decision-making. For the purposes of the present analysis, I define *leader identity* in terms of the set of social categories in terms of which leaders categorize themselves. These self-categorizations can be viewed functionally as helping – or, more neutrally, influencing how – leaders define themselves as leaders. Such self-categorizations include all of the category-based attributes (identity-relevant features and concerns) they find salient when thinking about themselves and their actions or inactions.

As with other forms of social identity, leader identities are presumably highly differentiated cognitive constructs with multiple, hierarchically arranged components. Thus, if asked to self-categorize, leaders might invoke a variety of different leadership categories. Additionally, leaders' self-categorizations presumably vary as a function of the situation or context in which they find themselves. For example, a leader of a Fortune 500 company who happens also to be an Hispanic female might find herself self-categorizing in different ways depending on the context in which that self-categorization is occurring. If, for example, she were attending an annual meeting of Fortune 500 CEOs, what might be most salient to her is the fact that she represents one of the newest of the Fortune 500 companies. If, alternatively, she were addressing a group of male executives who were interested in learning more about issues related to 'glass ceilings' in large organizations, she might think of herself primarily in terms of her gender. As these examples suggest, the salience of any particular leader identity may vary as a function of the features of the setting in which the leader is acting or located.

Some of a leader's self-categorizations obviously pertain to more central and enduring identities, while others will be perceived as more peripheral or transient. For example, some leaders may define themselves centrally in terms of their tenacity and ability to come back from a crisis, as did President Clinton. Clinton, in fact, frequently viewed himself as the 'Comeback Kid'. Even these central and core identities, however, are negotiated. Thus, leaders' success or failure at constructing and sustaining a desired valued or desired social identity depends, at least in part, on others' reactions to those identity affirmations and claims. Thus, the extent to which a given identity aspiration or claim can be registered convincingly depends, at least in part, on the reactions of important organizational constituents and audiences to that claim. In this sense, leaders' identities, as with other forms of social identity, are affirmed in and emerge through their interactions with other people, including especially audiences to whom those leaders feel particularly accountable (Ginzel, Kramer, and Sutton, 1993).

Social Identity and Decision-Making:
An Overview of Previous Theory and Research

Before elaborating on how identity might be linked to leader judgment and decision-making, it is useful first to say a few words about extant theory and research on social identity and decision-making more generally. Over the past several decades, there has been considerable research on the relationship between social identity and decision-making (Kramer and Brewer, 1984). One consistent finding that emerges from these studies is that the salience of a particular social identity affects judgment and choice in such situations. For example, in interpersonal bargaining contexts, the salience of a common or shared social identity has been shown to enhance concern with joint outcomes and fairness. In contrast, salience of distinctive or differentiating social identities has been shown to enhance more individualistic or competitive orientations. A second conclusion emerging from this research is that the decisions individuals make are sometimes construed as opportunities to affirm, validate, and project valued or cherished identities. As a consequence, when individuals are asked to explain *why* they selected a cooperative choice over an individualistic choice in a social dilemma situation, they typically do not say that they cooperated simply because doing so is a 'rational' decision. They do not invoke, in other words, the sort of calculative logic that a game theoretic or rational choice model of decision-making might posit. Instead, and revealingly, they often talk about their decisions in social terms (i.e., in terms of what it means for them as social actors embedded in a social context to make one choice over another).

The construction of identity through decision is only partially completed by individuals' idiosyncratic construal of their decisions, however. Individual self-categorizations thus tell only part of the causal story. A second major factor is the construal placed by others on an individual's decisions. Therefore, the specific identity-relevant implications of any given decision are determined, at least in part, through the sometimes tacit and often explicit negotiation over meaning or interpretation with audiences who also observe and evaluate their actions (Ginzel, Kramer, and Sutton, 1993; Weick, 1993).

Although previous research has demonstrated how social identities influence decision-making, this previous research suffers from at least two limitations. First, these previous studies have generally involved undergraduate students making decisions in artificial laboratory settings. These contexts have involved: (1) the manipulation of minimal and transient social identities and (2) low-cost and largely inconsequential decisions. Therefore, we know virtually nothing about whether any of these findings generalize to decisions involving real leaders and the more consequential decisions they confront in organizational settings.

To address some of these limitations, and to extend existing theory and research on the relationship between social identity and decision-making, I have been conducting a study of presidential identity and decision-making. At first glance, it might seem rather peculiar to talk about presidential identity as a form of social identity. However, if we revisit Hogg and Terry's (2001b) definition of social identity in terms of 'a social category ... *within which one falls*, and *to which one feels one belongs*, [and which] *provides a definition of who one is* in terms of the defining characteristics of the category' (p. 3, emphases added), then the presidency clearly qualifies as a form of social identity. The presidency is a social category, both from the standpoint of those who occupy the position and those who observe it. Moreover, nested within this generic, superordinate category is an impressively differentiated set of psychologically and socially salient subcategories. Presidents can categorize themselves as, among other things, Republican versus Democratic, liberal versus conservative, crooked or honest, flandering versus nonflandering, and so on. Any one or more of these categories might be salient to a president at a given moment of decision or indecision.

For those individuals who have occupied the office of the presidency, identity issues have been very salient, at least as evidenced by the large number of self-categorizations they express. Presidents make many statements, both privately and in public, regarding how they define themselves as leaders, noting the categories they include themselves in and exclude themselves from (see, for instance, Henggeler, 1991). For example, they often compare themselves to other presidents, noting how they are similar to those presidents. Similarly, they frequently talk about the ways in which they are unique and distinctive from former presidents.

Lyndon Johnson's presidential identity and the Vietnam decisions

Few instances of leader decision-making have attracted the level of attention of the Vietnam decisions and the individual who made them – Lyndon Baines Johnson. They have been the focus of enormous scholarly scrutiny – not only because of their intrinsic historical importance, but also because of their perplexing character. The perplexing character of Johnson's Vietnam decisions stems, in part, from the seeming disjunction between the attributes of the decision-maker and the decisions made. Few US presidents entered office with a clearer perception of their ultimate goals and ambitions. Moreover, few individuals who have taken on the duties of president have seemed better positioned to maneuver the vast machinery of Washington in fulfillment of their ambitions. Lyndon Johnson was widely regarded as one of the most capable wielders of power ever to have assumed the presidency. He was a master politician who understood better than almost anyone else alive at the time how Washington worked.

The record of Johnson's first months in office also contribute to our perplexity regarding the Vietnam decisions. Shortly after assuming the presidency, Johnson performed flawlessly, winning over a wary Congress and a sceptical public. After only a few months in office, he was elected to the presidency on his own in 1964 with the then-largest popular mandate in US history. On the basis of this early White House performance, it looked as if Johnson might be remembered in history as one of the great presidents, especially if judged primarily by his legislative accomplishments with respect to advances in civil rights, health care, education, and the war against poverty. The Vietnam decisions are perplexing also because there is substantial evidence that Johnson's initial assessments of the Vietnam situation were remarkably prescient. He foresaw the prospect of becoming mired in a costly, fruitless escalating conflict with little upside. He felt the conflict in Vietnam was not worth the shedding of a single American youth's blood (see, for instance, Johnson's remarks, recorded in his taped conversations; Beschloss, 1997, 2001).

Relative to Johnson's initial perceptive assessments of Vietnam, his presidential decisions during the 1964–68 period remain a conundrum to scholars. These were decisions that, all too obviously, went terribly awry, undoing first Johnson's beloved domestic programs, then his presidency, and ultimately the legacy he had fought for so long and so hard to create. Perhaps it is for this reason that these decisions have attracted so much scholarly scrutiny.

Previous scholarship on the Johnson Vietnam decisions has focused primarily on several social psychological accounts. One influential account has been *groupthink* (Janis, 1983). Another has been escalation of commitment (Staw, 1976) and psychological entrapment (Brockner and Rubin, 1986). In this chapter, I try to approach the Vietnam decisions from an identity perspective. To explicate how identity and decision collided dramatically and with devastating consequence, I first provide a brief characterization of how Lyndon Johnson self-categorized as president. I then examine in detail his cognitive responses to the identity-threatening predicament posed by his Vietnam decisions.

Lyndon Johnson's core identity

Lyndon Johnson was remarkably articulate about the core identity that he cherished and energetically sought to project as president, both to himself and to others (e.g., Henggeler, 1991; Kearns-Goodwin, 1976; Valenti, 1977). His views surfaced frequently in both his public pronouncements and his private ruminations with close confidantes and aides. Always foremost in his mind was furthering his ambition of becoming one of the greatest presidents in American history. As his aide Jack Valenti put it, 'He had one goal: to be the greatest president doing the greatest good in the history of the nation' (quoted in Middleton, 1990, p. 24). He wanted, in his own words, to be 'the greatest father the country had ever had' (quoted in Gruber, 1991). He once expressed the view that he aspired – figuratively at least – to have his visage placed alongside the other great figures looking out from Mount Rushmore.

In Johnson's eyes, presidential greatness had two cornerstones. The first was a record of historic domestic achievement. Here Johnson sought, as Nicholas Lemann once aptly commented, to 'set world records in politics the way a star athlete would in sports' (quoted in Dallek, 1991, p. 109). In pursuit of this goal, Johnson displayed a whirlwind of legislative genius, passing more sweeping domestic legislation than any president in history. He was determined to rival the record of Franklin Roosevelt as a president who knew how to throw the great machinery of government into high gear in pursuit of great, if difficult, aims. In this spirit, he embarked on a broad set of initiatives that he brought together under the umbrella of what he called the Great Society programme. In large measure, he felt the program would be the capstone of his presidency, the banner on which he would hang the legacy of his presidential achievement. The second cornerstone to presidential greatness in Johnson's eyes was the ability of a president to keep his country out of harm's way and conquer aggression. No US president, he knew, had achieved greatness without successfully waging war against its adversaries.

If Johnson entertained a clearly defined vision of the identity he sought as president, he knew just as clearly how he would achieve that identity. He knew from his reading of history and his intense study of the presidency the kind of president it would take to achieve such stunning accomplishments. As Kearns-Goodwin (1976) put it, Johnson believed that, 'If you had the energy and drive to work harder than everyone else you would achieve what you set out to accomplish.' Johnson, she went on to note, 'held before him the image of the daring cowboy, the man with the capacity to outrun the wild herd, riding at a dead run in the dark of the night' (p. 343–344). He drew a distinction between those leaders who were the 'doers' and those he dismissed as the 'thinkers' and 'talkers' of the world. Thus, Johnson's identity was just as sharply defined in the realm of means as it was with respect to the ends he would pursue.

It is within the context of this finely and sharply drawn identity portrait that the Vietnam decisions of the Johnson presidency can – and should – be placed. With respect to his Vietnam decisions, Johnson saw little upside. In his view, he had inherited the dilemma of Vietnam just as he had inherited his presidency – on a tragic moment's notice on November 22, 1963. From the instant of that assumed presidency, Johnson clearly recognized the threat that Vietnam posed to his legacy (Beschloss, 1997, 2001).

In terms of furthering his ambitions, unfortunately, none of the alternatives presented to Johnson regarding Vietnam seemed attractive or viable. 'I feel like a hound bitch in heat in the country,' he poignantly complained. 'If you run, they chew your tail off. If you stand still, they slip it to you' (Berman, 1989, p. 183). The thought of 'cutting and running', as he once put it, was anathema to a man with such a keenly developed image of what great presidents do in moments of crisis or challenge.

In Johnson's eyes, the Vietnam decisions also directly threatened his ability to implement his broad Great Society initiatives. In his view, it was these Great Society decisions that would enable him to demonstrate to the American public the sweep and grandeur of his presidential vision. He envisioned a revitalized and eventually completed America, where people would be judged by the 'quality of their minds', and not merely by the 'quantity of their goods' (Gruber, 1991). He described the program as being like a beautiful woman that the American people would love (Kearns-Goodwin, 1976). Thus, the Great Society decisions constituted, in Johnson's eyes, an identity-enhancing opportunity.

The intensity of the conflict between the identity Johnson hoped to affirm to himself and that he hoped to project to others through his Vietnam decisions intensified as the war drained economic and attentional resources from the Great Society. The program that he had earlier characterized as a young and beautiful woman now withered in Johnson's eye under the economic hardships imposed by the Vietnam War: 'She's getting thinner and thinner and uglier and uglier all the time ... Soon she'll be so ugly the American people will refuse to look at her; they'll stick her in a closet to hide her away and there she'll die. *And when she dies, I, too, will die*' (quoted in Kearns-Goodwin, 1976, p. 286–287, emphases added).

In Johnson's mind, the threat to his identity was intensified by the sudden disaffection of large segments of the American public – the same public that, only months ago, had made Lyndon Johnson one of the most popular and admired and beloved presidents in US history. As Berman (1989) noted, 'It pained him that those he believed had been helped most by his presidency [e.g., students, blacks, and educators] were leading the opposition to his war' (p. 183).

Johnson's cognitive responses to the identity-threat posed by his Vietnam decisions

How did Johnson respond to the identity-threatening predicament he perceived in his Vietnam decisions? Initially, his response was characterized by extremely vigilant and mindful information processing of the sort described by Janis (1989) in his classic work on high quality decision-making. Johnson studied all of the details of these decisions and vigorously pressed his Secretary of Defence Robert McNamara and his other advisors to consider every implication of every decision:

> What I would like to know is what has happened in recent months that requires this kind of decision on my part. What are the alternatives? I want this discussed in full detail, from everyone around this table ... what are the compelling reasons [for this decision]? What results can we expect? Again, I ask you, what are the alternatives? I don't want us to make snap judgments. I want us to consider all our options ...
>
> (Valenti, 1975, p. 259–26)

As the puzzle of Vietnam continued to defy his ability to resolve it, he displayed two less adaptive cognitive responses. The first cognitive response is what Janis (1989) identified as hyper-vigilant information processing.

> If Ronald Reagan was the Teflon president, to whom nothing stuck, Johnson was the flypaper president, to whom everything clung. A compulsive reader, viewer, and listener who took every criticism personally and to heart, he was at first intent on, and then obsessed with, answering every accusation, responding to every charge.
>
> (Herring, 1993, p. 95)

A second dysfunctional cognitive response evidenced by Johnson was intense and intrusive dysphoric rumination about Vietnam. 'If Johnson was unhappy thinking about Vietnam,' Kearns-Goodwin (1976) once noted, 'he was even less happy not thinking about it' (p. 299). Johnson often 'consciously and deliberately decided not to think another thought about Vietnam, yet discussions that started on poverty or education invariably ended up on Vietnam ... he found himself unwilling, and soon unable, to break loose from what had become an obsession' (Kearns-Goodwin, 1976, p. 299). In particular, he tended to ruminate at length about his deteriorating image as a leader and as president. This led Johnson to begin to imagine a vast web of conspiracy by powerful forces, including his many perceived political enemies, who he felt were lined up against him with the common aim of denying him the presidential legacy he sought (see, e.g., Califano, 1991; Dallek, 1991; Goodwin, 1988). As he put it, even years later, 'They'll get me anyhow, no matter how hard I try ... the reviews are in the hands of my enemies – the *New York Times* and my enemies – so I don't have a chance' (quoted in Kearns-Goodwin, 1976, p. 357).

In terms of protecting Johnson's identity, there were two interesting cognitive responses evidenced in the archival data. Both of these constitute attempts at re-categorizing himself and the decisions he was making. The first pattern that emerged entails what might be thought of as *selective self-categorizations*. Selective self-categorizations have been defined as decision-makers' attempts to cognitively focus on self-enhancing facets of their identities, while downplaying or minimizing attention to less flattering facets (Elsbach and Kramer, 1996). For example, when challenged by critics and advisors about the wisdom of his Vietnam policy, Johnson would remind them of all he had done for civil rights, poverty, education, and health care reform (Beschloss, 2001). According to his friend, Governor John Connally, he carried in his breast pocket a list of all his legislative accomplishments, which he would pull out and read off as if it were a baseball card (Gruber, 1991).

A second cognitive tactic much in evidence in the archival data is selective self-categorization through what might be thought of as 'strategic' (motivated or self-enhancing) social comparisons. Thus, in interpreting his dilemmas, Johnson continually compared himself to other US presidents, particularly Roosevelt and Lincoln. For example, in justifying his persistence in Vietnam, despite evidence that the war was not progressing favorably, Johnson argued that, 'You see, I deeply believe we are quarantining aggressors over there ... *Just like FDR [did with] Hitler, just like Wilson [did] with the Kaiser.* You've simply got to see this thing in historical perspective' (quoted in Kearns-Goodwin, 1976, p. 313, emphases added). Similarly, when friends, aides, advisors, and critics suggested to him that he might be perceived as a greater president if he decisively ended such an unpopular conflict, Johnson recoiled. 'Everything I know about history,' he asserted, 'proves this absolutely wrong. It was our lack of strength and failure to show stamina, our hesitancy, vacillation, and love of peace being paraded so much that caused all our problems before World War I, World War II, and Korea' (p. 313).

Johnson drew solace in repeated comparisons with Abraham Lincoln and the unpopular decisions he had made, 'I read all about the troubles Lincoln had in conducting the Civil War. Yet he persevered and history rewarded him for his perseverance' (Kearns-Goodwin, 1976, p. 314). 'We're going to have our troubles,' he acknowledged, but 'we're not running from nothing … *And remember old Abraham Lincoln …*' (quoted in Bechloss, 2001, p. 136). As he admonished his confidantes, 'They [the public] don't ever remember many of these presidents from Jackson to Lincoln. They don't remember many from Lincoln to Roosevelt. The ones they remember are those that stood up …' (quoted in Bechloss, 2001, p. 136).

Implications and Conclusions

As noted at the beginning of this chapter, there exists a rather substantial literature on the determinants of leader decision-making. A primary aim of the present chapter was to contribute to this literature by explicating the role that identity-related psychological and social processes play in such decisions. Approaching leader decision-making from a social identity perspective illuminates, I have argued, how leaders' core identities influence the manner in which they frame or construe the decisions they confront. Leaders' decisions, in turn, have important implications for their identity aspirations and claims. In particular, the ability of leaders to construct and sustain valued or desired identities (also see Chapters 15 and 16) depends on the consequences of the decisions they make. The research described above indicates some of the ways in which decisions represent important routes of leader identity construction and maintenance through either identity-enhancement or identity-threat.

The analysis represented in this chapter suggests that decisions can constitute identity-threatening predicaments in at least two ways. First, decisions can challenge or invalidate leaders' self-perceptions of their core identities. Leader decisions can create, in this sense, an internal 'credibility gap' in so far as they call into question desired or cherished self-categorizations. Second, decisions can threaten or call into question a leader's public or social claims regarding their core identities. Leaders care not only about their private identities, but also about the social images they project to others. When decisions cause important constituents to question a leader's intentions, motives, actions, competence then the leader is in crisis.

The present analysis also identifies two cognitive responses leaders make to identity-threatening predicaments that arise from their decisions. The first tactic involves *selective self-categorizations* that highlight alternate and attractive identity attributes. A second cognitive tactic for dealing with identity-threatening predicaments entails *selective social comparisons* that highlight alternate comparison groups for leaders to invoke when trying to make sense of their predicament. Selective social comparison can be viewed as a form of 're-categorization' in terms of a selective subset of comparison others within one's perceived social identity group. In discussing the adaptive value of this psychological tactic,

Frey and Ruble (1990) have proposed that, 'healthy [psychological] functioning may depend on the ability to exhibit flexibility in the choice of evaluative comparisons in order to maintain a sense of competence and high self-esteem' (p. 169). Both of these tactical responses can be thought of as re-categorization efforts in the service of identity maintenance and repair tactics.

A social identity perspective on leader decision-making also helps illuminate some of the reasons why leaders sometimes make the decisions they do. Such a perspective suggests, further, why leaders might persist with a chosen course of action even when the consequences of their decisions seem catastrophically flawed and self-defeating from the perspective of any reasonable rational calculation of advantage. Thus, although intended to resolve an identity threat, leaders' responses sometimes act instead to increase threat, as they invite further hostile or critical scrutiny. In this respect, the present research also contributes to our understanding of why leaders sometimes make disastrous or self-defeating decisions. A social identity-based model of leader decision-making thus complements and extends our understanding of previous work on this relationship.

In closing, I would argue that a perspective on leader decision-making grounded in conceptions of identity moves us closer to a richer and more evocative understanding of the psychological and social complexity of the decision-making process as it unfolds in complex organizations and institutions. It helps us appreciate more fully the intense affective responses leaders have to the decision dilemmas they confront. When decisions are coded by leaders in terms of affirmations or repudiations of a core sense of self, it is hardly suprising that they produce such intense and persistent responses. The leader's life is lived largely in a fishbowl, and this applies to their identity aspirations, attempts at identity construction and identity maintenance. As Pfeffer (1992) observed, 'To be in power is to be watched more closely, and this surveillance affords one the luxury of few mistakes' (p. 302).

Author's Acknowledgment

This chapter was written while the author was Visiting Professor of Public Policy and Management at the John F. Kennedy School of Government, Harvard University.

15 On the Science of the Art of Leadership

STEPHEN REICHER AND NICK HOPKINS

No area of modern social thought has escaped the shadow of the holocaust. The issues that we prioritize, the questions that we ask and the perspectives that we employ all changed irrevocably as a result of the slaughter. Leadership research is a case in point.

Prior to the Second World War, many thinkers were fascinated and attracted by forceful charismatic leaders who were seen as saving society from a dull mechanical future. Such figures stamped some agency, artistry and imagination on what Max Weber described as 'the routinized economic cosmos' (quoted in Lindholm, 1990, p. 27). However, after Hitler, 'the triumph of the will' acquired different connotations. The focus shifted from what was added by the leader to what was taken away from everyone else and hence the savior became Satan.

Thus, in the post-war period, there were a plethora of clinical studies which diagnosed charismatic leaders as suffering from a range of psychotic and personality disorders (Bion, 1961; Chessick, 1979; Kohut, 1985). The irony is that, once powerful leaders are diagnosed as insane, they are denied the very agency which first made them attractive. So is it possible to allow agency to the leader without removing it from everybody else? Can we conceive of leadership in such a way as to allow other possibilities beyond stultifying dullness and absolute tyranny? More specifically, does social psychology provide us with a way beyond such unattractive alternatives?

In broad terms, the trend within psychology matches the general trend without. An emphasis on the personality traits which characterize the effective leader in the pre-war period gave way to contingency theories which examine the situations in which different individuals rise to the fore (Fiedler and House, 1994; Gibb, 1954). The implication of such models is that no-one, whatever their qualities, can make the world as they will. While leaders might hold sway under particular circumstances, it is context which determines their influence rather than they who create their own contexts. But, despite this emphasis, contingency models tend to neglect the fact that the key context in which leaders operate is the group. There is no recognition of the interdependence between leadership and followership. Consequently, such models do not represent an extension of agency from leaders to followers, for how can those who are absent be agents? Rather they represent a partial restriction of even that agency which is allowed to leaders.

In recent years social identity theorists have sought to relocate the study of leadership within the field of group research. A leader is viewed as someone who represents a collective constituency. The term 'represents' has a double meaning here – as someone who is accorded the position of representative and as someone who reflects that which characterizes the group as a distinctive entity. The core claim of social identity approaches is that leaders acquire the mantle of being representatives in the first sense because they are representative in the second sense.

This position is already implicit in the very concept of social identity as the psychological basis of group behavior. As Turner (1982) argues, group membership depends upon a cognitive act of self-categorization. Only to the extent that we identify ourselves in terms of a particular self-category will we start acting on the basis of that category membership. Indeed, such social identification leads to a process of self-stereotyping: we seek to conform to the norms, beliefs and values which characterize the relevant category. Thus only those who identify with the social category will be subject to influence, only messages which are consonant with the category definition will be influential and only those who are in a position to define the nature of the category will be in a position to influence others. Most obviously, those whose credentials as group members are most secure will be best placed to achieve influence. The most typical group member has the most potential to achieve influence.

The wider significance of these arguments becomes clearer by a simple act of rephrasing: first, the extent of participation in common collective action will depend upon the boundaries of category inclusion; second, the form taken by common collective action will depend upon the content of the category definition; third, the ability to control common collective action will depend upon being seen as prototypical of the category (cf. Reicher and Hopkins, 1996a; Reicher, Drury, Hopkins and Stott, 2001). Social categorization is the psychological underpinning of mass social action.

More recently, these ideas – and the third premise in particular – have been developed into an explicit theory of leadership (Hogg, 2001; Chapter 3; also see Chapters 4 and 10). The basic premise is that, in salient groups, effective leadership depends upon the extent to which an individual is perceived as prototypical of the category. Empirical support has been provided by a series of studies by Hogg and his colleagues using both laboratory and field studies. As group membership becomes more salient, so individuals who embody group norms become preferred as leaders (Fielding and Hogg, 1997; Hains, Hogg and Duck, 1997).

Overall, as Haslam (2001) puts it, leadership centers around a partnership in a social self-categorical relationship. The leader and other group members are mutually bound together in a shared sense of 'we-ness'. One might conclude from this that there will be as many specifications of the ideal leader as there are social categories in the world. However, things are even more contingent than that, for the social identity tradition in general, and self-categorization theory in particular, stresses that group prototypes are not fixed but vary as a function of who we compare ourselves with: who 'we' are depends upon which 'they' is being considered. If the leadership is a function of prototypicality and if prototypes are a function of context it follows that leadership will also vary as a function of context. To be more specific, since the group prototype is the position that best distinguishes the ingroup from the outgroup, the leader who best represents the characteristics which render the group distinctive in context will be favored (cf. Turner and Haslam, 2000).

To date, then, work within the social identity perspective has concentrated on demonstrating how different types of leader come to the fore in different group contexts. This has principally been studied using experimental methods in which the parameters of context are set by the experimenter. Participants are then asked to choose, evaluate or respond to different would-be leaders who stand in different relations to the ingroup prototype. In these studies the world is taken as a given, identity is given by that world, and human action is a reflection of identity. If one stopped at this, such work would provide a strangely passive and reactive portrait of leadership. Leaders would not only have lost the ability to create contexts; they would also have lost the autonomy to direct others as they will within a given context, for their authority is limited to expressions of the group prototype. Indeed, one would be left with the impression that people do nothing to seek out the mantle of leadership but that the mantle simply flits amongst them, resting temporarily on those shoulders which happen, for a brief moment, to best fit with the group prototype.

While such a position represents total defeat for the heroic view of leadership, it also renders the masses passive. Like their leaders, followers seem to act in terms of an identity which is determined by context rather than themselves. They may confer approval on prototypical leaders, but they are accorded little choice in the matter. So, while leaders and followers are bound together, it is not that the will of the leader is counter-balanced against the will of the followers but rather that both appear as puppets of group processes. It is less that agency and imagination have been redistributed than that they have been obliterated.

Of course such a portrait is a caricature. Social identity theorists are well aware that leadership is an active process (cf. Hogg, 1996). Haslam (2001) is particularly emphatic in stressing that: 'the leader is an *active* constituent of the group, who is simultaneously defining of and defined by the group' (p. 69, emphasis in the original). He goes further and stresses that leaders and followers are mutually bound together in this process. While leaders may go out to define the meaning of the group identity and hence set the parameters for group action, followers are equally involved in deciding whether to accept the formulations offered to them.

Such a position has the attraction of limiting the autonomy of the leader by extending agency from leaders to followers. It characterizes the process of leadership as an interplay between agents. It also defines the field on which this relationship is played out – the shared sense of group identity. Thus, the social identity tradition potentially provides a way out of the dualism between the leader as agent and followers as passive depending on how active group members are allowed to be in the definition of context and hence identity. While there is a recognition *in theory* that any account of leadership which excludes such activity is necessarily deficient, it is rarely addressed *in practice*. In this sense, social identity research reflects one of the most remarkable tendencies of leadership research in general. That is, precious little work looks at what leaders actually do. The focus is primarily on what leads people to be endorsed as leaders by others. At most, people are presented with specific leadership acts and their response is sought. With very rare exceptions, the ways in which leaders go out to solicit support is ignored.

In sum, there is an urgent need to analyse the active dimensions of leadership. However, this is more than a matter of doing in practice what is stressed in theory. For, even if social identity theorists recognize the self-evident inadequacy of any account which ignores the way in which leaders shape context and identity, this recognition sits uneasily with the conventional emphases within social identity and self-categorization theories. Therefore, before being able to restore the active side of leadership to its rightful position centre-stage, it is necessary to revisit the theories themselves and, more particularly, to look at the way in which they characterize the relationship between context and categorization.

Constructing Categories and Mobilizing Masses

At a meta-theoretical level, one of the most significant contributions of the social identity tradition is to reassess the relationship between categorization and social reality as it is conceived in social psychology. Whereas categories have conventionally been treated as a distortion of social reality, self-categorization theorists in particular have stressed the importance of understanding categories as integrally linked to the organization of the social world (Oakes, Haslam and Turner, 1993): we see people as category members to the extent that they are organized categorically in reality. Thus the emphasis has tended to be on the determination of categories by context. Both in theory and in the practice of research, context is generally treated as a given and categories are viewed as an outcome. More generally, the approach could be described as perceptualist. It views the process of categorization in terms of how we perceive the existing world. In temporal terms, the process is very much rooted in the present: categories reflect what exists in the here and now. It is this which underlies the difficulties in developing an active model of leadership, for, if categorization is rigidly tied to the present, how can one explain how leaders (and followers) deploy categories in the making of the future?

In our own work, we argue that the social identity tradition needs to develop its conception of the category – context relationship. For us, this relationship is constituted through action rather than perception. Hence it is necessarily two-sided. On the one hand, as self-categorization theorists stress, categories do indeed reflect the existing organization of social action in context. However, on the other hand, categories also serve to organize social action and hence to (re)constitute contexts. Thus category definitions are as much about organizing the future as about the organization of the present. The implication of this is that, even in the same context, the relevant social categories can always be construed in many different ways. While there may be only one contemporaneous reality, there are always many possible futures. Accordingly, we would expect those with different visions of 'what should be' to advance different constructions of the categories into which people fall. Social identities, we argue, relate to their *projects* as much as to their percepts (Hopkins and Reicher, 1997; Reicher, Drury, Hopkins and Stott, 2001; Reicher and Hopkins, 1996a, 2001a; Reicher, Hopkins and Condor, 1997).

However, it is not simply that definitions of social categories relate to visions of the future. More significantly, they have to do with the mobilization of such social forces as will bring these futures into being. If, as self-categorization theory suggests, the definition of self-categories determines the parameters of collective action, then it is by construing these definitions that it is possible to shape collective mobilization. To be more precise, if the limits of participation depend upon category boundaries, the forms of action depend upon category content, and the control of action depends upon category prototypes, then leaders will be successful to the extent that they are able to construe themselves and their audience as sharing a common social identity and also to construe their proposals and policies as embodying in concrete form the norms, values and beliefs that characterize the identity. For us, then, effective leaders should be understood as 'entrepreneurs of identity' (cf. Besson, 1991).

Their entrepreneurship consists in two registers of activity. As we have already implied, one of these registers is rhetorical. Leaders need to be skilled in the arts of performance and representation in order to present their audience with a convincing account of the social world. However, rhetoric alone is not enough. It may lead people into action and it may initiate attempts to transform the social world, but, unless it is possible to organize the structure of activity in ways that mirror the rhetorical definition of social categories, then such definitions are likely to be rejected as – quite literally – useless. In the longer term the aim is characteristically the organization of the whole society; in the shorter term it is important to realize the rhetorical vision in the internal organization of the movement itself.

In this regard, the role of ritual and ceremonial is crucial but sadly overlooked in psychological literature – through not outside. For instance Ozouf (1989) shows how the leaders of the French Revolution set about creating a set of new festivals to replace those of the ancient regime: organization in terms of fixed social status gave way to inherently transitory categories such as age. There is clearly much to be done in developing the practical–experiential dimension of categorization and in examining its relationship to the rhetorical. Indeed, it is hard to separate the two. However, for the present our focus is principally on the latter.

Much of our research to date has looked at the uses of national identity – not least because in such a domain it is hard to ignore the fact that categories relate to the future as much as the past: nationalism is not only a reflection of the nation state but it also serves to create nation states. In the contemporary world, national categories often both reflect a world organized into nations and also seek to reorganize relations within and between nations. The use of national categories is particularly widespread in electoral politics since electorates are generally organized on the level of the nation state, and hence the entire electorate can be addressed through the use of these categories. In order to gain the widest support for any policies it is necessary to invoke national identity. In Scotland, for instance, we have found that those seeking parliamentary office, whatever their hue – whether they are in favor of greater national independence or enhanced union in Britain – all proclaim their deep sense of Scottishness. Where they differ is in how they ascribe content to Scottish identity and hence how they characterize the relationship of their own policies (and those of their rivals) to the national identity (Hopkins and Reicher, 1997; Reicher and Hopkins, 2001a).

For the left, Scottishness is characterized in terms of egalitarianism and communalism. These values are exemplified by key moments of Scottish history from the Declaration of Arbroath in 1320 to the radical Trades Unionism of Red Clydeside in the twentieth century. They are expressed in the welfarist and redistributionist policies of the left parties. For the right, however, all that is alien to the Scots, who are truly a nation of entrepreneurs and self-made men, as exemplified by such as Andrew Carnegie and as embodied in national myths such as 'the lad of pairts' who rises by his efforts from humble beginnings to glory. This version of identity is therefore to be realized through the anti-statist and business-friendly policies of the right parties.

The use of national categories depends less on the ends to which one is mobilizing people than the audience one is seeking to mobilize. The implication is that when one aims at a sub- or supra-national mobilization then national categories will be inappropriate if not actively counter-productive. Thus, at the start of the Gulf Conflict of 1990–91, American President George Bush initially referred to the threat to American oil interests – a position which placed Arab oil producers as a potential or actual outgroup and which became a political millstone as soon as US strategy became centered on building an international coalition with troops based in Saudi Arabia. Hence, in his famous 'New World Order' speech to the UN on October 1, 1990, the sides in this fight were redefined such that they were no longer the US against the oil producers. Rather 'the world's quarrel is with the dictator who ordered that invasion [of Kuwait]' (Reicher, 1991). Herein the US and Arab countries were included together as part of the world that opposed Saddam Hussein and the rhetorical and practical aspects of mobilization were put back in alignment.

These various examples have been provided in order to sustain our various claims about the science of categorization and leadership. They demonstrate that categories are about creating, rather than reflecting, reality – about 'becoming' more than 'being'. They show how there can be multiple competing category definitions of the same context and that these are tied to the different projects held by different actors or even the same actor at different times. They also show the attempts by leaders to establish a consonance between themselves, their parties, their policies and the identity of the group to which they appeal. In other words, they point to generic aspects of the relationship between futures, rhetoric and identity in the performance of leadership.

However, our examples also show something of *how* leaders construe reality so as to present their proposals as realizations of the values and aspirations of those they address. They show the importance of linguistic tropes such as Saddam Hussein as standing for the entire Iraqi enemy. They show the invocation of history, whether it be the Declaration of Arbroath or Red Clydeside. In short, they point to the importance of understanding leadership as an art and they show the centrality of an artistic imagination in effective leadership.

The importance of imagination is all the greater because of the competing versions of categories in circulation. Leaders are rarely, if ever, in a position to solicit support for their projects without having to deal with rivals who seek to advance alternative projects. Hence, it is not enough to state one's case – to assert the consonance between identity and policy. Rather, the case has to be made convincing using the various resources we have pointed to (linguistic tropes; the use of history, and of cultural myths) and others besides (cf. Reicher and Hopkins, 2001a). Yet, even as politicians argue with their rivals, they are not seeking to persuade each other. Rather, their aim is to be overheard and supported by the electorate.

What concerns leaders is ultimately the imagination of their potential followers, and their arguments with rivals constitute the modality through which they negotiate with followers about the meaning of identity. When leaders offer particular definitions, they may be challenged, modified or rejected by their audience. For instance, the independence-supporting Scottish National Party tends to employ an inclusive 'civic' definition of nationhood: everyone who lives in and is committed to Scotland as Scottish. However our evidence suggests that many Scots are unwilling to accept this definition but rather accept as 'true Scots' only those born and bred in the country – preferably of parents with similar credentials.

More generally, while our studies of followers are only just beginning, it is already clear that they are as able as leaders to draw upon language, history and culture in order to debate the nature of identity. That is to say, there is the potential for them to participate, along with their leaders, in a democratic process of identity definition and policy consideration. This potential for active democracy, which engages the imagination of all, derives precisely from basing the influence process on what people share in common (their social identity) rather than what divides them (differences in individual characteristics or personal power) and in acknowledging that identity definition is an interpretative, rather than a perceptual, process. Yet to suggest that there is a potential for a democratic dialogue is not the same as claiming that this potential is always realized in practice. Leaders may actively use their skills to limit the participation of followers and constrict their ability to exercise choice. As we shall argue in the next section, the ways in which they do so relate to the different ways in which it is possible to establish the relationship between oneself, one's policies and the group identity.

Essentialized Identities and Undemocratic Leadership

There are two powerful ways of denying choice to others. One is to hide the existence of alternatives. The other is to limit who is in a position to define the alternatives. The former relates to the way in which leaders characterize their category versions. The latter relates to the way in which leaders characterize themselves. We shall briefly consider each in turn.

In his discussion of the modes of operation of ideology, Thompson (1990) refers to reification as a means by which transitory states of being can be represented as permanent, and hence alternatives to the status quo can be ruled out. He identifies three strategies of reification. These are: naturalization, in which social creations are treated as natural events; eternalization, in which social–historical phenomena are treated as permanent, unchanging and everlasting; and nominalization/passivization, which are linguistic devices whereby human creations are turned into objective entities which exist independently of a subject who creates them. Each of these strategies can be applied to the ways in which leaders seek to make their own contingent constructions of identity into something self-evident and unchallengable.

Naturalization is to be found in the ways that identities in general, and national identities in particular, are often ascribed to aspects of the physical environment. For instance, Franco made use of the writer Miguel de Unamuno to suggest that true Spaniards were a hard and wiry race, toasted by the summer sun, frozen by winter frosts, suited to the poverty of life and totally unsuited to a soft and alien liberalism (Richards, 1996). By contrast, radical Scots argue that the harsh Scottish climate creates a cooperative and communal people better suited to more left-wing policies (Reicher and Hopkins, 2001a). The point, then, is not that a given landscape inherently lends itself to a given construction of identity, but rather that the use of landscape provides a rhetorical means of naturalizing any construction of identity.

Eternalization is best illustrated by the uses of history to which we have already alluded. As Thompson puts it 'customs, traditions and institutions which seem to stretch indefinitely into the past, so that any trace of their origin is lost and any question of their end is unimaginable, acquire a rigidity which cannot be easily disrupted' (1990, p. 66). In turn, the timelessness of these customs, traditons and institutions can help establish a rigid and unimpeachable definition of collective identity. If Czechs can be shown to be an inherently revolutionary people wherever one looks in their history then the claim is not an arbitrary assumption but a timeless truth. The same goes for the alternative claim that Czechs are an inherently democratic people as founded on an alternative reading of history. It will come as no surprise that the former version was advanced by the Communist regime and the latter by those who challenged and destroyed that regime. In the words of Holy (1996), national history: 'is a history of rewriting its history'.

Finally, the strategies of nominalization and passivization can be found both in the employment of specific devices within leadership rhetoric and in the overall organization of speeches. For instance, in her address to the Conservative Party Conference concerning the miners' strike of 1984, Margaret Thatcher structures the whole speech in terms of an attack on democracy by terrorism. Democracy is invoked as the quintessential quality of the British nation and is represented by those opposed to the strikers. Terrorism is invoked as the expression of an alien tradition and is represented by those prosecuting the strike. Thus national categories underlie the entire argument, but in the body of the speech they are referred to only by indirect means such as the use of symbols. For instance, strike-breakers are characterized as (British) 'lions'. Only in the very last paragraph is the national dimension given explicit mention. Instead of being presented as a contingent frame of interpretation used by the speaker, the categories are finally revealed as if a neutral naming of the reality that has been previously evoked (Reicher and Hopkins, 1996a).

These various techniques of reification can be used to make it more difficult for followers to challenge the categorical formulations of leaders, both by suggesting that there is no alternative and by obscuring the assumptions on which these formulations are based. But such techniques do not outlaw the very attempt to mount a challenge. There is another element in Thatcher's rhetoric which comes close to doing so. At both the start and the end of the speech, the contrast between democracy and terrorism is made tangible in the struggle between the ruling Conservative Party and its enemies (either the IRA, which the previous night had bombed Thatcher's hotel, or the executive of the National Union of Miners). Hence the Conservative government is elided with democracy and with the nation. Thatcher's final words make the elision of these three elements quite clear: 'This government will not weaken. This nation will meet that challenge. Democracy will prevail' (Reicher and Hopkins, 1996a, p. 362). Once this has been done, then any attack upon the government becomes an attack upon democracy and the nation. Ironically, the language of democracy is used to outlaw democratic dissent.

This act of elision goes beyond making the particular (i.e., the government) a typical or even prototypical instance of the category (i.e., the British nation). Rather it becomes the concrete manifestation of the category. Instead of being one amongst several actual or potential voices who are qualified to speak, the government becomes a unique manifestation of the category's voice. Moreover, there is no need for the category incarnate to justify what is said as according with the categorical identity since, by definition, what is said defines that identity.

The example we have used so far concerns the relationship between an organization and a category. However the more usual examples of elision concern the relationship between leaders and categories. Indeed, we would argue that instances of charismatic leadership are those where precisely such an elision has been made. Charismatic phenomena do not derive from the actual characteristics of the leader but rather from an active creation whereby all elements of the leader – physical appearance, dress, personality, personal history, lineage and so on – are constructed so as to mesh with the myths of the category itself (cf. Wallis, 1984). What makes a charismatic leader, as indeed any leader, will therefore be dependent upon the nature of the categories involved. The act of construction will need to be all the more elaborate insofar as all aspects of individual and collective history need to be merged.

Wilner (1984), for instance, details the way in which the Indonesian leader Sukharno came to be represented as Bima, the legendary hero and demi god of Javanese and Balinese mythology. This was achieved along multiple dimensions. The tale of Sukharno's career was told so as to emphasize Bima's two key attributes – bravery and a stubborn will. The parallels between Bima's and Sukharno's muscular appearance were pointed up and made central to visual representations of the leader. Sukharno spoke in a booming voice and a low Javanese dialect that violated the norms of Indonesia's dominant cultural groups but which resonated with Bima's usage. Sukharno even alluded to Bima's association with the colour black (which symbolizes strength) by invariably carrying a black baton which, for some Indonesians, was a repository of sacred power.

Sukharno was also linked to Arjuna, incarnation of the god Wishnu, in legend a figure of such immense charm that all women were drawn to him. Sukharno's representation as Arjuna's incarnation was supported by tales of his immense sexual potency. Sukharno came to personify the fertility of the realm and thereby became a symbol of the land and the soil. Of course, many male leaders are endowed in myth with immense sexual power, to the extent that it is sometimes argued that this is a generic symbol of their power (cf. Schiffer, 1973). However, in this regard it is worth pointing out that Ghandi, who sought to personify the asceticism which is central to certain Hindu traditions, circulated stories of his own prodigious sexual abstinence from the age of 37 to the end of his life 41 years later. Once again, what guarantees charisma is not any quality in itself, but use of the quality in linking the myth of the individual to the myth of the category.

This link is at its most powerful when it can be expressed in the simplest terms and enacted in the simplest rituals wherein all the layers of construction have become habitual and can be taken for granted. Kershaw (1987) notes how the 'Hitler' myth was consciously promoted by the Nazi regime as an integrating force. This mythology was rich and varied. It drew upon a volkish-nationalist strain within the German history of ideas in which the cult of the nation, an ethnic definition of inclusion and exclusion (most notably reflected in anti-semitism) and the idea of 'heroic leadership' are all central ideas (Greenfeld, 1992). Within this framework Hitler became a blend of the great German heroes actual and mythical – a mixture of Siegfried and Frederick the Great (Kershaw, 1987). He was portrayed as the expression of the German racial spirit, he was the 'executor of the people's will' (quoted in Kershaw, 1987, p. 78) or, as Rudolf Hess asserted in his final words to the 1934 Nuremburg Rally: 'The Party is

Hitler. But Hitler is Germany, just as Germany is Hitler! Sieg Heil!' (Kershaw, 1987, p. 69). This elision between country, party and individual was the source of Hitler's authority. It made his voice the German voice and made his every utterance authoritative.

Clearly, in the Nazi case, authority was defended with force, and any dissent was subject to ruthless repression. However, in many cases people willingly surrendered themselves to the leader. From a social identity perspective this becomes explicable when one considers that the relationship between leaders and followers is mediated by their identification with a common social category. Where leaders are construed as the embodiment of the category, then, if followers internalize the category as part of their self-definition, the leader becomes part of who they are. Followers become defined in and through the leader. Indeed, the leader is in a better position to know who they are and what they want than they are themselves. One would therefore expect, firstly, that in such cases followers would experience a very immediate relationship with the leader; secondly, the relationship would be very intense and, thirdly, the leader would be experienced as an overwhelmingly controlling force: the leader's voice would become one's own voice, the leader's choices, one's own choices, the leader's will, one's own will. There is evidence from studies of followers in charismatic relations that supports all three of these propositions (e.g. Abel, 1986; Kershaw, 1987; Lindholm, 1990; Schiffer, 1973; Willner, 1984).

Many Germans report that, even in the context of mass events, they had a sense of the Fuhrer looking at them personally and addressing them personally. As one youth put it: 'I looked at him as he passed by and felt that he met my glance. All who have ever seen him must have felt the same way' (Abel, 1986, p. 271). Frequently, this relationship with Hitler went way beyond that of an acquaintance briefly glimpsed. In Kershaw's terms, Hitler was the recipient of a 'daily torrent of adulation' (1987: 81). In one letter, which Kershaw cites as representative of many, an old Nazi writes to his 'beloved' Hitler that 'I feel compelled by unceasing love to thank our creator daily for, through his grace, giving us and the entire German people such a wonderful Fuhrer' (ibid). The experience of being in Hitler's presence was yet more intense. Kurt Ludecke writes that: 'I experienced an exaltation that could be likened only to religious conversion' (cited in Lindholm, 1990 102). In the same quote, Ludecke refers to Hitler's 'intense will', and the way it 'seemed to flow from him into me'. That is also a common reaction of those who witnessed him speak. Abel quotes one convert as saying that: 'the German soul spoke to German manhood in his words. From that day on I could never violate my allegiance to Hitler' (ibid., pp. 152–3). Rauschning is referring to women when he describes the relationship of the audience to Hitler as one of 'rapturous self-surrender' (265), but the terms accords with the self-descriptions of both men and women.

These testimonies from the Nazi period are far from unique. There is evidence from studies of cults that the internalization of the leader and hence subordination to the leader's will can go even further. As one of Charles Manson's devotees put it: 'I became Charlie. Everything I once was, was Charlie. There was nothing left of me anymore' (from Bugliosi, 1974. Cited in Lindholm, 1990,

p. 132). At this point the ability of followers to question and challenge, let alone to replace the leader's definition of the group and of group activity, is totally lost. The relationship between the two has passed from democracy and dialogue to autocracy and monologue. The mass has indeed become an inert substance that can be fashioned at will by the leader (also see Chapter 13).

Conclusion

We have now come full circle. We both started and finished with a focus on the creative and dominant leader. In between, the question we have sought to answer is whether these qualities are fatally inextricable, or whether it is possible to have creativity and imagination without autocracy and domination.

Our answer is a firm (but qualified) affirmative. We suggest that leaders and followers are bound together through their identification with a common social category (the social identity approach) and that the definition of social categories involves a process of imagination oriented as much to the creation of future realities as the perception of present reality (an activist conception of social identity processes). This conception allows for the possibility of leader-follower relations that are both creative and democratic. However, it does not guarantee them. Whether leadership is democratic or autocratic depends upon the way in which social identity is defined. More precisely, it depends upon two inter-linked issues. On the one hand, is there a recognition that any identity has multiple possible definitions or is there both an insistence that there is a single 'authentic' definition and an attempt to claim authenticity for particular versions of the shared identity? On the other hand, is it accepted that all members have the right to participate in the process of collective self-definition or else is that right restricted to a particular subgroup, or even a particular individual? Democracy depends upon the premise that that 'we' may be many things. Democracy also depends upon an active attempt to involve all category members in an open process of category definition.

In this regard, the first step towards autocracy lies in the very assumption that there exists a single or 'true' version of identity just waiting to be revealed. So, perhaps the most important contribution that psychology can make to the study of leadership is to stress the multiple versions of identity that exist in relation to different visions of the future and to expose the means by which our choice between versions may be denied. Sadly, however, psychology tends in precisely the opposite direction to the extent that it shares and underpins the assumption of singularity in theory rather than exposing how the illusion of singularity is achieved in practice (Reicher and Hopkins, 2001b).

There is one final point that comes out of our analysis. An analysis of leadership, particularly of charismatic leadership, points to the need for social psychological research to come to terms with the issue of depth. The relationship with these leaders is not simply a matter of intellectual perspective and the consequence is not simply a matter of social influence. It is something that evokes immense passions. It is something that can affect one's very notion of oneself as a bounded agent. Traditionally these phenomena have been used to propose a purely irrationalist notion of leadership and collective action. We are certainly not proposing a return to such models. However, just as it is wrong to invoke passion so as to ignore the ideological and social cognitive dimensions of leadership, so it would be wrong to invoke the latter so as to marginalize the former. When we look at the fascinating and powerful phenomena of leadership, it becomes clear that this is a domain in which we can, and indeed must, put together ideology and depth, social categorization and emotion, perhaps even social psychology and psychopathology. However those are tasks for another day.

16 Identity, Power, and Strategic Social Categorizations: Theorizing the Language of Leadership

SCOTT A. REID AND SIK HUNG NG

Leaders emerge and fall from power based on their relationship with followers. Because leadership is a collective and dynamic process it is highly dependent on language and social identity. Leaders cannot exist without followers, and so they must use language to define themselves, their ingroup, and relevant outgroups. A basic goal of such discursive positioning is the mobilization of group identity. To galvanize a group for action, leaders will need to take advantage of followers' social psychological motives. These include: the desire for group distinctiveness, positive social identity, a coherent understanding of social events, and justifications for group actions (see Tajfel, 1981). In our view, the strategic exploitation of these social psychological motivations is fundamentally a power process mediated by language. Hence, in this chapter we focus on the communicative processes that leaders use to create, maintain, and conceal power in the mobilization of group identity.

While group mobilization has been, and continues to be, addressed within the social identity perspective, it remains that basic motivational (i.e., social identity theory; Tajfel and Turner, 1979), and/or social–cognitive (i.e., self-categorization theory; Turner, 1987) processes have captured theoretical and empirical attention. On the one hand this has been useful; the social identity approach recognizes the socially contingent nature of identity – social identity is malleable, fluid, and contextually variable. Yet, at the same time, the active and strategic elements of identity construction that lend it power remain to be elaborated. How is it that identity is constructed and manipulated with *strategic* intent? (also see Chapters 14 and 15). Castells (1997) makes this point succinctly: 'It is easy to agree on the fact that, from a sociological perspective, all identities are constructed. The real issue is how, from what, by whom, and for what?' (p. 7). Our assertion is that these questions are every bit as pertinent to a social psychological analysis of identity.

Following Ng (1996), we would contend that the social identity perspective has yet to articulate a meaningful approach to the question of power.

Both social identity theory and self-categorization theory furnish a passive approach to influence, power, and by extension group mobilization – social change is something that happens to you, it is not something that you *do*. Another way of putting this is that the social identity approach treats social psychological phenomena as a reflection of social contextual realities (cf. Hopkins and Reicher 1997; Reicher and Hopkins, 1996; Chapter 16). For example, according to social identity theory people act with reference to their perceptions of the stability and legitimacy of group status, and the possibility of shifting between groups. However, an important yet simple question remains: how is it – in the first instance – that masses of people come to view social arrangements as stable, legitimate, or otherwise? Our argument is that to answer such a question we will need to consider the use of language (as power) to create, conceal, and routinize social contextual information.

In the remainder of this chapter we will substantiate these assertions in the context of a theoretical elaboration of Hogg and Reid's (2001) model of leadership and power. We will describe the role of language in the theory, and provide examples of real-world intergroup processes that illustrate the centrality of language to leadership, power, and identity.

The Social Identity Theory of Leadership

The social identity approach contributes to the study of leadership through its description of social contextual influences on collective self-perception (see Hogg, 2001; Chapter 3; Chapter 4). Leaders emerge and are perceived as effective insofar that they provide a faithful rendition of ingroup identity in relation to significant outgroups. Such representations are context dependent: they change depending upon the outgroup used for comparison, and they reflect the form of the (cooperative or competitive) relations between groups. These collective representations are described by prototypes. Prototypes are clusters of group-defining traits that simultaneously maximize intragroup similarities and intergroup differences associated with particular ingroup–outgroup social comparisons. As the frame of reference changes, new ingroup–outgroup comparisons become relevant, and hence the prototypical traits that describe the ingroup in that context change. Prototypical representations can be internalized as self-definitions, and are for this reason influential. When internalized, prototypes describe and prescribe thoughts, feelings, and beliefs that rationalize contextually salient intergroup comparisons. Consequently, people who embody the ingroup by possessing prototypical traits stand a strong chance of emerging and being endorsed as leaders (Hains, Hogg, and Duck, 1997; Hogg, Hains, and Mason, 1998; Platow and van Knippenberg, 2001; Chapter 10).

Extending the Social Identity Theory of Leadership: Leadership and Power

It is obvious that there are situations where leaders will behave as benevolent visionaries, just as there are situations where leaders will abuse their power in the most ruthless and despicable ways imaginable. The question is, which social psychological processes might enable a theoretical understanding of these different forms of behavior? In first attempting an answer to this question, it becomes clear that one will need to consider: (1) how leadership evolves over time, (2) how a leader or leadership clique might come to gain power within and across groups, (3) the circumstances that would lead to the exercise of that power, and (4) what effects such an exercise of power might have for the leader. To take account of these processes we integrated ideas from the social identity theory of leadership (Hogg, 2001), theory and research on power (French and Raven, 1959; Mulder, 1977; Reid and Ng, 1999, 2000), and the concept of idiosyncrasy credit (Hollander, 1958, 1985), and, critically, placed these processes within a diachronic framework. (For an elaboration of the background to this theory see Hogg and Reid, 2001.) Essentially, we described four stages of leadership: (1) leader emergence; (2) stabilization of the leadership position, (3) intragroup leader–follower power differentiation, and (4) the abuse of power.

Elaborating the role of language in the leadership-power process

In this section we extend Hogg and Reid's (2001) model of leadership and power by elaborating the role of language in the strategic manipulation of identity for power. More specifically, following Ng and Bradac (1993; see also Ng and Reid, 2001; Reid and Ng, 1999) we will demonstrate the role of language in revealing, creating, concealing, and routinizing a leader's power. We will do this in the context of the four stages of leadership just described.

First, it is necessary to describe the relationships between language and power. The power *behind* language describes the subordinate relation of language to power. This idea is captured in Mao's famous adage: 'power comes from the barrel of a gun'. From this perspective, language merely reflects or reveals an actor's power base. But language does not simply serve as a passive channel for the exercise of power and influence; language is an active co-player in social action. The power of language describes this active contribution of language to power. Language can be used to create material power, to conceal or mask the exercise of power when it might be perceived as undesirable, and it can contribute to making a dominance relationship appear natural.

Language and the autocatalytic relations of prototypicality and power

According to Hogg and Reid (2001) the theoretical mechanism that makes it possible to develop and maintain the leadership position is an autocatalytic relation between prototypicality and the exercise of influence and power. By occupying the prototypical ingroup position, an emergent leader gains the legitimacy to innovate from the ingroup norm (cf. Platow and van Knippenberg, 2001; Hollander, 1958, 1985); by engaging in innovation, the leader will enhance his or her power bases; these power bases can be used in turn to control the prototypical ingroup position, and this makes it possible to secure further power bases.

The means of this process is yet to be described. Our argument is that language enables this process as follows:

(1) Prototypicality is the crucial resource that bonds a leader to the group, but prototypicality is realized, maintained, and stabilized through the creative and dynamic use of linguistic social categorizations;

(2) Linguistically constructed (yet contextually grounded) categorizations enable the leader to broaden his or her power base – both in reality (by adding reward and coercive power), and as conceived social–psychologically in the minds of followers (by adding legitimate, informational, referent, and expert power);

(3) The inflation of these power bases feeds back into control of the prototypical ingroup position, and thus the ability to maintain the leadership position. This is because:

   (a) support from followers aids the task of linguistically manipulating ingroup and outgroup prototypes (followers are more likely to ascribe to the leader's definition of reality) such that the prototypical ingroup position remains focused upon the leader; and,

   (b) because it makes it possible to side-line pretenders to the leadership position.

This process continues unless it is countered by a leader's complacency (and thus inadvertent loss of power), broad and sweeping social changes that wrest the leader's control of the prototypical position, the opposing power of a conflictual outgroup, or an aspiring prototypical ingroup leader. The only antidote to power is counter power.

The language and power of leader emergence

Ariel Sharon's rise to Prime Minister of Israel illustrates the active, strategic, and constructive use of language and communication in leadership emergence. First,

Sharon engaged in behaviors designed to inflame social tensions and heighten social instability leading up to the February 2001 general election. This effectively changed Israeli-Palestinian relations, and made the relatively dovish Ehud Barak a non-prototypical leader. Second, Sharon engineered a new image of himself as the leader to resolve those very social tensions that he was instrumental in creating. Sharon gained leadership with an unprecedented margin.

Specifically, in his role as opposition leader of the right-wing Likud party, Sharon made a highly controversial visit to the Temple Mount (the al-Aksa Mosque for Muslims) in late September of 2000. This event took place in a context where the then Prime Minister Ehud Barak had been engaged (apparently at least) in an attempt to bring peace to the Middle East by offering concessions to the Egyptians, Syrians, Lebanese, Jordanians, and, in particular, the Palestinians. In July of 2001 Barak and Arafat met at Camp David and discussed the terms of a possible peace settlement. Barak, for example, proposed that Israel would exchange sovereignty in Jerusalem for Palestinian control of the West Bank. However, Arafat was unwilling or unable to accept Barak's offer; the summit was ultimately unsuccessful, and tensions between Palestinians and Israelis became, once again, inflamed.

Sharon's visit to the Temple Mount took place in the context of this volatile situation. In fact, immediately after his visit violent Palestinian demonstrations took place in the West Bank and Gaza Strip that led to the deaths of 40 rioters (BBC news, October 2, 2000). It is worth asking: was this visit instrumental in sparking off the violence? Given the symbolism associated with the Temple Mount, and the proximity of the action to the general election, we would suggest that the answer is yes. In fact, at the time of Sharon's visit, visits by Jews to the Temple Mount were banned by the rabbinical council of Judea, Samaria, and Gaza (the ban has since been rescinded). This ban reflected the fact that this particular site is a focus for the Israeli–Palestinian territorial dispute. Indeed, the Temple Mount can be taken to represent a focus of Palestinian–Israeli tensions insofar as it serves as a metaphor for the groups' negative interdependence over territory, as well as religious, and political differences. By visiting this site, Sharon was in effect communicating a simple proposition: 'this land belongs to Israel'. That Sharon was at least aware that his visit would spark tensions is clear from his remark to BBC reporters during his visit: 'there's no provocation here, the provocation is only on the other side' (BBC news, September 28, 2000). The fact that Sharon made his visit surrounded by armed guards seems to further corroborate this interpretation.

This action accomplished two goals: first, by further inflaming tensions, and demonstrating how quickly Palestinians were to engage in violent protest, Sharon was able to create the legitimacy required to engage in further conflict. As a result, a leader would need to be seen to respond appropriately to the Palestinian violence. Second, this served to polarize the prototype away from the relatively moderate Barak whose dovish approach to the group relations suddenly became incompatible with the reality of the intergroup conflict.

Although Sharon's action was highly effective in inflaming tensions with the Palestinians, the Israeli public was not looking for a figure who would lead them into further conflict; quite the contrary, the will of the constituent was still in favour of peace. Because of this, Sharon still had work to do leading up to the election to re-engineer his image. Specifically, Sharon diffused an image of himself as a fatherly protector of Israel. For example, campaign adverts showed Sharon playing with children (grandfather image), archive pictures of Sharon in military uniform (military hero), while being told that 'only Sharon will bring peace' and 'protect us'. In Sharon's (January, 2001) words:

> We all want peace, true peace. Peace with security. Peace that will protect us. There isn't a part of the society that wants peace and another that doesn't – and therefore we must pursue peace through unity. This unity will allow us to advance with courage towards peace with our neighbors and will allow us to firmly stand together regarding the things which are most vital to us. We are a nation, a state, and a people who desire peace: the most precious gift. With an experienced leadership, responsible and trustworthy in the truth and its path, we will succeed and reach peace, security, financial prosperity – and a richly diverse yet united and more balanced society. I ask for your trust and support.

Indeed, the success of Sharon's rhetoric is in some regards an impressive accomplishment. The images of Sharon that have been socially diffused among the general public, along with the voters' desire to believe, seem to have been enough to counter his well-known hawkish character.

In fact, a proof that Sharon's image as a peace-maker was linguistically and strategically constructed is not difficult. Quite simply, Sharon was known as an extremely hawkish politician and soldier – the reverse to his campaign image as a dovish instigator of social stability. For example (and the list is much longer than this – see BBC news, 7 February, 2001 profile), Sharon joined the Haganah at age 14 (see Israel ministry of foreign affairs, 1999); a military organization that, ironically, engaged in terrorist activities to prevent the deportation of Jews from Palestine by the British (Britannica, 2001); he fought in the Arab–Israeli war of 1948–49; was instrumental in attacks on Egyptian military units stationed in the Gaza Strip in the 1950s; was the mastermind of the Israeli invasion of Lebanon in 1982; and was removed from office in 1983 having been found indirectly responsible for the massacre of 'between 800 and 1500 Palestinians' (BBC news, 28 November, 2001) in a Beirut refugee camp by Lebanese Christian Militia at a time that the Israeli army controlled the area (while under the command of Sharon). In his role as minister of construction and housing (1990–92) Sharon presided over an unprecedented installation of Israeli settlements in newly captured land, and earned himself the nickname 'bulldozer'.

This demonstrates very clearly that emergence as the prototypical group member is not a passive process. If the social context was to provide a match with the most prototypical group member, it would not be Sharon. Indeed, Sharon diffused a prototypical image of himself, quite in contrast to that suggested by his deeds.

In sum, Sharon emerged as leader because he was able to encourage violence from the Palestinians, which he then used to justify attacking them further.

Additionally, Sharon was able to create, or at least intensify, the social uncertainties in his own constituency and to capitalize by diffusing an image of himself as the 'man to bring peace and security' – and all this despite well known evidence of his Hawkish character. Sharon's form of engineered persuasion is consistent with Lukes' (1974) three-dimensional conception of power:

> A may exercise power over B by getting him to do what he does not want to do, but he also exercises power over him by influencing, shaping or determining his very wants. Indeed, is it not the supreme exercise of power to get another or others to have the desires you want them to have – that is, to secure their compliance by controlling their thoughts and desires? (p. 23)

The language and power of leadership maintenance/stabilization

Regardless of the stage of leadership, the autocatalytic process that ties power resources to prototypicality operates as the mechanism of leadership; what does differ across stages is a leader's degree of control over resources and hence the prototypical position. Leaders who are relatively well established generally have at their disposal greater power than emergent leaders (military coups being an obvious exception). This makes the question of maintaining leadership one of mobilizing power and constructing and justifying its use through language.

The re-election of the Liberal–National coalition and John Howard as Prime Minister in Australia in November 2001 provides an illustrative example.

On August 26, 2001, a 20-metre fishing boat carrying 438 refugees (mostly nationals of Afghanistan and Iraq) from Indonesia was stranded and beginning to sink approximately 140 kilometres off the coast of Christmas Island (an Australian territory, 1,400 km off north-western Australia). The refugees and crew were rescued by a Norwegian container ship, the *Tampa*. The refugees, having boarded the *Tampa*, were reported to have demanded to be taken to Christmas Island: 'Five men went to the ship's bridge and threatened to jump overboard if the *Tampa* set course for Indonesia' (Douez, August 28, 2001).

Although the *Tampa* was relatively close to Christmas Island, where there were facilities for processing the refugees, the Howard government refused to allow the ship to land. In fact, the Australian government sent SAS commandos to Christmas Island to prevent the *Tampa* from entering Australian waters, and to board the ship if it did cross (which it did). Further, the parliament rushed through a bill (following 50 minutes of debate) that was designed to: (1) prevent legal challenge against the Howard government, (2) protect Australian officials from civil or criminal legal action, and (3) make it possible not to process the refugees while they were in Australian waters (see Hudson, 2001). Further still, the government sent four RAAF P3 Orion maritime surveillance aircraft, three frigates, a refuelling ship, and a troop carrier to the waters south of Indonesia for the purpose of discouraging further craft from attempting to cross into Australian waters. In addition to marshalling legal and military power, the government organized the processing of 150 refugees offshore in New Zealand, and the rest on the tiny island republic of Nauru some 6,000 km away – the latter including the building of detention centres and 30 million dollars in aid for development programs. It was estimated that this 'Pacific solution' cost 500 million Australian dollars (Oxfam, 2002).

While the mobilization of all of these forms of power are in themselves impressive, they would have been meaningless if not communicated with vigor to the electorate. Indeed, part of the rationale for mobilizing such force may have been to ensure the government intensive media coverage.

Instrumental to the resurgence of the government was the manner in which they managed various media images. In short, Prime Minister Howard, Minister of Immigration Phillip Ruddock, and Minister of Foreign Affairs Alexander Downer, were unanimous in: (1) their construal of the situation as an international crisis, (2) the view that Australia was under threat from mass illegal migrations, (3) the representation of Australia as a highly caring country with an almost unmatched record of compassion to refugees, and (4) categorizations of the refugees at various stages as (a) hijackers, (b) illegal immigrants, (c) queue jumpers, and (d) as having paid 'large sums of money' to 'people smugglers' when, (e) free to travel. These categorizations can all be understood as fulfilling one or more of the social functions of stereotypes proposed by Tajfel (1981); namely, these categorizations serve to inflame and reduce uncertainties about a threatening social situation, justify the actions of the government, and highlight the positive dimensions of Australian identity. But more than that, we would suggest that these categorizations possess an additional, but critical, feature – that of control.

Linguistic categorizations are controlling for two reasons. First, by producing an accepted categorization, the connotations that follow serve to create an image that was not produced in the initial words. A stereotypical image can be invoked with relatively few words, but the rest of the stereotype is then automatically invoked and assumed to be equally diagnostic of the person or persons described. Second, when such categorizations are widely diffused, they are controlling insofar that they produce a definition of reality – a definition that may require considerable effort to overturn, especially if it becomes generally accepted. To take an example, Phillip Ruddock, in a television interview, stated:

> The important point here is that this group of people put the captain of this vessel under duress because they wanted to come to Australia. And one understands that, they've paid large amounts of money, had been free enough to travel. They didn't wish to return to Indonesia. It wasn't because of issues of safety, it was because they see Australia as a migration destination primarily … I mean, it's akin to hijacking if you look at it in terms of what happened in this particular case. (September 2, 2001)

These categorizations serve a number of the purposes discussed above. First, the image that is invoked from hearing these words is not of a group of refugees fleeing persecution, hunger, or disease; rather, the image is of a group of self-interested, relatively wealthy terrorists who would prefer to live in Australia because it is a nicer place than Indonesia. To those who accept this definition of reality, there is a strong justification for preventing these people from landing on Australian territory; there is a positive reflection on Australia in relation to Indonesia; and there is a ready explanation that might be used to explain further actions the government might engage in to prevent such people making it to Australia.

A second incident occurred on October 6. In this instance the Australian Navy fired across the bow of a refugee ship to discourage it from entering Australian waters off the coast of Christmas Island. The ship was later boarded and the tough new penalties for 'people smuggling' into Australian territory explained. A critical event then allegedly took place. According to Minister Ruddock, some of the approximately 300, mainly Iraqi, asylum seekers started to throw children wearing life jackets into the water in the hope that they would be rescued by the Australian Navy. In commenting, Mr. Ruddock stated: 'It would be unfortunate if the steps being taken by the passengers lead to a loss of life but we will do our best to ensure that doesn't happen' (BBC news, 7 October, 2001). In this particular case, the implication is that asylum seekers packed onto decrepit boats are devious and reckless 'passengers' – the image of a group of people so desperate to save their children that they might engage in such behavior was not mentioned. Indeed, this is not surprising – evidence has emerged that this incident was misrepresented by the Howard government (ABC news, February 18, 2002). At the time of writing (February 17, 2002) there are calls for a senate inquiry into the evidence of these claims. The evidence so far suggests, at best, the Howard government made these claims while uninformed of the truth, and, at worst, engineered the scandal to increase their votes in the general election. Regardless of the truth on this matter, there is certainly evidence that the scandal was instrumental in the re-election of the Howard government.

Morgan polls conducted over the period (Roy Morgan research, 2001) show that prior to any major social events, the Labour Party was 10 percentage points ahead of the Liberal–National Party coalition, and was predicted to gain a landslide win if the election had taken place at that time. However, it can be seen that this 10 per cent difference is quickly attenuated to four over the initial four-to-five day period that the Tampa crisis was covered in the media. Although this was an ongoing crisis, throughout this period the Beazley Labor Party adopted the strategy of mirroring the coalition in their treatment of the refugees. And, initially, this seemed to have been a useful strategy, because by September 8/9 the Labour Party lead was restored. The next major event was the terrorist attacks on the United States on September 11. The social uncertainties produced by these events, together with Prime Minister Howard's presence in Washington, the rapid commitment of Australian troops to the war in Afghanistan, and the ongoing illegal immigration 'crisis', led to gains for the coalition that brought them neck-to-neck with Labour by October 6/7. This lead was once again taken by Labour following the televised debate of John

Howard and Kim Beazley on October 14. However, the coalition continued with the claims that asylum seekers were deliberately manipulating the Australian navy, knowing that they would be saved if they disabled their ships. On November 8, just two days prior to the election, the Howard government released a videotape taken by the Australian navy that allegedly showed children being thrown overboard from a refugee ship. The government was voted back to power.

The language of intra- and inter-group differentiation

One of the concerns of the leadership-power theory is in understanding the processes that might induce a leader to abuse power over followers. The proposal is that the social–cognitive and power differentiation of the leader from followers produces an embryonic inter-group categorization that can transform the leader–follower relationship from an intra- to an inter-group relation (cf. Mulder, 1977). By gaining more power within the group, the leader becomes more likely to subscribe to such a categorization. However, this process of intra-group differentiation is tied to the leader's exercise of power in inter-group social contexts – the leader gains power by successfully mobilizing the group in relation to relevant outgroups (see also Hogg, 2001). For this reason, we will focus upon intergroup linguistic processes and their concomitant effects on intra-group power differentiation.

An illustrative example can be found in the American Civil Rights Movements of the 1960s. By the mid-1960s, many black Americans had become dissatisfied with the progress of Martin Luther King's moderate and non-violent approach to civil rights. This dissatisfaction was compounded by a series of factors: several years of integrationist rhetoric, non-violent protest, some failed campaigns (e.g., the March, 1965 Selma Alabama demonstrations where King turned his followers back from a line of state troopers brandishing clubs and tear gas); the critical observation that many black Americans were still living in oppressive conditions; and the fact that many protestors suffered imprisonment and beatings at the hands of white police (e.g., in Birmingham, Alabama in spring 1963). These events created the context required for a more aggressive approach to civil rights issues. Capitalizing on this discontent, Stokely Carmichael redefined the direction of the Civil Rights Movement by taking a militant stand – by criticizing the integrative strategies of King for achieving justice and an end to oppression, espousing a national/separatist approach to black–white relations, self-defence, economic control, and the creation of positive black stereotypes. Instrumental in the success of this counter movement was the 'Black power' slogan, and the accompanying symbol of the raised fist.

Carmichael's militancy towards white authority is captured in his rhetoric at Greenwood, Mississippi on June 17, 1966. Carmichael was released from arrest just minutes prior to giving his address to a rally of some 3,000 people:

When Stokely moved forward to speak, the crowd greeted him with a huge roar. He acknowledged his reception with a raised arm and clenched fist. Realizing that he was in his element, with his people, Stokely let it all hang out. 'This is the twenty-seventh time I have been arrested – and I ain't going to jail no more!' The crowd exploded into cheers and clapping. 'The only way we gonna stop them white men from whuppin' us is to take over. We have been saying freedom for six years and we ain't got nothin. What we gonna start saying now is BLACK POWER!' The crowd was right with him. They picked up his thoughts immediately. 'BLACK POWER!' they roared in unison. Willie Rickes, who was as good at orchestrating the emotions of a crowd as anyone I have ever seen, sprang into action. Jumping to the platform with Stokely, he yelled to the crowd, 'What do you Want?' 'BLACK POWER!' 'What do you want?' 'BLACK POWER!' 'What do you want?' 'BLACK POWER!' 'BLACK POWER!' 'BLACK POWER!' Everything that happened afterward was a response to that moment. More than anything, it assured that the Meredith March Against Fear would go down in history as one of the major turning points in the black liberation struggle.

(quoted by Stewart, 1997, p. 433–434)

Carmichael did not emerge with a new strategy for achieving equality or an end to exploitation. His strategy was to move from town to town and to communicate the views of militancy. He did not form a new movement to focus the fervor, nor did he particularly care to take a leadership role (in fact, he left for Guinea, West Africa in 1969 and changed his name to Kwame Toure). Nevertheless, Carmichael was successful in capitalizing on, and transforming, the discontent, and forming it into the sentiment of black pride. He changed the meaning of being black in America; for example, the word 'negro' was no longer to be a group-defining term. At the same time, however, this had an effect on intragroup relations. By taking a militant stand, black identity in America became more tightly focused around a militant/conflictual prototype. In fact, this prototypical image of a black militant was specifically that of a *male* black militant. Women in the movement were all but relegated to a secondary role. Reflecting this change, Carmichael was reputed to have remarked, when reacting to a paper on 'the position of women in the SNCC', that 'the only position for women in the SNCC is prone'.

Carmichael's militancy can be understood as an intergroup process. By taking a militant stance, he was in effect enhancing the bargaining power of moderates such as King (cf. Killian, 1972). This is the case because white Americans, when being confronted by an image of angry and threatening black Americans, will categorize moderates as ingroup members more so than if the context of comparison was simply between whites and moderate blacks (without militant blacks as the second outgroup). Further, the militant approach can provide a potent basis for the mobilization of black interests around the tightly focused group prototype, and the sense of esteem that can be gained for new members. However, this is not to say that the effects of moderate-militant categorizations will necessarily all be positive. If whites were to feel too threatened, and if solutions to resolving the conflict were seen as too difficult, then negative sanctions could be anticipated. Indeed, 'the black voices of the 1960s have been eliminated; virtually all the leaders of the black movement are in jail, in exile or are dead' (Borden, 1973, p. 423).

Language and the exercise of naked power

When the leader has acquired a great deal of power within the group, and when he or she feels sufficiently threatened, the exercise of power can shift from normative social influence that flows from group consensus, to a direct unmasked attempt to maintain position through force. In Russell's (1938) words:

> As the beliefs and habits which have upheld traditional power decay, it gradually gives way to power based upon some new belief, or to 'naked' power, i.e., to the kind that involves no acquiescence on the part of the subject. Such is the power of the butcher over the sheep, of an invading army over a vanquished nation, and of the police over detected conspirators. The power of the Catholic Church over Catholics is traditional, but its power over heretics who are persecuted is naked. (p. 57)

Traditional power is exercised within the confines of an ingroup normative consensus. Leaders can be influential with ingroup members, but they cannot expect to be influential by using coercive power. However, the shift from traditional to naked power (i.e., from normative influence to coercion) is not a simple matter of ingroup–outgroup relations (cf. Turner, 1991). The Catholic Church does not have a pre-given ingroup–outgroup relation with true believers and heretics, these categories are created when the need arises. Again, language is crucial to the exercise of naked power, because it is necessary to use language to construct the 'other' to justify the exercise of power. But more than this, coercive power can be used covertly to control the information that is presented to ingroup members. Thus, coercion can create the conditions for influence when the exercise of that power is concealed.

The situation that led up to the Zimbabwe national elections on March 9–10 2002 provides an illustrative example. President Mugabe has pushed through three new bills (out of four proposed) in a thinly veiled attempt to ensure success in the coming election. The 'freedom of information and right to privacy bill' ensures control over journalists. To be a journalist in Zimbabwe now requires state accreditation, and there are stiff penalties for those who might 'spread rumors or falsehoods that cause alarm and despondency under the guise of authentic reports' (BBC news, February 5, 2002) – penalties include a fine up to Z\$100,000 or two years' imprisonment. How this might occur is not entirely clear, given that the bill also bars journalists from publishing 'unauthorized' reports of cabinet deliberations and policy advice. The Public Order and Security Act makes it illegal to 'undermine the authority of the president or engender hostility towards him', or to 'perform acts, utter words, distribute or display any writing, sign or other visible representation that is obscene, threatening, abusive, insulting or intended to provoke a breach of peace' (BBC news, February 5, 2002). The punishment for breaking this law ranges from heavy fines, imprisonment, through to execution. Finally, the General Laws Amendment Act makes it difficult for people to register to vote. This bill effectively removes a number of votes from the opposition party through control of postal votes: 'postal votes are restricted to diplomats and members of the armed forces, disenfranchizing millions of students and workers living abroad' (BBC news, February 5, 2002).

These bills demonstrate the centrality of language in maintaining the leadership position. Indeed, the very content of these bills suggests that Mugabe will not cede power even if the opposition were to gain more votes – he will be able, 'legally', to treat any opposition claims of an electoral victory as an attempt to 'undermine the authority of the president'. So, on the one hand, these words appear to be no more than a reflection of Mugabe's governmental power. These laws make it possible to prevent the dissent of challengers to the government position. However, there is also power in the wording of these bills. Each bill comes with words vague enough to make it possible to construe the behavior of challengers as illegal; it is this obfuscated language that makes the requisite 'othering' of opposition figures possible before sending them to prison or the executioner's block.

A second linguistic strategy of the Mugabe government is to control and disseminate state propaganda within the media. Because foreign journalists have been banned from Zimbabwe, the main sources of information about the government are to be found in the state media. Winter (2002) reports the 'absurd Orwellian significance' of these broadcasts: 'His Excellency the president, Comrade Robert Mugabe has opened a dam in Masonaland ...', 'The opposition MDC have been denounced as traitors ...' The significance of such control is not in its immediate effects – indeed, it may result in quite negative reactions when seen as obvious propaganda. The effect of such language is cumulative: when no alternative version of reality is apparent over a period of time (dissent is illegal after all), and when the official line has been presented with clarity and consistency long enough, the cumulative result is the routinization of the status quo. Through systematic deletion of alternative views, and a consistent message, the effect can be psychological exhaustion and an inability to conceive of reality in any other way. Indeed, Winter (2002) comments: 'I tried to ignore this form of psychological pressure while I was there but after a few months it did start to wear me down.'

Indeed, time has borne out our (a priori) analysis. Robert Mugabe won power in a highly controversial election (BBC news, March 13, 2002), following which his chief rival Morgan Tsvangirai was fined 1.5 million Zimbabwean dollars, was ordered to surrender property and his passport, and faces trial for treason. If found guilty, Tsvangirai may be executed (BBC news, March 20, 2002).

Concluding Comments

Our discussion of leadership and power has centered around several interconnected processes: collective self-definition as a group member, leadership, leader–follower interdependence, the bases and exercise of power, and, importantly, the central role of language. Indeed, the mechanism that makes power come to life is communicative: to ensure success leaders must use language to create, justify, depoliticize, and routinize power. Language is not a passive by-product of power bases or social cognitive mechanisms – it is an active co-player in the realization of power. Language *is* the power process in action (for elaboration see Reid and Ng, 1999). In illustrating this process we hope to have gone beyond the static and passive view that relates social psychological processes directly to patterns of intergroup relations but stops short of elaborating the actual *doing* of identity, power, and intergroup conflict.

At the same time we believe we have gone beyond the perspective that conceives the language–power relationship as 'the power *behind* language' – as if language were entirely incidental to the 'real' variables of power and identity. Furthermore, we hope to have gone beyond the perspective that conceives the relationship as 'the power *of* language' – as if language were the sole component of power in action (for further discussion of these perspectives, see Ng and Bradac, 1993; Ng and Reid, 2001). Rather, we hope to have demonstrated, in principle at least, that power bases and the power *of* language are interdependent constructs. At present, research aimed at testing the full model is yet to be conducted, but we believe many of the crucial processes have been illustrated.

References

ABC news (February 18, 2002). *PM's Dept head knew children overboard claims were wrong.* http://abc.net.au/news/australia/2002/02/item20020218131816_1.htm

Abel, T. (1986). *Why Hitler came to power.* Cambridge, MA: Harvard University Press.

Abrams, D., and Hogg, M.A. (2001). Collective identity: Group membership and self-conception. In M.A. Hogg and R.S. Tindale (eds), *Blackwell handbook of social psychology: Group processes* (pp. 425–60). Oxford: Blackwell.

Abrams, D., Wetherell, M., Cochrane, S., Hogg, M.A., and Turner, J.C. (1990). Knowing what to think by knowing who you are: Self-categorisation and the nature of norm formation, conformity and group polarisation. *British Journal of Social Psychology, 29,* 97–119.

Adams, J.S. (1965) Inequity in social exchange. In L. Berkowitz (ed.), *Advances in experimental social psychology* (Vol. 2, pp. 267–99). New York: Academic Press.

Adler, N.J. (1999). Global leaders: Women of influence. In G.N. Powell (ed.), *Handbook of gender and work* (pp. 239–61). Thousand Oaks, CA: Sage.

Adler, N.J., and Izraeli, D.N. (1994). *Competitive frontiers: Women managers in a global economy.* Cambridge, MA: Blackwell Business.

Alimo-Metcalfe, B., and Alban-Metcalfe, R.J. (2001). The development of a new transformational leadership questionnaire. *Journal of Occupational and Organizational Psychology, 74,* 1–27.

Allport, G.W. (1954). *The nature of prejudice.* Reading, MA: Addison-Wesley.

Anderson, D.L. (1993). *Shadow on the White House: Presidents and the Vietnam war.* Lawrence, Kansas: University of Kansas Press.

Antaki, C., Condor, S., and Levine, M. (1996). Social identities in talk: Speakers' own orientations. *British Journal of Social Psychology, 35,* 473–492.

Aries, E. (1996). *Men and women in interaction: Reconsidering the differences.* New York: Oxford University Press.

Aron, A., and Aron, E.N. (1997). Self-expansion motivation and including other in the self. In S. Duck (ed.), *Handbook of personal relationships: Theory, research and interventions* (2nd ed., pp. 251–270). New York: John Wiley & Sons, Inc.

Aron, A., Aron, E.N., Tudor, N., and Nelson, G. (1991). Close relationships as including other in the self. *Journal of Personality and Social Psychology, 60,* 241–53.

Aron, A., and Fraley, B. (1999). Relationship closeness as including other in the self: Cognitive underpinnings and measures. *Social Cognition, 17*(2), 140–60.

Ashforth, B.E., and Mael, F. (1989). Social identity theory and the organization. *Academy of Management Review, 14,* 20–39.

Astin, A.W., Parrott, S.A., Korn, W.S., and Sax, L.J. (1997). *The American freshman: Thirty year trends.* Los Angeles: Higher Education Research Institute, University of California, Los Angeles.

Atwater, L.E., Carey, J.A., and Waldman, D.A. (2001). Gender and discipline in the workplace: Wait until your father gets home. *Journal of Management, 27,* 537–61.

Avolio, B., Bass, B., and Jung, D.I. (1995). *MLQ Multifactor Leadership Questionnaire: Technical report*. Palo Alto, CA: Mind Garden.

Ayman, R., Chemers, M.M., and Fiedler, F.E. (1998). The contingency model of leadership effectiveness: Its levels of analysis. In F. Dansereau and F.J. Yammarino (eds), *Leadership: The multiple-level approaches*. Stamford, CT: JAI Press.

Bacharach, S.B., and Lawler, E.J. (1981). *Bargaining*. San Francisco: Jossey-Bass.

Bandura, A. (1997). *Self-efficacy: The exercise of control*. New York: W.H. Freeman.

Barber, J.D. (1972). *The presidential character: Predicting performance in the White House*. Englewood Cliffs, NJ: Prentice-Hall.

Bardach, J.L., and Eccles, R.G. (1989). Price, authority, and trust. *Annual Review of Sociology*, 15, 97–118.

Baron, R.S., Inman, M., and Kao, C.F. and Logan, H. (1992). Negative emotion and superficial social processing. *Motivation and Emotion*, 16, 323–46.

Baron, R.S., Van Dello, J. and Brunsman, B. (1996). The Forgotten Variable in Conformity Research: The Impact of Task Importance on Social Influence. *Journal of Personality and Social Psychology*, 71, 915–27.

Baron, R.S. (1986). Distraction-conflict theory: Progress and problems. In L. Berkowitz (ed.). *Advances in experimental social psychology*. 19, 1–40, New York: Academic Press.

Baron, R.S. (2000). Arousal, capacity and intense indoctrination. *Personality and Social Psychology Review*, 4, 3: 238–54.

Barrett, D.M. (1993) *Uncertain warriors: Lyndon Johnson and his Vietnam advisors*. Lawrence, KS: Kansas University Press.

Barron, S. (1991). *'Degenerate art': The fate of the avant-garde in Nazi Germany*. Los Angeles, CA: Harry N. Abrams, Inc.

Barry, B., and Shapiro, D.L. (1992). Influence tactics in combination: The interactive effects of soft versus hard influence tactics and rational exchange. *Journal of Applied Social Psychology*, 22, 1429–41.

Barsalou, L.W. (1983). Ad hoc categories. *Memory and Cognition*, 11, 211–27.

Bass, B.M. (1985). *Leadership and performance beyond expectations*. New York: Free Press.

Bass, B.M. (1988). Evolving perspectives on charismatic leadership. In J.A. Conger and R.N. Kanungo (eds), *Charismatic leadership: The elusive factor in organizational effectiveness* (pp. 40–77). San Francisco, CA: Jossey-Bass.

Bass, B.M. (1990). *Bass and Stogdill's handbook of leadership: Theory, research and managerial applications* (3rd edn). New York: The Free Press.

Bass, B.M. (1990). From transactional to transformational leadership: Learning to share the vision. *Organizational Dynamics*, 18, 19–31.

Bass, B.M. (1998). *Transformational leadership: Industry, military, and educational impact*. Mahwah, NJ: Erlbaum.

Bass, B.M., and Avolio, B.J. (1993). Transformational leadership: A response to critiques. In M.M. Chemers and R.A. Ayman (eds), *Leadership theory and research: Perspectives and directions* (pp. 49–80). London: Academic Press.

Bass, B.M., and Avolio, B.J. (1997). *Full range leadership development: Manual for the Multifactor Leadership Questionnaire*. San Francisco, CA: MindGarden Inc.

Baumeister, R.F., and Leary, M.R. (1995). The need to belong: Desire for interpersonal attachments as a fundamental human motivation. *Psychological Bulletin*, 117, 497–529.

BBC News (September 28, 2000). *Ariel Sharon makes his fateful visit to Jerusalem*. http://news.bbc.co.uk/hi/english/in_depth/middle_east/2001/tv_and_radio_reports/newsid_1691000/1691972.stm

BBC News (October 2, 2000). *Israel apportions blame*. http://news.bbc.co.uk/hi/english/world/monitoring/media_reports/newsid_953000/953507.stm

BBC News (February 7, 2001). *Arial Sharon: Controversial hardliner*. http://news.bbc.co.uk/hi/english/world/middle_east/newsid_1154000/1154622.stm

BBC News (October 7, 2001). *Refugee children 'thrown from ship'*. http://news.bbc.co.uk/hi/english/world/asia-pacific/newsid_1584000/1584024.stm

BBC News (November 28, 2001). *Court postpones Sharon ruling*. http://news.bbc.co.uk/hi/english/world/middle_east/newsid_1680000/1680577.stm

BBC News (February 5, 2002). *Zimbabwe's controversial laws*. http://news.bbc.co.uk/hi/english/world/africa/newsid_1748000/1748979.stm

BBC News (March 13, 2002). *Rival rejects Mugabe win*. http://news.bbc.co.uk/hi/english/world/africa/newsid_1871000/1871392.stm

BBC News (March 20, 2002). *Mugabe rival charged with treason*. http://news.bbc.co.uk/hi/english/world/africa/newsid_1884000/1884191.stm

Beersma, B., and De Dreu, C.K.W. (2002). Integrative and distributive negotiation in small groups: Effects of task structure, decision rule, and social motive. *Organizational Behavior and Human Decision Processes*, 87, 227–52.

Ben-Yoav, O., and Pruitt, D. (1984). Resistance to yielding and the expectation of cooperative future interaction in negotiation. *Journal of Experimental Social Psychology*, 34, 323–35.

Berger, J. and Zelditch, M. (1998). *Status, power, and legitimacy: Strategies and theories*. New Brunswick, NJ: Transaction Press.

Berger, J., Cohen, B.P., and Zelditch, M. (1972). Status characteristics and social interaction. *American Sociological Review*, 37, 241–55.

Berger, J., Fisek, H., Norman, R., and Zelditch, M. (1977). *Status characteristics and social interaction*. New York: Elsevier.

Berger, J., Norman, R.Z., Balkwell, J.W., and Smith, L. (1992). Status inconsistency in task situations: A test of four status processing principles. *American Sociological Review*, 57, 843–55.

Berger, J., Ridgeway, C.L., Fisek, M.H. and Norman, R.Z. (1998). The legitimation and delegitimation of power and prestige orders. *American Sociological Review*, 63, 379–405.

Berger, J., Ridgeway, C.L., and Zelditch, M. (2002). Construction of status and referential structures. *Sociological Theory*, 20, 157–79.

Berman, L. (1982). *Planning a tragedy: The Americanization of the war in Vietnam*. New York: Norton.

Berman, L. (1988). Lyndon B. Johnson: Paths chosen and opportunities lost. In F.I. Greenstein (ed.), *Leadership in the modern presidency*. Cambridge, MA: Harvard University Press.

Berman, L. (1989). *Lyndon Johnson's War*. New York: Norton.

Beschloss, M.R. (1997). *Taking charge: The Johnson White House tapes, 1963–1964*. New York: Simon & Schuster.

Beschloss, M.R. (2001). *Reaching for glory: Lyndon Johnson's secret White House tapes, 1964–1965*. New York, London: Simon & Schuster.

Besson, Y. (1991). *Identités et conflits au proche orient*. Paris: L'Harmattan.

Biernat, M. and Kobrynowicz, D. (1997). Gender and race-based standards of competence: lower minimum standards but higher ability standards for devalued groups. *Journal of Personality and Social Psychology*, 72, 544–57.

Biernat, M. and Vescio, T.K. (1993). Categorisation and stereotyping: Effects of group context on memory and social judgment. *Journal of Experimental Social Psychology*, 29, 166–202.

Bies, R.J. and Moag, J.F. (1986). Interactional justice: Communication criteria of fairness. In R.J. Lewicki, B.H. Sheppard, and M.H. Bazerman (eds), *Research on negotiations in organizations* (Vol. 1, pp. 43–55). Greenwich, CT: JAI Press.

Biesanz, J.C., Neuberg, S.L., Smith, D.M., Asher, T., and Judice, T.N. (2001). When accuracy-motivated perceivers fail: Limited attentional resources and the re-emerging self-fulfilling prophecy. *Personality and Social Psychology Bulletin*, 27, 621–9.

Bion, W. (1961). *Experiences in Groups*. New York: Basic Books.

Blair, I.V., and Banaji, M.R. (1996). Automatic and controlled processes in stereotype priming. *Journal of Personality and Social Psychology*, 70, 1142–63.

Blau, P. (1964). *Exchange and power in social life*. New York: Wiley.

Bodenhausen, G.V. (1993). Emotions, arousal and stereotypic judgements: A heuristic model of affect and stereotyping. In D.M. Mackie and D.L. Hamilton (eds), *Affect, cognition and stereotyping* (pp. 13–37). New York: Academic Press.

Bodenhausen, G.V., and Macrae, C.N. (1998). Stereotype activation and inhibition. In R.S. Wyer, Jr (ed.), *Stereotype activation and inhibition.* (pp. 1–52). Mahwah, NJ: Erlbaum.

Boldry, J., Wood, W., and Kashy, D.A. (2001). Gender stereotypes and the evaluation of men and women in military training. *Journal of Social Issues*, 57, 689–706.

Bond R., and Smith P.B. (1996). Culture and conformity: A meta analysis of studies using the Asch's line judgement task. *Psychological Bulletin*, 119, 111–37.

Borden, K.W. (1973). Black rhetoric in the 1960's: Sociohistorical perspectives. *Journal of Black Studies*, 3, 423–31.

Branscombe, N.R., Ellemers, N., Spears, R., and Doosje, B. (1999). The context and content of social identity threat. In N. Ellemers, R. Spears and B. Doosje (eds), *Social identity: Context, commitment, content* (pp. 35–58). Oxford: Blackwell.

Brennan, J.G., Miller, L.E., and Seltzer, J. (1993). Influence tactics and effectiveness. *Journal of Social Psychology*, 133, 747–8.

Brewer, M. (1979). Ingroup bias in the minimal intergroup situation: A cognitive–motivational analysis. *Psychological Bulletin*, 86, 307–24.

Brewer, M.B. (1988). A dual process model of impression formation. In T.K. Srull and R.S. Wyer, Jr (eds). *A dual process model of impression formation* (pp. 1–36). Hillsdale, NJ: Erlbaum.

Brewer, M.B. (1991). The social self: On being the same and different at the same time. *Personality and Social Psychology Bulletin*, 17, 475–82.

Brewer, M.B., and Brown, R.J. (1998). Intergroup relations. In D.T. Gilbert, S.T. Fiske, and G. Lindzey (eds), *The handbook of social psychology* (4th ed., Vol. 2, pp. 554–94). New York: McGraw-Hill.

Brewer, M.B., and Gardner, W. (1996). Who is this 'we'? Levels of collective identity and self representations. *Journal of Personality and Social Psychology*, 71(1), 83–93.

Brewer, M.B., and Pickett, C.L. (1999). Distinctiveness motives as a source of the social self. In T.R. Tyler, R.M. Kramer and O.P. John (eds), *The psychology of the social self*. Mahwah, NJ: Erlbaum.

Brockner, J., and Rubin, J. (1985). *Entrapment in escalating conflicts*. New York: Springer-Verlag.

Brown, D.E. (1991). *Human universals*. Philadelphia, PA: Temple University Press.

Brown, D.J., Lord, R.G., Hanges, P.E., and Hall, R.J. (2002). *Leadership perceptions: A dynamic perspective*. (Manuscript submitted for publication.)

Brown, J.D. (1990). Evaluating one's abilities: Shortcuts and stumbling blocks on the road to self-knowledge. *Journal of Experimental Social Psychology*, 26, 149–67.

Browne, K. (1998). *Divided labours: An evolutionary view of women at work*. New Haven, CT: Yale University Press.

Bruins, J. (1997). *Predicting the use of influence tactics: A classification and the role of group membership*. Paper presented at the European Congress on Work and Organisational Psychology, Verona, Italy.

Bruins, J.J., and Wilke, H.A. (1993). Upward power tendencies in a hierarchy: Power Distance Theory versus bureaucratic rule. *European Journal of Social Psychology*, 23, 239–54.

Bruner, J.S. (1957). On perceptual readiness. *Psychological Review*, 64, 123–51.

Bueno de Mesquita, B. (1981). Risk, power distributions and the likelihood of war. *International Studies Quarterly*, 25, 541–68.

Burgess, D., and Borgida, E. (1999). Who women are, who women should be: Descriptive and prescriptive gender stereotyping in sex discrimination. *Psychology, Public Policy, and Law*, 5, 665–92.

Burke, J.P., and Greenstein, F.I. (1989). *How presidents test reality: Decisions on Vietnam, 1954 and 1965*. New York: Russell Sage Foundation.

Burns, J.M. (1978). *Leadership*. New York: Harper & Row.

Burt, R.S., Jannotta, J.E., and Mahoney, J.T. (1998). Personality correlates of structural holes. *Social Networks*, 20, 63–87.

Buss, D.M., Gomes, M., Higgins, D.S., and Lauterbach, K. (1987). Tactics of manipulation. *Journal of Personality and Social Psychology*, 52, 1219–29.

Butz, D.A., Vescio, T.K., and Snyder, M. (2002, February). Leadership style and stereotype-based hypothesis testing. Poster session presented at the annual meeting of the Society of Personality and Social Psychology, Savannah, GA.

Byrnes, J.P., Miller, D.C., and Schafer, W.D. (1999). Gender differences in risk taking: A meta-analysis. *Psychological Bulletin*, 125, 367–83.

Calder, B.J. (1977). An attributional theory of leadership. In B.M. Staw and G.R. Salancik (eds), *New directions in organizational behavior* (pp. 179–204). Chicago, IL: St. Clair Press.

Califano, J.A. (1991). *The triumph and tragedy of Lyndon Johnson*. New York: Simon & Schuster.

Caporael, L.R., Dawes, R.M., Orbell, J.M., and Van de Kragt, A.J. (1989). Selfishness examined: Cooperation in the absence of egoistic incentives. *Behavioral and Brain Sciences*, 12, 683–739.

Carli, L.L. (2001). Gender and social influence. *Journal of Social Issues*, 57, 725–41.

Caro, R.A. (1982). *The path to power: The years of Lyndon Johnson*. New York: Vintage Books.

Carter, L.F., and Nixon, M. (1949). An investigation of the relationship between four criteria of leadership ability for three different tasks. *Journal of Psychology*, 27, 245–61.

Cartwright, D. (ed.) (1959). *Studies in social power*. Ann Arbor, MI: University of Michigan Press.

Castells, E. (1997). *The power of identity*. Malden, MA: Blackwell.

Catalyst. (2000). *Census of women corporate officers and top earners*. New York: Catalyst.

Catalyst. (2002). *Fact sheet: Women CEOs*. Retrieved on October 6, 2002 from Catalyst website, http://www.catalystwomen.org/press_room/factsheets/fact_women_ceos.htm.

Cejka, M.A., and Eagly, A.H. (1999). Gender-stereotypic images of occupations correspond to the sex segregation of employment. *Personality and Social Psychology Bulletin*, 25, 413–23.

Center for the American Woman and Politics. (2001). *Fact sheet*. Retrieved June 6, 2001, from Rutgers University, Eagleton Institute of Politics, Center for the American Woman and Politics Web site: http://www.rci.rutgers.edu/~cawp/pdf/elective.pdf.

Chaiken, S. (1987). The heuristic model of persuasion. In M.P. Zanna, J.M. Olson and C.P. Herman (eds), *Social influence: The Ontario symposium* (Vol. 5, pp. 3–39). Hillsdale, NJ: Erlbaum.

Chan, K.Y. and Drasgow, F. (2001). Toward a theory of individual differences and leadership: Understanding the motivation to lead. *Journal of Applied Psychology*, 86, 481–98.

Charity Frauds Bureau (1974) Final Report of the Children of God to Honorable Louis J. Lefkowitz, Attorney General of the State of New York. (unpublished report: State of New York.

Chemers, M.M. (2001). Leadership effectiveness: An integrative review. In M.A. Hogg and S. Tindale (eds), *Blackwell handbook of social psychology: Group processes* (pp. 376–99). Maulden, MA: Blackwell.

Chemers, M.M., Watson, C.B., and May, S.T. (2000). Dispositional affect and leadership effectiveness: A comparison of self-esteem, optimism, and efficacy. *Personality and Social Psychology Bulletin*, 26, 267–77.

Chemers, M.M. (1987). Leadership processes: Intrapersonal, interpersonal, and societal influences. In C. Hendrick (ed.), *Review of Personalty and Social Psychology* (Vol. 8, pp. 252–77). Newbury Park, CA: Sage.

Chessick, R. (1979). A practical approach to the psychotherapy of the borderline patient. *American Journal of Psychotherapy*, 33, 531–46.

Chin, M.G., and McClintock, C.G. (1993). The effects of intergroup discrimination and social values on level of self-esteem in the minimal group paradigm. *European Journal of Social Psychology*, 23, 63–75.

Cialdini, R.B., and Trost, M.R. (1998). Social influence: Social norms, conformity, and compliance. In D.T. Gilbert, S.T. Fiske and G. Lindzey (eds), *The handbook of social psychology* (4th ed., Vol. 2, pp. 151–92). Boston: McGraw-Hill.

Cleveland, J.N., Stockdale, M., and Murphy, K.R. (2000). *Women and men in organizations: Sex and gender issues at work.* Mahwah, NJ: Erlbaum.

Clifford, C. (1991). *Counsel to the president.* New York: Random House.

Cogliser, C.C., and Schriesheim, C.A. (2000). Exploring work unit context and leader–member exchange: A multi-level perspective. *Journal of Organizational Behavior*, 21, 487–511.

Colquitt, J.A., Conlon, D.E, Wesson, M.J., Porter, C.O.L.H., and Ng, K.Y. (2001) Justice at the millennium: A meta-analytic review of 25 years of organizational justice research. *Journal of Applied Psychology*, 86, 425–45.

Conger, J.A., and Kanungo, R.N. (1987). Toward a behavioral theory of charismatic leadership in organizational settings. *Academy of Management Review*, 12, 637–47.

Conger, J.A., and Kanungo, R.N. (1988). Conclusion: patterns and trends in studying charismatic leadership. In J.A. Conger and R.N. Kanungo (eds), *Charismatic leadership: The elusive factor in organizational effectiveness* (pp. 324–36). San Fransisco: Jossey-Bass.

Conger, J.A., and Kanungo, R.N. (1998). *Charismatic leadership in organizations.* Thousand Oaks, CA: Sage.

Conway, M., Pizzamiglio, M.T., and Mount, L. (1996). Status, communality, and agency: Implications for stereotypes of gender and other groups. *Journal of Personality and Social Psychology*, 71, 25–38.

Cronshaw, S.F., and Lord, R.G. (1987). Effects of categorization, attribution, and encoding processes on leadership perceptions. *Journal of Applied Psychology*, 72, 97–106.

Cropanzano, R., and Greenberg, J. (1997). Progress in organizational justice: Tunneling through the maze. In C. Cooper and I. Robertson (eds), *International review of industrial and organizational psychology* (pp. 317–372). New York: Wiley.

Dallek, R. (1991). *Lone star rising: Lyndon Baines Johnson.* New York: Oxford University Press.

Dansereau, F., Cashman, J., and Graen, G. (1973). Instrumentality theory and equity theory as complementary approaches in predicting the relationship between leadership and turnover among managers. *Organizational Behavior and Human Performance*, 13, 46–78.

Dansereau, F., Graen, G.B., and Haga, W. (1975). A vertical dyad linkage approach to leadership in formal organisations: A longitudinal investigation of the role making process. *Organizational Behavior and Human Performance*, 13, 46–78.

Darley, J.M. (1966). Fear and social comparison as determinants of conformity behavior. *Journal of Personality and Social Psychology*, 4, 73–8.

Dasgupta, P. (1988). Trust as a commodity. In D. Gambetta (ed.), *Trust: Making and breaking cooperative relations* (pp. 49–72). Oxford: Basil Blackwell.

Davis, D. (1984). *The Children of God: The inside story*. Grand Rapids, MI: Zondervan.

Davison, H.K., and Burke, M.J. (2000). Sex discrimination in simulated employment contexts: A meta-analytic investigation. *Journal of Vocational Behavior*, 56, 225–48.

De Cremer, D. (2000). Leadership selection in social dilemmas – not all prefer it: The moderating role of social value orientation. *Group Dynamics: Theory, Research and Practice*, 4, 330–7.

De Cremer, D. (2002a). Respect and cooperation in social dilemmas: the importance of feeling included. *Personality and Social Psychology Bulletin*, 28, 1335–41.

De Cremer, D. (2002b). Charismatic leadership and cooperation in social dilemmas: A matter of transforming motives? *Journal of Applied Social Psychology*, 32, 997–1016.

De Cremer, D. (2002c). *The importance of respect as a function of belongingness needs: A relational equilibrium model.* (Manuscript submitted for publication.)

De Cremer, D. (2002d). *Cooperation as a function of belongingness needs, respect and status within the group: A relational equilibrium model.* Unpublished manuscript, Maastricht University, The Netherlands.

De Cremer, D. (in press). Exploring the instrumental versus non-instrumental aspects of procedural fairness: The usefulness of a person x situation approach. In F. Columbus (ed.), *Advances in psychology research.* New York: NOVA science publishers.

De Cremer, D., Snyder, M., and Dewitte, S. (2001). The less I trust the less I contribute (or not?): The effect of trust, accountability and self-monitoring in social dilemmas. *European Journal of Social Psychology*, 31, 93–107.

De Cremer, D., and van den Bos, K. (2001). Relational Concerns and Leadership in Social Dilemmas: Interdependent Self-Construal and Procedural Fairness Effects on Cooperation With Leaders. Unpublished Manuscript, Maastricht University, The Netherlands.

De Cremer, D., and van Dijk, E. (2002). Reactions to group success and failure as a function of identification level: A test of the goal-transformation hypothesis in social dilemmas. *Journal of Experimental Social Psychology*, 38, 435–42.

De Cremer, D., and van Knippenberg, D. (2002). How do leaders promote cooperation? The effects of charisma and procedural fairness. *Journal of Applied Psychology*, 87, 858–66.

De Cremer, D., and van Lange, P. (2001). Why prosocials exhibit greater cooperation than proselfs: The role of responsibility. *European Journal of Personality*, 15, S5 –S18.

De Cremer, D., van Vugt, M. (1999). Social identification effects in social dilemmas; A transformation of motives. *European Journal of Social Psychology*, 29, 871–93.

De Cremer, D., and van Vugt, M. (2002). Intergroup and intragroup aspects of leadership in social dilemmas: A relational model of cooperation. *Journal of Experimental Social Psychology*, 38, 126–36.

De Dreu, C.K.W. (1995). Coercive power and concession making in bilateral negotiation. *Journal of Conflict Resolution*, 39, 646–70.

De Dreu, C.K.W., Giebels, E., and van de Vliert, E. (1998). Social motives and trust in integrative negotiation: Disruptive effects of punitive capability. *Journal of Applied Psychology*, 83, 408–22.

De Dreu, C.K.W., and McCusker, C. (1997). Gain-loss frames in two-person social dilemmas: A transformational analysis. *Journal of Personality and Social Psychology*, 72, 1093–106.

De Dreu, C.K.W., Nauta, A., and van de Vliert, E. (1995). Self-serving evaluation of conflict behavior and escalation of the dispute. *Journal of Applied Social Psychology*, 25, 2049–66.

De Dreu, C.K.W., and van Kleef, G.A. (2002). *The influence of power on information search, impression formation, and concession making in negotiation.* Unpublished manuscript, University of Amsterdam.

De Dreu, C.K.W., and van Lange, P.A.M. (1995). Impact of social value orientation on negotiator cognition and behavior. *Personality and Social Psychology Bulletin*, 21, 1178–88.

De Dreu, C.K.W., Weingart, L.R., and Kwon, S. (2000). Influence of social motives on integrative negotiation: A meta-analytical review and test of two theories. *Journal of Personality and Social Psychology*, 78, 889–905.

de Zárate, R.O. (2002). *Women world leaders: 1945–2002.* Retrieved on October 6, 2002 from http://www.terra.es/personal2/monolith/00women.htm.

Deaux, K. (1996). Social identification. In E.T. Higgins and A.W. Kruglanski (eds), *Social psychology: Handbook of basic principles* (pp. 777–98). New York: Guilford Press.

Deaux, K., and Lewis, L.L. (1984). Structure of gender stereotypes: Interrelationships among components and gender label. *Journal of Personality and Social Psychology*, 46, 991–1004.

Deaux, K., Reid, A., Mizrahi, K., and Cotting, D. (1999). Connecting the person to the social: The functions of social identification. In T.R. Tyler, R.M. Kramer, and O.P. John (eds), *The psychology of the social self* (pp. 91–113). Mahwah, NJ: Lawrence Erlbaum Associates.

Deci, E.L. (1980). *The psychology of self-determination.* Lexington, MA: Lexington.

Deci, E.L., and Ryan, R.M. (2000). The what and why of goal pursuits: Human needs and the self-determination of behavior. *Psychological Inquiry*, 11, 227–68.

Deluga, R.J., and Souza, J. (1991). The effects of transformational and transactional leadership styles in the influencing behaviour of subordinate police officers. *Journal of Occupational Psychology* 64, 49–55.

Den Hartog, D.N., House, R.J., Hanges, P.J., Ruiz-Quintanilla, S.A., Dorfman, P.W., and Associates (1999). Culture specific and cross-culturally generalizable implicit leadership. *Leadership Quarterly*, 10, 219–56.

Déprét, E., and Fiske, S.T. (2000). Perceiving the powerful: Intriguing individuals versus threatening groups. *Journal of Experimental Social Psychology*, 35, 461–80.

Deutsch, M. (1958). Trust and suspicion. *Journal of Conflict Resolution*, 2, 265–79.

Deutsch, M. (1973). *The resolution of conflict: Constructive and destructive processes.* New Haven: Yale University Press.

Devine, P.G., Hamilton, D.L., and Ostrom, T.M. (eds) (1994). *Social cognition: Impact on social psychology.* San Diego, CA: Academic Press.

Diekman, A.B., and Eagly, A.H. (2000). Stereotypes as dynamic constructs: Women and men of the past, present, and future. *Personality and Social Psychology Bulletin*, 26, 1171–81.

Dienesch, R.M., and Liden, R.C. (1986). Leader–member exchange model of leadership: A critique and further development. *Academy of Management Review*, 11, 618–34.

Dijksterhuis, A., and van Knippenberg, A. (1998). The relation between perception and behavior, or how to win a game of Trivial Pursuit. *Journal of Personality and Social Psychology*, 74, 865–77.

Dirks, K.T. (2000). Trust in leadership and team performance: Evidence from NCAA basketball. *Journal of Applied Psychology*, 85, 1004–12.

Dolinski, D., and Nawrat, R. (1998). 'Fear-then-relief' procedure for producing compliance: Beware when the danger is over. *Journal of Experimental Social Psychology*, 34, 27–50.

Douez, S, (2001, August 28). *How captain took on a human cargo*. http:// www.theage.com. au/news/national/2001/08/28/FFXTTNRBVQC.html

Dovidio, J.F., Brown, C.E., Heltman, K., Ellyson, S.L., and Keating, C.F. (1988). Power displays between women and men in discussions of gender linked tasks: A multi-channel study. *Journal of Personality and Social Psychology*, 55, 580–7.

Driskell, J.E., and Mullen, B. (1990). Status, expectations, and behavior: A meta-analytic review and test of the theory. *Personality and Social Psychology Bulletin* 16, 541–53.

Duchon, D., Green, S., and Taber, T.D. (1986). Vertical dyad linkage: A longitudinal assessment of antecedents, measures, and consequences. *Journal of Applied Psychology*, 71, 56–60.

Duck, J.M., and Fielding, K.S. (1999). Leaders and subgroups: One of us or one of them? *Group Processes and Intergroup Relations*, 2, 203–30.

Dunning, D., and Sherman, D.A. (1997). Stereotypes and tacit inference. *Journal of Personality and Social Psychology*, 73, 459–71.

Eagly, A.H. (1987). *Sex differences in social behavior: A social-role interpretation*. Hillsdale, NJ: Erlbaum.

Eagly, A.H. (in press). Prejudice: Toward a more inclusive understanding. In A.H. Eagly, R.M. Baron and V.L. Hamilton (eds), *The social psychology of group identity and social conflict: Theory, application, and practice*. Washington DC: APA Books.

Eagly, A.H., and Johannesen-Schmidt, M.C. (2001). The leadership styles of women and men. *Journal of Social Issues*, 57, 781–97.

Eagly, A.H., Johannesen-Schmidt, M.C., and van Engen, M. (2003). Transformational, transactional, and laissez-faire leadership styles: A meta-analysis comparing women and men. *Psychological Bulletin*, 129, 569–91.

Eagly, A.H., and Johnson, B.T. (1990). Gender and leadership style: A meta-analysis. *Psychological Bulletin*, 108, 233–56.

Eagly, A.H., and Karau, S.J. (1991). Gender and the emergence of leaders: A meta-analysis. *Journal of Personality and Social Psychology*, 60, 685–710.

Eagly, A.H., and Karau, S.J. (2002). Role congruity theory of prejudice toward female leaders. *Psychological Review*, 109, 573–98.

Eagly, A.H., Karau, S.J., and Makhijani, M.G. (1995). Gender and the effectiveness of leaders: A meta-analysis. *Psychological Bulletin*, 117, 125–45.

Eagly, A.H., Makhijani, M.G., and Klonsky, B.G. (1992). Gender and the evaluation of leaders: A meta-analysis. *Psychological Bulletin*, 111, 543–88.

Eagly, A.H., and Mladinic, A. (1989). Gender stereotypes and attitudes toward women and men. *Personality and Social Psychology Bulletin*, 15, 543–58.

Eagly, A.H., and Mladinic, A. (1994). Are people prejudiced against women? Some answers from research on attitudes, gender stereotypes, and judgments of competence. In W. Stroebe and M. Hewstone (eds), *European review of social psychology* (Vol. 5, pp. 1–35). New York: Wiley.

Eagly, A.H., and Steffen, V.J. (1984). Gender stereotypes stem from the distribution of women and men into social roles. *Journal of Personality and Social Psychology*, 46, 735–54.

Eagly, A.H., Wood, W., and Diekman, A. (2000). Social role theory of sex differences and similarities: A current appraisal. In T. Eckes and H.M. Trautner (eds), *The developmental social psychology of gender* (pp. 123–74). Mahwah, NJ: Erlbaum.

Eckes, T. (1994). Explorations in gender cognition: Content and structure of female and male subtypes. *Social Cognition*, 12, 37–60.

Ehrhart, M.G., and Klein, K.J. (2001). Predicting followers' preferences for charismatic leadership: the influence of follower values and personality. *Leadership Quarterly*, 12, 153–79.

Ellemers, N., Spears, R., and Doosje, B. (eds) (1999). *Social identity*. Oxford: Blackwell.

Elsbach, K.D., and Kramer, R.M. (1996). Members' responses to organizational identity threats: Encountering and countering the Business Week rankings. *Administrative Science Quarterly*, 41, 442–76.

Epitropaki, O., and Martin, R. (1999). The impact of relational demography on the quality of leader–member exchanges (LMX) and employees' work attitudes and well being. *Journal of Occupational and Organizational Psychology*, 72, 237–40.

Erber, R., and Fiske, S.T. (1984). Outcome dependency and attention to inconsistent information. *Journal of Personality and Social Psychology*, 47, 709–26.

Erez, M., and Earley, P.C. (1993). *Culture, self-identity, and work*. New York: Oxford University Press.

Erez, M., Rim, Y., and Keider, I. (1986). The two sides of the tactics of influence: Agent vs target. *Journal of Occupational Psychology*, 59, 25–39.

Eysenck, M.W. (1977). *Human memory: theory, research, and individual differences*. Oxford: Pergamon.

Falbo, T. (1977). Multidimensional scaling of power strategies. *Journal of Personality and Social Psychology*, 35, 537–47.

Falbo, T., and Peplau, L.A. (1980). Power strategies in intimate relationships. *Journal of Personality and Social Psychology*, 38, 618–28.

Farmer, S.M., Maslyn, J.M., Fedor, D.B., and Goodman, J.S. (1997). Putting upward influence strategies in context. *Journal of Organizational Behavior*, 18, 12–42.

Fein, S., and Spencer, S.J. (1997). Prejudice as self-image maintenance: Affirming the self through derogating others. *Journal of Personality and Social Psychology*, 73, 31–44.

Fiedler, F.E. (1964). A contingency model of leadership effectiveness. In L. Berkowitz (ed.), *Advances in experimental social psychology* (Vol. 1, pp. 149–90) New York: Academic Press.

Fiedler, F.E. (1967). *A theory of leadership effectiveness*. New York: McGraw-Hill.

Fiedler, F.E., and House, R.J. (1994) Leadership theory and research: a report of progress. In C. Cooper and I. Robertson (eds) *Key reviews in managerial psychology* (pp. 97–116). New York: Wiley.

Fielding, K.S., and Hogg, M.A. (1997). Social identity, self-categorization, and leadership: A field study of small interactive groups. *Group Dynamics: Theory, Research, and Practice*, 1, 39–51.

Fisek, M.H., Berger, J., and Norman, R.Z. (1991). Participation in heterogeneous and homogeneous groups: A theoretical integration. *American Journal of Sociology*, 97, 114–42.

Fiske, S.T. (1993). Controlling other people: The impact of power on stereotyping. *American Psychologist*, 48, 621–8.

Fiske, S.T. (1998). Stereotyping, prejudice, and discrimination. In D.T. Gilbert, S.T. Fiske and G. Lindzey (eds), *The handbook of social psychology* (4th ed., Vol. 2, pp. 357–411). Boston, MA: McGraw-Hill.

Fiske, S.T., Bersoff, D.N., Borgida, E., Deaux, K., and Heilman, M.E. (1991). Social science research on trial: Use of sex stereotyping research in Price Waterhouse vs. Hopkins. *American Psychologist*, 46, 1049–60.

Fiske, S.T., Lin, M., and Neuberg, S.L. (1999). The continuum model: Ten years later. In S. Chaiken and Y. Trope (eds) *Dual-process theories in social psychology* (pp. 231–54). New York: The Guilford Press.

Fiske, S.T., and Neuberg, S.L. (1990). A continuum model of impression formation: From category-based to individuating processes as a function of information, motivation, and attention. In M.P. Zanna (ed.), *Advance in experimental psychology* (Vol. 23, pp. 1–108). San Diego, CA: Academic Press.

Fiske, S.T., Neuberg, S.L., Beattie, A.E., and Milberg, S.J., (1987). Category-based and attribute-based reactions to others: Some informational conditions of stereotyping and individuating processes. *Journal of Experimental Social Psychology*, 23, 399–427.

Fiske, S.T., and Stevens, L.E. (1993). What's so special about sex? Gender stereotyping and discrimination. In S. Oskamp and M. Costanzo (eds), *Gender issues in contemporary society: Applied social psychology annual* (pp. 173–96). Newbury Park, CA: Sage.

Fleishman, E.A., and Harris, E.F. (1962). Patterns of leadership behavior related to employee grievances and turnover. *Personnel Psychology*, 15, 43–56.

Florian, V., and Mikulincer, M. (1997). Fear of death and judgement of social transgressions: A multidimensional test of terror management theory. *Journal of Personality and Social Psychology*, 24, 1104–12.

Foddy, M., and Platow, M.J. (2001). *Rethinking reputation: Group membership and trustworthiness*. Paper presented at the Fourth Annual Conference of the Asian Association of Social Psychology, Melbourne, Australia.

Foddy, M., Platow, M.J., and Yamagishi, T. (2001). *Group-based trust in strangers: Evaluations or expectations?* (Manuscript under review).

Folger, R. (1977). Distributive and procedural justice: Combined impact of 'voice' and improvement of experienced inequity. *Journal of Personality and Social Psychology*, 35, 108–19.

Fondas, N. (1997). Feminization unveiled: Management qualities in contemporary writings. *Academy of Management Review*, 22, 257–82.

Forsyth, D. (1999). *Group Dynamics* (3rd edn) Belmont, CA: Wadsworth.

Foschi, M. (1989). Status characteristics, standards, and attributions. In J. Berger, M. Zelditch, Jr and B. Anderson (eds), *Sociological theories in progress: New formulations*, (pp. 58–72). Newbury Park, CA: Sage.

Foschi, M. (2000). Double standards for competence: Theory and research. *Annual Review of Sociology*, 26, 21–42.

Freese, L. and Cohen, B.P. (1973). Eliminating status generalization. *Sociometry* 36, 177–93.

French, J.R.P., and Raven, B. (1959). The bases of social power. In D. Cartwright (ed.), *Studies in social power* (pp. 150–67). Ann Arbor, MI: University of Michigan Press.

Frey, B.S. (1997). *Not just for the money: An economic theory of personal motivation*. Cheltenham, UK: Edward Elgar.

Frey, K.S., and Ruble, D.N. (1990). Strategies for comparitive evaluation: Maintaining a sense of competence across the life span. In R.J. Sternberg and J. Kolligan (eds), *Competence considered*. New Haven: Yale University Press.

Fry, W.R., Firestone, I.J., and Williams, D.L. (1984). Negotiation process and outcome of stranger dyads and dating couples: Do lovers lose? *Basic and Applied Social Psychology*, 4, 1–16.

Fu, P.P., and Yukl, G. (2000). Perceived effectiveness of influence tactics in the United States and China. *Leadership Quarterly*, 11(2), 251–66.

Gaertner, S.L., and Dovidio, J.F. (2000). *Reducing intergroup bias: The common ingroup identity model*. Philadelphia, PA: Psychology Press.

Galanter, M. (1989). *Cults: Faith, Healing, and Coercion*. Oxford and New York: Oxford University Press.

Garvin, D.A. (1993). Building a learning organization. *Harvard Business Review*, 71(4), 78–91.

George, A. (1980). *Presidential decision-making in foreign policy: The effective use of information and advice*. Boulder, CO: Westview.

Georgesen, J.C. (2001). Power and evaluative effects: The power-as-threat theory. Dissertation Abstracts International, 61(7–B), 3900.

Georgesen, J.C., and Harris, M.J. (1998). Why's my boss always holding me down? A meta-analysis of power effects on performance evaluations. *Personality and Social Psychology Review*, 2, 184–95.

Georgesen, J.C., and Harris, M.J. (2000). The balance of power: Interpersonal consequences of differential power and expectations. *Personality and Social Psychology Bulletin*, 26, 1239–57.

Gerstel, D. (1982). *Paradise Incorporated: Synanon*. Novato, CA: Presidio Press.

Gerstner, C.R., and Day, D.V. (1994). Cross-cultural comparison of leadership prototypes. *Leadership Quarterly*, 2, 121–34.

Gerstner, C.R., and Day, D.V. (1997). Meta-analytic review of leader–member exchange theory: Correlates and construct issues. *Journal of Applied Psychology*, 82, 827–45.

Gibb, C.A. (1954). Leadership. In G. Lindzey (ed.) *Handbook of social psychology* (Vol. 2, pp. 877–920). Cambridge, Mass: Addison Wesley.

Giebels, E., De Dreu, C.K.W., and Van de Vliert, E. (1998). The alternative negotiator as the invisible third at the table: The impact of potency information. *The International Journal of Conflict Management*, 9, 5–21.

Giebels, E., De Dreu, C.K.W., and Van de Vliert, E. (2000). Interdependence in negotiation: Impact of exit options and social motives on distributive and integrative negotiation. *European Journal of Social Psychology*, 30, 255–72.

Gilbert, D.T., and Malone, P.S. (1995). The correspondence bias. *Psychological Bulletin*, 117, 21–38.

Ginzel, L.E., Kramer, R.M., and Sutton, R.I. (1993). Organizational impression management as a reciprocal influence process: The neglected role of the organizational audience. In L.L. Cummings and B.M. Staw (eds), *Research in organizational behavior*, 15, 227–66. Greenwich, CT: JAI Press.

Glick, P., and Fiske, S.T. (1996). The Ambivalent Sexism Inventory: Differentiating hostile and benevolent sexism. *Journal of Personality and Social Psychology*, 70, 491–512.

Gold, M. (1999) (ed.). *The complete social scientist: A Kurt Lewin Reader*. Washington DC: American Psychological Association.

Goodwin, R.N. (1988). *Remembering America: A voice from the sixties*. New York: Harper & Row.

Goodwin, S.A., Gubin, A., Fiske, S.T., and Yzerbyt, V.Y. (2000). Power can bias impression processes: Stereotyping subordinates by default and by design. *Group Processes & Intergroup Relations*, 3, 227–56.

Goodwin, S.A., Operario, D., and Fiske, S.T. (1998). Situational power and interpersonal dominance facilitate bias and inequality. *Journal of Social Issues*, 54, 677–98.

Grace, D.M., and David, B. (2001). Sources of influence in preschoolers' use of gender categories. *Australian Journal of Psychology*, 53 (supplement), 115.

Graen, G., and Scandura, T.A. (1987). Toward a psychology of dyadic organizing. *Research in Organizational Behavior*, 9, 175–208.

Graen, G.B. (1976). Role-making processes within complex organizations. In M.D. Dunnette (ed.), *Handbook of industrial and organizational psychology* (pp. 1201–45). Chicago, IL: Rand McNally.

Graen, G.B., and Cashman, J. (1975). A role-making model of leadership in formal organisations: A developmental approach. In J.G. Hunt and L.L. Larseon (eds), *Leadership frontiers* (pp. 143–165). Kent, OH: Kent State University Press.

Graen, G.B., Scandura, T., and Graen, M.R. (1986). A field experimental test of the moderating effects of growth need strength on productivity. *Journal of Applied Psychology*, 71, 484–91.

Graen, G.B., and Uhl-Bien, M. (1995). Relationship-based approach to leadership: Development of leader–member exchange (LMX) theory of leadership over 25 years: Applying a multi-level multi-domain perspective. *Leadership Quarterly*, 6, 219–47.

Grams, W.C., and Rogers, R.W. (1990). Power and personality: Effects of Machiavellianism, need for approval, and motivation to use influence tactics. *The Journal of General Psychology*, 117, 71–82.

Green, S.G., and Mitchell, T.R. (1979). Attributional processes of leaders in leader–member interactions. *Organizational Behavior and Human Performance*, 23, 429–58.

Greenfeld, L. (1992) *Nationalism*. Cambridge, MA: Harvard University Press.

Greenwald, A. (1980). The totalitarian ego: Fabrication and revision of personal history. *American Psychologist*, 35, 603–18.

Griffin, R.N. (1981). Relationships among individual, task design, and leader behavior variables. *Academy of Management Journal*, 23, 665–83.

Gruber, D. (1991). *LBJ: A biography (video)*. Dallax, TX: North Texas Public Broadcasting.

Hackman, J.R. (1987). The design of work teams. In J.W. Lorsch (ed.), *Handbook of organizational behavior* (pp. 315–42). Englewood Cliffs, NJ: Prentice Hall.

Hackman, J.R., and Oldham, G.R. (1976). Motivation through the design of work: Test of a theory. *Organizational Behavior and Human Performance*, 16, 250–79.

Hains, S.C., Hogg, M.A., and Duck, J.M. (1997). Self-categorization and leadership: Effects of group prototypicality and leader stereotypicality. *Personality and Social Psychology Bulletin*, 23, 1087–1100.

Halberstam, D. (1972). *The best and the brightest*. New York: Random House.

Hall, J.A., and Friedman, G.B. (1999). Status, gender, and nonverbal behavior: A study of structured interactions between employees of a company. *Personality and Social Psychology Bulletin*, 25, 1082–91.

Hall, R.J. and Lord, R.G. (1995). Multi-level information-processing explanations of followers' leadership perceptions. *Leadership Quarterly*, 6, 265–87.

Halls R.J., Makiney, J.D., Marchioro, C.A., and Philips, J. (2002) A social relationship analysis of the antecedents of leadership perceptions. Unpublished paper, University of Akron, Akron, Ohio.

Hall, R.J., Philips, J., Makiney, J.D., and Marchioro, C.A. (2002). *A social relations analysis of leadership and group citizenship in a small group context*. Working paper. University of Akron.

Hall, R.J., Workman, J.W. and Marchioro, C.A. (1998). Sex, task, and behavioral flexibility effects on leadership perceptions. *Organizational Behavior and Human Decision Processes*, 74, 1–32.

Hamilton, D.L., and Sherman, J.W. (1994). Stereotypes. In R.S., Wyer, Jr and T.K. Srull, (eds), *Handbook of social cognition* (Vol. 2, 2nd ed., pp. 1–68). Hillsdale, NJ: Lawrence Erlbaum.

Hamilton, D.L., and Sherman, S.J. (1996). Perceiving persons and groups. *Psychological Review*, 103, 336–55.

Hanges, P.J., Lord, R.G., and Dickson, M.W. (2000). An information-processing perspective on leadership and culture: A case for connectionist architecture. *Applied Psychology: An International Review*, 49, 133–61.

Haslam, S.A. (2001). *Psychology in organisations: The social identity approach*. London: Sage.

Haslam, S.A., McGarty, C., Brown, P.M., Eggins, R.A., Morrison, B.E., and Reynolds, K.J. (1998). Inspecting the emperor's clothes: Evidence that random selection of leaders can enhance group performance. *Group Dynamics: Theory, Research, and Practice*, 2, 168–84.

Haslam, S.A., and Platow, M.J. (2001a). The link between leadership and followership: How affirming social identity translates vision into action. *Personality and Social Psychology Bulletin* 27, 1469–79.

Haslam, S.A., and Platow, M.J. (2001b). Your wish is our command: The role of shared social identity in translating a leader's vision into followers' action. In M.A. Hogg and D. Terry (eds), *Social identity processes in organisations* (pp. 213–28). New York: Psychology Press.

Haslam, S.A., Platow, M.J., Turner, J.C., Reynolds, K.J., McGarty, C., Oakes, P.J., Johnson, S., Ryan, M.K., and Veenstra, K. (2001). Social identity and the romance of leadership: The importance of being seen to be doing it for us. *Group Processes and Intergroup Relations*, 4, 191–205.

Heath, J. (1975). *Decade of disillusionment: The Kennedy-Johnson years*. Bloomington, IN: Indiana University Press.

Hedges, L.V., and Nowell, A. (1995). Sex differences in mental test scores, variability, and numbers of high-scoring individuals. *Science*, 269, 41–45.

Heilman, M.E. (1983). Sex bias in work settings: The lack of fit model. *Research in Organizational Behavior*, 5, 269–98.

Heilman, M.E. (2001). Description and prescription: How gender stereotypes prevent women's ascent up the organizational ladder. *Journal of Social Issues*, 57, 657–74.

Heilman, M.E., Block, C.J., and Martell, R.F. (1995). Sex stereotypes: Do they influence perceptions of managers? *Journal of Social Behavior and Personality*, 10, 237–52.

Heilman, M.E., Block, C.J., Martell, R.F., and Simon, M.C. (1989). Has anything changed? Current characterizations of men, women, and managers. *Journal of Applied Psychology*, 74, 935–42.

Heine, Lehman, Markus, and Kitayama, (1999). Is there a universal need for positive self-regard? *Psychological Review*, 106, 766–94.

Henggeler, P.R. (1991). *In his steps: Lyndon Johnson and the Kennedy mystique*. Chicago, IL: Dee.

Herring, G.C. (1993). The reluctant warrior: Lyndon Johnson as Commander in Chief. In D.L. Anderson (ed.), *Shadow on the White House: Presidents and the Vietnam war, 1945–1975*, pp. 87–112. Kansas: University of Kansas Press.

Higgins, E.T. (1997). Beyond pleasure and pain. *American Psychologist*, 52, 1280–300.

Hinkle, L.E., and Wolff, H.G. (1956). Communist interrogation and indoctrination of 'Enemics of the State'. *Archives of Neurology and Psychiatry*, 76, 115–74.

Hirokawa, G., and Miyahara, A. (1986). A comparison of influence strategies utilized by managers in American and Japanese organizations. *Communication Quarterly*, 34, 250–65.

Hoffer, E. (1951). *The true believer*. New York: Mentor.

Hoffman, M.L. (2000). *Empathy and moral development*. Cambridge: Cambridge University Press.

Hofstede, G. (1980). *Culture's consequences: International differences in work-related values*. Beverly Hills, CA: Sage.

Hogan, R., Curphy, G.J., and Hogan, J. (1994). What we know about leadership: Effectiveness and personality. *American Psychologist*, 49, 493–504.

Hogg, M.A. (1992). *The social psychology of group cohesiveness: From attraction to social identity*. Hemel Hempstead, UK. Harvester Wheatsheaf.

Hogg, M.A. (1993). Group cohesiveness: A critical review and some new directions. *European Review of Social Psychology*, 4, 85–111.

Hogg, M.A. (1996). Intragroup processes, group structure and social identity. In W.P. Robinson (ed.). *Social groups and identities: Developing the legacy of Henri Tajfel* (pp. 65–93). Oxford: Butterworth-Heinemann.

Hogg, M.A. (2000). Social identity and social comparison. In J. Suls and L. Wheeler (eds), *Handbook of social comparison: Theory and research* (pp. 401–21). New York: Kluwer/Plenum.

Hogg, M.A. (2001). A social identity theory of leadership. *Personality and Social Psychology Review*, 5, 184–200.

Hogg, M.A. (2001b). Social identity and the sovereignty of the group: A psychology of belonging. In C. Sedikides and M.B. Brewer (eds), *Individual self, relational self, collective self* (pp. 123–43). Philadelphia, PA: Psychology Press.

Hogg, M.A. (2001c). Social categorization, depersonalization, and group behavior. In M.A. Hogg and R.S. Tindale (eds), *Blackwell handbook of social psychology: Group processes* (pp. 56–85). Oxford: Blackwell.

Hogg, M.A. (2001d). From prototypicality to power: A social identity analysis of leadership. In S.R. Thye, E.J. Lawler, M.W. Macy, and H.A. Walker (eds), *Advances in group processes* (Vol. 18, pp. 1–30). Oxford: Elsevier.

Hogg, M.A. (2002). Social identity. In M.R. Leary and J.P. Tangney (eds), *Handbook of self and identity* (pp. 462–79). New York: Guilford.

Hogg, M.A. (in press a). Uncertainty and extremism: Identification with high entitativity groups under conditions of uncertainty. In V. Yzerbyt, C.M. Judd and O. Corneille (eds), *The psychology of group perception: Contributions of the study of homogeneity, entitativity, amd essentialism* (pp. 401–18). New York: Psychology Press.

Hogg, M.A. (in press b). Social identity and leadership. In D.M. Messick and R. Kramer (eds), *The psychology of leadership: Some new approaches.* Mahwah, NJ: Erlbaum.

Hogg, M.A., and Abrams, D. (1988). *Social identifications: A social psychology of intergroup relations and group processes.* London: Routledge.

Hogg, M.A., Hains, S.C., and Mason, I. (1998). Identification and leadership in small groups: Salience, frame of reference, and leader stereotypicality effects on leader evaluations. *Journal of Personality and Social Psychology*, 75, 1248–63.

Hogg, M.A., and Martin, R. (2003). Social identity analysis of leader–member relations: Reconciling self-categorization and leader-member exchange theories of leadership. In S.A. Haslam, D. van Knippenberg, M.J. Platow and N. Ellemers (eds), *Social identity at work: Developing theory for organizational practice.* Philadelphia, PA: Psychology Press.

Hogg, M.A., Martin, R., Weeden, K., and Epitropaki, O. (2001). *Effective leadership in salient groups: Revisiting leader–member exchange theory from the perspective of the social identity theory of leadership.* Manuscript submitted for publication: University of Queensland.

Hogg, M.A., and Mullin, B.A. (1999). Joining groups to reduce uncertainty: Subjective uncertainty reduction and group identification. In D. Abrams, and M.A. Hogg (eds), *Social identity and social cognition* (pp. 249–79). Oxford: Blackwell Publishers.

Hogg, M.A., and Reid, S.A. (2001). Social identity, leadership, and power. In A.Y. Lee-Chai and J.A. Bargh (eds), *The use and abuse of power: Multiple perspectives on the causes of corruption* (pp. 159–80). Philadelphia, PA: Psychology Press.

Hogg, M.A., and Terry, D.J. (2000). Social identity and self-categorization processes in organizational contexts. *Academy of Management Review*, 25, 121–40.

Hogg, M.A., and Terry, D.J. (eds) (2001a). *Social identity processes in organizational contexts.* Philadelphia, PA: Psychology Press.

Hogg, M.A., and Terry, D.J. (2001b). Social identity theory and organizational processes. In M.A. Hogg and D.J. Terry (eds), *Social identity processes in organizational contexts* (pp. 1–12). Philadelphia, PA: Psychology Press.

Hogg, M.A., and van Knippenberg, D. (2003). Social identity and leadership processes in groups. In M. P. Zanna (ed.), *Advances in experimental social psychology* (Vol. 35) (pp. 1–52). San Diego, CA: Academic Press.

Hollander, E.P. (1958). Conformity, status, and idiosyncrasy credit. *Psychological Review*, 65, 117–27.

Hollander, E.P. (1978). *Leadership dynamics: A practical guide to effective relationships*. New York: Free Press.

Hollander, E.P. (1985). Leadership and power. In G. Lindzey and E. Aronson (eds), *The handbook of social psychology* (Vol. 2, 2nd ed., pp. 485–537). New York: Random House.

Hollander, E.P. and Julian, J.W. (1969). Contemporary trends in the analysis of leadership perceptions. *Psychological Bulletin*, 71, 387–97.

Hollander, E.P., and Julian, J.W. (1970). Studies in leader legitimacy, influence, and innovation. In L. Berkowitz (ed.), *Advances in experimental social psychology* (Vol. 5, pp. 34–69). New York: Academic Press.

Hollander, E., and Julian, J.W. (1978). Studies in leader legitimacy, influence, and innovation. In L. Berkowitz (ed.), *Group processes*. New York: Academic Press.

Holy, L. (1996) *The little Czech and the great Czech nation: National identity and the post-communist transformation of society*. Cambridge: Cambridge University Press.

Hopkins, N. and Reicher, S. (1997) The construction of social categories and processes of social change. In G. Breakwell and E. Lyons (eds) *Changing European identities*. London: Butterworth.

Hopkins, N., and Reicher, S.D. (1997). Social movement rhetoric and the social psychology of collective action: A case study of anti-abortion mobilization. *Human Relations*, 50(3), 261–86.

House, R.J. (1971). A path–goal theory of leader effectiveness. *Administrative Science Quarterly*, 16, 321–38.

House, R.J. (1977). A 1976 theory of charismatic leadership. In J.G. Hunt and L.L. Larson (eds), *Leadership: The cutting edge* (pp. 189–207). Carbondale, IL: Southern Illinois University Press.

House, R.J., and Aditya, R.N. (1997). The social scientific study of leadership: Quo vadis? *Journal of Management*, 23, 409–73.

House, R.J., and Baetz, M.L. (1979). Leadership: Some empirical generalizations and new research directions. *Research in Organizational Behavior*, 1, 341–423.

House, R.J. and Mitchell, T.R. (1974). Path–goal theory of leadership. *Journal of Contemporary Business*, 3, 81–98.

House, R.J., and Shamir, B. (1993). Toward the integration of Transformational, Charismatic and Visionary Theories. In M.M. Chemers and R. Ayman (eds) *Leadership theory and research: perspectives and directions*. San Diego, CA: Academic Press.

House, R.J., Woycke, J., and Fodor, E.M. (1988). Charismatic and noncharismatic leaders: Differences in behavior and effectiveness. In J.A. Conger and R.N. Kanungo (eds), *Charismatic leadership: The elusive factor in organizational effectiveness* (pp. 99–121). San Francisco, CA: Jossey-Bass.

Hudson, P. (2001, Aug. 30). *Bill allows use of force on refugees*. http://www.theage.com.au/news/national/2001/08/30/FFXF0QKQYQC.html

Hughes, R.L., Ginnett, R.C., and Gurphy, G.J. (1999). *Leadership: Enhancing the lessons of experience*. Boston, MA: McGraw Hill.

Ibarra, H. (1999). Provisional selves: Experimenting with image and identity in professional adaptation. *Administrative Science Quarterly*, 44, 764–91.

Israel Ministry of Foreign Affairs (1999). *Ariel Sharon, MK Prime Minister of Immigrant Absorption (Likud)*. http://www.mfa.gov.il/mfa/go.asp?MFAH00ge0

Jacobsen, C., and House, R.J. (2001). Dynamics of charismatic leadership: A process theory, simulation model, and tests. *Leadership Quarterly*, 12, 75–112.

Jacobsen, J.P. (1998). *The economics of gender* (2nd ed.). Malden, MA: Blackwell.

James, K., and Cropanzano, R. (1994). Dispositional group loyalty and individual action for the benefit of an ingroup: Experimental and correlational evidence. *Organizational Behavior and Human Decision Processes*, 60, 179–205.

Janis, I.L. (1983). *Groupthink* (2nd ed.). Boston, MA: Houghton Mifflin.

Janis, I.L. (1989). *Crucial decisions*. New York: Free Press.

Jervis, R. (1976). *Perception and misperception in international politics*. Princeton, NJ: Princeton University Press.

Jervis, R. (1992). Implications of loss aversion for political psychology. *Political Psychology*, 13, 187–204.

Johnson, T., and Graen, G.B. (1973). Organizational assimilation and role rejection. *Organizational Behavior and Human Performance*, 10, 72–8.

Johnston, L., and Macrae, N. (1994). Changing social stereotypes: The case of the information seeker. *European Journal of Social Psychology*, 24, 581–92.

Jonas, K., Broemer, P., and Diehl, M. (2000). Attitudinal ambivalence. In W. Stroebe and M. Hewstone (eds), *European review of social psychology* (Vol. 11, pp. 35–74). Chichester, UK: John Wiley.

Jost, J.T., and Banaji, M.R. (1994). The role of stereotyping in system-justification and the production of false consciousness. *British Journal of Social Psychology*, 33, 1–27.

Jost, J.T., Burgess, D., and Mosso, C.O. (2001). Conflicts of legitimation among self, group, and system: The integrative potential of system justification theory. In J. Jost and B. Major, (eds), *The psychology of legitimacy: Emerging perspective on ideology, justice, and intergroup relations* (pp. 363–90). New York: Cambridge University Press.

Juran, J.M. (1988). *Juran on planning for quality*. New York: Free Press.

Katz, D. (1964). The motivational basis of organizational behavior. *Behavioral Science*, 9, 131–46.

Katz, D., and Kahn, D. (1978). *The social psychology of organizing*. New York: McGraw Hill.

Katz, I., and Hass, G.R., (1988). Racial ambivalence and American value conflict: Correlational and priming studies of dual cognitive structures. *Journal of Personality & Social Psychology*, 55, 893–905.

Kearns-Goodwin, D. (1976). *Lyndon Johnson and the American dream*. New York: New American Library.

Keinan, G., Friedland, N., and Even-Haim, G. (2000). The effect of stress and self-esteem on social stereotyping. *Journal of Social and Clinical Psychology*, 19(2), 206–19.

Keller, T., and Dansereau, F. (2000). The effects of adding items to scales: An illustrative case of LMX. *Organizational Research Methods*, 4, 131–43.

Kelley, D.M. (1995). Waco: The massacre, the aftermath. *First Things*, May 1995.

Kelley, H.H., and Thibaut, J. (1978). *Interpersonal relations: A theory of interdependence*. New York: Wiley.

Kelman, H.C. (1958). Compliance, identification, and internalization: Three processes of attitude change. *Journal of Conflict Resolution*, 2, 51–60.

Kelman, H.C. and Hamilton, V.L. (1989). *Crimes of obedience*. New Haven: Yale University Press.

Keltner, D., Capps, L., Kring, A.M., Young, R.C., and Heerey, E.A. (2001). Just teasing: A conceptual analysis and empirical review. Psychological Bulletin. Mar Vol 127(2), 229–48.

Keltner, D., Gruenfeld, D.H., and Anderson, C. (2003). Power, approach, and inhibition. *Psychological Review*.

Kershaw, I. (1987) *The Hitler Myth*. Oxford: Clarendon Press.

Killian, L.M. (1972). The significance of extremism in the black revolution. *Social Problems*, 20, 41–9.

Kim, P.H. (1997). Strategic timing in group negotiations: The implications of forced entry and forced exit for negotiators with unequal power. *Organizational Behavior and Human Decision Processes*, 71, 263–86.

Kinicki, A.J., and Vecchio, R.P. (1994). Influences on the quality of supervisor–subordinate relations: The role of time-pressure, organizational commitment, and locus of control. *Journal of Organizational Behavior*, 15, 75–82.

Kipnis, D. (1976). *The powerholders*. Chicago, Ill: University of Chicago Press.

Kipnis, D. (1984). The use of power in organizations and in interpersonal settings. *Applied Social Psychology Annual*, 5, 179–210.

Kipnis, D., and Schmidt, S.M. (1988). Upward influence styles. *Administrative Science Quarterly*, 33, 528–42.

Kipnis, D., Schmidt, S.M., and Wilkinson, I. (1980). Intraorganizational influence tactics: Explorations in getting one's way. *Journal of Applied Psychology*, 65, 440–52.

Kohut, H. (1985) *Self-Psychology and the Humanities*. New York: Norton.

Komorita, S.S., Chan, D.K.S. and Parks, C.D. (1993). The effects of reward structure and reciprocity in social dilemmas. *Journal of Experimental Social Psychology*, 29, 252–67.

Komorita, S.S., and Parks, C.D. (1994). *Social dilemmas*. Dubuque, IA: Brown and Benchmark.

Komorita, S.S., Parks, C.D. and Hulbert, L.G. (1992). Reciprocity and the induction of cooperation in social dilemmas. *Journal of Personality and Social Psychology*, 62, 607–17.

Konrad, A.M., Ritchie, J.E. Jr, Lieb, P., and Corrigall, E. (2000). Sex differences and similarities in job attribute preferences: A meta-analysis. *Psychological Bulletin*, 126, 593–641.

Krackhardt, D. (1990). Assessing the political landscape: Structure, cognition, and power in organizations. *Administrative Science Quarterly*, 35, 342–69.

Kramer, R.M. (1994). The sinister attribution error: Origins and consequences of collective paranoia. *Motivation and Emotion*, 18, 199–230.

Kramer, R.M., and Brewer, M.B. (1984). Effects of group identity on resource use in a simulated commons dilemma. *Journal of Personality and Social Psychology*, 46, 1044–57.

Kramer, R.M., Pommerenke, P. and Newton, E. (1993). The social context of negotiation. *Journal of Conflict Resolution*, 37, 633–54.

Langford, T., and MacKinnon, N.J. (2000). The affective bases for the gendering of traits: Comparing the United States and Canada. *Social Psychology Quarterly*, 63, 34–48.

Latane, B., and Darley, J. (1970). *The unresponsive bystander: Why doesn't he help?* New York: Appleton-Century-Crofts.

Lawrence, P.R. and Lorsch, J.W. (1967). *Organization and environment*. Cambridge, MA: Harvard University Press.

Layton, D. (1998). *Seductive poison*. New York: Doubleday.

Lee, F. and Tiedens, L.Z. (2001). Is it lonely at the top? The independence of power holders. *Research in Organizational Behavior*, 23, 43–91.

Lee-Chai, A.Y., and Bargh, J.A. (2001). *The use and abuse of power: Multiple perspectives on the causes of corruption*. Philadelphia, PA: Psychology Press.

Leming M.R. and Smith, T.C. (1974). The Children of God as a social movement. *Journal of Voluntary Action Research*, 3, 77–83.

Leventhal, G.S. (1980). What should be done about equity theory? New approaches to the study of fairness in social relationships. In K. Gergen, M. Greenberg, and R. Willis (eds), *Social exchange: Advances in theory and research* (pp. 27–55). New York: Plenum.

Levi, M. (1997). *Consent, dissent, and patriotism*. Cambridge: Cambridge University Press.

Levine, J.M., and Moreland, R.L. (1995). Group processes. In A. Tesser (ed.), *Advanced Social Psychology* (pp. 419–66). New York: McGraw-Hill.

Lewicki, R.J., and Bunker, B.B. (1995). Trust in relationships: A model of development and decline. In B.B. Bunker, J.Z. Rubin and associates (eds), *Conflict, cooperation, and justice: Essays inspired by the work of Morton Deutsch* (pp. 133–74). San Francisco: Jossey-Bass.

Leyens, J-Ph., Yzerbyt, V.Y., and Schadron, G., (1992). The social judgeability approach to stereotypes. In W. Stroebe, and M. Hewstone (eds), *European review of social psychology* (Vol. 3, pp. 91–120). New York: John Wiley & Sons.

Liden, R.C., and Graen, G.B. (1980). Generalizability of the Vertical Dyad Linkage model of leadership. *Academy of Management Journal*, 23, 451–65.

Liden, R.C., Sparrowe, R.T., and Wayne, S.J. (1997). Leader–Member Exchange theory: The past and potential for the future. *Research in Personnel and Human Resources Management*, 15, 47–119.

Lifton, R.J. (1961). *Thought reform and the psychology of totalism: A study of brainwashing in China*. New York: Holt.

Lind, E.A. (2001). Fairness heuristic theory: Justice judgments as pivotal cognitions in organizational relations. In J. Greenberg and R. Cropanzano (eds), *Advances in organizational justice* (pp. 56–88). Stanford, CA: Stanford University Press.

Lind, E.A. and Tyler, T.R. (1988). *The social psychology of procedural justice*. New York: Plenum.

Lindholm, C. (1990) *Charisma*. Oxford: Blackwell.

Lipman-Blumen, J. (1996). *The connective edge: Leading in an interdependent world*. San Francisco, CA: Jossey-Bass.

Locke, E.A., and Latham, G.P. (1990). *A theory of goal setting and performance*. Englewood Cliffs, NJ: Prentice-Hall.

Lord, R.G. (1977). Functional leadership behavior: Measurement and relation to social power and leadership perceptions. *Administrative Science Quarterly*, 22, 114–33.

Lord, R.G. (1985). An information processing approach to social perception, leadership and behavioral measurement in organizations. *Research in Organizational Behavior*, 7, 87–128.

Lord, R.G., and Brown, D.J. (2003). *Leadership and follower identity*. Mahwah, NJ: Lawrence Erlbaum Associates.

Lord, R.G., Brown, D.J., and Freiberg, S.J. (1999). Understanding the dynamics of leadership: The role of follower self-concepts in the leader/follower relationship. *Organizational Behavior and Human Decision Processes*, 78, 1–37.

Lord, R.G., Brown, D.J., Harvey, J.L., and Hall, R.J. (2001). Contextual constraints on prototype generation and their multi-level consequences for leadership perceptions. *Leadership Quarterly*, 12, 311–28.

Lord, R.G., De Vader, C.L., and Alliger, G.M. (1986). A meta-analysis of the relation between personality traits and leadership perceptions: An application of validity generalization procedures. *Journal of Applied Psychology*, 71, 402–10.

Lord, R.G., Foti, R.J., and DeVader, C.L. (1984). A test of leadership categorization theory: Internal structure, information processing, and leadership perceptions. *Organizational Behavior and Human Performance*, 34, 343–78.

Lord, R.G., and Maher, K.J. (1991). *Leadership and information processing: Linking perception and performance*. Winchester, MA: Unwin Hyman.

Lord, R.G., and Smith, W.G. (1998). Leadership and the changing nature of work performance. In D.R. Ilgen and E.D. Pulakos (eds), *The changing nature of work performance: Implications for staffing, personnel decisions, and development*. San Francisco, CA: Jossey-Bass.

Lowe, K.B., Kroeck, K.G., and Sivasubramaniam, N. (1996). Effectiveness correlates of transformational and transactional leadership: A meta-analytic review of the MLQ literature. *Leadership Quarterly*, 7, 385–425.

Luce, R.D., and Raiffa, H. (1957). *Games and decisions: Introduction and critical survey.* London: John Wiley and Sons.

Lukes, S. (1974). *Power: A radical view.* London: Macmillan Press, Ltd.

Maaga, M.M. (1998) *Hearing the voices of Jonestown.* Syracuse, NY: Syracuse University Press.

Mackie, D.M., Worth, L.T., and Asuncion, A.G. (1990). Processing of persuasive in-group messages. *Journal of Personality and Social Psychology*, 58, 812–22.

Mael, F., and Ashforth, B.E. (1995). Loyal from day one: Biodata, organizational identification, and turnover among newcomers. *Personnel Psychology*, 48, 309–33.

Major, D.A., Kozlowski, S.W.J., Chao, G.T., and Gardner, P.D. (1995). A longitudinal investigation of newcomer expectations, early socialization outcomes, and the moderating effects of role development factors. *Journal of Applied Psychology*, 80, 418–31.

March, J.G. (1994). *A primer on decision making.* New York: Free Press.

Markus, H., and Kitayama, S. (1991). Culture and the self: Implications for cognition, emotion and motivation. *Psychological Review*, 98, 224–53.

Markus, H., and Wurf, E. (1987). The dynamic self-concept: A social psychological perspective. *Annual Review of Psychology*, 38, 299–338.

Marques, J.M., Abrams, D., Páez, D., and Hogg, M.A. (2001). Social categorization, social identification, and rejection of deviant group members. In M.A. Hogg and R.S. Tindale, (eds), *Blackwell handbook of social psychology: Group processes* (pp. 400–24). Oxford: Blackwell.

Matthews, A.M., Lord, R.G., and Walker, J.B. (1990). *The development of leadership perceptions in children.* Unpublished manuscript. University of Akron.

Maume, D.J. (1999). Glass ceilings and glass escalators: Occupational segregation and race and sex differences in managerial promotions. *Work and Organizations*, 26, 483–509.

Maurer, T.J., and Lord, R.G. (1991). An exploration of cognitive demands in group interaction as a moderator of information processing variables in perceptions of leadership. *Journal of Applied Social Psychology*, 21, 821–39.

McClintock, C. (1977). Social motivations in settings of outcome interdependence. In D. Druckman (ed.), *Negotiation: Social psychological perspectives* (pp. 49–77). Beverly Hills, CA: Sage.

McCusker, C., and Carnevale, P.J. (1995). Framing in resource dilemmas: Loss aversion and the moderating effects of sanction. *Organizational Behavior and Human Decision Processes*, 61, 190–201.

McGarty, C. (1999). *Categorization in social psychology.* London: Sage.

McGarty, C., Haslam, S.A., Hutchinson, K.J., and Turner, J.C. (1994). The effects of salient group memberships on persuasion. *Small Group Research*, 25, 267–93.

Meindl, J.R. (1993). Reinventing leadership: A radical, social psychological approach. In J.K. Murnighan (ed.), *Social psychology in organizations: Advances in theory and research* (pp. 89–118). Englewood Cliffs, NJ: Prentice Hall.

Messick, D.M., Bloom, S., Boldizar, J.P., and Samuelson, C.D. (1985). Why we are fairer than others? *Journal of Experimental Social Psychology*, 21, 213–25.

Messick, D.M., Wilke, H.A.M., Brewer, M.B., Kramer, R.M., Zemke, P.E., and Lui, L. (1983). Individual adaptations and structural change as solutions to social dilemmas. *Journal of Personality and Social Psychology*, 44, 294–309.

Michener, H.A., and Lawler, E.J. (1975). Endorsement of formal leaders: An integrative model. *Journal of Personality and Social Psychology*, 31, 216–23.

Miller, D.T. (1999). The norm of self-interest. *American Psychologist*, 54, 1–8.

Miller, D.T. and Turnbull, W. (1986). Expectancies and interpersonal processes. *Annual Review of Psychology*, 37, 233–256.

Miller, M. (1980). *Lyndon: An oral biography*. New York: Ballantine.

Molm, L.D., Peterson, G., and Takahashi, N. (1999). Power and negotiated and reciprocal exchange. *American Sociological Review*, 64, 876–90.

Moore, J.C. (1968). Status and influence in small group interactions. *Sociometry* 31, 47–63.

Morrison, A.M., White, R.P., and Van Velsor, E. (1987). *Breaking the glass ceiling*. Reading, MA: Addison-Wesley.

Moskowitz, D.W., Suh, E.J., and Desaulniers, J. (1994). Situational influences on gender differences in agency and communion. *Journal of Personality and Social Psychology*, 66, 753–61.

Mulder, L., Wilke, H., van Dijk, E., and De Cremer, D. (2002). Ondermijning van vertrouwen en coöperatie: De paradox van sanctiesystemen in sociale dilemma's [Undermining trust and cooperation: The paradox of surveillance systems in social dilemmas]. In Stapel, D., van Dijk, E., and Hagedoorn, M. (eds). *Jaarboek Sociale Psychologie*. Delft: Eburon

Mulder, M. (1977). *The daily power game*. Leiden, NL: Martinus Nijhoff Social Sciences Division.

Nauta, A., De Dreu, C.K.W., and Van der Vaart, T. (2002). Social value orientation, organizational goal concerns and interdepartmental problem solving. *Journal of Organizational Behavior*, 23, 199–213.

Nauta, A., De Vries, J., and Wijngaard, J. (2001). Power and biased perceptions of interdepartmental negotiation behavior. *Group Processes and Intergroup Relations*, 4, 263–70.

Neale, M.A., and Bazerman, M.H. (1991). *Rationality and cognition in negotiation*. New York: Free Press.

Nemeth, C.J., and Staw, B.M. (1989). The tradeoffs of social control and innovation in groups and organizations. *Advances in Experimental Social Psychology*, 22, 175–210.

Neuberg, S.L. (1989). The goal of forming accurate impressions during social interactions: Attenuating the impact of negative expectancies. *Journal of Personality & Social Psychology*, 56, 374–86.

Neuberg, S., and Fiske, S.T. (1987). Motivational influences on impression formation: Outcome dependency, accuracy-driven attention, and individuating processes. *Journal of Personality and Social Psychology*, 53, 431–44.

Neustadt, R.E. (1990). *Presidential power and the modern presidents*. New York: Free Press.

Newport, F. (2001, February 21). *Americans see women as emotional and affectionate, men as more aggressive*. Gallup Poll News Service. Retrieved August 18, 2001 from http://www.gallup.com/poll/releases/pr010221.asp

Ng, S.H. (1996). Power: An essay in honour of Henri Tajfel. In W.P. Robinson (ed.), *Social identity: The developing legacy of Henri Tajfel* (pp. 191–215). Oxford: Butterworth-Heinemann.

Ng, S.H., and Bradac, J.J. (1993). *Power in language: Verbal communication and social influence*. Newbury Park, CA: Sage.

Ng, S.H., and Reid, S.A. (2001). Power. In W.P. Robinson and H. Giles (eds), *The new handbook of language and social psychology* (pp. 357–70). Chichester, UK: John Wiley & Sons.

Noel, J.G., Wann, D.L., and Branscombe, N.R. (1995). Peripheral ingroup membership status and public negativity towards outgroups. *Journal of Personality and Social Psychology*, 68, 127–37.

Norris-Watts, C., and Lord, R.G. (2001). *The cognitive and perceptual mechanisms underlying stereotype threat*. The University of Akron. (Unpublished manuscript.)

Nye, J.L., and Simonetta, L.G. (1996). Followers' perceptions of group leaders: The impact of recognition-based and inference-based processes. In J.L. Nye and A.M. Bower (eds), *What's social about social cognition: Research on socially shared cognition in small groups* (pp. 124–53). Thousand Oaks, CA: Sage.

Oakes, P.J. (1987). The salience of social categories. In J.C. Turner, M.A. Hogg, P.J. Oakes, S.D. Reiche and M.S. Wetherell, *Rediscovering the social group: A self-categorization theory* (pp. 117–41). Oxford: Blackwell.

Oakes, P.J., Haslam, S.A., and Turner, J.C. (1994). *Stereotyping and social reality*. Oxford: Blackwell.

Offermann, L.R., Kennedy, J.K. Jr, Wirtz, P.W. (1994). Implicit leadership theories: Content, structure, and generalizability. *Leadership Quarterly*, 5, 43–58.

Ofshe, R. (1980). The social development of the Synanon cult: the managerial strategy of organizational transformation. *Sociological Analysis.* 41, 109–27.

Onorato, R.S., and Turner, J.C. (2001). The 'I,' the 'me,' and the 'us': The psychological group and self-concept maintenance and change. In C. Sedikides and M.B. Brewer (eds), *Individual self, relational self, collective self* (pp. 147–70). Philadelphia, PA: Psychology Press.

Organ, D.W. (1990). The motivational basis of organizational citizenship behavior. In L.L. Cummings and B.M. Staw (eds), *Research in organizational behavior* (Vol. 12, pp. 43–72). Greenwich, CT: JAI Press.

Overbeck, J.R., and Park, B. (2001). When power does not corrupt: Superior individuation processes among powerful perceivers. *Journal of Personality & Social Psychology*, 81, 549–65.

Oxfam (2002). *Adrift in the Pacific: The implications of Australia's Pacific refugee solution.* http://www.caa.org.au/campaigns/refugees/pacificsolution/

Ozouf, M. (1989) *Festivals and the French Revolution*. Cambridge, MA: Harvard University Press.

Pfeffer, J. (1981). Management as symbolic action. In L.L. Cummings and B.M. Staw (eds), *Research in organizational behavior* (Vol. 3, pp. 1–52). Greenwich, CT: JAI Press.

Pfeffer, J. (1992). *Managing with power*. Cambridge, MA: Harvard Business School Press.

Pfeffer, J. (1998). *New directions for organization theory: Problems and prospects*. Oxford: Oxford University Press.

Pfeffer, J., and Cialdini, R.B. (1998). Illusions of influence. In R.M. Kramer and M.A. Neale (eds), *Power and influence in organizations* (pp. 1–20). Thousand Oaks, CA: Sage Publications.

Phillips, G.M. (2000). Perceived organizational support: An extended model of the mediating and moderating effects of self-structures. Unpublished doctoral dissertation. University of Akron, Akron, Ohio.

Phillips, G.M. and Hall, R.J. (2001). Perceived organizational support: The mediating role of self-structures. 16th Annual conference of the society for Industrial and Organizational Psychology, San Diego, CA.

Pierce, K.P., and Brewer, M.B. (May, 2002). When more means less: The effect of irrelevant individuating information on stereotype use. Paper presented at the annual meeting of the Midwestern Psychological Association, Chicago, IL.

Piliavin, I.M., Piliavin, J.A., and Rodin, J. (1975). Cost, diffusion, and the stigmatized victim. *Journal of Personality and Social Psychology*, 32, 429–38.

Pillai, R., Schriesheim, C.A., and Williams, E.S. (1999). Fairness perceptions and trust as mediators for transformational and transactional leadership: A two-sample study. *Journal of Management*, 25, 897–933.

Pittman, T.S. (1975). Attribution of arousal as a mediator in dissonance reduction.

Platow, M.J., Durante, M., Williams, N., Garrett, M., Walshe, J., Cincotta, S., Lianos, G., and Barutchu, A. (1999). The contribution of sport fan social identity to the production of prosocial behaviour. *Group Dynamics: Theory, Research, and Practice*, 3, 161–9.

Platow, M.J., Harley, K., Hunter, J.A., Hanning, P., Shave, R., and O'Connell, A. (1997). Interpreting ingroup-favouring allocations in the minimal group paradigm. *British Journal of Social Psychology*, 36, 107–18.

Platow, M.J., Hoar, S., Reid, S., Harley, K., and Morrison, D. (1997). Endorsement of distributively fair and unfair leaders in interpersonal and intergroup situations. *European Journal of Social Psychology*, 27, 465–94.

Platow, M.J., Mills, D., and Morrison, D. (2000). The effects of social context, source fairness, and perceived self-source similarity on social influence: A self-categorisation analysis. *European Journal of Social Psychology*, 30, 69–81.

Platow, M.J., O'Connell, A., Shave, R., and Hanning, P. (1995). Social evaluations of fair and unfair allocators in interpersonal and intergroup situations. *British Journal of Social Psychology*, 34, 363–81.

Platow, M.J., Reid, S., and Andrew, S. (1998). Leadership endorsement: The role of distributive and procedural behaviour in interpersonal and intergroup contexts. *Group Processes and Intergroup Relations*, 1, 35–47.

Platow, M.J., and van Knippenberg, D. (2001). A social identity analysis of leadership endorsement: The effects of leader in-group prototypicality and distributive intergroup fairness. *Personality and Social Psychology Bulletin*, 27, 1508–19.

Platow, M.J., van Knippenberg, D., Haslam, S.A., van Knippenberg, B., and Spears, R. (2001). *A special gift we bestow on you for being representative of us: Considering leader charisma from a self-categorization perspective*. Unpublished manuscript, La Trobe University.

Platow, M.J., Wenzel, M., and Nolan, M. (2003). The importance of social identity and self-categorization processes for creating and responding to fairness. In S.A. Haslam, D. van Knippenberg, M.J. Platow and N. Ellemers (eds), *Social identity at work: Developing theory for organisational practice*. Brighton, UK: Psychology Press.

Podsakoff, P.M., and Schriescheim, C.A. (1985). Field studies of French and Raven's bases of power: Critique, reanalysis, and suggestions for future research. *Psychological Bulletin*, 97, 387–411.

Pondy, L. (1992). Reflections on organizational conflict. *Journal of Organizational Behavior*, 13, 257–61.

Pool, G.J., Wood, W., and Leck, K. (1998). The self-esteem motive in social influence: Agreement with valued majorities and disagreement with derogated minorities. *Journal of Personality and Social Psychology*, 75, 967–75.

Powell, G.N., and Butterfield, D.A. (1994). Investigating the 'glass ceiling' phenomenon: An empirical study of actual promotions to top management. *Academy of Management Journal*, 37, 68–86.

Praslova, L. and Hall, R.J. (2002). Collectivist antecedents of organizational citizenship behaviors: The Russian case. 17th Annual conference of the society for Industrial and Organizatinal Psychology, Toronto, Canada.

Pratkanis, A.R., and Aronson, E. (2000). *Age of Propaganda* (2nd ed.). New York: Freeman.

Price Waterhouse vs. Hopkins, 109 S. Ct. 1775 (1989).

Pruitt, D.G. (1981). *Negotiation Behavior*. New York: Academic Press.

Pruitt, D.G., and Carnevale, P.J.D. (1993). *Negotiation and Mediation*. London: Open University Press.

Rauschning, H. (1940). *The Voice of Destruction*. New York: Putnam.

Raven, B.H. (1992). A power/interaction model of interpersonal influence: French and Raven thirty years later. *Journal of Social Behavior and Personality*, 7, 217–44.

Reavis, D.J. (1998). *The Ashes of Waco: An Investigation*. Syracuse, New York: Syracuse University Press.

Reicher, S. (1991) *Mad dogs and Englishmen: Telling tales from the Gulf*. Paper presented to the British Association 'Science '91' meeting. Plymouth.

Reicher, S., Drury, J., Hopkins, N. and Stott, C. (2001). A Model of Crowd Prototypes and Crowd Leadership. In C. Barker, A. Johnson and M. Lavalette (eds) *Leadership and social movements* (pp. 178–195). Manchester: Manchester University Press.

Reicher, S. and Hopkins, N. (1996a). Constructing categories and mobilising masses: An analysis of Thatcher's and Kinnock's speeches on the British miners' strike 1984–5. *European Journal of Social Psychology*, 26, 353–71.

Reicher, S., and Hopkins, N. (2001a) *Self and nation*. London: Sage.

Reicher, S., and Hopkins, N. (2001b) Psychology and the end of history: a critique and a proposal for the psychology of social categorisation. *Political Psychology*, 22, 383–407.

Reicher, S., Hopkins, N. and Condor, S. (1997). Stereotype construction as a strategy of influence. In R. Spears, P. Oakes, A. Haslam and N. Ellemers (eds) *Stereotyping and social identity*. Oxford: Blackwell.

Reicher, S.D. (1987). Crowd behavior as social action. In J.C. Turner, M.A. Hogg, P.J. Oakes, S.D. Reicher, and M.S. Wetherell. *Rediscovering the social group: A self-categorization theory* (pp. 171–202). Oxford: Blackwell.

Reicher, S.D., and Hopkins, N. (1996). Seeking influence through characterizing self-categories: An analysis of anti-abortionist rhetoric. *British Journal of Social Psychology*, 35(2), 297–311.

Reid, S.A., and Ng, S.H. (1999). Language, power, and intergroup relations. *Journal of Social Issues*, 55, 119–39.

Reid, S.A., and Ng, S.H. (2000). Conversation as a resource for influence: Evidence for prototypical arguments and social identification processes. *European Journal of Social Psychology*, 30, 83–100.

Reynolds, K.J., Turner, J.C., Haslam, S.A., and Ryan, M.K. (2001). The role of personality and group factors in explaining prejudice. *Journal of Experimental Social Psychology*, 37, 427–34.

Rich, F. (2001, September 30). The father figure. *New York Times Magazine*, p. 23.

Richards, M. (1996). Constructing the Nationalist State: Self-sufficiency and regeneration in the early Franco years. In C. Mar-Molinero and A. Smith (eds) *Nationalism and the Nation in the Iberian Peninsula: Competing and conflicting identities* (pp. 149–67). Oxford: Berg.

Ridgeway, C.L. (1981). Nonconformity, competence, and influence in groups. *American Sociological Review*, 46, 333–47.

Ridgeway, C.L. (1997). Interaction and the conservation of gender inequality: Considering employment. *American Sociological Review*, 62, 218–35.

Ridgeway, C.L. (2001a). Gender, status, and leadership. *Journal of Social Issues*, 57, 637–55.

Ridgeway, C.L. (2001b). Social status and group structure. In M.A. Hogg and S. Tindale (eds), *Blackwell handbook of social psychology: Group processes*, (pp. 352–75). Maulden, MA: Blackwell.

Ridgeway, C.L., and Berger, J. (1986). Expectations, legitimation, and dominance behavior in groups. *American Sociological Review*, 51, 603–17.

Ridgeway, C.L., Boyle, E.H., Kuipers, K., and Robinson, D. (1998). How do status beliefs develop? The role of resources and interaction. *American Sociological Review*, 63, 331–50.

Ridgeway, C.L., and Erickson, K.G. (2000). Creating and spreading status beliefs. *American Journal of Sociology*, 106, 579–615.

Ridgeway, C.L., Johnson, C., and Diekema, D. (1994). External status, legitimacy, and compliance in male and female groups. *Social Forces*, 72, 1051–77.

Ridgeway, C.L., and Smith-Lovin, L. (1999). The gender system and interaction. *Annual Review of Sociology*, 25, 191–216.

Robinson, P. and Darley, J. (1995). *Justice, liability, and blame*. Boulder, CO.: Westview.

Rodriguez-Bailon, R., Moya, M., and Yzerbyt, V. (2000). Why do superiors attend to negative stereotypic information about their subordinates? Effects of power legitimacy on social perception. *European Journal of Social Psychology*, 30, 651–71.

Rosch, E. (1978). Principles of categorization. In E. Rosch and B.B. Lloyd (eds), *Cognition and categorization*. Hillsdale, NJ: Erlbaum.

Ross, L. (1977). The intuitive psychologist and his shortcomings. In L. Berkowitz (ed.), *Advances in experimental social psychology* (Vol. 10, pp. 174–220). New York: Academic Press.

Ross, M., and Sicoly, F. (1979). Egocentric biases in availability and attribution. *Journal of Personality and Social Psychology*, 37, 322–36.

Rousseau, D.M. (1995). *Psychological contracts in organizations: Understanding written and unwritten agreements*. Thousand Oaks, CA: Sage.

Roy Morgan Research (2001). *2001 Morgan polls archive*. http://www.roymorgan.com/polls/2001/

Rubin, J., Pruitt, D.G., and Kim, S. (1994). *Social conflict: Escalation, stalemate, and settlement*. New York: McGraw Hill.

Ruddock, P. (2001, September 2). *Illegal immigration—MV Tampa. Transcript of television interview*. Australian Department of Foreign Affairs and Trade: http://www.dfat.gov.au/media/tampa.html

Rudman, L.A., and Glick, P. (1999). Feminized management and backlash toward agentic women: The hidden costs to women of a kinder, gentler image of middle management. *Journal of Personality and Social Psychology*, 77, 1004–10.

Rudman, L.A., and Glick, P. (2001). Prescriptive gender stereotypes and backlash toward agentic women. *Journal of Social Issues*, 57, 743–62.

Rule, B.G., Bisanz, G.L., and Kohn, M. (1985). Anatomy of persuasion schema: Targets, goals and strategies. *Journal of Personality and Social Psychology*, 48, 1127–40.

Rusbult, C., and van Lange, P. (1996). Interdependence processes. In E.T. Higgins and A.W. Kruglanski (eds), *Social psychology*. New York: Guilford.

Ruscher, J.B., and Fiske, S.T. (1990). Interpersonal competition can cause individuating processes. *Journal of Personality and Social Psychology*, 58, 832–43.

Russell, B. (1938). *Power: A new social analysis*. London: George Allen & Unwin.

Rutte, C.G., and Wilke, H.A.M. (1985). Preference for decision structures in a social dilemma situation. *European Journal of Social Psychology*, 15, 367–70.

Samuelson C.D., and Messick D.M. (1986). Inequities in access to and use of shared resource in social dilemmas. *Journal of Personality and Social Psychology*, 51, 960–7.

Sanbonmatsu, D.M., and Kardes, F.R. (1988). The effects of physiological arousal on information processing and persuasion. *Journal of Consumer Research*, 15, 379–85.

Sargant, W. (1957). *Battle for the mind: How evangelists, psychiatrists, politicians, and medicine men can change your beliefs and behavior*. Garden City, NY: Doubleday.

Sattler, D.N., and Kerr, N.L. (1991). Might versus morality explored: Motivational and cognitive bases for social motives. *Journal of Personality and Social Psychology*, 60, 756–65.

Scandura, T.A., and Graen, G.B. (1984). Moderating effects of initial leader–member exchange status on the effects of a leadership intervention. *Journal of Applied Psychology*, 69, 428–36.

Scandura, T.A. (1999). Rethinking leader–member exchange: An organizational justice perspective. *Leadership Quarterly*, 10, 25–40.

Schein, E.H., Schneier, I., and Barker, C.H. (1961). *Coercive persuasion: A socio-psychological analysis of the 'brainwashing' of American civilian prisoners by the Chinese communists.* New York: W. W. Norton.

Schein, V.E. (1975). The relationship of sex role stereotypes and requisite management characteristics among female managers. *Journal of Applied Psychology*, 60, 340–4.

Schein, V.E. (2001). A global look at psychological barriers to women's progress in management. *Journal of Social Issues*, 57, 675–88.

Schiffer, I. (1973). *Charisma.* Toronto: University of Toronto Press.

Schriesheim, C.A., Castro, S.L., and Cogliser, C.C. (1999). Leader–member exchange (LMX) research: A comprehensive review of theory, measurement, and data-analytic practices. *Leadership Quarterly*, 10, 63–113.

Schriesheim, C.A., Castro, S.L., and Yammarino, F.J. (2000). Investigating contingencies: An examination of the impact of span of supervision and upward controllingness on leader–member exchange using traditional and multivariate within- and between-entities analysis. *Journal of Applied Psychology*, 85, 659–77.

Schriesheim, C.A., and Hinkin, T.R. (1990). Influence tactics used by subordinates: A theoretical and empirical analysis and refinement of the Kipnis, Schmidt, and Wilkinson subscales. *Journal of Applied Psychology*, 75, 246–57.

Sedikides, C., and Brewer, M.B. (2001). *Individual self, relational self, collective self.* Philadelphia, PA: Psychology Press.

Shamir, B., House, R.J., and Arthur, M.B. (1993). The motivational effects of charismatic leadership: A self-concept based concept. *Organizational Science*, 4, 577–94.

Sharon, A. (January, 2001). *Arial Sharon Campaign 2001.* http://www.sharon2001.com.

Sharon, A. *Encyclopaedia Britannica* (2001, CD-ROM).

Shaw, M.E. (1981). *Group dynamics: The psychology of small group behavior* (2nd edn). New York: McGraw-Hill.

Sherif, M. (1936). *The psychology of social norms.* New York: Harper & Row.

Sherif, M., Harvey, O.J., White, B.J., Hood, W.R., and Sherif, C.W. (1961). *Intergroup conflict and cooperation: The Robbers' Cave experiment.* Norman, OK: University Book Exchange.

Sherman, J.W. and Klein, S.B. (1994). Development and representation of personality impressions. *Journal of Personality and Social Psychology* 67, 972–83.

Sidanius, J., and Pratto, F. (1999). *Social dominance: An intergroup theory of social hierarchy and oppression.* New York: Cambridge University Press.

Siegel, A.E., and Fouraker, L.E. (1960). *Bargaining and group decision making.* New York: McGraw-Hill.

Simmons, W.W. (2001, January 11). *When it comes to choosing a boss, Americans still prefer men.* Gallup Poll News Service. Retrieved August 18, 2001 from http://www.gallup.com/poll/releases/pr010111.asp.

Sinclair, L., and Kunda, Z. (2000). Motivated stereotyping of women: She's fine if she praised me but incompetent if she criticized me. *Personality and Social Psychology Bulletin*, 26, 1329–42.

Singer, M. (1995). *Cults in our midst.* San Francisco: Jossey-Bass.

Smith, E.R., and DeCoster, J. (1998). Knowledge acquisition, accessibility, and use in person perception and stereotyping: Simulation with a recurrent connectionist network. *Journal of Personality and Social Psychology*, 74, 21–35.

Smith, E.R., and Henry, S. (1996). An in-group becomes part of the self: Response time evidence. *Personality and Social Psychology Bulletin*, 22, 635–42.

Smith, J.A., and Foti, R.J. (1998). A pattern approach to the study of leader emergence. *Leadership Quarterly*, 9, 147–60.

Smith, K.G., Carroll, S.J., and Ashford, S.J. (1995). Intra- and interorganizational cooperation: Toward a research agenda. *Academy of Management Journal*, 38, 7–23.

Smith, P.M. (1995). Leadership. In A.S.R. Manstead and M. Hewstone (eds), *The Blackwell encyclopaedia of social psychology* (pp. 358–62). Cambridge, MA: Blackwell.

Snyder, M. (1992). Motivational foundations of behavioral confirmation. *Advances in Experimental Social Psychology*, 25, 67–114.

Sparrowe, R.T., and Liden, R.C. (1997). Process and structure in leader–member exchange. *Academy of Management Review*, 22, 522–52.

Spence, J.T., and Helmreich, R. (1978). *Masculinity and femininity: Their psychological dimensions, correlates, and antecedents.* Austin, TX: University of Texas Press.

Stahelski, A.J., and Paynton, C.F. (1995). The effects of status cues on choices of social power and influence strategies. *Journal of Social Psychology*, 135, 553–60.

Staw, B.M. (1976). Knee-deep in the big muddy: A study of escalating commitment to a chosen course of action. *Organizational Behavior and Human Performance*, 16, 27–44.

Steele, C.M. (1988). The psychology of self-affirmation: Sustaining the integrity of the self. In L. Berkowitz (ed.), *Advances in experimental social psychology*, 21, 261–302. New York: Academic Press.

Steele, C.M., Spencer, S.J., and Lynch, M. (1993). Self-image resilience and dissonance: The role of affirmational resources. *Journal of Personality and Social Psychology*, 64, 885–96.

Steensma, H. (1995). Influence tactics used by managers. In J. Boonstra (chair), Power Dynamics and Organizational Change I, Symposium held at the seventh European Congress on Work and Organizational Psychology, Györ, Hungary.

Stern, J.P. (1984). *Hitler: The Fuhrer and the people.* London: Flamingo.

Stewart, C.J. (1997). The evolution of a revolution: Stokely Carmichael and the rhetoric of black power. *Quarterly Journal of Speech*, 83, 429–46.

Stogdill, R. (1974). *Handbook of leadership.* New York: Free Press.

Strodtbeck, F.L., James R.M., and Hawkins, C. (1957). Social status in jury deliberations. *American Sociological Review*, 22, 713–19.

Suls, J., and Wheeler, L. (eds) (2000). *Handbook of social comparison: Theory and research.* New York: Kluwer/Plenum.

Swann, W.B. (1987). Identity negotiation: Where two roads meet. *Journal of Personality and Social Psychology*, 53, 1038–51.

Swim, J., Borgida, E., Maruyama, G. and Meyers, D.G. (1989). Joan McKay versus John McKay: Do gender stereotypes bias evaluations? *Psychological Bulletin*, 105, 409–29.

Tajfel, H. (1981). Social stereotypes and social groups. In J.C. Turner and H. Giles (eds), *Intergroup behaviour* (pp. 144–67). Oxford: Blackwell.

Tajfel, H. (ed.). (1982). *Social identity and intergroup relations.* Cambridge: Cambridge University Press.

Tajfel, H. and Turner, J.C. (1979). An integrative theory of intergroup conflict. In W.G. Austin and S. Worchel (eds), *The social psychology of intergroup relations* (pp. 33–47). Monterey, CA: Brooks/Cole.

Tajfel, H., and Turner, J. (1986). The social identity theory of intergroup behavior. In W.G. Austin, and S. Worchel (eds), *Psychology of intergroup relations.* Chicago, IL: Nelson-Hall.

Tannen, D. (1994). *Talking from 9 to 5: Women and men in the workplace: Language, sex, and power.* New York: William Morrow.

Taylor, S., and Brown, J.D. (1988). Illusion and well-being: A social psychological perspective on health. *Psychological Bulletin*, 103, 193–210.

Tenbrunsel, A.E. and Messick, D.M. (1999). Sanctioning systems, decision frames, and cooperation. *Administrative Science Quarterly*, 44, 684–707.

Tepper, B.J., Brown, S.J., and Hunt, M.D. (1993). Strength of subordinates upward influence tactics and gender congruency effects. *Journal of Applied Social Psychology*, 23, 1903–19.

Tesser, A. and Moore, J. (1990). Independent threats and self-evaluation maintenance processes. *Journal of Social Psychology*, 130, 677–89.

Tetlock, P.E. (1992). The impact of accountability on judgment and choice: Toward a social contingency model. In L. Berkowitz (ed.), *Advances in experimental social psychology* (v. 25), (pp. 331–376). New York: Academic Press.

Tetlock, P.E. (1999). Accountability theory: Mixing properties of human agents with properties of social systems. In L.L. Thompson, J.M. Levine and D. Messick (eds), *Shared cognition in organizations: The management of knowledge* (pp. 117–37). Mahwah, NJ: Lawrence Erlbaum.

The corporate woman: A special report. (March 24, 1986). *Wall Street Journal*, 32-page supplement.

Thibaut, J.W., and Kelly, H.H. (1959, reprinted 1986). *The social psychology of groups*. New Brunswick, NJ: Transaction Publishers.

Thibaut, J., and Walker, L. (1975). *Procedural justice: A psychological analysis*. Hillsdale, NJ: Erlbaum.

Thomas, K.W. (1992). Conflict and negotiation processes in organizations. In M.D. Dunnette and L.M. Hough (eds), *Handbook of industrial and organizational psychology* (2nd ed., pp. 651–717). Palo Alto, CA: Consulting Psychologists Press.

Thompson, J. (1990) *Ideology and Modern Culture*. Oxford: Polity.

Thompson, L., and Loewenstein, G. (1992). Egocentric interpretations of fairness and interpersonal conflict. *Organizational Behavior and Human Decision Processes*, 51, 176–97.

Tjosvold, D. (1985). Power and social context in superior-subordinate interaction. *Organizational Behavior and Human Decision Processes*, 35, 281–93.

Townsend, J., Phillips, J.S., and Elkins, T.J. (2000). Employee retaliation: The neglected consequence of poor leader–member exchange relations. *Journal of Occupational Health Psychology*; 5, 457–63.

Triandis, H.C. (1989). The self and social behavior in differing cultural contexts. *Psychological Review*, 96, 506–20.

Tripp, T.M. (1993). Power and fairness in negotiation. *Social Justice Research*, 6, 19–38.

Tropp, L.R., and Wright, S.C. (2001). Ingroup identification as inclusion of ingroup in the self. *Personality and Social Psychology Bulletin*, 27, 585–600.

Turner, J.C. (1982) Towards a cognitive redefinition of the social group. In H. Tajfel (ed.) *Social identity and intergroup relations*. Cambridge: Cambridge University Press.

Turner, J.C. (1985). Social categorization and the self-concept: A social cognitive theory of group behavior. In E.J. Lawler (ed.), *Advances in group processes* (Vol. 2, pp. 77–122). Greenwich, CT: JAI.

Turner, J.C. (1987). A self-categorization theory. In J.C. Turner, M.A. Hogg, P.J. Oakes, S.D. Reicher and M.S. Wetherell. *Rediscovering the social group: A self-categorization theory* (pp. 24–67). Oxford: Blackwell.

Turner, J.C. (1991). *Social influence*. Buckingham, UK: Open University Press.

Turner, J C., and Giles, H. (eds). (1981). *Intergroup behaviour*. Oxford: Blackwell.

Turner, J.C., and Haslam, S.A. (2001). Social identity, organizations, and leadership. In M.E. Turner (ed.), *Groups at work: Theory and research* (pp. 25–65). Mahway, NJ: Erlbaum.

Turner, J.C., Hogg, M., Oakes, P.J., Reicher, S. and Wetherell, M. (1987). *Rediscovering the social group: A self-categorization theory*. Oxford: Blackwell.

Turner, J.C., and Onorato, R.S. (1999). Social identity, personality, and the self-concept: A social categorization perspective. In T.R. Tyler, R.M. Kramer and O.P. John (eds), *The psychology of the social self*. Mahwah, NJ: Erlbaum.

Turner, K.J. (1985). *Lyndon Johnson's dual war: Vietnam and the press*. Chicago, IL: University of Chicago Press.

Twenge, J.M. (1997). Changes in masculine and feminine traits over time: A meta-analysis. *Sex Roles*, 36, 305–25.

Twenge, J.M. (2001). Changes in women's assertiveness in response to status and roles: A cross-temporal meta-analysis, 1931–93. *Journal of Personality and Social Psychology*, 81, 133–45

Tyler, T.R. (1984). Justice in the political arena. In R. Folger (ed.), *The sense of injustice* (pp. 189–225). New York: Plenum Press.

Tyler, T.R. (1988) What is procedural justice? *Law and Society Review*.

Tyler, T.R. (1990). *Why people obey the law*. New Haven: Yale.

Tyler, T.R. (1997). The psychology of legitimacy: A relational perspective on voluntary deference to authorities. *Personality and Social Psychology Review*, 1, 323–45.

Tyler, T.R. (1999). Why people cooperate with organizations: An identity-based perspective. *Research in Organizational Behavior*, 21, 201–46.

Tyler, T.R. and Bies, R.J. (1990). Beyond formal procedures: The interactional context of procedural justice. In J.S. Carroll (ed.), *Applied social psychology and organizational settings* (pp. 77–98). Hillsdale, NJ: Erlbaum.

Tyler, T.R., and Blader, S. (2000). *Cooperation in groups: Procedural justice, social identity, and behavioral engagement*. Philadelphia: Taylor & Francis.

Tyler, T.R., and Dawes, R.M. (1993). Fairness in groups: Comparing the self-interest and social identity perspectives. In B.A. Melkers and J. Baron (eds), *Psychological perspectives on justice: Theory and applications* (pp. 87–108). Cambridge, NY: Cambridge University Press.

Tyler, T.R., and Degoey, P. (1995). Collective restraint in social dilemmas: Procedural justice and social identification effects on supports of authorities. *Journal of Personality and Social Psychology*, 69, 482–97.

Tyler, T.R., and Degoey, P. (1996). Trust in organizational authorities: The influence of motive attributions on willingness to accept decisions. In R.M. Kramer and T.R. Tyler (eds), *Trust in organizations: Frontiers of theory and research* (pp. 331–56). Thousand Oaks, CA: Sage.

Tyler, T.R., Degoey, P., and Smith, H. (1996). Understanding why the justice of group procedures matter: A test of the psychological dynamics of the group-value model. *Journal of Personality and Social Psychology*, 70, 913–30.

Tyler, T.R. and Kramer, R. (1996). *Trust in organizations*. Thousand Oaks, CA: Sage.

Tyler, T.R., and Lind, E.A. (1992). A relational model of authority in groups. In M. Zanna (ed.), *Advances in experimental social psychology* (Vol. 25, pp. 115–91). New York: Academic Press.

Tyler, T.R., Rasinski, K., and McGraw, K. (1985). The influence of perceived injustice on support for political authorities. *Journal of Applied Social Psychology*, 15, 700–25.

Tyler, T.R., and Smith, H.J. (1999). Justice, social identity, and group processes. In T.R. Tyler, R.M. Kramer and O.P. John (eds), *The psychology of the social self* (pp. 223–64). Mahaw, NJ: Lawrence Erlbaum Associates, Inc.

US Bureau of Labor Statistics. (2001). *Annual average tables from the January 2001 issue of Employment and Earnings* (Table 11. Employed persons by detailed occupation, sex, race, and Hispanic origin). Retrieved August 18, 2001, from http://www.bls.gov/cpsaatab.htm.

US Department of Education, Office of Educational Research and Improvement, National Center for Educational Statistics. (2000). *NAEP trends in academic progress: Three decades of student performance* (NCES 2000–469, by J.R. Campbell, C.M. Hombo, and J. Mazzeo). Washington, DC: Author. Retrieved May 15, 2001, from http://nces.ed.gov/NAEP/site/home.asp.

US Bureau of Labor Statistics. (2002). *News: The employment situation: January 2002* (Table A-1. Employment status of the civilian population by sex and age). Retrieved August 18, 2001, from http://www.bls.gov/news.release/pdf/empsit.pdf.

United Nations Development Programme. (2001). *Human development report 2001*. New York: Oxford University Press.

USA Today (2001, September 14). *Defining moments in the bully pulpit*, p. 4a.

Useem, M. (1998). *The leadership moment*. Times Business Books.

Valenti, J. (1977). *A very human president*. New York: W. W. Norton.

van Knippenberg, B. (1999). *Determinants of the use of influence tactics*. Leiden University, Leiden.

van Knippenberg, B., and Steensma, H. (2003). Future interaction expectation and the use of hard and soft influence tactics. *Applied Psychology: An International Review*, 52, 55–67.

van Knippenberg, B., van Eijbergen, R., and Wilke, H.A.M. (1999). The use of soft and hard influence tactics in cooperative task groups. *Group Processes and Intergroup Relations*, 2, 321–244.

van Knippenberg, B., and van Knippenberg, D. (2000). *Social identity issues in leaders' use of influence tactics*. Paper presented at the small group meeting of the European Association of Experimental Social Psychology on social identity processes in organisations, Amsterdam, The Netherlands.

van Knippenberg, B., and van Knippenberg, D. (2001). Leaders' use of influence tactics, prototypicality and their effects on subordinates' perceptions and performance. Unpublished manuscript.

van Knippenberg, B., van Knippenberg, D., Blaauw, E., and Vermunt, R. (1999). Relational considerations in the use of influence tactics. *Journal of Applied Social Psychology*, 29, 806–19.

van Knippenberg, B., van Knippenberg, D., and Wilke, H.A.M. (2001). Power use in cooperative and competitive settings. *Basic and Applied Social Psychology*, 23, 293–302.

van Knippenberg, D. (1999). Social identity and persuasion: Reconsidering the role of group membership. In D. Abrams and M.A. Hogg (eds), *Social identity and social cognition*, (pp. 315–31). Oxford: Blackwell.

van Knippenberg, D. (2000). Group norms, prototypicality, and persuasion. In D.J. Terry and M.A. Hogg (eds), *Attitudes, behavior, and social context: The role of norms and group membership*, (pp. 157–70). Mahwah, NJ: Erlbaum.

van Knippenberg, D. (2000). Work motivation and performance: A social identity perspective. *Applied Psychology: An International Review*, 49, 357–71.

van Knippenberg, D., and Hogg, M. (eds). (2001). Social identity processes in organizations. *Group Processes and Intergroup Relations*, 4, 185–9.

van Knippenberg, D., Lossie, N., and Wilke, H. (1994). In-group prototypicality and persuasion: Determinants of heuristic and systematic message processing. *British Journal of Social Psychology*, 33, 289–300.

van Knippenberg, D., van Knippenberg, B., and van Dijk, E. (2000). Who takes the lead in risky decision making? Effects of group members' risk preference and prototypicality. *Organizational Behavior and Human Decision Processes*, 83, 213–34.

van Lange, P.A.M., and Kuhlman, M.D. (1994). Social value orientations and impressions of partner's honesty and intelligence: A test of the might versus morality effect. *Journal of Personality and Social Psychology*, 67, 126–41.

van Lange, P.A.M., Otten, W., De Bruin, E.N.M., and Joireman, J.A. (1997). Development of prosocial, individualistic, and competitive orientations: Theory and preliminary evidence. *Journal of Personality and Social Psychology*, 73, 733–46.

van Overwalle, F., Drenth, T., and Mausman, G. (1999). Spontaneous trait inference. *Personality and Social Psychology Bulletin*, 25, 450–62.

van Vianen, A.E.M. (2000). Person-organization fit: The match between newcomers' and recruiters' preferences for organizational cultures. *Personnel Psychology*, 53, 113–49.

van Vugt M, and De Cremer D. (1999). Leadership in social dilemmas: The effects of group identification on collective actions to provide public goods. *Journal of Personality and Social Psychology*, 76, 587–99.

Vecchio, R.P. (1982). A further test of leadership effects due to between-group and within-group variation. *Journal of Applied Psychology*, 67, 200–8.

Vecchio, R.P. (1998). Leader–member exchange, objective performance, employment duration, and supervisor ratings: Testing for moderation and mediation. *Journal of Business and Psychology*, 12, 327–41.

Vecchio, R.P., and Gobdel, B.C. (1984). The vertical dyad linkage model of leadership: problems and prospects. *Organizational Behavior*, 34, 5–20.

Vecchio, R.P., and Sussmann, M. (1991). Choice of influence tactics: Individual and organizational determinants. *Journal of Organizational Behavior*, 12, 73–80.

von Hippel, W., Sekaquaptewa, D., and Vargas, P. (1995). On the role of encoding processes in stereotype maintenance. In M. Zanna (ed.), *Advances in experimental social psychology* (Vol. 27, pp. 177–254). San Diego, CA: Academic Press.

Vonk, R. (1999). The slime effect: Suspicion and dislike of likeable behavior towards superiors. *Journal of Personality and Social Psychology*, 74, 849–64.

Vroom, V.H. (1964). *Work and motivation*. New York: Wiley.

Vroom, V.H. and Yetton, P.W. (1973). *Leadership and decision-making*. Pittsburgh, PA: University of Pittsburgh Press.

Wagner, D.G., and Berger, J. (1997). Gender and interpersonal task behaviors: Status expectation accounts. *Sociological Perspectives*, 40, 1–32.

Wagner, J.A., and Moch, M.K. (1986). Individualism-collectivism: Concept and measure. *Group and Organization Studies*, 11, 280–304.

Wallis, R. (1984) *The elementary forms of the new religious life*. London: Routledge and Kegan Paul.

Walster, E., Berscheid, E., and Walster, G. W. (1976). New directions in equity research. In L. Berkowitz and E. Walster (eds), *Advances in experimental social psychology* (pp. 1–42). New York: Academic Press.

Watson, C.B., Chemers, M.M., and Preiser, N. (2001). Collective efficacy: A multilevel analysis. *Personality and Social Psychology Bulletin*, 27, 1057–68.

Wayne, S.J., and Ferris, G.R. (1990). Influence tactics, affect, and exchange quality in supervisor–subordinate interactions. *Journal of Applied Psychology*, 75, 487–99.

Wayne, S.J., Shore, L.M., and Liden, R.C. (1997). Perceived organizational support and leader–member exchange: A social exchange perspective. *Academy of Management Journal*, 40, 82–111.

Weber, M. (1947). *The theory of social and economic organization*. (A.M. Henderson and T. Parsons, trans., T. Parsons, ed.). New York: Free Press. (Original work published 1924)

Webster, M. (1977). Equating characteristics and social interaction: Two experiments. *Sociometry*, 40, 41–50.

Webster, M., and Driskell, J.E. (1978). Status generalization: A review and some new data. *American Sociological Review*, 43, 220–36.

Webster, M., and Driskell, J.E. (1983). Beauty as status. *American Journal of Sociology*, 89, 140–65.

Webster, M. and Foschi, M. (1988). Overview of status generalization. In M. Webster and M. Foschi, (eds), *Status generalization: New theory and research* (pp, 1–22). Stanford, CA: Stanford University Press.

Weick, K.E. (1993). Sensemaking in organizations. In J.K. Murnighan (ed.), *Social psychology in organizations: Advances in theory and practice*. Englewood Cliffs, NJ: Prentice-Hall.

Weightman, J.M. (1984). *Making sense of the Jonestown suicides*. New York: Mellon.

Whyte, M.K. (1978). *The status of women in preindustrial societies*. Princeton, NJ: Princeton University Press.

Wilke, H.A.M. (1991). Greed, efficiency and fairness in resource management situations. In W. Stroebe and M. Hewstone (eds), *European Review of Social Psychology* (Vol. 2, pp. 165–87). Chichester, UK: Wiley.

Williams, C. (1992). The glass escalator: Hidden advantages for men in the 'female' professions. *Social Problems*, 39, 41–57.

Williams, C. (1995). *Still a man's world: Men who do women's work*. Berkeley, CA: University of California Press.

Williamson, O.E. (1993). Calculativeness, trust, and economic organization. *Journal of Law and Economics*, 36, 453–86.

Wilner, R. (1984) *The Spellbinders: Charismatic political leadership*. New Haven: Yale University Press.

Winter, J. (2002, 9 January). *The perils of reporting in Zimbabwe*. BBC news: http://news.bbc.co.uk/hi/english/world/africa/newsid_1751000/1751402.stm.

Wittenbrink, B., Judd, C.M. and Park, B. (2001). Spontaneous prejudice in context: Variability in automatically activated attitudes. *Journal of Personality and Social Psychology*, 81, 815–27.

Wood, W., Christensen, P.N., Hebl, M.R., and Rothgerber, H. (1997). Conformity to sex-typed norms, affect, and the self-concept. *Journal of Personality and Social Psychology*, 73, 523–35.

Xin, K.R., and Tsui, A.S. (1996). Different strokes for different folks? Influence tactics by Asian-American and Caucasian-American managers. *Leadership Quarterly*, 7(1), 109–32.

Yamagishi, T. (1986). The structural goal/expectation theory of cooperation in social dilemmas. *Advances in Group Processes*, 3, 51–87.

Yamagishi, T., and Yamagishi, M. (1994). Trust and commitment in the United States and Japan. *Motivation and Emotion*, 18, 129–66.

Yee, M. (1997). Charles Dederich, founder of cult-like religious group Synanon, dies at 83. *The Associated Press*, March 5, 1997.

Yoder, J.D. (2001). Making leadership work more effectively for women. *Journal of Social Issues*, 57, 815–28.

Yorges, S.L., Weiss, H.M., and Strickland, O.J. (1999). The effect of leader outcomes on influence, attributions, and perceptions of charisma. *Journal of Applied Psychology*, 84, 428–36.

Yukl, G.A. (1974). The effects of situational variables and opponent concessions on a bargainer's perception, aspirations, and concessions. *Journal of Personality and Social Psychology*, 29, 227–36.

Yukl, G. (1971). Toward a behavioral theory of leadership. *Organizational Behavior and Human Performance*, 6, 414–40

Yukl, G. (1998). *Leadership in organizations* (4th ed.). New Jersey: Prentice Hall.

Yukl, G. (1999). An evaluation of conceptual weaknesses in transformational and charismatic leadership theories. *Leadership Quarterly*, 10, 285–305.

Yukl, G., and Falbe, C.M. (1990). Influence tactics and objectives in upward, downward, and lateral influence attempts. *Journal of Applied Psychology*, 75, 132–40.

Yukl, G., Falbe, C.M., and Youn, J.Y. (1993). Patterns of influence behavior for managers. *Group & Organization Management*, 18, 5–28.

Yukl, G., Guinan, P.J., and Sottolano, D. (1995). Influence tactics used for different objectives with subordinates, peers and superiors. *Group & Organization Management*, 20, 272–96.

Yukl, G., Kim, H., and Falbe, C.M. (1996). Antecedents of influence outcomes. *Journal of Applied Psychology*, 81(3), 309–17.

Yukl, G., and Tracy, J.B. (1992). Consequences of influence tactics used with subordinates, peers, and the boss. *Journal of Applied Psychology*, 77, 525–35.

Zaccaro, S.J., Foti, R.J., and Kenny, D.A. (1991). Self-monitoring and trait-based variance in leadership: an investigation of leader flexibility across group situations. *Journal of Applied Psychology*, 76, 308–15.

Zelditch, M. (2001). Theories of legitimacy. In J. Jost and B. Major, (eds), *The psychology of legitimacy: Emerging perspective on ideology, justice, and intergroup relations* (pp. 33–53). New York: Cambridge University Press.

Zelditch, M., and Walker, H.A. (1984). Legitimacy and the stability of authority. In E.J. Lawler, (ed.), *Advances in group processes*, (Vol 1, pp. 1–25). Greenwich, CT: JAI Press.

Index